Simulation Techniques of Digital Twin in Real-Time Applications

Scrivener Publishing
100 Cummings Center, Suite 541J
Beverly, MA 01915-6106

Publishers at Scrivener
Martin Scrivener (martin@scrivenerpublishing.com)
Phillip Carmical (pcarmical@scrivenerpublishing.com)

Simulation Techniques of Digital Twin in Real-Time Applications

Design Modeling and Implementation

Edited by

Abhineet Anand

*Computer Science and Engineering, Bahara University, Waknaghat,
Himachal Pradesh, India*

Anita Sardana

*Dept. of Computer Science and Engineering, Jaypee University
of Information Technology, Solan, Himachal Pradesh, India*

Abhishek Kumar

University of Castilla-La Mancha (UCLM), Toledo, Spain

Srikanta Kumar Mohapatra

*Chitkara University Institute of Engineering and Technology, Chitkara University,
Punjab, India*

and

Shikha Gupta

*Dept. of Computer Science Engineering, Chandigarh University,
Mohali, Punjab, India*

Scrivener
Publishing

This edition first published 2024 by John Wiley & Sons, Inc., 111 River Street, Hoboken, NJ 07030, USA
and Scrivener Publishing LLC, 100 Cummings Center, Suite 541J, Beverly, MA 01915, USA
© 2024 Scrivener Publishing LLC
For more information about Scrivener publications please visit www.scrivenerpublishing.com.

Wiley Global Headquarters
111 River Street, Hoboken, NJ 07030, USA

For details of our global editorial offices, customer services, and more information about Wiley products visit us at www.wiley.com.

Limit of Liability/Disclaimer of Warranty
While the publisher and authors have used their best efforts in preparing this work, they make no representations or warranties with respect to the accuracy or completeness of the contents of this work and specifically disclaim all warranties, including without limitation any implied warranties of merchantability or fitness for a particular purpose. No warranty may be created or extended by sales representatives, written sales materials, or promotional statements for this work. The fact that an organization, website, or product is referred to in this work as a citation and/or potential source of further information does not mean that the publisher and authors endorse the information or services the organization, website, or product may provide or recommendations it may make. This work is sold with the understanding that the publisher is not engaged in rendering professional services. The advice and strategies contained herein may not be suitable for your situation. You should consult with a specialist where appropriate. Neither the publisher nor authors shall be liable for any loss of profit or any other commercial damages, including but not limited to special, incidental, consequential, or other damages. Further, readers should be aware that websites listed in this work may have changed or disappeared between when this work was written and when it is read.

Library of Congress Cataloging-in-Publication Data

ISBN 978-1-394-25697-6

Cover image: Pixabay.Com
Cover design by Russell Richardson

Set in size of 11pt and Minion Pro by Manila Typesetting Company, Makati, Philippines

Printed in the USA

10 9 8 7 6 5 4 3 2 1

Dedication

For our gurus, parents, and God, we dedicate our book. Their blessings are the reason for our motivation.

Contents

6   Digital Twin Application on System Identification and Control 123
Rakesh Kumar Pattanaik and Mihir Narayan Mohanty

Part 2: Real Time Applications of Digital Twin   163

Preface

Currently, a great amount of research is invested in the development of models and exploring their implementation. Digital twin technology is just the replica of an object in digital form. Generally, this technology improves the capability to receive real-time data and produce the data pool of the original object. This book is for researchers of diversified technologies, and the main objective is to showcase the proposed research models to a real-world audience.

This book collects a significant number of important research articles from domain-specific experts to present their works to the readers. A useful platform for both researchers and readers, this book gives a better understanding of how Digital twin technology may be the next big thing in the context of sustainable sectors to industrial sectors. This book sheds light on the various techniques of digital twin that are implemented in various application areas. It emphasizes error findings and respective solutions before the actual thing happens. Most of the aspects in this book are the implementation of strategies in real-time applications. Various real-life experiences are taken to show the proper implementation of simulation technologies. Overall, the book is for the readers to manage real-time applications or problems with the help of replicated models or digital twin technologies.

The book shows how authors of any technology can input their research ideas to convert to real scenarios by using replicas. Hence, the book has a collection of research articles from various authors with expertise in different technologies from many regions of the world. It will give an idea to implement the real-time data embedded into technologies.

Specifically, the chapters herein relate to the auto landing and cruising features in aerial vehicles, automated coal mining simulation strategy, the enhancement of workshop equipment, and implementation in power energy management for urban railways. This book also describes the coherent mechanism of digital twin technologies with deep neural networks and artificial intelligence.

Overall, the book gives a complete idea about the implementation of digital twin technology in real-time scenario. Furthermore, it emphasizes how this technology can be embedded with running technologies to solve all other issues.

This book comprises two parts: Part 1—"A Guide to Simulated Techniques in Digital Twin" and Part 2—"Real-Time Applications of Digital Twin". In Part 1, Chapter 1 introduces digital twin modeling. Furthermore, it specifies that engineers and designers employ simulation, a key step in the development of digital twins, to generate and test various scenarios in a secure and controlled environment. Many simulation techniques are widely used in the development of digital twins, including FEA, CFD, DES, MBD, MCS, and ABM. There are pros and cons to each of these techniques, but they may all be used to imitate and enhance particular aspects of the physical system. As digital twin technology advances, new simulation techniques and tools will emerge, allowing engineers to create more accurate and comprehensive models.

Chapter 2 shines light on the future of today's manufacturing lines. Furthermore, it clarifies that twin model is clearly headed toward advanced real-time simulation frameworks taking the lead. These frameworks, built on the digital twin principles, have ushered in a new era where real-time data synthesis and prompt feedback are not just useful but essential. Production simulations are now more realistic, precise, and comprehensive thanks to digital twin. The growing use of digital twin of traditionally physical systems has enabled industries to predict issues, make precise predictions, and base decisions on real-time data.

Chapter 3 discusses an air purifier system. The air quality, energy use, and cost-effectiveness of the air purifier system are all predicted by the LabVIEW simulation model. The digital twin concept can improve the efficiency, effectiveness, and cost-effectiveness of air purifier systems. The most effective and affordable air purifier system layouts can be found through analysis using the digital twin approach. The digital twin model might simulate how pollutants impact air quality and air treatment technologies. Research may enhance air quality, energy effectiveness, cost effectiveness, and air purification innovation.

Chapter 4 generated results that indicate that the suggested model did well on the classification dataset. It has very good accuracy, precision, recall, specificity, and F1-scores (between 96.85 and 99.3). The findings demonstrate that the model can accurately distinguish between those who genuinely have the illness and those who do not. The healthy class showed positive results, indicating that the model successfully distinguishes between healthy (normal) and damaged leaves.

Chapter 5 discusses various signaling methods, including BDPSK, BPSK, BFSK, QPSK, NCFSK, MPSK, MQAM, DQPSK, MDPSK, and NCMFSK over F fading channel, which have had error rate equations calculated for them in this study. The asymptotic, tightly bound, and approximate expressions of ABER have now been calculated. Additionally, the many expressions of capacities have been discovered. For the purposes of generalization and validation, a few reduction examples are also described. The analytical results have been acquired, and simulation results support them.

Chapter 6 looks at the effectiveness of the F model when combined with MGF. The expression for MGF is first derived. We have determined the expression for BER utilizing a variety of signaling schemes, including BDPSK, NBFSK, BPSK, BFSK, MSK, MAM, Square MQAM, MPSK, and NMFSK, using the suggested MGF. Additionally, the ORA and CIFR capacity expressions are computed. Through the use of Monte Carlo simulations and special case outcomes, the accuracy of the result has been verified. According to the study, higher-fading severity parameters perform better in terms of BER and channel capacity than lower ones.

To begin Part 2, Chapter 7 works on the creation of virtual replicas of real cars which is made possible by the use of digital twin technology, enabling prolonged testing in a controlled environment. By modeling numerous scenarios and driving conditions, developers can evaluate the performance and capabilities of autonomous driving systems without the need for real-world testing. This avoids wasting time and money and guarantees that the technology is thoroughly tested before being used on public roads.

Chapter 8 summarizes the study's major conclusions and learnings in digital twin modeling. Real-time information, including voltage, current, and temperature, are gathered by sensors for transformer condition monitoring. Therefore, this information is sent to the computer. The use of a MATLAB-based ANN-based intelligent monitoring system that is connected with the hardware to produce digital twins demonstrates tremendous potential for enhancing the precision and effectiveness of power transformer failure analysis through temperature monitoring.

Chapter 9 gives a thorough explanation of the integrated deep learning digital twin approach. For the purpose of advancing digital twin technology, authors have examined several forms of digital twins and the ways that deep learning techniques are applied in various simulation models. They have researched a variety of current publications that use deep learning to enhance the functionality of digital twin models.

Chapter 10 discloses an online system identification or virtual modeling approach. There is huge potential for the use of digital twin (DT) in dynamical systems, including active control, health monitoring, diagnostics, prognosis, and computation of remaining useful life. However, the implementation of this technology in real time has lagged behind schedule, largely because there is a dearth of data pertinent to the application being used.

Chapter 11 describes UAVs that use digital twin-based techniques, which have a great chance of performing autonomous takeoff, landing, and cruising. The findings of this study add to the body of knowledge already available on UAV autonomy and highlight the need for more research in this field. Overcoming the challenges and researching the suggested future courses are necessary to fully realize the promise of digital twin-based autonomous operations and drastically transform how they are used in many businesses and sectors.

Chapter 12 explains digital twins and artificial intelligence (AI)-powered algorithms to increase productivity, safety, and sustainability in the mining industry, as the adoption of such a system alters coal mining operations. Overall, the DT is making headway, and thanks to its almost endless potential, it is becoming a more significant and well-liked competitor in the race. The authors are one step closer to making actual DTs with the development of its underlying technologies, which are constantly evolving.

Chapter 13 analyzes real-time data from the aircraft's sensors and systems. Digital twins can foresee likely defects or maintenance needs. This proactive approach helps to reduce unscheduled downtime, enhance maintenance schedules, and improve aircraft availability and reliability. By combining digital twin technology with artificial intelligence and machine learning methods, the prediction abilities of Digital Twins will be enhanced.

Chapter 14 relates to energy consumption, which is closely related to power consumption in urban trains. The system's energy performance demonstrates that energy in both reference instances is gradually rising. An error result of less than 1% is also displayed to demonstrate accuracy. Therefore, the aspect of concern is power consumption or energy utilization. The involved railroad authorities may find these results helpful in describing the user-label experience. These results also demonstrate that the simulation can use certain preventative measures.

Chapter 15 describes pipedream, which is a cutting-edge system that enables real-time hydraulic state forecasting and interpolation for urban fast-flood nowcasting. The pipedream toolset's data assimilation method can be utilized by emergency management to estimate localized floods at ungauged locations, enabling rapid flood response and targeted emergency service dispatch.

We would like to express our gratitude to the writers and contributors for their efforts as well as to Wiley and Scrivener Publishing for their cooperation and assistance in the timely publication of this book.

The Editors
March 2024

Part 1

A GUIDE TO SIMULATED TECHNIQUES IN DIGITAL TWIN

Introduction to Different Simulation Techniques of Digital Twin Development

Suvarna Sharma and Chetna Monga*

Chitkara University Institute of Engineering and Technology, Chitkara University, Rajpura, Punjab, India

Abstract

Virtual models of actual systems, processes, or products are known as "digital twins" in technology. It replicates an object or system's behavior, functionality, and responsiveness to various circumstances using a software version of the real-world counterpart. In addition to manufacturing, healthcare, construction, aerospace, and transportation, there are numerous additional sectors that use the technology. With the use of digital twins, businesses may increase productivity, decrease downtime, maximize resource use, and enhance decision-making. The following simulation methodologies can be applied in digital twin technology: computational fluid dynamics (CFD), finite element analysis (FEA), agent-based modeling (ABM), multi-body dynamics (MBD), discrete event simulation (DES), and monte Carlo simulation. The foundations of digital twin technology are covered in this chapter, along with the benefits they offer to real-world research applications. This chapter also discusses several simulation methods for the practical uses, advantages, and disadvantages that will be covered in later chapters.

Keywords: Digital-twin technology, agent-based modeling (ABM), finite element analysis (FEA), discrete event simulation (DES), computational fluid dynamics (CFD), Monte Carlo simulation, multi-body dynamics (MBD)

Corresponding author: chetna@chitkara.edu.in

Abhineet Anand, Anita Sardana, Abhishek Kumar, Srikanta Kumar Mohapatra and Shikha Gupta (eds.) Simulation Techniques of Digital Twin in Real-Time Applications: Design Modeling and Implementation, (3–24) © 2024 Scrivener Publishing LLC

1.1   Introduction

Digital twins are frequently described as "a digital representation of a real world object with focus on the object itself" [13]. Figure 1.1 illustrates the extensive application areas of digital twin technology across various industries [1]. This visualization showcases the diverse utilization of digital twins in sectors such as manufacturing, healthcare, and urban planning, highlighting their significance in enhancing operational efficiency and facilitating predictive analysis.

A. Digital twin features
Technologies for creating, managing, and analyzing digital twins—virtual representations of actual systems or processes—are known as "digital twin technologies." Among the crucial elements of digital twin technologies are the following:

Data integration: Digital twin technologies combine information from several sources, such as IoT devices, sensors, and other systems, to create a full image of the physical system or process.

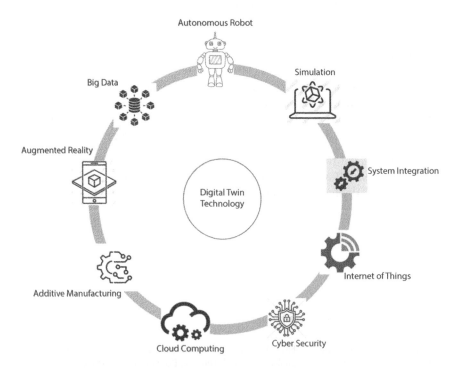

Figure 1.1 Different application areas of digital twin.

Simulated and modeled learning: In order to build virtual representations of actual systems or processes, digital twin technologies employ simulation and modeling approaches. With the help of these models, the behavior of the physical system under various conditions may be forecasted and studied.

Real-time monitoring: Digital twin technologies offer real-time observation of the physical system or process using data from sensors and other gears. Engineers and operators can now quickly identify and deal with any new issues as they arise.

Prevention-based maintenance: Based on information gathered from sensors and other devices, digital twin technology may be used to forecast when maintenance is necessary for the physical system or process. By doing so, downtime may be cut down and overall productivity can rise.

Optimization: The functionality of a physical system or process could be improved using technologies like digital twins through data analysis and the identification of issue areas. Increased effectiveness and lower costs may result from this.

Collaboration: Communication between numerous teams and departments is made feasible by digital twin technologies' shared image of the physical system or process. This can improve dialogue and facilitate problem-solving.

Machine learning and artificial intelligence: By analyzing data and making predictions about how a physical system or process will behave, digital twin technologies may make use of machine learning and artificial intelligence algorithms. Making decisions will be more accurate and effective as a result.

The ability to create and maintain virtual representations of actual systems or activities is provided through a number of capabilities provided by digital twin technologies, which are used by engineers and operators. These characteristics can help with cost reductions, performance improvements, and efficiency increases.

B. Digital twin classification

Digital twin instance (DTI): A certain type of digital twin is referred to as a "digital twin instance" when it continuously depicts its physical counterpart across time in line with its specification [14]. As a result, the physical twin is continuously monitored, and any adjustments or changes it goes through will affect the digital twin. In this perception, the aim keeps track of and predicts the behavior of a process or product from the moment of its conception until the end of its existence. Validating a product's or object's predicted performance and behavior is helpful.

Digital twin prototype (DTP): A digital twin prototype gathers and stores important information and features about a product's physical counterpart when it comes to the design and production of that product. Diagrams, computer-aided designs (CADs), and even information connecting persons involved in the production chain with the manufacturing process are examples of data [14]. Before the actual manufacturing process begins, the DTP may simulate production situations and carry out validation testing, assessments, and even quality control testing in accordance with DT requirements. By detecting defects or potential dangers in the physical twin before manufacturing, this method efficiently minimizes production costs and operating time. DTPs are also sometimes referred to as experimentable DTs in this sense, where, in accordance with [15], it is possible to access a virtual prototype whose degree of detail grows over time, and virtual test results offer an adequate evaluation of the design's quality while reducing the need for normally affluent hardware archied types.

Performance digital twin (PDT): More realistic and unforeseen situations can be monitored, collected, and evaluated by the PDT than they can by physical twins [14]. The PDT can analyze the data being tracked from the physical equivalent by fusing its smart capabilities. The processing yields useful information that may be applied to design optimization, the creation of maintenance plans, and the drawing of inferences from a product's capability [16].

1.2 Literature Review

A. Digital twin technology: Based on the fact that DT technology is still in its infancy, it will be crucial to overcome the many obstacles that a contemporary DT deployment faces, such as costs, information complexity and maintenance, a lack of standards and legislation, issues with cybersecurity and communications, and issues with standards and regulations. When assessing DTs in the three areas of technology, social readiness, and maturity, the maturity spectrum examination of major publications, as well as the TRL, SRL, and maturity analysis, are all very beneficial. The evolution of DT technology and maturity has only just started for the vast majority of applications. Although advanced DT uses are addressed in [1], more work has to be done before DTs may be fully enabled, accepted, and sustained in practical settings. The development of DTs will be aided by technologies and techniques for data processing and analysis. To address the issues brought up in this paper, future research should concentrate on the following areas: 1) computing complexity reduction through simulation and modeling, 2) 5G communication, 3) data from the Internet of Things can be processed and analyzed using big data, machine learning, and artificial intelligence, 4) the capacity of simulation, modeling, analysis, and visualization software to cooperate and integrate, and 5) recent technical advances including, but not limited to, the inclusion of edge and cloud computing potentialities in current microprocessors. One will be able to make a more accurate assessment of the current state of the art and the direction that technology is moving if they are aware of the whole picture of DTs across many crucial fields. It is crucial to take on the suggested research projects if DTs are to completely deliver on their promise for the future.

In [2], the conclusions are as follows:

(1) A variety of naval equipment can be built using the full digital twin (DT) architecture, and the DT approach demonstrated for the horizontal axis tidal turbine (HATT) performs well in simulations and tank tests. Instructions for the DT model may be broadcast to the outside world in order to achieve self-learning, and data can be utilized to translate changes in the physical environment to the digital environment.

(2) After several mechanical learning sessions, the substantial error in the DT data that the interpolation approach produced was decreased to less than 10%, which is regarded as being within an acceptable range and can be used as engineering reference values. The monitoring and performance assessment process for any marine equipment might be covered by this system.

(3) Supercomputing is used to run a variety of simulations, develop a turbine DT full life cycle decision support system, and perform quick interpolation and data extraction. These systems also enable online monitoring of physical parameters like flow rate and pressure. Machine learning is combined with the optimization procedure for data with significant comparison result curve deviation.

B. Finite element analysis: The finite element analysis (FEA) method is used in the simulation model in conjunction with real-time data from the assembly line. Innovative engineering methods and open-source development have also made it easier for field engineers and operators to use technology. As the digital twin is expanded to additional production lines, there is a good chance that Arçelik's manufacturing facilities may employ technology more frequently in the future. As a result, the overall cost of production and labor needs for refrigerators have decreased [3].

In [4], the use of a machine learning algorithm (decision tree) and digital twin technologies enables personalized medical care. The patient's historical and real-time data are both captured by the model. In order to forecast, monitor, and create a model that might be used for additional diagnostics, doctors, healthcare organizations, nurses, and patients will follow the observations. With the use of these technologies, effective and customized medical care may be created, and patients will have access to more individualized care. Cybersecurity is the main issue one could run into when utilizing digital twin technology. Data loss is a result of the rise in cybercrimes. The enormous amount of data is being gathered from multiple sources, all of which could be potential weak points. Cloud-based simulation software and storage can be utilized to address these difficulties and stop data loss and leakage. HIPPA-like regulations, for example, can be used to impose data governance. If properly implemented, these techniques may lower the likelihood of data loss.

In [5], the measured current was the input used by the FEA model. Temperature estimates at the same spot as the sensor-probed point were made in the simulation; readings had a significant correlation with dimensions (maximum error of 9.5%). Additional support for the DT theory came from simulations that looked at temperature distribution, torque profile, resistive losses, and stator copper conductivity—parameters that are challenging to measure but have a strong correlation with the motor's operating state. By demonstrating behavior that was consistent with theory and consistent with observations in the literature, these results provided support for the numerical model that had been created. The technique offers a tool that will aid in the monitoring of induction motor status in the future and produces accurate results under a continuous regime. The industry also benefits greatly from the advanced understanding because it means that the motor is only shut off when necessary for maintenance, which lowers expenses.

C. Computational fluid dynamics: Precision medicine's goal is to provide treatments that are customized for each patient. This goal is made possible by our growing capacity to collect vast data on each patient. In [6], the second enabling aspect for achieving this aim, in the opinion of some, is the capacity of computers and algorithms to learn about, comprehend, and produce a patient's "digital twin." Future treatments will consider more factors in addition to the patient's health right now and the information that is now accessible, but also a precise projection of the various routes for restoring health provided by model projections. The ability to make diagnoses and prognoses is being improved by computational models. Cardiovascular imaging and computational fluid dynamics can be utilized to provide diagnostic metrics and non-invasively characterize flow fields in the contexts of coronary artery disease, aortic aneurysm, aortic dissection, valve prosthesis, and stent design.

In [6], to give precision cardiology, information will be integrated with inductive and deductive reasons that are incorporated in each patient's digital twin. Accurate predictions of the underlying causes of sickness and the best cures or treatments for health maintenance or restoration will serve as the cornerstone for treating and preventing cardiovascular diseases. In the domains of coronary artery disease, aortic aneurysm, aortic dissection, valve prosthesis, and stent design, non-invasive flow fields are characterized and diagnostic metrics are computed using cardiovascular imaging and computational fluid dynamics. Mechanistic and statistical models will work together in a synergistic manner to develop and validate these predictions. Although the first steps have already been made in this direction, the next ones will depend on a coordinated effort by stakeholders in the scientific, clinical, industrial, and regulatory areas to gather the necessary data and address the organizational and social problems described below.

D. Discrete event simulation: The need to predict asset behavior and make decisions practically instantly has caused DES to develop into an essential component of what are now known as the digital twins (DTs) in the Logistics 4.0 era [7]. Using real-time data produced by IoT devices implanted on the physical twin, or the automation, discrete event simulation programs, which act as the cyber twin, are utilized to run simulation software queries and update the simulation to the consequent system state. The integration of the real and virtual warehouse is made possible by DTs, which promote speedy and effective decision-making, planning, and management in the warehouse. Future DES and DT systems will have the ability to do simulations in real time and provide results that are almost real time, when "sensing" shop floor data is widely available, improving the efficiency of both production and logistics processes.

Article [6] develops the concept of a digital twin (DT) of medical services using a mix of discrete event simulation (DES) and the Internet of Things (IoT), which is a novel methodology described in this work. Real-time services data from several systems and devices are used to construct a predictive decision support model. By employing this technique, it is feasible to assess both the results of service improvements and the efficacy of the present healthcare delivery systems without having an impact on the hospital's normal operations. A digital twin, also known as a virtual equivalent of the hospital, was developed to imitate a variety of crucial hospital healthcare services utilizing vital data that is obtained in real time. Despite the fact that the model first imitates four significant services to illustrate the idea, it also offers a core framework that may be adjusted to suit more services. By giving management and practitioners the opportunity to assess any model changes in order to predict the effectiveness or efficiency of services before they are put into practice, the proved proof-of-concept reveals how it enhances resource use and planning.

The overall patient count for each scenario, both input and output, is depicted in Figure 1.3, as evidenced by the fact that the number of patients serviced changes whenever resources vary. Similar to this, a hospital's increased resources enhance the number of patients it can serve. The amount of staff members required in the hospital twin might also be simulated and tested. One may have observed that the number of inputs and patients are not equal. It is possible that some patients were still getting care at the conclusion of the simulation period, which would account for this. The 3D simulation model for hospital patient pathways is depicted in Figure 1.2. For each scenario in Table 1.1, Figure 1.2 describes the altered

Table 1.1 Description of each scenario's available objects [8].

	Scenario 1	Scenario 2	Scenario 3	Scenario 4
Number of Receptionist	1	1	1	1
Number Physicians	1	1	1	2
Number RNs	1	1	1	2
Number of Exam Rooms (Exam Tables)	1	2	6	6
Number of Xray	1	1	1	1
Number of triage	1	1	1	1
Number of wheelchair	1	1	1	1
Number of waiting room	1	1	1	1
Number of patient Arrive door	1	1	1	1
Number of patient Exit door	1	1	1	1
Number of item queuing	1	1	1	1
Number of item processing	1	1	1	1

necessary resources. Variables may, of course, be changed to better reflect the resources used in this simulation—for instance, the number of input and output patients might be equalized without affecting the level of care.

Figure 1.2 details the patients' wait periods along their treatment pathway. The length of time the participants in this simulation wait depends on a number of parameters as was previously shown—for instance, beds or waiting areas as well as nurses and doctors.

In scenario 2, there is a longer line at the patients' vital sign station, as seen in Figure 1.3. The fact that there is just one registered nurse (RN) is the cause of this. Additionally, in scenarios 3 and 4, nearly no time has

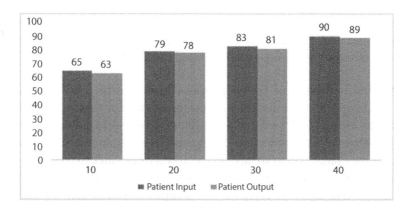

Figure 1.2 Patient chart input–output [8].

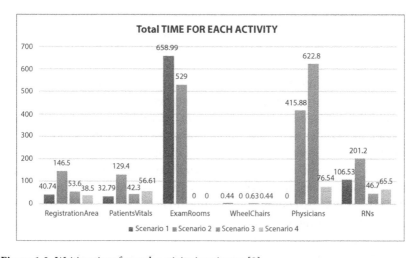

Figure 1.3 Waiting time for each activity in minutes [8].

passed while people have been waiting in the Exam Room area. This raises the issue of the six exam rooms present here as opposed to one or two in other settings.

E. Agent-based modeling: The biggest challenges of today are dealing with uncertainty and numerous threats that can cause the network to collapse at any point while developing and running systems that can swiftly and efficiently manufacture a wide range of customized products. Due to agents' potential ability to accurately represent this environment, agent-based models can solve optimization problems. A number of things may be accomplished using the virtual model, including comprehending the traits and connections between the system's agents, assessing and predicting specific system qualities, and identifying and fixing flaws. Generally speaking, in many application fields, the interaction of autonomous agents can be demonstrated using an agent-based model [9, 46].

F. Multi-body dynamics: The root-mean-square metrics used to pinpoint the defects demonstrate that the root-mean-square characteristic metrics of the digital twin model perform better than those of the traditional model. The problem of data collection during real gear equipment degradation must be resolved. In order to be resolved, it will be possible to conduct additional research on planetary gear predictive maintenance on the basis of this model. The author created a more accurate model of digital twin gear depreciation in place of utilizing inadequate testing. Positive derivation and inverse identification are employed to extract precise meshing parameters, gearbox defects, and other mechanical data during the fault progression [10]. The aerospace and automotive industries, as well as large-scale industrial equipment, can all benefit from the answers provided by this research in terms of problem identification and preventative maintenance.

G. Monte Carlo simulation: The thorough part digital twin model (PDTM), which has been put forth [11], integrates many heterogeneous geometric models and converts assembly information from assembly semantics to geometry components in order to increase the effectiveness of assembly simulation. As a result, parts are automatically positioned during assembly. Calculating the impact on the assembled product's important components takes into consideration manufacturing mistakes, assembly alignment difficulties, and mating surface distortion. A combination of the small displacement torsor (SDT) theory and the Monte Carlo method based on the modeling of the mating surfaces' actual real-world mating state is used to mimic the uncertainty of the assembly position in a real assembly. The precision of the analytical results can be increased by superimposing the assembly-gap calculation result on the deformation of the mating surface. The effectiveness of the recommended strategy is illustrated using a case study that uses a prototype system and a load-sensitive multi-way valve assembly process.

Real-time Monte Carlo simulation models of operations with unknown operators may now be generated automatically, thanks to the development of a technology. The resulting real-time locating systems (RTLS)-based digital twin is flexible due to its real-time connections to the manufacturing execution system (MES), enterprise resource planning system (ERP), and real-time locating systems (RTLS) databases. The placement of workstations, how they are used, and the flow of manufacturing materials may all be learned from position and vibration data by applying data mining techniques. One may consider the online usage of this data in simulation software as a versatile depiction of the manufacturing process. A real-time digital twin's output can be used to monitor productivity, particularly when activities are finished by personnel.

Digital twins that combine simulations with current sensor and production data should be the foundation of cyber-physical model-based solutions. The benefits of employing real-time locating systems (RTLS) to combine information are explored in the study [12], and it is shown how the examination of product-specific activity periods using simulation may be accomplished using position and acceleration data. The suggested digital twin is able to forecast the state of production in real time and offer data for assessing the effectiveness of the production process. RTLS and adaptable simulation model connections in real time are really appreciated. In the industrial case study that serves as the basis for this paper, we demonstrate how the notion of Simulation 4.0 aids in an analysis of the efficacy of human resources (HRE) in an assembly process.

1.3   Digital Twin Simulation Techniques

1.3.1   Finite Element Analysis Simulation

The combination of the power of computational modeling with real-time data integration has increased the accuracy and efficiency of finite element analysis (FEA) simulations with digital twin technology. An illustration of a digital twin simulation utilizing finite element analysis is the following:

Data collection: In order to get started, the digital twin collects real-time data from the physical system's embedded sensors. Temperature, pressure, strain, and displacement are a few examples of characteristics that might be included in this data. Continuous data transfers are made to the digital twin platform [28].

Initialization of the model: The physical system is represented by a 3D model that includes information about its shape and composition. There are finite elements that make up the model, and these elements are joined at particular nodes [17].

Material characterization: Based on the physical characteristics of the actual system, each element is given a unique set of material qualities, such as elastic modulus, Poisson's ratio, and thermal conductivity. Testing of the material or already-existing data sources are two ways to get this information.

Boundary conditions: The boundary conditions seen in the physical system are included into the digital twin. Forces, displacements, or heat inputs are a few examples of these situations. In order to depict the system's current condition properly, sensor data is used [22].

Model-data integration: The FEA solver's simulated results are combined with the real-time data received from the physical system through a process known as model-data integration. With the aid of this integration, which enables the digital twin to modify and update its model in response to observable behavior, the simulation can be validated to make sure it properly reflects the actual system [32].

Analysis and design optimization: The digital twin platform examines the simulation results to spot possible problems, gauge the effectiveness of the system, and improve its layout. As a result, preventative maintenance and performance enhancements are possible. It can also forecast how the system will behave in certain conditions [32].

Visualization and reporting: The simulation results and analytical findings are given in clear visualizations and reports so that stakeholders may comprehend the system's behavior and make wise decisions about upkeep, design modifications, or other actions [26].

1.3.2   Computational Fluid Dynamics Simulation

To produce precise and dynamic simulations of fluid systems, computational fluid dynamics (CFD) simulation with respect to digital twin technology makes use of real-time data integration and sophisticated fluid flow modeling. Here is a CFD simulation utilizing digital twin technology as an example:

Data collection: The real-time data that is collected by the physical system's sensors, which are utilized to monitor various parameters, includes flow rates, pressures, temperatures, and velocities. These data are delivered in real-time to the digital twin platform.

Geometry modeling: A 3D model of the fluid system's geometry is made, including all necessary pipes, valves, pumps, and other geometric elements. The model can be generated from current data sources or constructed using CAD tools [37].

Mesh generation: The fluid system's shape is discretized into smaller parts using a computational mesh that is produced by the digital twin. The mesh needs to be fine enough to correctly depict the flow behavior's finer characteristics. There are several meshing methods that may be used, including structured and unstructured meshes.

Fluid properties and boundary conditions: The simulation model's digital twin takes boundary conditions and fluid properties into consideration. Examples of these fluid qualities include density, viscosity, and thermal conductivity. Additionally, the relevant regions of the computational domain are subjected to the boundary conditions found in the physical system, such as inflow rates, temperatures, and pressure boundaries.

Initialization of the solver: The governing equations, including the Navier–Stokes equations for fluid flow, are repeatedly solved over discrete time steps in order to simulate the behavior of the fluid system [23].

Simulation of fluid flow: The CFD solver calculates the properties of the flowing fluid, such as velocity profiles, pressure distributions, temperature gradients, turbulence patterns, and other pertinent flow parameters. The solver takes into consideration variables including fluid viscosity, temperature impacts, and turbulence models to properly depict the flow behavior [2].

Data incorporation and validation: Along with the simulated outcomes from the CFD solver, real-time data gathered from the physical system is also incorporated. Through continual updating and model adjustments based on observed flow behavior, with the aid of this connection, the digital twin is able to update and evaluate the simulation, guaranteeing correctness and reliability [28].

Analysis and optimization: The effectiveness of the system is evaluated by the digital twin platform using the results of the simulation, spot any possible problems, and improve the fluid system's conception and operation. Different scenarios may be simulated, and the effects of configuration modifications can be examined, resulting in insights that can be used to increase operating performance and efficiency while also reducing energy consumption [18].

Reporting and visualization: Reports and visualizations are used to communicate the outcomes of the simulation, the analysis, and the performance metrics. This enables stakeholders to comprehend the flow behavior, pinpoint areas for improvement, and make data-driven choices about system optimization, maintenance, or operational modifications [29].

1.3.3   Discrete Event Simulation

The capabilities of simulation modeling and real-time data integration are used in discrete event simulation (DES). It uses digital twin technology to portray complicated systems in a way that is dynamic and lifelike. As an example of a discrete event simulation based on a digital twin, consider the following:

Data collection: Sensors and other embedded data sources in the physical system are used to gather real-time data. This information could contain elements like the condition of the equipment, output rates, queue lengths, or resource use. The digital twin platform receives the data on a constant basis.

Model initialization: A simulation model capturing the physical system's structure, operations, resources, and decision-making principles is developed. With the help of a simulation software, the model may be constructed utilizing components like entities, events, queues, and resources.

A connection is made between the simulation model and real-time data collected from the physical system. Due to this link, the accuracy of the digital twin's representation of the system's current status and of dynamic changes occurring in real time is ensured [43].

Event-driven simulation: The simulation model employs a discrete event approach, in which activities inside the system are initiated by events that take place at certain periods in time. The model replicates how things (such as items and consumers) move through different processes, capturing resource allocation, queueing behavior, and system interactions [42].

Real-time control and decision-making: Real-time data is used by the digital twin platform to operate the simulation model and make decisions that follow established rules or algorithms. Based on observed circumstances in the physical system, it may, for instance, alter resource allocation, give orders top priority, or start maintenance procedures [45].

Performance analysis: During the simulation run, the simulation model generates performance measures such as throughput, cycle time, waiting periods, or resource consumption. These indicators reveal the behavior of the system, its bottlenecks, and its potential areas of development [44].

Optimization and what-if analysis: The digital twin platform enables scenario analysis and optimization by changing the simulation model's parameters, rules, or resource allocations. As a result, users may investigate various operational methods, assess the effects of changes, and find the best configurations or rules [21, 30].

Reporting and visualization: Reports and visualizations are used to display the outputs of the analysis, performance measurements, and simulation results. As a result, stakeholders are better able to comprehend the behavior of the system, evaluate performance, and decide how to enhance processes, allocate resources, or make operational changes.

1.3.4 Agent-Based Modeling Simulation

Using agent-based modeling (ABM) simulation, which is based on digital twin technology, complex systems may be accurately and dynamically simulated. Simulating agent-based modeling (ABM) blends real-time data integration with ABM's modeling capabilities. This simulation makes use of agent-based modeling and digital twin technologies.

Data collection: Data is gathered in real time through sensors, IoT gadgets, or other data sources that are integrated into the physical system. The variables in this data include things like customer interactions, agent conduct, and environmental and resource circumstances. To the digital twin platform, the data is continually transferred.

Initialization of the model: A simulation model simulating the behavior of various actors or entities in the system is built, including agents that replicate their behavior. In addition to the environment in which the agents function, the model also depicts the structure, rules, and interactions among the agents [25].

Agent definition: According to their traits, activities, rules for making decisions, interactions with other agents, and interactions with their surroundings, agents are defined. Because of the fact that these characteristics are drawn from actual data and subject matter expertise, the behavior of the physical system can be accurately replicated by the digital twin.

Integration of real-time data: The simulation model is combined with the real-time data that has been gathered from the physical system. By adding real-time changes in agent behavior, environmental circumstances, or resource availability, this integration makes sure that the digital twin accurately depicts the system's present state [38].

Execution of the simulation model: The simulation model may be run in real time or accelerated mode, enabling the agents to interact and make decisions in accordance with predefined rules and up-to-date information. The model accurately depicts the dynamics of the system, including agent mobility, decision-making procedures, resource distribution, and emergent behaviors at the systemic level [19].

Performance analysis: The simulation generates performance measures such as agent productivity, system throughput, client satisfaction, or resource use. These measurements show patterns in the system's behavior, point out bottlenecks, and emphasize areas that need development [35].

Optimization and what-if analysis: The digital twin platform enables what-if analysis and scenario optimization by changing agent behaviors, environmental factors, or resource distributions inside the simulation model. Users are able to investigate various operational tactics, assess the effects of adjustments, and find the best configurations or rules as a result [20].

Reporting and visualization: Reports and visualizations are used to display the simulation results, performance data, and analytical findings. Individual agent behavior may be observed, system-level trends can be examined, and stakeholder-level choices about process optimization, resource allocation, or policy changes can be made with full knowledge of the situation [34].

1.3.5   Multi-Body Dynamics Simulation

Using digital twin technology, multi-body dynamics (MBD) simulation creates precise and dynamic models of mechanical systems by combining the capabilities of real-time data integration with multi-body dynamics modeling. Using digital twin technology, following is the process of simulation of multi-body dynamics:

Data collection: Information about the location, velocity, acceleration, and forces acting on various parts of the physical system is captured in real time by sensors integrated into the system. The digital twin platform receives this information on a constant basis.

Model initialization: The mechanical system's shape, parts, and connections are represented by a 3D model that is built. Model elements such as bodies, joints, contacts, and forces are used to describe the system's physical characteristics and restrictions. It may either be created with CAD software or retrieved from already existing data sources.

Integration of real-time data: In addition to the real-time data obtained from the physical system, the simulation model is merged with it. This integration guarantees that the digital twin appropriately depicts the system's current state, taking into account changes in locations, velocities, forces, or other pertinent characteristics in real time [33].

Kinematics and dynamics modeling: The multi-body dynamics theory is used by the digital twin platform to describe the mechanical system's motion and interactions. Incorporating constraints, joint behaviors, and external forces, the model accurately depicts the kinematics (motion) and dynamics (forces and torques) of the system [24].

Initialization of the solver: The simulation is started utilizing the integrated model and real-time data by the MBD solver. It determines the motion and forces in the system by resolving the motion equations while taking into account elements like mass, inertia, contact forces, and friction.

Execution of simulation: The MBD simulation is executed by the digital twin, replicating the mechanical system's behavior over time. The dynamics of the system are correctly simulated by taking into account the interactions between various parts, joints, connections, and outside influences [39].

Performance analysis: The simulation produces performance measures such as component stresses, displacements, velocities, accelerations, or contact forces. These metrics shed light on the behavior of the system, point out problem areas, and assess how well it performs under various loading scenarios [10].

Reporting and visualization: Reports and visualizations are used to display the simulation results, performance data, and analytical findings. The motion of various parts may be observed, stress distributions can be analyzed, and stakeholders can decide on system optimization, design modifications, or maintenance procedures with knowledge.

1.3.6 Monte Carlo Simulation

To produce reliable and accurate models of complex systems, Monte Carlo simulation based on digital twin technology combines the strength of probabilistic modeling with real-time data integration. An illustration of a Monte Carlo simulation utilizing Digital Twin technology is shown below:

Data collection: Sensors and other embedded data sources in the physical system are used to gather real-time data. These variables include things like component qualities, operational circumstances, environmental influences, and input parameters. The digital twin platform receives the data on a constant basis.

Initialization of the model: Probabilistic distributions are included into a simulation model that represents the physical system. The link and dependence between variables, as well as their effect on system behavior, are captured by the model. It may be created with simulation software, applying statistical models and probability distributions [31].

Real-time data integration: The simulation model is combined with the real-time data gathered from the physical system. With the inclusion of real-time changes in input parameters, environmental factors, or component characteristics, this integration makes sure that the digital twin properly captures the system's current state [27].

Monte Carlo sampling: By selecting samples from the specified probability distributions, the digital twin platform uses Monte Carlo sampling to produce numerous sets of input parameters. Each set depicts a unique collection of system circumstances or potential outcomes.

Execution of the simulation model: The simulation model is run for each set of sampled input variables. The digital twin repeats the simulation several times, producing a vast number of simulations that reflect the system's unpredictability and uncertainty. Based on the sampled input parameters and system behavior, the model calculates the outputs or performance metrics of interest [31, 47].

Performance analysis: Data from the Monte Carlo runs' simulations is gathered and examined. It is possible to quantify risks or uncertainties related to system performance by using statistical approaches to investigate the distribution of outputs, evaluate variability, find sensitivity to various input factors, and estimate risk [40].

Decision-making and optimization: The digital twin platform enables decision-making and optimization based on the findings of Monte Carlo simulations. Users may investigate many situations, evaluate the effects of adjustments, and come to wise conclusions about the operational plans, risk management, and resource allocation [36].

Reporting and visualization: Reports and visualizations are used to show the outputs of statistical analyses, the simulation results, and the risk assessment. In order to increase system dependability, performance, and decision-making, stakeholders may comprehend the variability in system performance, evaluate risk levels, and make data-driven decisions [41].

1.4 Conclusion

In order to build and test different situations in a safe and controlled environment, engineers and designers use simulation, which is a crucial part of the creation of digital twins. FEA, CFD, DES, MBD, MCS, and ABM are a few of the simulation methods frequently utilized in the creation of digital twins. Each of these methods may be used to simulate and improve certain facets of the physical system, but each has specific benefits and drawbacks. New simulation methods and tools will appear as digital twin technology develops further, allowing engineers to produce models that are more precise and complete.

References

1. Botín-Sanabria, D.M., Mihaita, A.S., Peimbert-García, R.E., Ramírez-Moreno, M.A., Ramírez-Mendoza, R.A., Lozoya-Santos, J.D.J., Digital twin technology challenges and applications: A comprehensive review. *Remote Sens.*, 14, 6, 1335, 2022.
2. Cao, Y., Tang, X., Gaidai, O., Wang, F., Digital twin real time monitoring method of turbine blade performance based on numerical simulation. *Ocean Eng.*, 263, 112347, 2022.
3. Turan, E., Konuşkan, Y., Yıldırım, N., Tuncalp, D., Inan, M., Yasin, O., Turan, B., Kerimoğlu, V., Digital twin modelling for optimizing the material consumption: A case study on sustainability improvement of thermoforming process. *Sustain. Comput. Inf. Syst.*, 35, 100655, 2022.
4. Chandrasekaran, S., Dutt, V., Vyas, N., Kumar, R., Student Sentiment Analysis Using Various Machine Learning Techniques. *2023 International Conference on Artificial Intelligence and Smart Communication (AISC)*, Greater Noida, India, pp. 104–107, 2023, doi: 10.1109/AISC56616.2023.10085018.
5. Dos Santos, J.F., Tshoombe, B.K., Santos, L.H., Araújo, R.C., Manito, A.R., Fonseca, W.S., Silva, M.O., Digital twin-based monitoring system of induction motors using iot sensors and thermo-magnetic finite element analysis. *IEEE Access*, 11, 1682–1693, 2022.
6. Kumar, A., Kumar, S.A., Dutt, V., Dubey, A.K., Narang, S., A hybrid secure cloud platform maintenance based on improved attribute-based encryption strategies. *Int. J. Interact. Multimed. Artif. Intell.*, 8, 8, 150–157, 2023.
7. Agalianos, K., Ponis, S.T., Aretoulaki, E., Plakas, G., Efthymiou, O., Discrete event simulation and digital twins: review and challenges for logistics. *Proc. Manuf.*, 51, 1636–1641, 2020.
8. Karakra, A., Fontanili, F., Lamine, E., Lamothe, J., Taweel, A., Pervasive computing integrated discrete event simulation for a hospital digital twin, in: *2018 IEEE/ACS 15th International Conference on Computer systems and Applications (AICCSA)*, 2018, October, IEEE, pp. 1–6.
9. Huang J, Cui Y, Zhang L, Tong W, Shi Y, Liu Z. An overview of agent-based models for transport simulation and analysis. *J. Adv. Transp.*, 2022, Article ID 1252534, 17 pages, 2022. https://doi.org/10.1155/2022/1252534.
10. Kumar, A., Kumar, S. A., Dutt, V., Shitharth, S., & Tripathi, E., IoT based arrhythmia classification using the enhanced hunt optimization-based deep learning. *Expert Syst.*, 40, 7, 2023.
11. Wang, K., Liu, D., Liu, Z., Wang, Q., Tan, J., An assembly precision analysis method based on a general part digital twin model. *Robot. Comput. Integr. Manuf.*, 68, 102089, 2021.
12. Ruppert, T. and Abonyi, J., Integration of real-time locating systems into digital twins. *J. Ind. Inf. Integr.*, 20, 100174, 2020.

13. Canedo, A., Industrial IoT lifecycle via digital twins, in: *Proceedings of the Eleventh IEEE/ACM/IFIP International Conference on Hardware/Software Codesign and System Synthesis*, 2016, October, pp. 1–1.

14. Dutt, V., and Sharma, S., Artificial intelligence and technology in weather forecasting and renewable energy systems: emerging techniques and worldwide studies. *Artif. Intell. Renew. Energy Syst.*, 2022, 189–207, 2022.

15. Dahmen, U. and Rossmann, J., Experimentable digital twins for a modeling and simulation-based engineering approach, in: *2018 IEEE International Systems Engineering Symposium (ISSE)*, 2018, October, pp. 1–8, IEEE.

16. Kumar, A., Kumar, S., Dutt, V., Dubey, A.K., García-Díaz, V., IoT-based ECG monitoring for arrhythmia classification using Coyote Grey Wolf optimization-based deep learning CNN classifier. *Biomed. Signal Process. Control*, 76, 103638, 2022.

17. Singh, S., Weeber, M., Birke, K.P., Advancing digital twin imple- mentation: A toolbox for modelling and simulation. *Proc. CIRP*, 99, 567–572, 2021.

18. Reyes Yanes, A., Abbasi, R., Martinez, P., Ahmad, R., Digital twinning of hydroponic grow beds in intelligent aquaponic systems. *Sensors*, 22, 19, 7393, 2022.

19. He, B. and Bai, K.J., Digital twin-based sustainable intelligent manufacturing: A review. *Adv. Manuf.*, 9, 1–21, 2021.

20. Orozco-Romero, A., Arias-Portela, C.Y., Saucedo, J.A.M., The use of agent-based models boosted by digital twins in the supply chain: A literature review, in: *Intelligent Computing and Optimization: Proceedings of the 2nd International Conference on Intelligent Computing and Optimization 2019 (ICO 2019)*, pp. 642–652, 2020, Springer International Publishing.

21. Lim, K.Y.H., Zheng, P., Chen, C.H., A state-of-the-art survey of Digital Twin: techniques, engineering product lifecycle management and business innovation perspectives. *J. Intell. Manuf.*, 31, 1313–1337, 2020.

22. Liang, Z., Wang, S., Peng, Y., Mao, X., Yuan, X., Yang, A., Yin, L., The process correlation interaction construction of Digital Twin for dynamic characteristics of machine tool structures with multi-dimensional variables. *J. Manuf. Syst.*, 63, 78–94, 2022.

23. Zohdi, T.I., A digital-twin and machine-learning framework for precise heat and energy management of data-centers. *Comput. Mech.*, 69, 6, 1501–1516, 2022.

24. Kumar, A., Rathore, P. S., Dubey, A. K., Agrawal, R., & Sharma, K. P., LTE-NBP with holistic UWB-WBAN approach for the energy efficient biomedical application. *Multimed. Tools Appl.*, 82, 25, 39797–39811, 2023.

25. Vogel-Heuser, B., Ocker, F., Scheuer, T., An approach for leveraging Digital Twins in agent-based production systems. *at-Automatisierungstechnik*, 69, 12, 1026–1039, Scheuer2021.

26. Li, L., Aslam, S., Wileman, A., Perinpanayagam, S., Digital twin in aerospace industry: A gentle introduction. *IEEE Access*, 10, 9543–9562, 2021.

27. Wei, Y., Hu, T., Yue, P., Luo, W., & Ma, S., Study on the construction theory of digital twin mechanism model for mechatronics equipment. *Int. J. Adv. Manuf. Technol.*, 2022, 1–19, 2022.

28. Zhang, T., Li, Y., Cai, J., Meng, Q., Sun, S., Li, C., A digital twin for unconventional reservoirs: A multiscale modeling and algorithm to investigate complex mechanisms. *Geofluids*, 2020, 1–12, 2020.

29. Xia, J. and Zou, G., Operation and maintenance optimization of off- shore wind farms based on digital twin: A review. *Ocean Eng.*, 268, 113322, 2023.

30. Leng, J., Yan, D., Liu, Q., Zhang, H., Zhao, G., Wei, L., Zhang, D., Yu, A., Chen, X., Digital twin-driven joint optimisation of packing and storage assignment in large-scale automated high-rise warehouse product-service system. *Int. J. Comput. Integr. Manuf.*, 34, 7-8, 783–800, 2021.

31. van Dinter, R., Tekinerdogan, B., & Catal, C., Predictive maintenance using digital twins: A systematic literature review. *Inf. Softw. Technol.*, 151, 107008, 1–20, 2022.

32. Tao, F., Sui, F., Liu, A., Qi, Q., Zhang, M., Song, B., Guo, Z., Lu, S.C.Y., Nee, A.Y., Digital twin-driven product design framework. *Int. J. Prod. Res.*, 57, 12, 3935–3953, 2019.

33. Benkhaddra, I., Kumar, A., Setitra, M.A. *et al.*, Design and development of consensus activation function enabled neural network-based smart healthcare using BIoT. *Wirel. Pers. Commun.*, 130, 1549–1574, 2023. https://doi.org/10.1007/s11277-023-10344-0.

34. Marah, H. and Challenger, M., An Architecture for Intelligent Agent-Based Digital Twin for Cyber-Physical Systems, in: *Digital Twin Driven Intelligent Systems and Emerging Metaverse*, pp. 65–99, Springer Nature, Singapore, 2023.

35. Latsou, C., Farsi, M., Erkoyuncu, J.A., Digital twin-enabled automated anomaly detection and bottleneck identification in complex manufacturing systems using a multi-agent approach. *J. Manuf. Syst.*, 67, 242–264, 2023.

36. Züst, S., Züst, R., Züst, V., West, S., Stoll, O., Minonne, C., A graph based Monte Carlo simulation supporting a digital twin for the curatorial management of excavation and demolition material flows. *J. Clean. Prod.*, 310, 127453, 2021.

37. Gambitta, M., Beirow, B., & Schrape, S., A Digital Twin of Compressor Blisk Manufacturing Geometrical Variability for the Aeroelastic Uncertainty Quantification of the Aerodynamic Damping, in: *Turbo Expo: Power for Land, Sea, and Air*, vol. 86069, p. V08AT21A021, American Society of Mechanical Engineers, Rotterdam, Netherlands, 2022.

38. Cioara, T., Anghel, I., Antal, M., Antal, C., Arcas, G.I., Croce, V., An Overview of Digital Twins Application in Smart Energy Grids, in: *2022 IEEE 18th International Conference on Intelligent Computer Communication and Processing (ICCP)*, 2022, September, IEEE, pp. 25–30.

39. Li, J., Wang, S., Yang, J., Zhang, H., Zhao, H., A digital twin-based state monitoring method of gear test bench. *Appl. Sci.*, 13, 5, 3291, 2023.

41. Wang, M., Wang, C., Hnydiuk-Stefan, A., Feng, S., Atilla, I., Li, Z., Recent progress on reliability analysis of offshore wind turbine support structures considering digital twin solutions. *Ocean Eng.*, 232, 109168, 2021.

42. Srivastav, A., Markandeya, Patel, N. *et al.*, Concepts of circular economy for sustainable management of electronic wastes: Challenges and management options. *Environ. Sci. Pollut. Res.*, 30, 48654–48675, 2023. https://doi.org/10.1007/s11356-023-26052-y.

43. Aheleroff, S., Zhong, R.Y., Xu, X., A digital twin reference for mass personalization in industry 4.0. *Proc. Cirp*, 93, 228–233, 2020.

44. Pillai, R. and Babbar, H., Digital Twin for Edge Computing in Smart Vehicular Systems, in: *2023 International Conference on Advancement in Computation & Computer Technologies (InCACCT)*, 2023, May, IEEE, pp. 1–5.

45. Bhola, J., Shabaz, M., Dhiman, G., Vimal, S., Subbulakshmi, P., Soni, S.K., Performance evaluation of multilayer clustering network using distributed energy efficient clustering with enhanced threshold protocol. *Wirel. Pers. Commun.*, 126, 3, 2175–2189, 2022.

46. Ilyas, B., Kumar, A., Setitra, M.A., Bensalem, Z.E.A., Lei, H., Prevention of DDoS attacks using an optimized deep learning approach in blockchain technology. *Trans. Emerging. Telecommun. Technol.*, 34, 4, e4729, 2023.

47. Monga, C., Raju, K. S., Arunkumar, P. M., Bist, A. S., Sharma, G. K., Alsaab, H. O., & Malakhil, B., Secure techniques for channel encryption in wireless body area network without the certificate. *Wirel. Commun. Mob. Comput.*, 2022, 1–11, 2022.

2

Comprehensive Analysis of Error Rate and Channel Capacity of Fisher Snedecor Composite Fading Model

Hari Shankar* and Yogesh

Department of Computer Science and Engineering, Chitkara University Institute of Engineering and Technology, Chitkara University, Rajpura, Punjab, India

Abstract

Signal characterization is very important in different propagation environments such as urban and suburban, and it may become distorted due to variations in time domain and shadowing effects through the surrounding objects. Fisher Snedecor fading is an accurate and simple model for next-generation wireless communication technology, more specifically for device to device (D2D) communication. In this paper, the expressions of the average bit error rate (ABER) for binary and multilevel signaling are derived. We also derive the approximate, tightly bound, and asymptotic error rate expressions for some signaling schemes. Thereafter, the capacity expressions using different adaptive transmission techniques are derived. We also compute the capacity expression for both low and high signal-to-noise ratio (SNR) values. Furthermore, to cross-verify the computed expressions, simulation technique is used.

Keywords: Average bit error rate, multipath fading, shadowing, signal-to-noise ratio, channel capacity

2.1 Introduction

In a wireless system, fading is defined as the variation, which is random in nature, in the received signal that occurs due to the combined effect of

---

*Corresponding author: hari.shankar55@gmail.com

Abhineet Anand, Anita Sardana, Abhishek Kumar, Srikanta Kumar Mohapatra and Shikha Gupta (eds.) Simulation Techniques of Digital Twin in Real-Time Applications: Design Modeling and Implementation, (25–56) © 2024 Scrivener Publishing LLC

time and frequency variations. It can be defined in two ways: short-term fading and long-term fading (shadowing). The characterization of the fading channel has an important role in system performance improvement. Generally, the transmitted signal may go through the small-scale faded/shadowed environment. In this case, the composite fading model is most useful [1]. The lognormal distribution-based composite fading models are much more complex; it is also difficult to analyze their performance matrices in the wireless communication system. Some composite fading models based on lognormal distribution are Rayleigh lognormal [2], Rice lognormal [3], Nakagami-m lognormal [4], and κ-μ/lognormal [5]. On other hand, Gamma, inverse Gamma, and inverse Gaussian-based composite fading model are simple and mostly presented in the closed form. The composite fading models based on these shadowing distributions are Rayleigh gamma [6], Nakagami-m/Gamma [7], κ-μ/gamma [8], Nakagami-m/inverse Gaussian [9], κ-μ/inverse gamma [10], η-μ/inverse Gamma [10], etc. A well-known fading distribution, that is, Fisher Snedecor model, has been proposed in [11] and has better characterization for wearable or D2D communication systems [12]. The BER and channel capacity are most important performance matrices in wireless communication systems [13, 14].

In mobile communication systems, the composite fading model was first introduced in [2] and coined as Rayleigh-lognormal. After that, in [4], the Nakagami-m lognormal (NLN) model was introduced. A Rayleigh Gamma or K distribution was proposed in [6], which is most suitable for radar application. A generalized K (GK) model was proposed in [7], which is the generalization of [6]. The presented model was simple and has a closed-form solution. The author in [7] further derived the expressions of the amount of fading (AF) and ABER for BPSK signaling. The performance analysis over the GK fading channel was also presented in [15–18]. In [9], Nakagami-m inverse Gaussian model was introduced. The expressions of capacity for various adaptive protocols under Fox's H function channels were computed in [19].

The work on the recently proposed Fisher Snedecor channels has been presented in various literatures [20–29]. The performances of the switch diversity system for F fading channels were analyzed in [20, 21]. The capacity performance for different adaptive methods was analyzed in [22]. The energy detection-based performance analysis over the F channel has been elaborated in [23]. The performances of MRC receiving diversity over the

F channel were analyzed in [24, 25]. The effective rate analysis over the F channel was performed in [26]. The performance of secure communication in the form of secrecy capacity for the F model was analyzed in [27]. The effective capacity analysis for the F channel was presented in [28].

It is noted that, in [11], the author obtained the ABER expressions only for BPSK (asymptotic not exact analysis) and differential phase shifting keying (DPSK) using the MGF method. Moreover, in [29], the author computed the average channel capacity and ASER expressions for MQAM and MAM. The expressions derived in [29] are given in Fox H function form which is not directly available in well-known software tools like MAPLE and MATLAB. Moreover, the obtained expressions in [29] are unnecessarily too lengthy, which become tedious when elaborating the results.

This paper presents the ABER expressions for binary and multilevel modulations using PDF method over the F channels. We also derive the approximate, tightly bound, and asymptotic expressions of ABER/ASER for some signaling schemes. Thereafter, we compute the capacity expressions for four transmission protocols. The capacity expressions for some limited regions are also computed in further extension. The use of Monte Carlo simulation provides the truthiness of the computed expressions.

We have organized the paper as follows. The density function of the F model is presented in Section 2.2. The ABER for different signaling and capacity expressions for four protocols are derived in Section 2.3. The results of the works are illustrated in Section 2.4. The whole work is concluded in Section 2.5.

2.2   Fisher Snedecor Composite Fading

The PDF of the envelope signal (r) is [11, Equation (2.3)]:

$$f_R(r) = \frac{2m^m \cdot (m_s\Omega)^{m_s} r^{2m-1}}{B(m,m_s)(m_s\Omega + mr^2)^{m+m_s}} \tag{2.1}$$

where $B(\cdot,\cdot)$ is beta function [30], and m and m_s is the fading severity and shadowing parameter, respectively. As $m_s \to 0$, the rms signal power undergoes heavy shadowing, and with $m_s \to \infty$ no shadowing occurs [11]. $\Omega = E[r^2]$ is the mean power of the envelope signal.

The SNR PDF is [13]:

$$f_\gamma(\gamma) = f_r\left(\sqrt{\frac{\Omega\gamma}{\bar{\gamma}}}\right) \bigg/ \left(2\sqrt{\frac{\bar{\gamma}\gamma}{\Omega}}\right) \tag{2.2}$$

where $\bar{\gamma} = \Omega E_s/N_0$, N_0 is the noise power, E_s is the energy symbol, and $\Omega = E[R^2]$.

By using (2.1) and (2.2), the PDF of γ is obtained as [11, Equation (2.5)]:

$$f_\gamma(\gamma) = \frac{m^m \cdot (m_s\bar{\gamma})^{m_s} \gamma^{m-1}}{B(m,m_s)(m\gamma + m_s\bar{\gamma})^{m+m_s}} \tag{2.3}$$

where instantaneous SNR (γ) is defined as $\gamma = \bar{\gamma} \cdot R^2 / \Omega$, and $\bar{\gamma} = E[\gamma]$ is the average instantaneous SNR.

2.3   Mathematical Analysis

2.3.1   Error Rate Analysis

The ABER is formulated as [1]:

$$P_e(E) = \int_0^\infty P_e(E/\gamma)f_\gamma(\gamma)d\gamma \tag{2.4}$$

where $P_e(E/\gamma)$ represents the conditional bit error rate (BER) over the AWGN channel.

2.3.1.1   NCBFSK and BDPSK

The conditional BER for NCBFSK ($A = 0.5$, $B = 0.5$) and BDPSK ($A = 0.5$, $B = 1$) can be defined as [31]:

$$P_e(E/\gamma) = A\exp(-B\gamma) \tag{2.5}$$

where exp(.) is the exponential function [30].

The average BER for the F composite model can be obtained by putting (2.3) and (2.5) in (2.4); hence, we get:

$$P_e(E) = \int_0^\infty A\exp(-B\gamma)\frac{m^m(m_s\bar{\gamma})^{m_s}\gamma^{m-1}}{B(m,m_s)(m\gamma + m_s\bar{\gamma})^{m+ms}}d\gamma \qquad (2.6)$$

As we know that [1, Equation (4.268)]:

$$\exp(-Bx) = G_{0,1}^{1,0}\left(Bx\left|\begin{array}{c}-\\0\end{array}\right.\right) \qquad (2.7)$$

It is noted that $G_{p,q}^{m,n}[\cdot|\cdot]$ defines the Meijer G function [30]. By substituting (2.7) into (2.6), we get:

$$P_e(E) = \frac{A(m_s\bar{\gamma})^{m_s}}{B(m,m_s)m^{m_s}}\int_0^\infty G_{0,1}^{1,0}\left(Bx\left|\begin{array}{c}-\\0\end{array}\right.\right)\frac{\gamma^{m-1}}{(\gamma + m_s\bar{\gamma}/m)^{m+ms}}d\gamma \quad (2.8)$$

By using [30, p.852, Equation (7.811.5)] and after canceling out the same term in the numerator and denominator, the solution of the preceding expression becomes:

$$P_e(E) = \frac{A}{\Gamma(m+m_s)B(m,m_s)}G_{1,2}^{2,1}\left(\frac{Bm_s\bar{\gamma}}{m}\left|\begin{array}{cc}1-m\\m+m_s-m & 0\end{array}\right.\right) \qquad (2.9)$$

2.3.1.2   BPSK, BFSK, and QPSK

The conditional error probability for BPSK ($A = 0.5$, $B = 1$), BFSK ($A = 0.5$, $B = 0.5$), and QPSK ($A = 1$, $B = 0.5$) is given by [31]:

$$P_e(E/\gamma) = A\,erfc(\sqrt{B\gamma}) \qquad (2.10)$$

where erfc(.) is the complementary error function. By using (2.3), (2.4), and (2.10), we get:

$$P_e(E) = \int_0^\infty A erfc\left(\sqrt{B\gamma}\right) \frac{m^m (m_s \bar{\gamma})^{m_s} \gamma^{m-1}}{B(m,m_s)(m\gamma + m_s \bar{\gamma})^{m+m_s}} d\gamma \quad (2.11)$$

As we know that [1, Equation (4.274)]:

$$erfc(\sqrt{B\gamma}) = \frac{1}{\sqrt{\pi}} G_{0,1}^{1,0}\left(B\gamma \left| \begin{matrix} 1 \\ 0.5 \quad 0 \end{matrix} \right. \right) \quad (2.12)$$

Thus, by substituting (2.12) in (2.11), we get:

$$P_e(E) = \frac{A m^m (m_s \bar{\gamma})^{m_s}}{\sqrt{\pi} B(m,m_s)} \int_0^\infty G_{0,1}^{1,0}\left(Bx \left| \begin{matrix} 1 \\ 0.5 \quad 0 \end{matrix} \right. \right) \frac{\gamma^{m-1}}{(m\gamma + m_s \bar{\gamma})^{m+m_s}} d\gamma \quad (2.13)$$

By using [30, p.852, Equation (7.811.5)] and after algebraic calculation, we get the preceding expression as:

$$P_e(E) = \frac{A}{\sqrt{\pi} \cdot \Gamma(m+m_s)B(m,m_s)} G_{2,3}^{3,1}\left(\frac{Bm_s \bar{\gamma}}{m} \left| \begin{matrix} 1-m \quad 1 \\ m_s \quad 0.5 \quad 0 \end{matrix} \right. \right) \quad (2.14)$$

where $\Gamma(.)$ is the Gamma function.

2.3.1.3   MQAM

The conditional error rate (AWGN) for MQAM is [13]:

$$P_e(E/\gamma) = 4\left(1 - \frac{1}{\sqrt{M}}\right) Q\left(\sqrt{\frac{3\gamma}{M-1}}\right) - 4\left(1 - \frac{1}{\sqrt{M}}\right)^2 Q^2\left(\sqrt{\frac{3\gamma}{M-1}}\right) \quad (2.15)$$

The exact closed-form SER expression using MQAM, in terms of bivariate Fox H-function, for the F model is given in [29]. The main drawback of this function is that it is not available in well-known software tools like MATHEMATICA and MATLAB. The exact expression for SER using MQAM in [29] is unnecessarily too lengthy, which becomes tedious when elaborating the result. Therefore, we will derive alternative approximate and tightly bound BER expression for MQAM.

Approximate Analysis: An alternate approximate conditional BER is [13]:

$$P_e(E/\gamma) = 2\left(1 - \frac{1}{\sqrt{M}}\right) erfc\left(\sqrt{\frac{3\gamma}{2(M-1)}}\right) \qquad (2.16)$$

On plugging (2.3) and (2.16) into (2.4), we get the ABER over Fisher fading channel as:

$$P_e(E) = 2\left(1 - \frac{1}{\sqrt{M}}\right) \int_0^\infty erfc\left(\sqrt{\frac{3\gamma}{2(M-1)}}\right) \frac{m^m (m_s\bar{\gamma})^{m_s} \gamma^{m-1}}{B(m,m_s)(m\gamma + m_s\bar{\gamma})^{m+m_s}} d\gamma$$

$$(2.17)$$

Following the similar steps from (2.11)–(2.14), the solution of (2.17) becomes:

$$P_e(E) = \frac{2}{\Gamma(m+m_s)\sqrt{\pi} \cdot B(m,m_s)} \cdot \left(1 - \frac{1}{\sqrt{M}}\right) G_{2,3}^{3,1}\left(\frac{3m_s\bar{\gamma}}{2m(M-1)} \middle| \begin{array}{ccc} 1-m & & 1 \\ m_s & 0.5 & 0 \end{array}\right)$$

$$(2.18)$$

Tightly bound analysis: A tight upper-bound conditional error rate is [32]:

$$P_e(E/\gamma) \leq \frac{1}{5}\exp\left(\sqrt{\frac{1.5\gamma}{M-1}}\right), \qquad \gamma \geq 0, M \geq 4 \qquad (2.19)$$

By substituting (2.3) and (2.19) in (2.4), we obtained:

$$P_e(E) = 0.2\int_0^\infty \exp\left(-\frac{1.5\gamma}{(M-1)}\right) \frac{m^m (m_s\bar{\gamma})^{m_s} \gamma^{m-1}}{B(m,m_s)(m\gamma + m_s\bar{\gamma})^{m+ms}} d\gamma$$

$$(2.20)$$

After going through the same steps from (2.6) to (2.9), we get:

$$P_e(E) = \frac{0.2}{B(m,m_s)\Gamma(m+m_s)} G_{1,2}^{2,1}\left(\frac{1.5m_s\bar{\gamma}}{(M-1)m} \middle| \begin{matrix} 1-m \\ m+m_s-m \quad 0 \end{matrix} \right) \quad (2.21)$$

2.3.1.4   MPSK

The conditional ASER expression for M-ary Phase Shifting Keying (MPSK) is [13]:

$$P_e(E/\gamma) = \frac{1}{\pi} \int_0^{(M-1)\pi/M} \exp\left(-\frac{b\gamma}{\sin^2(\theta)} \right) d\theta \quad (2.22)$$

where $b = \log_2(M)\sin^2(\pi/M)$

By plugging (2.3) and (2.22) in (2.4), we get:

$$P_e(E) = \frac{1}{\pi} \int_0^{\infty} \int_0^{(M-1)\pi/M} \exp\left(-\frac{b\gamma}{\sin^2(\theta)} \right) d\theta \, \frac{m^m(m_s\bar{\gamma})^{m_s} \gamma^{m-1}}{B(m,m_s)(m\gamma + m_s\bar{\gamma})^{m+ms}} d\gamma$$

$$(2.23)$$

or

$$P_e(E) = \frac{m^m(m_s\bar{\gamma})^{m_s}}{\pi B(m,m_s)} \int_0^{(M-1)\pi/M} \left\{ \int_0^{\infty} \exp\left(-\frac{b\gamma}{\sin^2(\theta)} \right) \frac{\gamma^{m-1}}{(m\gamma + m_s\bar{\gamma})^{m+ms}} d\gamma \right\} d\theta$$

$$(2.24)$$

After going through the same steps from (2.6) to (2.9), we get:

$$P_e(E) = \frac{1}{\pi\Gamma(m+m_s)B(m,m_s)} \int_0^{(M-1)\pi/M} G_{1,2}^{2,1}\left(\frac{bm_s\bar{\gamma}}{\sin^2(\theta)m} \middle| \begin{matrix} 1-m \\ m+m_s-m \quad 0 \end{matrix} \right) d\theta$$

$$(2.25)$$

Equation (2.25) is in finite integral form. The approximate error rate expression of MPSK signaling is given as [12, p. 202, Equation (8.31)]:

$$P_e(E/\gamma) \approx \frac{2}{\max(\log_2 M, 2)} \sum_{k=1}^{\max(M/4,1)} Q\left(\sqrt{2\gamma \log_2(M)} \sin\left(\frac{(2k-1)\pi}{M}\right)\right)$$

(2.26)

where Q(.) is the Q function. Now, for large SNR and M > 4, (2.26) can be further simplified to [12, p.202, Equation (8.32)]:

$$P_e(E/\gamma) \approx \frac{2}{\log_2 M} Q\left(\sqrt{2\gamma \log_2(M)} \sin(\pi/M)\right) = \frac{1}{\log_2 M} erfc\left(\sqrt{\gamma \log_2 M} \sin(\pi/M)\right)$$

(2.27)

By substituting (2.3) and (2.27) in (2.4), the ABER for MPSK (M > 4) for large SNR is given as:

$$P_e(E) = \int_0^\infty \frac{1}{\log_2 M} erfc\left(\sqrt{(\log_2 M)\gamma} \sin(\pi/M)\right) \frac{m^m \gamma^{m-1} (m_s \bar{\gamma})^{m_s}}{(m\gamma + m_s \bar{\gamma})^{m+m_s} B(m, m_s)} d\gamma$$

(2.28)

After going through the same steps from (2.11) to (2.14), (2.28) becomes:

$$P_e(E) = \frac{1}{\Gamma(m+m_s)B(m,m_s)\log_2(M)\sqrt{\pi}} G_{2,3}^{3,1}\left(\frac{m_s \bar{\gamma} \sin^2(\pi/M)\log_2(M)}{m} \middle| \begin{matrix} 1-m & 1 \\ m_s & 0.5 & 0 \end{matrix}\right)$$

(2.29)

2.3.1.5   MDPSK

The error rate for the MDPSK modulation scheme is [13]:

$$P_e(E/\gamma) = \frac{1}{\pi} \int_0^{(M-1)\pi/M} \exp\left(-\frac{\gamma \sin^2(\pi/M)}{1 + \cos(\pi/M)\cos(\theta)}\right) d\theta$$ (2.30)

On substituting (2.30) in (2.4), we get ASER (MDPSK) of the F composite fading model as:

$$P_e(E) = \frac{m^m \cdot (m_s \bar{\gamma})^{m_s}}{\pi B(m, m_s)} \int_0^\infty \int_0^{(M-1)\pi/M} \frac{\gamma^{m-1}}{(m\gamma + m_s \bar{\gamma})^{m+m_s}} \exp\left(-\frac{\gamma \sin^2(\pi/M)}{1+\cos(\pi/M)\cos(\theta)}\right) d\theta d\gamma$$

(2.31)

or

$$P_e(E) = \frac{m^m \cdot (m_s \bar{\gamma})^{m_s}}{\pi B(m, m_s)} \int_0^{(M-1)\pi/M} \left\{ \int_0^\infty \frac{\gamma^{m-1}}{(m\gamma + m_s \bar{\gamma})^{m+m_s}} \exp\left(-\frac{\gamma \sin^2(\pi/M)}{1+\cos(\pi/M)\cos(\theta)}\right) d\gamma \right\} d\theta$$

(2.32)

After going through the same steps from (2.6) to (2.9), (2.32) becomes:

$$P_e(E) = \frac{1}{\pi\Gamma(m+m_s)B(m,m_s)} \int_0^{(M-1)\pi/M} G_{1,2}^{2,1}\left(\frac{m_s \bar{\gamma} \sin^2(\pi/M)}{m(1+\cos(\pi/M)\cos(\theta))} \Bigg| \begin{matrix} 1-m \\ m+m_s-m \quad 0 \end{matrix} \right) d\theta$$

(2.33)

The solution of (2.33) can be obtained directly by using simulation software like MATHEMATICA and MAPLE.

Asymptotic analysis: The conditional approximate asymptotic ASER is given as [33, 12]:

$$P_e(E/\gamma) = \sqrt{\frac{1+\cos(\pi/M)}{2\cos(\pi/M)}} erfc\left(\sqrt{\gamma(1-\cos(\pi/M))}\right)$$

(2.34)

where $M > 3$

On plugging (2.3) and (2.34) into (2.4), we get ASER for MDPSK as:

$$P_e(E) = \sqrt{\frac{1+\cos(\pi/M)}{2\cos(\pi/M)}} \frac{m^m \cdot (m_s\bar{\gamma})^{m_s}}{B(m,m_s)} \int_0^\infty \frac{\gamma^{m-1} erfc\left(\sqrt{\gamma(1-\cos(\pi/M))}\right)}{(m\gamma + m_s\bar{\gamma})^{m+m_s}} d\gamma$$

(2.35)

After going through the same steps from (2.11) to (2.14), (2.35) becomes:

$$P_e(E) = \frac{\sqrt{1 + \cos(\pi / M)}}{B(m, m_s) \cdot \Gamma(m + m_s)\sqrt{2\pi \cos(\pi / M)}} G_{2,3}^{3,1}\left(\frac{(1 - \cos(\pi / M))m_s\bar{\gamma}}{m} \Bigg| \begin{array}{ccc} 1 - m & 1 & \\ m_s & 0.5 & 0 \end{array} \right)$$

$$(2.36)$$

This is an asymptotic ASER for MDPSK over the F composite fading channel.

2.3.1.6   NCMFSK

The conditional SER for NCMFSK is [34]:

$$P_e(E / \gamma) = \frac{1}{M} \sum_{i=2}^{M} (-1)^i \binom{M}{i} \exp\left(-\left(1 - \frac{1}{i}\right)\gamma \right) \qquad (2.37)$$

By substituting (2.3) and (2.37) in (2.4), we get:

$$P_e(E) = \frac{(m_s\bar{\gamma})^{m_s}}{Mm^{m_s}B(m, m_s)} \sum_{i=2}^{M} (-1)^i \binom{M}{i} \int_0^\infty \exp\left(-\left(1 - \frac{1}{i}\right)\gamma \right) \frac{\gamma^{m-1}}{(\gamma + m_s\bar{\gamma}/m)^{m+m_s}} d\gamma$$

$$(2.38)$$

After going through the same steps from (2.6) to (2.9), we get:

$$P_e(E) = \frac{1}{M \cdot \Gamma(m + m_s)B(m, m_s)} \sum_{i=2}^{M} (-1)^i \binom{M}{i} G_{1,2}^{2,1}\left(\left(1 - \frac{1}{i}\right)\frac{m_s\bar{\gamma}}{m} \Bigg| \begin{array}{cc} 1 - m & \\ m + m_s - m & 0 \end{array} \right)$$

$$(2.39)$$

2.3.1.7   DQPSK

The error rate for DQPSK is [12, 35]:

$$P_e(E / \gamma) = Q(a, b) - \frac{1}{2} I_0(ab) \exp\left(-\frac{a^2 + b^2}{2} \right) \qquad (2.40)$$

where $a = \sqrt{\gamma(2-\sqrt{2})}$, $b = \sqrt{\gamma(2+\sqrt{2})}$, and $I_0(.)$ and $Q(a, b)$ represent the modified Bessel function and Marcum Q-function, respectively. In simplified infinite series form, an alternative expression of BER for DQPSK is given by [13]:

$$P_e(E/\gamma) = \exp(-2\gamma) \left[\sum_{k=0}^{\infty} I_k(\sqrt{2}\gamma) \left(\sqrt{\frac{2-\sqrt{2}}{2+\sqrt{2}}} \right)^k - \frac{I_0(\sqrt{2}\gamma)}{2} \right]$$

(2.41)

By substituting (2.41) in (2.4), we get:

$$P_e(E) = \sum_{k=0}^{\infty} \left(\sqrt{\frac{2-\sqrt{2}}{2+\sqrt{2}}} \right)^k \underbrace{\int_0^{\infty} \exp(-2\gamma) I_k(\sqrt{2}\gamma) f_\gamma(\gamma) d\gamma}_{T_1} - \frac{1}{2} \underbrace{\int_0^{\infty} \exp(-2\gamma) I_0(\sqrt{2}\gamma) f_\gamma(\gamma) d\gamma}_{T_2}$$

(2.42)

To obtain the analytical solution of BER, we have to solve the integral terms in (2.42) (i.e., T_1 and T_2):

$$T_1 = \int_0^{\infty} \exp(-2\gamma) I_k(\sqrt{2}\gamma) f_\gamma(\gamma) d\gamma$$

(2.43)

By the definition of Bessel function [30] and using (2.3), we get:

$$T_1 = \frac{(m_s\bar{\gamma}/m)^{m_s}}{B(m,m_s)} \sum_{n=0}^{\infty} \frac{1}{2^{n+k/2} n! \Gamma(n+k+1)} \int_0^{\infty} \frac{\gamma^{m+2n+k-1} \exp(-2\gamma)}{\left(\gamma + \frac{m_s\bar{\gamma}}{m} \right)^{m+m_s}} d\gamma$$

(2.44)

After going through the same steps from (2.6) to (2.9), (2.44) becomes:

$$T_1 = \sum_{n=0}^{\infty} \frac{\left(m_s\bar{\gamma}/m\right)^{2n+k}}{B(m,m_s)n!\Gamma(n+k+1)\cdot\Gamma(m+m_s)\cdot 2^{n+k/2}} G_{1,2}^{2,1}\left(\frac{2m_s\bar{\gamma}}{m}\left|\begin{array}{c}1-m-2n-k\\ m_s-2n-k \quad ,0\end{array}\right.\right)$$

(2.45)

In a similar way, T_2 becomes:

$$T_2 = \frac{1}{2}\sum_{n=0}^{\infty} \frac{\left(m_s\bar{\gamma}/m\right)^{2n}}{B(m,m_s)n!\Gamma(n+1)\cdot\Gamma(m+m_s)\cdot 2^{n}} G_{1,2}^{2,1}\left(\frac{2m_s\bar{\gamma}}{m}\left|\begin{array}{c}1-m-2n\\ m_s-2n \quad ,0\end{array}\right.\right)$$

(2.46)

On substituting (2.45) and (2.46) in (2.42) and after some algebraic calculations, we get:

$$P_e(E) = \sum_{n=0}^{\infty} \frac{\left(m_s\bar{\gamma}/m\right)^{2n}}{B(m,m_s)n!\Gamma(m+m_s)} \left\{ \sum_{k=0}^{\infty} \frac{\left(m_s\bar{\gamma}/m\right)^{k}}{\Gamma(n+k+1)\cdot 2^{n+k/2}} \left(\sqrt{\frac{2-\sqrt{2}}{2+\sqrt{2}}}\right)^{k} \right.$$

$$\left. G_{1,2}^{2,1}\left(\frac{2m_s\bar{\gamma}}{m}\left|\begin{array}{c}1-m-2n-k\\ m_s-2n-k \quad ,0\end{array}\right.\right) - \frac{1}{2^{n+1}\Gamma(n+1)} G_{1,2}^{2,1}\left(\frac{2m_s\bar{\gamma}}{m}\left|\begin{array}{c}1-m-2n\\ m_s-2n \quad ,0\end{array}\right.\right) \right\}$$

(2.47)

This is the exact analytical BER expression for DQPSK.

Approximate analysis: An approximate conditional BER is [35, Equation (2.8)]:

$$P_e\left(E/\gamma\right) = \frac{\left(\sqrt{2}+1\right)}{\sqrt{8\pi\gamma\sqrt{2}}}\exp\left(-\left(2-\sqrt{2}\right)\gamma\right)$$

(2.48)

By plugging (2.3) and (2.48) into (2.4), we get an approximate BER for DQPSK over the Fisher fading channel.

$$P_e(E) = \frac{(\sqrt{2}+1)}{B(m,m_s)\sqrt{8\pi\sqrt{2}}} \left(\frac{m_s\bar{\gamma}}{m}\right)^{m_s} \int_0^\infty \frac{\exp\left(-\left(2-\sqrt{2}\right)\gamma\right)}{(\gamma+m_s\bar{\gamma}/m)^{m+m_s}} \gamma^{m-3/2} d\gamma$$

(2.49)

Using (2.7), (2.49) becomes:

$$P_e(E) = \frac{(\sqrt{2}+1)}{B(m,m_s)\sqrt{8\pi\sqrt{2}}} \left(\frac{m_s\bar{\gamma}}{m}\right)^{m_s} \int_0^\infty \frac{\gamma^{m-3/2}}{(\gamma+m_s\bar{\gamma}/m)^{m+m_s}} G_{0,1}^{1,0}\left(\left(2-\sqrt{2}\right)\gamma\,\Big|\,0\right) d\gamma$$

(2.50)

By using [30, p.852, Equation (7.811.5)] and after algebraic calculation, the preceding expression becomes:

$$P_e(E) = \frac{(\sqrt{2}+1)}{\Gamma(m+m_s)\sqrt{8\pi\sqrt{2}}\,B(m,m_s)} \left(\frac{m_s\bar{\gamma}}{m}\right)^{-1/2} G_{1,2}^{2,1}\left(\left(2-\sqrt{2}\right)\frac{m_s\bar{\gamma}}{m}\,\Big|\,\begin{matrix}\frac{3}{2}-m\\ m_s+\frac{1}{2},\quad 0\end{matrix}\right)$$

(2.51)

2.3.2 Channel Capacity Analysis

The rate of transmission of maximum data through a wireless channel is termed as channel capacity. In a practical wireless communication system, the Shannon bound acts as optimum bound at minimum BER. The channel capacity in a wireless fading environment can be used more efficiently by varying the symbol rate, transmitting power level, and constellation size. Four different adaptive capacities will be derived in this section for the F fading model.

2.3.2.1   ORA

In optimal rate adaption (ORA) policy, the Rx knows the channel state information (CSI), and the transmitter sends the information with constant power. The capacity $\langle C \rangle_{ORA}$ (bps) over any fading channel is [14, Equation (2.29)],

$$\langle C \rangle_{ORA} = B \int_0^\infty \log_2(1+\gamma) f_\gamma(\gamma) d\gamma \qquad (2.52)$$

Now, by putting the PDF of instantaneous SNR (2.3) in (2.52), we get:

$$\langle C \rangle_{ORA} = \frac{1}{\log(2)} \int_0^\infty \log(1+\gamma) \frac{m^m \cdot (m_s \bar{\gamma})^{m_s} \gamma^{m-1}}{B(m,m_s)(m\gamma + m_s \bar{\gamma})^{m+m_s}} d\gamma \quad (2.53)$$

By taking the constant term outside integral and by converting $\log(1+\gamma)$ into Meijer G function [1, Equation (4.279)], we get:

$$\langle C \rangle_{ORA} = \frac{m^m \cdot (m_s \bar{\gamma})^{m_s}}{\log(2) B(m,m_s)} \int_0^\infty G_{2,2}^{1,2}\left(\gamma \left|\begin{matrix} 1 & 1 \\ 1 & 0 \end{matrix}\right.\right) \frac{\gamma^{m-1}}{(m\gamma + m_s \bar{\gamma})^{m+m_s}} d\gamma$$

$$(2.54)$$

By using [30, p.852, Equation (7.811.5)] and after mathematical calculation, we get the preceding expression as:

$$\langle C \rangle_{ORA} = \frac{1}{B(m,m_s)\log(2)\Gamma(m+m_s)} G_{3,3}^{2,3}\left(\frac{m_s \bar{\gamma}}{m} \left|\begin{matrix} 1-m & 1 & 1 \\ m_s & 1 & 0 \end{matrix}\right.\right)$$

$$(2.55)$$

High SNR regimes: The C_{ORA} at high SNR is [20]:

$$\langle C \rangle_{ORA}(HSNR) = B \int_0^\infty \log_2(\gamma) f_\gamma(\gamma) d\gamma \qquad (2.56)$$

By substituting (2.2) in (2.56), we get:

$$\langle C \rangle_{ORA}(HSNR) = \frac{(m_s \bar{\gamma}/m)^{m_s}}{B(m,m_s)} \int_0^\infty \log_2(\gamma) \frac{\gamma^{m-1}}{(\gamma + m_s \bar{\gamma}/m)^{m+m_s}} d\gamma$$

$$(2.57)$$

By using [36, p.489, Equation (2.6.4.7)] and after some algebraic calculations, we get:

$$\langle C \rangle_{ORA}(HSNR) = \frac{1}{\log(2)}\left[\log\left(\frac{m_s\bar{\gamma}}{m}\right) + \psi(m) - \psi(m_s)\right] \quad (2.58)$$

Low SNR regime: The C_{ORA} at low SNR is [37, Equation (2.11)]:

$$\langle C \rangle_{ORA}(LSNR) \approx B\int_0^\infty \gamma f_\gamma(\gamma)d\gamma \quad (2.59)$$

Therefore, (2.59) becomes:

$$\langle C \rangle_{ORA}(LSNR) \approx \frac{1}{\log(2)}\left(\frac{m_s\bar{\gamma}}{m}\right)\frac{B(m+1,m_s-1)}{B(m,m_s)} \quad (2.60)$$

2.3.2.2 OPRA

In the Optimal Simultaneous Power and Rate Adaption (OPRA) scheme, the CSI is known both at Tx and Rx. Since the transmitter knows the CSI, it can easily adapt its power as well as transmission rate. The channel capacity under OPRA schemes in bit per second is [14, Equation (2.7)]:

$$\langle C \rangle_{OPRA} = B\int_{\gamma_0}^\infty \log_2\left(\frac{\gamma}{\gamma_0}\right) \cdot f_\gamma(\gamma)d\gamma \quad (2.61)$$

where γ_0 is the optimal cutoff SNR.

The condition for adaptive transmission is given as [14, Equation (2.8)]:

$$\int_{\gamma_0}^\infty \left(\frac{1}{\gamma_0} - \frac{1}{\gamma}\right)f_\gamma(\gamma)d\gamma = 1 \quad (2.62)$$

Data transmission is suspended when the received instantaneous SNR level γ falls below γ_0. The relationship between γ_0 and $\bar{\gamma}$ for adaptive transmission can be achieved by deriving two integrals I_1 and I_2 (say) using [30, p.315, Equation (3.194.2)]:

$$I_1 = \int_{\gamma_0}^{\infty} f_{\gamma}(\gamma)d\gamma = \int_{\gamma_0}^{\infty} \frac{m^m \cdot (m_s\bar{\gamma})^{m_s} \gamma^{m-1}}{B(m,m_s)(m\gamma + m_s\bar{\gamma})^{m+m_s}} d\gamma = \frac{\gamma_0^{-m_s} \, _2F_1\left(m+m_s, m_s; m_s+1; \dfrac{-m_s\bar{\gamma}}{m\gamma_0}\right)}{B(m,m_s)(m/m_s\bar{\gamma})^{m_s} m_s}$$

(2.63)

where $_2F_1\left(\cdot,\cdot;\cdot;\cdot\right)$ is the Gauss hypergeometric function [30] and:

$$I_2 = \int_{\gamma_0}^{\infty} \frac{1}{\gamma} f_{\gamma}(\gamma)d\gamma = \int_{\gamma_0}^{\infty} \frac{m^m \cdot (m_s\bar{\gamma})^{m_s} \gamma^{m-2}}{B(m,m_s)(m\gamma + m_s\bar{\gamma})^{m+m_s}} d\gamma = \frac{\gamma_0^{-1-m_s} \, _2F_1\left(m+m_s, m_s+1; m_s+2; \dfrac{-m_s\bar{\gamma}}{m\gamma_0}\right)}{B(m,m_s)(m/m_s\bar{\gamma})^{m_s} (m_s+1)}$$

(2.64)

Now, putting the expression of (2.63) and (2.64) in (2.62), we get the condition for optimal adaptive data transmission as:

$$\frac{\gamma_0^{-1-m_s}}{(m/\bar{\gamma}m_s)^{m_s} B(m,m_s)} \left[\frac{_2F_1\left(m+m_s, m_s; 1+m_s; \dfrac{-m_s\bar{\gamma}}{m\gamma_0}\right)}{m_s} - \frac{_2F_1\left(m+m_s, 1+m_s; 2+m_s; \dfrac{-m_s\bar{\gamma}}{m\gamma_0}\right)}{(1+m_s)}\right] = 1$$

(2.65)

Now, by substituting (2.3) into (2.61), we get:

$$\langle C \rangle_{OPRA} = \frac{m^m (m_s\bar{\gamma})^{m_s}}{B(m,m_s)} \int_{\gamma_0}^{\infty} \log_2\left(\frac{\gamma}{\gamma_0}\right) \cdot \frac{\gamma^{m-1}}{(m\gamma + m_s\bar{\gamma})^{m+m_s}} d\gamma \quad (2.66)$$

Let $\gamma/\gamma_0 = x$ or $d\gamma = \gamma_0 dx$; thus, (2.66) becomes:

$$\langle C \rangle_{OPRA} = \frac{(m_s\bar{\gamma})^{m_s}}{\log(2)B(m,m_s)(\gamma_0 m)^{m_s}} \int_1^{\infty} \log(x) \cdot \frac{(x)^{m-1}}{\left(x + \dfrac{m_s\bar{\gamma}}{m\gamma_0}\right)^{m+m_s}} \gamma_0 d\gamma$$

(2.67)

By using integration property, we get:

$$\langle C \rangle_{OPRA} = \frac{(m_s\bar{\gamma})^{m_s}}{\log(2)(m\gamma_0)^{m_s}B(m,m_s)} \left[\underbrace{\int_0^{\infty} \log(x) \frac{(x)^{m-1}}{\left(x + \dfrac{m_s\bar{\gamma}}{m\gamma_0}\right)^{m+m_s}} d\gamma}_{I_3} - \underbrace{\int_0^1 \log(x) \frac{(x)^{m-1}}{\left(x + \dfrac{m_s\bar{\gamma}}{m\gamma_0}\right)^{m+m_s}} d\gamma}_{I_4} \right]$$

(2.68)

I_3 can be solved by using [36, p.489, Equation (2.6.4.7)]. Using the identity $\log(1 + x) = x \, _2F_1(1,1;2;-x)$ [30], I_4 can be computed using [38, p.317, Equation (2.26)]. On substituting the value of I_3 and I_4 in (2.68), we get the C_{OPRA} as:

$$\langle C \rangle_{OPRA} = \frac{1}{\log(2)} \left(\log\left(\frac{m_s\bar{\gamma}}{m\gamma_0}\right) + \psi(m) - \psi(m_s) \right.$$

$$\left. + \frac{_3F_2\left(m,m,m+m_s;1+m,1+m,-\dfrac{m\gamma_0}{m_s\bar{\gamma}}\right)}{m^2 B(m,m_s)} \left(\frac{m_s\bar{\gamma}}{m\gamma_0}\right)^{-m} \right)$$

(2.69)

where $\psi(m)$ is the psi function [30].

2.3.2.3   CIFR

The capacity under channel inversion with fixed rate (CIFR) is [14, Equation (2.46)]:

$$\langle C \rangle_{CIFR} = B \log_2 \left(1 + \frac{1}{\int_0^\infty \frac{f_\gamma(\gamma)}{\gamma} d\gamma} \right) \tag{2.70}$$

By substituting (2.3) in (2.70) and using [30, p.315, Equation (3.194)], we get:

$$\langle C \rangle_{CIFR} = B \log_2 \left(1 + \frac{B(m, m_s) m_s \bar{\gamma}}{m B(m-1, 1+m_s)} \right) \tag{2.71}$$

It is noted that (2.71) satisfies the condition $m + m_s > m - 1 > 0$.

2.3.2.4 TIFR

The capacity for the truncated CIFR (TIFR) schemes is given as [14, Equation (2.47)]:

$$\langle C \rangle_{TIFR} = B \log_2 \left(1 + \frac{1}{\int_{\gamma_0}^\infty \frac{P_\gamma(\gamma)}{\gamma} d\gamma} \right) (1 - P_{out}) \tag{2.72}$$

Considering the integral term in (2.72) as I:

$$I = \int_{\gamma_0}^\infty \gamma^{-1} P_\gamma(\gamma) d\gamma = \frac{m^m \cdot (m_s \bar{\gamma})^{m_s}}{(m_s \bar{\gamma})^{m+m_s} B(m, m_s)} \int_{\gamma_0}^\infty \frac{\gamma^{m-2}}{\left(1 + \frac{m\gamma}{m_s \bar{\gamma}} \right)^{m+m_s}} d\gamma$$

$$\tag{2.73}$$

Using [30], we get the preceding expression as:

$$I = \frac{\gamma_0^{-1-m_s} \, _2F_1\left(m+m_s, 1+m_s; 2+m_s; -\frac{m_s\bar{\gamma}}{m\gamma_0}\right)}{\left(m/m_s\bar{\gamma}\right)^{m_s}(m_s+1)B(m,m_s)} \tag{2.74}$$

By substituting (2.74) in (2.72), we get C_{TIFR}:

$$\langle C \rangle_{TIFR} = B\log_2\left(1+\frac{\left(m/m_s\bar{\gamma}\right)^{m_s} B(m,m_s)\cdot(m_s+1)}{\gamma_0^{-1-m_s} \, _2F_1\left(m+m_s, 1+m_s; 2+m_s; -\frac{\bar{\gamma}m_s}{\gamma_0 m}\right)}\right)(1-P_{out}) \tag{2.75}$$

where P_{out} represents the OP that has been proposed in [11, Equation (2.11)], and $_2F_1(.)$ is the hypergeometric function.

2.4   Numerical Results

The results of the error rate using several signaling scheme and capacity for various adaptive methods are presented in this section using different m and m_s parameters. The analysis has been performed using several signaling schemes as available in literature [1, 12, 39]. The validation of numerical results is achieved through Monte Carlo simulation. The m_s value depends on the environment condition, whether it is dense or not. The dense environment can have a heavy shadowing effect ($m_s \to 0$).

Figure 2.1 presents the ABER using BPSK schemes for $m = 1, 2$ under $m_s = 20$. In Figure 2.1, the ABER (BPSK) of the F composite model (continuous line) is compared with the ABER of existing models. In Figure 2.1, the larger value of m, m_s was kept constant here, has the lowest error rate because of least severity in multipath fading.

Figure 2.2 depicts the error rate of BFSK, BPSK, and QPSK signaling. We have used $m = 2$ and $m_s = 4$ to plot the BER curve for all three modulation schemes. From Figure 2.2, it is observed that the BFSK has a larger error rate because of non-linearity than BPSK signaling. The QPSK signaling also has less BER performance compared to the two others (BPSK and BFSK).

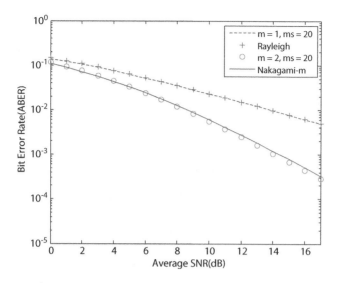

Figure 2.1 BER for BPSK and its comparison with Rayleigh and Nakagami-m.

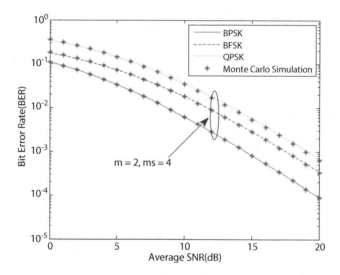

Figure 2.2 Error probability for basic signaling scheme.

Figure 2.3 depicts the error probability for NCBFSK/BDPSK having m and m_s distinct values. In Figure 2.3, the BDPSK has a lesser error rate than NCFSK. On increasing m, the error rate also becomes lower. However, on increasing m_s (between 0.5 and 2) while the fading severity parameter was

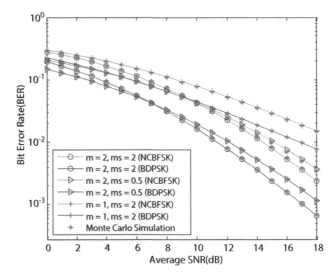

Figure 2.3 Average BER for NCBFSK and BDPSK for different m and m_s.

kept constant ($m = 2$), the BER performance for low SNR regime (say, 0 to 4 dB) gets decreased, and it increases for the high SNR regime (say, 14 to 18 dB).

Figure 2.4 shows the average BER for 4 QAM and 32 QAM modulation scheme with $m = 2$, 8 and $m_s = 1$ over the F composite fading channel. We have plotted the approximate (18) and exponential tightly bound (21) ABER results for the MQAM modulation scheme with $M = 4$ and 32. The simulation shows the correctness of the derived expression presented in (18) and (21). From Figure 2.4, we observed that, on varying m (2 to 8) with $m_s = 1$ and $M = 4$, the BER decreases. On varying M, the BER performance also degrades as expected.

Figure 2.5 is the error rate using 4 PSK and 16 PSK signaling for $m = 2$, 8 with heavy ($m_s = 0.5$), moderate ($m_s = 5$), and light shadowing environments ($m_s = 15$). We have used $M = 4$ and 16 to plot the BER curve for the MPSK modulation schemes (29). In Figure 2.5, on increasing m_s (0.5 to 15) with $m = 2$ (or 8) and $M = 4$ (or 16), the BER performance increases. Thus, it can be concluded that, in no shadowing or light shadowing environment, the error probability is lower than that of in heavy/moderate shadowing environment. Moreover, on increasing m, the error rate decreases. The study shows that, as M increases, the probability of error performance degrades as expected.

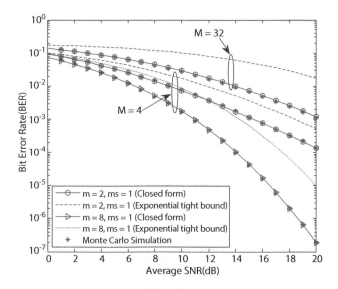

Figure 2.4 Error rate for MQAM including various *m*.

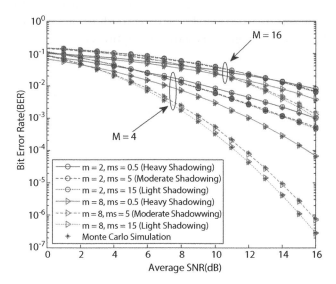

Figure 2.5 BER for MPSK with *M* = 4 and 16.

Figure 2.6 depicts the average BER for MDPSK modulation schemes with $m = 2, 20, m_s = 1, 20,$ and $M = 8, 16$. We have plotted the curve of asymptotic ABER for 8 DPSK and 16 DPSK (36). In Figure 2.6, on varying m (between 2 and 20) with constant m_s and M, the error rate performance improves because of degradation in fading severity. However, on increasing the shadowing parameter, from heavy shadowing ($m_s = 1$) to light shadowing ($m_s = 20$), we observed that the error rate performance increases slightly only at high SNR (>20).

Figure 2.7 depicts the error probability for NCMFSK modulation scheme (39) with $m = 2, 4, 12, m_s = 1,$ and $M = 8, 16,$ and 32. With $M = 2,$ the closed form ABER expression for NCMFSK (39) reduces to ABER for NCBFSK (9). In Figure 2.7, on increasing M, the error rate decreases as expected. Moreover, on increasing m with $m_s = 1$ and $M = 8$ (or 16 or 32), the BER performance increases.

Figure 2.8 presents the exact and approximate error rate for DQPSK with $m = 1, 2, 4, 8, 16$ and $m_s = 1, 20$. With $m = 1$ and light shadowing (that is larger m_s), the ABER using DQPSK (47) over the F channels converges to the corresponding Rayleigh fading [13]. Moreover, it is also observed that the error rate performance for the exact result is slightly higher compared to that of the approximate result. However, both results merge with each other at the high SNR region, as shown in Figure 2.8.

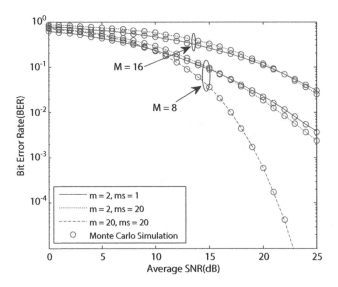

Figure 2.6 BER for MDPSK with $M = 8$ and 16.

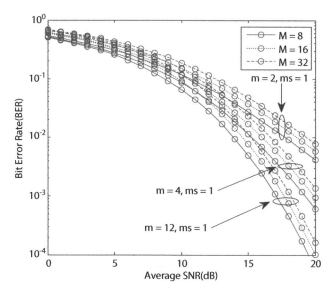

Figure 2.7 Average BER for NCMFSK with $M = 8$, 16, and 32.

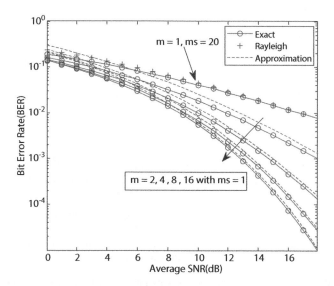

Figure 2.8 Error probability for DQPSK signaling.

Figure 2.9 shows the capacities for ORA, OPRA, CIFR, and TIFR. From Figure 2.9, it is clear that the capacity improves as the SNR (in decibel) increases. Moreover, the result shows that the channel capacity under the

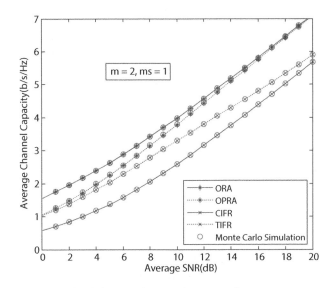

Figure 2.9 Capacity under different policies with $m = 2$ and $m_s = 1$.

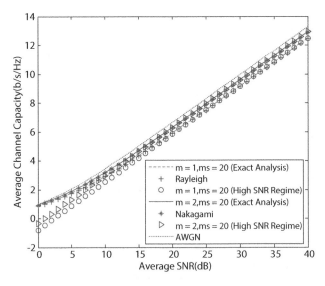

Figure 2.10 Comparison of the channel capacity for ORA with classical fading models.

ORA schemes (55) is higher compared to other policies like OPRA (39), CIFR (71), and TIFR (75). At the higher SNR, the C_{TIFR} meets with the C_{CIFR}. Because of constant transmitting power and data rates, the C_{ORA} has better performance than the capacity for other policies. On the other hand,

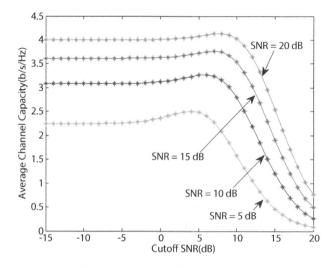

Figure 2.11 Capacity for TIFR *versus* cutoff SNR (γ_0) with $m = 4$, $m_s = 2$, and $\bar{\gamma} = 5$, 10, 15, and 20 dB.

the C_{CIFR} policy transfers a large amount of power without having knowledge of CSI; therefore, this scheme is suffering from large capacity penal. C_{TIFR} recovers this loss by truncating the SNR value below the threshold level.

Figure 2.10 depicts the C_{ORA} of the F composite model and its comparison with the capacity of the existing model. We have drawn the channel capacity (ORA) for both exact closed-form expression (55) and expression at high-SNR regime (58). For $m = 1$ and $m_s = 20$, (55) approaches to the capacity for Rayleigh fading [14]. Similarly, with $m = 2$ and $m_s = 20$ (light shadowing), (55) coincides with C_{ORA} of Nakagami-m fading [1, p.285, Equation (4.207)]. From Figure 2.10, as m increases, the capacity performance under ORA policy gets improved. It can be seen that the ideal AWGN channel has optimal capacity performance.

Figure 2.11 shows the plot of C_{TIFR} with different $\bar{\gamma}$, $m = 4$, and $m_s = 2$. In Figure 2.11, on increasing the average SNR with fixed optimal cutoff SNR, the capacity gets increased.

2.5   Conclusion

In this paper, the error rate expressions for different signaling schemes such as BDPSK, BPSK, BFSK, QPSK, NCFSK, MPSK, MQAM, DQPSK,

MDPSK, and NCMFSK over the F fading channel have been derived. Next, the approximate, tightly bound, and asymptotic expressions of ABER have been computed. Furthermore, different capacity expressions have been obtained. For insight study, we also derived capacity expressions at high and low SNR. Some reduction cases have also been mentioned for validation and generalization purposes. The analytical results have been obtained and corroborated with simulation. The study shows that the error rate and channel capacity performances improve by increasing m with fixed shadowing parameters (m_s). However, the slight performance improvements have been seen when switching from heavy shadowing ($m_s \to 0$) to light shadowing environment ($m_s \to \infty$) with constant m. Moreover, it is seen that the ORA policy has improved channel capacity compared to that of the three other policies since it requires fixed transmit power and data rate. However, the CIFR policy has higher capacity penalty than TIFR as it sends large transmitting power.

References

1. Shankar, P.M., *Fading and Shadowing in Wireless Systems*, Springer, New York, USA, 2012.
2. Suzuki, H., A statistical model for urban radio propagation. *IEEE Trans. Commun.*, 25, 673–680, 1977.
3. Corazza, G.E. and Vatalaro, F., A statistical model for land mobile satellite channels and its application to nongeostationary orbit systems. *IEEE Trans. Veh. Technol.*, 43, 738–742, 1994.
4. Tjhung, T.T. and Chai, C.C., Fade statistics in Nakagami-lognormal channels. *IEEE Trans. Commun.*, 47, 1769–1772, 1999.
5. Cotton, S.L., A statistical model for shadowed body-centric communications channels: Theory and validation. *IEEE Trans. Ant. Prop.*, 62, 1416–1424, 2014.
6. Abdi, A., Kaveh, M., K distribution: An appropriate substitute for Rayleigh-lognormal distribution in fading-shadowing wireless channels. *IET Electron. Lett.*, 34, 851–852, 1998.
7. Shankar, P.M., Error rates in generalized shadowed fading channels. *Wirel. Pers. Commun.*, 28, 233–238, 2004.
8. Yoo, S.K., Cotton, S.L., Sofotasios, P.C., Freear, S., Shadowed fading in indoor off-body communication channels: A statistical characterization using the κ-μ/gamma composite fading model. *IEEE Trans. Wirel. Commun.*, 15, 5231–5244, 2016.

9. Laourine, A., Alouini, M.S., Affes, S., Stéphenne, A., On the performance analysis of composite multipath/shadowing channels using the G-distribution. *IEEE Trans. Commun.*, 57, 1162–1170, 2009.

10. Yoo, S.K., Bhargav, N., Cotton, S.L., Sofotasios, P.C., Matthaiou, M., Valkama, M., Karagiannidis, G.K., The κ-μ/ inverse gamma and η-μ / inverse gamma composite fading models: Fundamental statistics and empirical validation. *IEEE Trans. Commun.*, 69, 8, 5514–5530, 2017, doi: 10.1109/TCOMM.2017.2780110.

11. Yoo, S.K., Cotton, S.L., Sofotasios, P.C., Matthaiou, M., Valkama, M., Karagiannidis, G.K., The Fisher-Snedecor F distribution: A simple and accurate composite fading model. *IEEE Commun. Lett.*, 21, 1661–1664, 2017.

12. Bhatia, H., Panda, S.N., Nagpal, D., Internet of Things and its Applications in Healthcare-A Survey, in: *IEEE International Conference on Reliability, Infocom Technologies and Optimization (Trends and Future Directions), (ICRITO)*, pp. 305–310, 2020.

13. Simon, M.K. and Alouini, M.S., *Digital Communication over Fading Channels*, John Wiley & Sons, New York, 2005.

14. Alouini, M.S. and Goldsmith, A., Capacity of Rayleigh fading channels under different adaptive transmission and diversity combining techniques. *IEEE Trans. Veh. Technol.*, 48, 1165–1181, 1999.

15. Bithas, P.S., Sagias, N.C., Mathiopoulos, P.T., Karagiannidis, G.K., Rontogiannis, A.A., On the performance analysis of digital communications over generalized-K fading channels. *IEEE Commun. Lett.*, 5, 353–355, 2006.

16. Laourine, A., Alouini, M.S., Affes, S., Stephenne, A., On the capacity of Generalized-K fading channels. *IEEE Trans. Wirel. Commun.*, 7, 2441–2445, 2008.

17. Efthymoglou, G.P., On the performance analysis of digital modulations in Generalized-K fading channels. *Wirel. Pers. Commun.*, 65, 643–651, 2008.

18. Efthymoglou, G.P., Ermolova, N.Y., Aalo, V.A., Channel capacity and average error rates in Generalised-K fading channels. *IET Commun.*, 4, 1364–1372, 2010.

19. Rahama, Y.A., Ismail, M.H., Hassan, M.S., Capacity of Fox's H-function fading channel with adaptive transmission. *IET Electron. Lett.*, 52, 976–978, 2016.

20. Cheng, W., Wang, X., Ma, T., Wang, G., On the performance analysis of switched diversity combining receivers over Fisher-Snedecor $\mathcal{F}$ composite fading channels. *Sensors*, 21, 3014, 2020.

21. Shankar, H., Performance analysis of switch and stay combining system over Fisher Snedecor (F) fading channels. *Wirel. Pers. Commun.*, 130, 113–141, 2023.

22. Zhao, H., Yang, L., Salem, A.S., Alouini, M.S., Ergodic capacity under power adaption over Fisher-Snedecor F fading channels. *IEEE Commun. Lett.*, 23, 3, 546–549, 2019.

23. Yoo, S.K., Cotton, S.L., Sofotasios, P.C., Muhaidat, S., Badarneh, O.S., Karagiannidis, G.K., Entropy and energy detection-based spectrum sensing over F composite fading channels. *IEEE J.*, 67, 7, 4641–4653, 2018.

24. Badarneh, O.S., da Costa, D.B., Sofotasios, P.C., Muhaidat, S., Cotton, S.L., On the sum of Fisher-Snedecor F variates and its application to maximal-ratio combining. *IEEE Wirel. Commun. Lett.*, 7, 966–969, 2018.

25. Shankar, H. and Kansal, A., Performance analysis of MRC receiver over fisher snedecor (F) composite fading channels. *Wirel. Pers. Commun.*, 117, 1337–1359, 2021.

26. Chen, S., Zhang, J., Karagiannidis, G.K., Ai, B., Effective rate of MISO systems over Fisher–Snedecor F Fading Channels. *IEEE Commun. Lett.*, 22, 2619–2622, 2018.

27. Kong, L. and Kaddoum, G., On physical layer security over the Fisher-SnedecorF wiretap fading channels. *IEEE Access*, 7, 39466–39472, 2018.

28. Almehmadi, F.S., Badarneh, O.S., On the effective capacity of Fisher–Snedecor F fading channels. *Electon. Lett.*, 54, 1068–1070, 2018.

29. Aldalgamouni, T., Ilter, M.C., Badarneh, O.S., Yanikomeroglu, H., Performance analysis of Fisher-Snedecor F composite fading channels. *IEEE Middle East and North Africa Commun. Conf. (MENACOMM)*, Jounieh, Lebanon, 2018.

30. Gradshteyn, I.S. and Ryzhik, I.M., *Table of Integrals, Series, and Products*, 7th ed, Academic Press, London, 2007.

31. Peppas, K.P., Nistazakis, H.E., Tombras, G.S., An overview of the physical insight and the various performance metrics of fading channels in wireless communication systems. *Adv. Trends Wirel. Commun.*, 2011. In Tech. DOI: 10.5772/15028

32. Hamed, A., Alsharef, M., Rao, R.K., MGF based performance analysis of digital wireless system in urban shadowing environment, in: *Proceedings of the World Congress on Engineering and Computer Science*, 2015.

33. Pawula, R.F., Asymptotics and error rate bounds for M-ary DPSK. *IEEE Trans. Commun.*, 32, 93–94, 1984.

34. Sun, J. and Reed, I.S., Performance of MDPSK, MPSK, and Noncoherent MFSK in wireless Rician fading channels. *IEEE Trans. Commun.*, 47, 813–816, 1999.

35. Ferrari, G., Corazza, G.E., Tight bounds and accurate approximations for DQPSK transmission bit error rate. *Electron. Lett.*, 40, 1284–1285, 2004.

36. Prudnikov, A.P., Brychkov, Y.A., Marichev, I., *Integrals and Series*, vol. 1, Gordon and Breach Science Publishers, New York, 1986.

37. Renzo, M.D., Graziosi, F., Santucci, F., Channel capacity over generalized fading channels: A novel MGF-based approach for performance analysis and design of wireless communication systems. *IEEE Trans. Veh. Technol.*, 59, 127–149, 2010.

38. Prudnikov, A.P., Brychkov, Y.A., Mariche, I., *Integrals and series*, vol. 3, Gordon and Breach Science Publishers, New York, 1986.
39. Kumari, S. and Singal, T.L., A Comprehensive review of modulation techniques used in long term evolution. *J. Today's Ideas-Tomorrow's Technol.*, 3, 83–93, 2015.

3

Implementation of Automatic Driving Car Test Approach Based on a Digital Twinning Technology and by Embedding Artificial Intelligence

Pranjal Shukla*, Chahil Choudhary, Anurag and Jatin Thakur

Department of Computer Science and Engineering, Chandigarh University, Mohali, Punjab, India

Abstract

Autonomous or self-driving vehicle testing is a process that evaluates and certifies the performance, safety, and reliability of a vehicle. Before the cars are put on the road, these tests ensure that the automatic driving system works as intended and complies with the rules. Testing of self-driving vehicles often involves a variety of assessments, including functionality, efficiency, safety, and real-life testing. The goal is to ensure that the autonomous system accurately recognizes its environment, makes intelligent decisions, and performs control actions in various driving situations. The term "automated passenger car test" refers to a system that uses digital twin technology and embedded artificial intelligence (AI) to improve autonomous vehicle testing. A digital twin creates a virtual copy or simulation of a real system or object. A virtual model that reproduces the parts, sensors, software, and environment of a car is called a "digital twin" in the context of automated vehicles. Using digital twin technology in the testing methodology, developers can reproduce and evaluate the behavior of an automated vehicle in a controlled virtual environment. This eliminates the need for physical prototypes or actual field testing, allowing extensive testing, scenario replication, and car performance. Artificial intelligence makes autonomous driving much easier. In the testing strategy, AI can be used to improve the simulation and evaluation process by integrating AI technologies into the digital twin. The test strategy can simulate real driving situations, evaluate the performance of the autonomous system, and find areas for improvement by

**Corresponding author*: pranjal.shukla.355@gmail.com

Abhineet Anand, Anita Sardana, Abhishek Kumar, Srikanta Kumar Mohapatra and Shikha Gupta (eds.) Simulation Techniques of Digital Twin in Real-Time Applications: Design Modeling and Implementation, (57–86) © 2024 Scrivener Publishing LLC

integrating artificial intelligence into the digital twin system. Overall, the approach to automated passenger car testing using digital twin technology and artificial intelligence creates a controlled and efficient environment for testing and fine-tuning an autonomous system. It allows developers to evaluate system capabilities, optimize algorithms, and build on existing systems to improve the efficiency and safety of autonomous vehicles before they are deployed in the real world.

Keywords: Autonomous, simulation, digital twin, optimize, artificial intelligence

3.1   Introduction

Automatic cars are a major implementation of artificial intelligence which are capable of being driven themselves without the need of any human driver [1]. Automobiles that can drive themselves are referred to as self-driving cars, autonomous vehicles, or self-driving autos. With the use of sophisticated technologies like sensors, cameras, radar systems, and computer algorithms, these vehicles can detect their environment, make decisions, and travel safely.

Self-driving cars are primarily designed to increase traffic efficiency, decrease accidents brought on by driver mistake, and improve traffic safety. These vehicles interpret their surroundings with the help of sensors and algorithms and then act in real time as a result [2]. Sensors gather data on the location of other vehicles, pedestrians, and road signs in the vicinity of the vehicle. The vehicle's internal computer system interprets the data that has been gathered, analyzes it using a variety of algorithms, and then decides

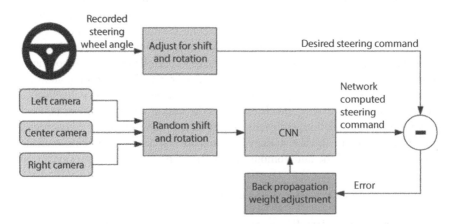

Figure 3.1 Automatic self-driving cars' working principle. https://miro.medium.com/v2/resize:fit:1400/format:webp/1*OeziRNGI1XspCf9RZCqyFA.png

what course of action is best for the vehicle, such as accelerating, braking, or changing lanes as mentioned in the Figure 3.1. The steering, throttle, and braking systems on the car are all automated and may be used without a driver's assistance. According to the Society of Automotive Engineers (SAE), autonomous vehicles can operate at various levels of autonomy. These levels start at level 0 (no automation) and go all the way up to level 5 (full automation), with each level denoting a higher degree of autonomy and less involvement from the driver. At level 5, fully autonomous self-driving vehicles are capable of performing all driving activities without any help from or intervention from humans. Even if the technology for self-driving cars has evolved greatly in recent years, fully autonomous vehicles are still not frequently used by consumers. To make self-driving car technology safer, more dependable, and more available to the general public, numerous businesses and researchers are working diligently to create and refine it [3].

*Main Idea Behind Automated Self-Driving Cars
Self-driving cars are primarily intended to be vehicles that can function autonomously, utilizing cutting-edge technologies and algorithms to perceive their surroundings, make judgments, and direct their movements. By lowering human error, enhancing traffic flow, and giving individuals who are unable to drive mobility options, the main goal is to increase safety, efficiency, and accessibility in transportation.

The following advantages of autonomous vehicles are their goals:

1. Safety: Accidents induced by human error, which is now a major factor in traffic accidents, have the potential to be considerably reduced in autonomous cars. Self-driving cars can reduce risks and increase road safety because of their capacity for environmental perception and decision-making based on real-time data.
2. Efficiency: By lowering traffic jams and trip times, self-driving cars have the potential to improve traffic flow. With their high vision abilities and ability to coordinate with other vehicles, they can improve traffic control systems and lessen inefficiencies caused by human driving behaviors.
3. Accessibility: People who are unable to drive, such as the elderly, the disabled, or those who lack a driver's license, may find that autonomous vehicles improve their possibilities for mobility. Self-driving cars can increase accessibility and independence for a variety of communities by providing dependable and safe transportation alternatives.

4. Sustainability: By promoting the use of electrified and shared transportation, self-driving cars can help achieve sustainability goals. They can aid in lowering greenhouse gas emissions and the impact of transport on the environment by enhancing routes, easing traffic, and facilitating effective car sharing.

5. Productivity: Autonomous vehicles have the ability to convert commuting time into productive time. Self-driving car users can perform work, pleasure, or other activities while traveling, boosting productivity and improving the entire trip experience.

The fundamental concept of self-driving cars is to use cutting-edge technologies to develop safer, more effective, accessible, and sustainable transportation solutions. However, the development and deployment of self-driving cars are still in the early stages.

*Working of Self-Driving Cars

Automated self-driving automobiles, sometimes referred to as autonomous vehicles (AVs), rely on a combination of cutting-edge technologies and sensors to function without the need for human interaction [4]. The underlying ideas that drive self-driving automobiles are summarized as follows:

1. Sensors: Self-driving cars utilize a variety of sensors to learn about their surroundings. Radar, LiDAR (laser-based detection), cameras, and ultrasonic sensors are some of these. They constantly scan their surroundings, picking up and following objects like other cars, people walking down the road, and road markings.

2. Perception and mapping: Complex computer vision and perception algorithms are used to process the sensor data. These algorithms examine the sensor data to recognize objects, comprehend their locations and motions, and build a thorough map of the immediate area.

3. Decision-making: The autonomous vehicle's software bases choices on this knowledge once the perception system has processed the sensor input and produced a representation of the surroundings. To identify the proper course of action, such as accelerating, braking, or steering, the software

employs machine learning algorithms, artificial intelligence, and rule-based systems.

4. Control systems: Through the use of the car's control systems, the decision-making outputs are then converted into actual physical actions. The accelerating, braking, and steering systems of the vehicle are controlled by these systems, which also comprise actuators and electronic controls, in order to carry out the intended operations.

5. Redundancy and safety: Redundancy is incorporated into the design of self-driving automobiles to ensure safety. They frequently have several sensors of the same kind to cross-validate data and lessen the effects of sensor failures. In order to increase safety and respond to new conditions, the software is also regularly updated and upgraded.

6. Connectivity: Real-time information and connection can be useful for autonomous cars. They have the ability to interact *via* vehicle-to-vehicle (V2V) and vehicle-to-infrastructure (V2I) systems with other cars and infrastructure systems. This connectivity may offer more details about the state of the roads, the flow of traffic, and any dangers.

7. Testing and validation: Before being used on open highways, self-driving cars must pass stringent testing and validation procedures. To evaluate their performance in a variety of situations and environments, this includes both simulated testing and real-world trials. To ensure the security and dependability of autonomous cars, regulatory organizations and industry standards are essential.

It is crucial to keep in mind that different manufacturers and developers may use different technologies and unique implementations of self-driving automobiles. In addition, since most automated vehicles on the road now operate at levels 2 or 3, human drivers must always be prepared to take over in an emergency. The deployment of completely autonomous vehicles on a large scale is still being developed, although steps are being taken to increase the automation levels.

*Digital Twinning and Embedded Method
Digital twinning technology and embedded artificial intelligence (AI) are used in the creation of an automatic driving car test approach to simulate and assess the performance and behavior of self-driving cars in a virtual environment [5]. It strives to offer a digital representation that closely

reflects its analogue in the physical world, allowing for real-time observation, analysis, and simulation. In most cases, the digital twin is produced by gathering and combining data from numerous sources, including sensors, IoT devices, and other data-generating systems connected to the physical object or system [6]. Using this information, a virtual model is built that, in terms of geometry, behavior, and properties, is an exact replica of the real-world object. Through the use of the digital twin, communication and interaction between the physical and digital worlds are made possible [7]. It permits both real-time monitoring of the physical object's performance and status and historical data analysis to learn more about the behavior and patterns of the object over time. Using digital twinning technology, a virtual duplicate or "twin" of a system or an object can be produced. A digital twin would be a computerized representation of the car, its sensors, and its surroundings in the context of self-driving cars. The presence of a digital twin makes it possible to model and forecast how the actual thing will behave in certain settings. This makes it possible to take preventative action, optimize, and debug without really affecting the physical system. A digital twin of a production line, for instance, can be used to optimize operations, model process modifications, and spot possible bottlenecks or problems before they arise in the industrial setting. Applications for digital twinning are found across a range of sectors, including manufacturing, healthcare, transportation, energy, and smart cities. Predictive maintenance is made possible, as is performance optimization, downtime reduction, efficiency improvement, and product development enhancement [8]. Through numerous driving circumstances, this virtual model may faithfully reproduce the behavior of the real car. Digital twinning allows scientists and engineers to thoroughly test and assess the algorithms and systems used in self-driving cars in a secure virtual environment. To evaluate the effectiveness and resilience of the autonomous driving system, they can simulate a variety of road conditions, traffic patterns, and potential risks.

AI technologies are integrated into the simulation to increase the digital twin's functionalities and make it more realistic and intelligent. The decision-making, perception, and reaction speeds of humans can all be imitated by AI systems in a virtual setting. In order to simulate driving circumstances more accurately and dynamically, this is possible. Researchers are able to evaluate the usefulness, safety, and dependability of self-driving car systems before they are put into use on actual roads by integrating digital twinning technology with AI. It aids in spotting and resolving possible problems, enhancing algorithms, and enhancing the capabilities of autonomous driving. In general, this method enables comprehensive testing and improvement of self-driving car technology in a controlled and scalable manner, lowering the hazards connected with real-world testing and hastening the development of secure and dependable autonomous vehicles [9].

*Positives of Self-Driving Cars

The Figure 3.2 describes numerous potential advantages of self-driving cars are why they are becoming more and more popular and advanced. These are a few of the major advantages of self-driving cars:

1. Enhanced safety: Human error, which is a major contributor to traffic accidents, has the potential to be considerably reduced by self-driving automobiles. The use of autonomous vehicles could result in safer roads and fewer accidents since they can constantly monitor their surroundings, react quicker than people, and carefully follow traffic regulations.
2. Improved traffic efficiency: Due to the ability of autonomous vehicles to communicate with one another and the surrounding infrastructure, traffic flow can be improved and congestion can be decreased. They can use cutting-edge algorithms to coordinate lane changes, acceleration, and deceleration, which could result in more efficient traffic patterns and faster travel times.
3. Increased accessibility: Those who are unable to drive owing to physical constraints, advanced age, or impairments may be able to travel thanks to self-driving automobiles. Many people, particularly the elderly and those who have mobility issues, can improve their quality of life as a result of this improved accessibility.

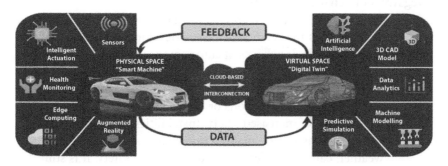

Figure 3.2 Digital twin structure. https://www.mdpi.com/2571-5577/5/4/65.

4. Fuel efficiency and environmental benefits: In order to maximize fuel efficiency, autonomous vehicles can be taught to drive more efficiently by optimizing their speed, acceleration, and route choices. This might result in lower fuel use and emissions, improving the air quality and helping the ecosystem stay sustainable.

5. Productivity and comfort: Autonomous vehicles allow passengers to make better use of their journey time. Instead of paying attention to driving, commuters can focus on business, recreation, or relaxation. In addition to making travel more comfortable overall, this can enhance productivity and reduce stress.

6. Potential for urban planning and infrastructure changes: Urban planning and infrastructure could be changed by self-driving autos. Cities might be able to reassign parking spots to other uses or restructure roadways to give priority to pedestrian and bike safety if parking demands are decreased and people can drop off passengers and continue without parking.

7. Reduced energy consumption: Autonomous vehicles can be incorporated into intelligent transportation systems, improving traffic flow and lowering idle time, which can result in overall energy savings and decreased fuel consumption.

It is important to keep in mind that while self-driving cars may offer these potential benefits, there are also difficulties and factors to be carefully taken into account in terms of technological advancement, legal frameworks, moral dilemmas, and societal impacts.

*Negatives of Self-Driving Cars
Self-driving cars have a lot of potential advantages, but there are also some issues and difficulties that come with their development and broad use. Here are some possible drawbacks of autonomous vehicles:

1. Safety and reliability concerns: Self-driving cars are not impervious to malfunctions or errors in technology despite the promise of increased safety. Instabilities in the environment, such as sensor malfunctions, software bugs, or bad weather, can be problematic and jeopardize safety. It is still very important to ensure the dependability and fail-safe features of autonomous systems.

2. Job displacement: In sectors that rely on human drivers, such as trucking, ride-hailing services, and delivery services, the widespread use of self-driving cars could result in major employment displacement. Affected workers may need assistance throughout this transition, which could necessitate taking steps to ease their entry into new fields of labor or industries.

3. Ethical and legal challenges: Complex moral and legal quandaries are brought up by self-driving cars. Autonomous systems, for instance, will have to decide in the split second whether to take one course of action over another, which might result in harm to occupants or pedestrians, when a collision is imminent. In accidents involving self-driving cars, determining blame and legal accountability might be difficult as well.

4. Data security and privacy: Self-driving cars produce and rely on enormous volumes of data, such as real-time sensor data, mapping data, and user-specific data. To safeguard the privacy and security of this data, as well as to guard against its possible misuse or unauthorized access, is essential to safeguarding the personal information of persons.

5. Technical and infrastructure challenges: There is still a big technical hurdle in creating completely autonomous vehicles that can function effectively and securely in all environments. The widespread use of self-driving cars also necessitates a strong and dependable communication infrastructure, including high-speed connectivity and well-maintained roadways, which could be problematic in some areas.

6. Hacking and cybersecurity risks: As self-driving cars become more interconnected and dependent on digital networks, they are at risk of being attacked by hackers. Potentially dangerous security hazards or unauthorized access to personal data could result from hackers taking advantage of communication or software flaws in the vehicle.

7. Cost and affordability: Although self-driving car technology is still growing, designing and producing these vehicles can be expensive at first. This may limit the availability and advantages of self-driving cars by making them unaffordable for many people.

To overcome these obstacles, it is necessary to continuously innovate, test, and validate new ideas thoroughly, work together with many stakeholders, and implement suitable rules and laws to ensure the safe and responsible use of self-driving cars.

*Future Scope

With so much promise, automated self-driving automobiles have the capacity to fundamentally alter both society and transportation [10]. The future of self-driving cars can be summed up by the following salient features:

1. Advancements in technology: Self-driving car technology will keep developing quickly. As sensors, computer vision algorithms, machine learning, and artificial intelligence advance, autonomous vehicles will be able to understand their surroundings more clearly, make better decisions, and negotiate challenging settings.

2. Increased safety: For autonomous vehicles, safety will always come first. Self-driving cars are anticipated to be substantially safer than human-driven cars as the technology develops and goes through intensive testing and validation. Self-driving cars have the potential to significantly lower traffic accidents and save lives because of less human error and quicker reaction times.

3. Urban mobility and ride-sharing: Urban mobility is predicted to change as a result of self-driving cars. To provide users with on-demand transportation, ride-sharing businesses may eventually shift to a fleet of autonomous vehicles. This change has the potential to decrease the number of privately owned automobiles, relieve traffic, and improve the road system.

4. Enhanced accessibility: For people who are unable to drive, such as the elderly, the disabled, and those without a driver's license, autonomous cars can improve their mobility alternatives. Their quality of life and social inclusion can be enhanced by having a convenient, independent access to transport services.

5. Integration with smart cities: Smart city initiatives will probably heavily rely on self-driving car technology. Autonomous vehicles can help make transportation networks more effective, consume less energy, and improve overall urban

planning by connecting with infrastructure systems, traffic management systems, and communication networks.

6. Self-driving technology has the potential to revolutionize public transportation. Taxis, shuttles, and autonomous vehicles can all run more effectively and provide commuters with affordable, adaptable transportation options. Self-driving technology can also offer dynamic routing and adaptability to shifting demand patterns, optimizing public transportation systems.

7. Last-mile distribution: The logistics and distribution sector may undergo a transformation thanks to self-driving cars. Robotic and autonomous delivery vehicles can efficiently move items, providing quicker and more affordable delivery services. This has the potential to change the e-commerce environment and increase last-mile delivery efficiency.

8. Regulations: To ensure the safe deployment of self-driving cars, governments and regulatory authorities are working hard to draft regulations. Regulations will continue to develop as technology advances in order to handle the ethical, safety, and legal issues related to autonomous vehicles.

Although automated self-driving cars have a bright future, it is crucial to acknowledge that there are still technical, societal, and governmental obstacles to be overcome. Realizing the full potential of self-driving cars will depend on ongoing research, collaboration, and public acceptance.

3.2   Literature Review

This section focuses on the previous research done on this topic: automatic self-driven car test. The table consist of all the information that are needed to check the previous research done. This section helps us to find the major research gap.

S. no.	Literature review
1.	Z. Lv *et al.* (2021) highlight its uses, data-related hurdles, interpretability worries, scalability problems, and ethical implications while providing an overview of the present status, challenges, and future research areas in the integration of artificial intelligence into digital twins.

(Continued)

(*Continued*)

2.	Q. Liu *et al.* (2021) provide a way to build and optimize a flow-type smart manufacturing system; the research article uses a digital twin-based methodology. It focuses on arrangement, movement, control, and optimization models and provides insights for effective system design and operation.
3.	Y. Lu *et al.* (2020) provide the idea of digital twin-driven smart manufacturing. A reference model is provided, and its applications and research challenges are covered. In order to enhance smart manufacturing systems, it highlights the need for digital twins in facilitating data-driven decision-making, optimization, and integration of production processes.
4.	M. Grau *et al.* (2021) use a computerized approach to develop a digital twin of a process plant using 3D scanning and artificial intelligence methods in the research study. The goal of the project is to incorporate these technologies to produce a precise and thorough digital replication of the plant for enhanced tracking and analysis.
5.	H. Aydemir *et al.* (2020) suggested an automated method employing computational intelligence and three-dimensional imaging to create a digital twin of a processing facility. The goal of the project is to integrate these technologies to produce a precise and thorough digital replication of the plant for improved monitoring and analysis.
6.	G. Chen *et al.* (2020) proposed the concepts of cyber-physical systems to offer a framework architecture for an intelligent production facility in the modular production industry. In order to establish an effective and adaptive manufacturing environment for better efficiency and decision-making, it focuses on integrating diverse technologies and components.
7.	O. Moztarzadeh *et al.* (2023) evaluate cervical vertebral maturation and enable enhanced medical diagnosis; "Metaverse and Medical Diagnosis" suggests a blockchain-based digital twin strategy. This approach utilizes the MobileNetV2 algorithm.
8.	J. Wang *et al.* (2022) use laser-driven aircraft innovation to build a digital twin for ground-based devices to simulate space debris, helping debris prevention efforts. Two methods were used and gave an average error of 8.13% for the neural network, and a 3.1% error is achieved for the simulation.

(*Continued*)

(*Continued*)

9.	M. Ebadpour *et al.* (2023) outline a digital twin strategy for metaverse unmanned electric vehicles that combines IoT and VR to improve performance and efficiency. It suggests that the digital twinning technique has a straightforward, no-auxiliary-infrastructures design that can decrease physical losses and strains and is better suited to IoUEVs.
10.	A. Jain *et al.* (2022) provide a way to increase the security and dependability of vehicle communications; "Improved a Recurrent Neural Network Schema for Validating Digital Signatures in VANET" offers an improved neural network schema for certifying digital signatures in vehicular *ad hoc* networks. The suggested solution outperformed previous methods in terms of computational overhead.
11.	J. Leng *et al.* (2020) examine a technique for quick reconfiguring of automated production lines that make use of digital twins and an open architectural approach, resulting in increased adaptability and efficiency. It primarily focuses on automating and quickly optimizing the reconfiguration process in order to decrease its overheads.
12.	M. Liu *et al.* (2021) give a thorough analysis of digital twin concepts, technological advances, and the vast range of industries in which they are employed, offering insightful information on both their potential merits and implementation issues. It presents the digital twin in different life cycle stages.
13.	R. Shen *et al.* (2022) examine how digital twin technology may be used to help with grid-connected dispatching of novel energy sources, delivering insights into the best ways to optimize energy distribution and boost efficiency in the context of integrating renewable energy.
14.	S. Sepasgozar *et al.* (2021) address how to use sophisticated digital technologies and processes to increase project efficiency, eliminate waste, and foster sustainability in sustainable construction. It focuses on the integration of lean practices, building information modeling (BIM), and digital twinning.

(*Continued*)

(*Continued*)

15.	K. Xia *et al.* (2021) focus on the environment, interfaces, and cognitive capacity for decision-making to optimize manufacturing processes and maximize efficiency. It also proposes a digital twin architecture to train advanced reinforcement learning robots for sophisticated production facilities.

3.3   Comparative Analysis

Autonomous driving technology has rapidly advanced over the years, with the aim of improving road safety, reducing traffic congestion, and enhancing overall transportation efficiency. Two prominent approaches in the development of autonomous driving systems are twinning technologies and artificial intelligence (AI). This comparative analysis explores the strengths, weaknesses, and key differences between these approaches.

Twinning technologies involve replicating real-world driving scenarios in a virtual environment. This approach utilizes a combination of high-fidelity simulators, advanced sensor systems, and detailed mapping data. The primary focus is on creating an accurate digital twin of the physical world for testing and training autonomous driving algorithms.

*Strengths
Safety: Twinning technologies enable extensive testing in virtual environments, allowing developers to identify and rectify potential risks and failures without endangering real-life road users.
Scalability: The virtual nature of twinning technologies enables the rapid creation of diverse scenarios, facilitating the testing of various edge cases and challenging driving conditions.
Cost-effectiveness: By reducing the reliance on physical prototypes and real-world testing, twinning technologies can significantly lower the development and deployment costs of autonomous driving systems.

*Weaknesses
Real-world variability: Although twinning technologies strive to simulate real-world conditions, there can be challenges in replicating the complexities, uncertainties, and dynamics of the physical environment accurately.
Sensor limitations: Twinning technologies heavily rely on sensor data to create virtual environments. The accuracy and limitations of sensors used

in these simulations can impact the fidelity and realism of the generated scenarios.

Ethical considerations: Creating accurate digital twins raises ethical questions concerning data privacy, potential biases in training data, and the implications of relying solely on simulations for decision-making algorithms.

*Artificial Intelligence

AI-based autonomous driving systems employ machine learning algorithms to process sensor data, make real-time decisions, and control the vehicle's actions. These systems learn from vast amounts of training data, adapt to various driving conditions, and continually improve their performance through reinforcement learning.

*Strengths

Adaptability: AI-based systems can learn and adapt to changing road conditions, new scenarios, and unexpected situations, enhancing their decision-making capabilities.

Real-time response: AI algorithms can process large amounts of data quickly, enabling rapid decision-making and response to dynamic driving environments.

Perception and interpretation: AI models can analyze sensor data from multiple sources, such as cameras, LiDAR, and radar, to accurately interpret the surrounding environment, identify objects, and predict their behavior.

*Weaknesses

Data dependence: AI models heavily rely on high-quality, diverse, and extensive training data to achieve optimal performance. Insufficient or biased training data can lead to suboptimal decision-making or unsafe behavior.

Explainability: The inherent complexity of deep learning algorithms often limits the interpretability of AI models. Understanding the reasoning behind specific decisions can be challenging, which raises concerns regarding accountability and trust.

Edge cases and novel situations: AI systems may struggle with rare or unprecedented situations that were not adequately covered in the training data. These edge cases require additional validation and testing to ensure safe operation.

Twinning technologies and AI represent two distinct approaches in the development of autonomous driving cars. Twinning technologies focus on creating realistic virtual environments for testing and training, offering benefits in safety, scalability, and cost-effectiveness. AI-based systems leverage machine learning algorithms to process sensor data, adapt to various scenarios, and enhance real-time decision-making capabilities. Both approaches have their strengths and weaknesses, emphasizing the need for a comprehensive and integrated approach to maximize the potential of autonomous driving technology while addressing safety, ethics, and reliability concerns. Future advancements are likely to happen, resulting in more accuracy.

Proposed Mythology
Problem Definition
Give an overview of self-driving technology and the role of twinning technology and artificial intelligence in boosting its capabilities. Define the methodology's goal: to create an efficient and safe autonomous driving system combining twinning technology and artificial intelligence.

Data Collection and Preprocessing
Identify and collect suitable data for training the AI model. Include a variety of circumstances, such as urban, highway, bad weather, and construction zones. Preprocess the obtained data to reduce noise, assure consistency, and improve quality for training purposes.
Twinning technology: Incorporate twinning technology into the self-driving system. Create a live link between the AI-controlled car and a human driver. To facilitate learning and decision-making, enable data interchange between the AI model and the human driver.

AI Model Development
Create an AI model that can receive sensory data, make choices, and operate the vehicle. Deep learning techniques including convolutional neural networks (CNNs), recurrent neural networks (RNNs), and transformers can be used. Train the AI model with the preprocessed data, taking both supervised and reinforcement learning methodologies into account. Improve the AI model's performance, accuracy, and responsiveness in real time.

Training and Validation
Divide the preprocessed data into two sets—training and validation. Continuously improve the AI model's capabilities by training it on the training set. Using the validation set, validate the model's performance to ensure that it fulfils safety and efficiency standards. Based on the validation findings, iteratively refine the AI model.

Real-Time Testing and Evaluation
Post training, the framework is subjected to a new collection of data known as the test dataset. This dataset is not utilized during the training process and is used to assess how well the model applies to new, previously unknown data. The way the model performs on the simulated dataset is an excellent predictor of how it will operate in real-world circumstances. The findings received during the testing phase may be compared using different epoch settings.

Feedback Loop With Twinning
Using twinning technology, collect real-time input from the human driver. Allow the human driver to intervene and amend the judgments of the AI model as needed. Use the feedback loop to enhance the AI model's performance and decision-making skills over time.

Regulatory Compliance and Safety
Ensure that autonomous driving systems comply with all applicable rules and safety requirements. To reduce the possibility of accidents or breakdowns, conduct extensive safety testing and risk assessment. To improve safety and security, implement fail-safe mechanisms, redundant systems, and cybersecurity measures.

Continuous Learning and Adaptation
Allow the self-driving system to adapt to and learn from fresh driving experiences. Continuously feed new data into the AI model to increase its performance and expand its capabilities. Real-world driving data is monitored and analyzed to uncover developing patterns and trends, which are then included into the AI model.

Deployment and Scalability
Deploy the autonomous driving system in a controlled environment after it has achieved suitable performance and safety standards. Expand the rollout gradually to broader regions, taking into account considerations such as infrastructural readiness and public approval. Monitor the system's performance in real-world scenarios, collect user input, and make any necessary scaling adjustments.

Conclusion
Summarize the process for constructing an autonomous driving system with twinning technology and artificial intelligence. Stress the need for continual improvement, safety, and regulatory compliance. Highlight the

potential advantages of self-driving vehicles, such as better road safety, decreased congestion, and improved transportation efficiency.

The Figure 3.3 describes the different phases involved in proposing the desired model.

Twinning technology with artificial intelligence (AI) can dramatically improve the operation of self-driving automobiles by boosting vision, decision-making, and control capabilities.

Twinning technology can generate a digital twin of a self-driving automobile that accurately matches its physical characteristics and behavior. The digital twin may produce synthetic sensor data using AI algorithms, mimicking different driving circumstances and complementing the real-world dataset. This updated dataset may be used to train perception models for item identification and recognition, lane detection, and traffic sign recognition, among other things. The use of both real-world and synthetic data allows the perception system to handle a broader range of events, increasing accuracy and resilience.

Decision-Making Improvement

AI algorithms mixed with twinning technology can improve self-driving car decision-making skills. The digital twin may be utilized to teach the decision-making system by simulating numerous driving conditions, including uncommon and risky incidents. By learning from both successful and unsuccessful simulations, reinforcement learning techniques may be used to optimize the decision-making process. The twin vehicle enables the AI

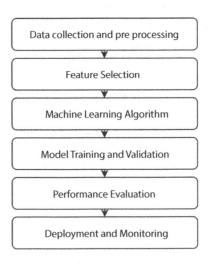

Figure 3.3 Steps of an algorithm.

system to make better and more informed judgments on the road by allowing for the safe and comprehensive testing of various techniques and policies.

Control Optimization

Twinning technology can be used to improve self-driving car control algorithms. Control algorithms may be fine-tuned and optimized to enhance handling, stability, and reaction by comparing the behavior of the digital twin to that of the real-world vehicle. The digital twin may also be used as a testing platform for comparing various control techniques and settings, allowing for quick iterations and improvements. Model predictive control, for example, may be used in conjunction with the twin vehicle to optimize control actions in real time based on sensor inputs and intended vehicle behavior.

Scenario Simulation and Testing

The combination of twinning technology and artificial intelligence allows for the comprehensive modeling and testing of self-driving automobile systems. The digital twin may be used to build virtual settings that mimic real-world driving situations, such as complicated traffic problems, inclement weather, and uncommon incidents. By simulating these scenarios, AI systems may learn and adapt to a wide range of settings, increasing the system's capacity to handle novel and difficult conditions. Before placing self-driving cars on the road, simulations give a safe and cost-effective means to test system performance, validate safety measures, and detect possible concerns.

Continuous Learning and Improvement

The combination of twinning technology with AI enables self-driving car systems to learn and improve continuously. The digital twin can collect real-time data from deployed cars, allowing AI algorithms to adapt and improve depending on driving experiences in the real world. This information may be utilized to uncover system flaws, handle edge cases, and improve perception, decision-making, and control components. The cumulative learning of the whole fleet can also assist self-driving cars since insights and improvements from one vehicle can be shared and applied to others.

Self-driving cars may accomplish increased vision, more intelligent decision-making, optimized control, comprehensive scenario testing, and continuous learning and development by utilizing twinning technology and AI. These developments help to make autonomous driving system safer, more efficient, and more dependable.

3.4   Result

The creation of self-driving automobiles has significantly advanced thanks to AI and twin technologies. It is crucial to remember that, based on the unique projects and businesses involved, the development and results may differ [11]. Here are some noteworthy results and advantages discovered in the field.

Perception and object detection have been significantly improved because of the use of AI and twinning technology in self-driving automobile systems. AI systems have shown improved item identification, recognition, and tracking skills when trained on large-scale datasets that include both real-world and synthetic data produced *via* twinning technology [24]. As a result, perception systems are now more precise and trustworthy, enabling autonomous cars to comprehend their surroundings and react properly as mentioned in the Result diagram 1.

Improved decision-making and planning: The fusion of AI with twinning technologies has improved self-driving car decision-making and planning. The ability to comprehend difficult driving situations and make wise judgments has improved for reinforcement learning systems that have been taught using simulations with digital twin cars [23]. Result diagram 2 presents route planning, lane switching, merging, and managing various traffic circumstances are some of the elements included in this.

Control systems and vehicle dynamics for self-driving automobiles have been optimized thanks, in a large part, to twinning technology and AI algorithms [12]. Control algorithms may be adjusted and improved by deploying digital twins that precisely mimic the behavior of the actual vehicle as

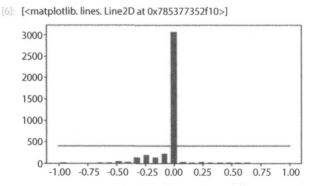

[6]: [<matplotlib. lines. Line2D at 0x785377352f10>]

Result diagram 1 An outline from Matplot.

Text (0.5, 1.0, 'Validation set')

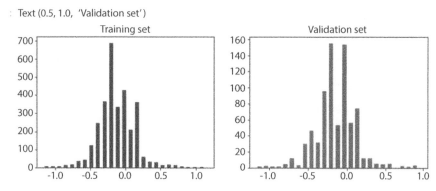

Result diagram 2 Training and validation set comparison.

Text (0.5, 1.0, 'Zoomed Image')

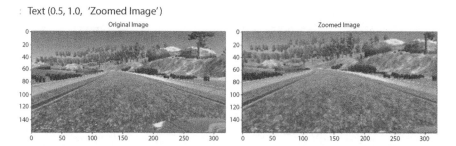

Result diagram 3 View before and after zooming.

described in the Result diagram 3. This leads to superior handling, more accurate control movements, and increased stability.

Robust performance in difficult situations: AI and twinning technologies have been used to enhance the resilience and performance of self-driving automobiles in difficult situations. The Result diagram 4 tells that developers may design and test edge situations, unfavorable weather conditions, and uncommon events that are hard to meet in real-world testing through simulations employing digital twin cars [13].

Continuous learning and adaptation: The capacity to enable continuous learning and adaptation in self-driving automobiles is one of the primary advantages of twinning technology and AI [14]. The AI algorithms may learn from actual driving experiences because of the digital twin's ability to gather real-time data from deployed automobiles. The system may develop over time, solve new problems, and include updates and optimizations thanks to this iterative learning process as mentioned in the Result diagram 5.

: Text (0.5, 1.0, 'Panned Image')

Result diagram 4 View before and after panning.

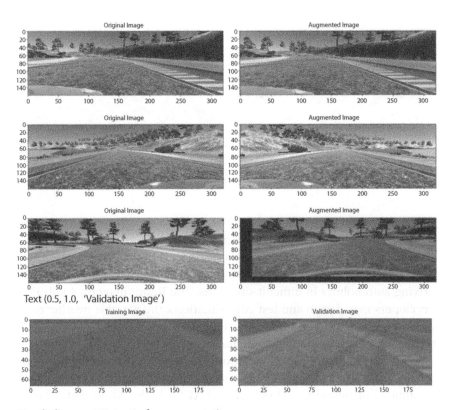

Text (0.5, 1.0, 'Validation Image')

Result diagram 5 Images after augmentation.

It is vital to remember that the autonomous driving industry is developing quickly and that, since my knowledge cutoff, particular outcomes and developments may have advanced farther [22]. The advancement and improvement of self-driving cars that use twinning technology and AI are being fueled by ongoing research, development, and real-world deployments as described in the Result diagram 6.

Text (0.5, 1.0, 'Preprocessed Image')

Result diagram 6 Images after preprocessing.

Error

The term "error" in machine learning describes the discrepancy between a model's projected output and the actual or desired output. A machine learning model is trained with the intention of minimizing this error, which shows that the model is capable of accurate prediction.

The type of machine learning task and the chosen evaluation metric determine the precise estimate of error. Let us get into more detail about how error is calculated for various machine learning issues.

The most common way of finding the error is by using the given formula:

Error = (number of incorrect predictions)/(number of total predictions)

1. Regression problems: The objective of regression problems is to forecast a continuous numerical value. Mean squared error (MSE) and mean absolute error (MAE) are two most often used error measures in regression.
   a. Mean squared error (MSE): MSE is derived by averaging the squared discrepancies between each data point's expected and actual values. The MSE equation is:

$$MSE = (1/n) * \Sigma(y_i - \bar{y})^2$$

In this instance, y_i stands for the actual value, $\bar{y}$ for the predicted value, and n for the total number of data points. Larger errors are penalized more severely than smaller errors using the squared difference.

b. Mean absolute error (MAE): The MAE is calculated by averaging the absolute discrepancies between each data point's expected and actual values. The MAE equation is:

$$MAE = (1/n) * \Sigma \, | \, y_i - \bar{y} \, |$$

MAE is less susceptible to outliers than MSE because it does not square the differences.

2. Classification problems: Predicting a categorical label or class is the aim of tasks involving classification. The comparison between the anticipated labels and the actual labels serves as the foundation for the classification error computation.

a. Accuracy: One typical statistic in categorization is accuracy. Out of all the guesses, it determines the percentage of labels that were successfully predicted. The accuracy equation is the number of accurate forecasts divided by the total number of predictions.

The accuracy would be 85%, for instance, if you made 100 forecasts and 85 of them came true.

b. Log loss (cross-entropy loss): Cross-entropy loss, commonly referred to as log loss, is frequently employed in binary and multi-class classification problems. It quantifies the discrepancy between the actual distribution of the labels and the projected probability distribution.

Log loss is equal to $-(1/n)*(y_i{}^*\log(p_i) + (1-y_i)^*\log(1-p_i))$

Here p_i stands for the anticipated probability, y_i stands for the actual label (0 or 1), and n stands for the total number of data points. A logarithmic loss function called "log loss" severely penalizes confidently wrong predictions while rewarding them when they are correct.

Depending on the requirements of the classification problem, additional evaluation measures, such as F1 score, precision, recall, and area under the ROC curve (AUC-ROC), may also be utilized.

It is significant to remember that the error measure selected depends on the issue at hand and the desired evaluation standards. Different metrics capture various facets of a model's performance, and the selection should be in line with the task's particular objectives and specifications. Here in our model or problem, the model will predict the performance by seeing how the model predicts the outcomes and how close it is to the actual value.

[29]: Text (0.5, 0, 'Epoch')

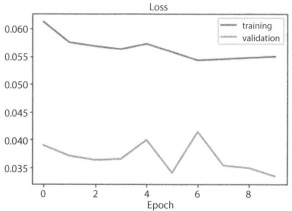

Result diagram 7 Validation data.

The preceding graph shows how the model is working, and the curves define how close or far the values are from each other, hence defining the accuracy of the model as mentioned in the Result diagram 7.

The following table defines all the entities mentioned for finding the error in the model predictions:

S. no.	Test	Value
1.	RMSE	7.23
2.	MSE	6.91
3.	MAE	7.11

Thus, it shows that they are that low, but then the errors are also not that much impactful on the outcomes. By all these, we can calculate the accuracy of the model which is approximately 83%, which is a very good accuracy for the model.

3.5   Concluding Remarks and Future Scope

Finally, implementing an automated driving car test technique based on digital twinning technology and incorporating artificial intelligence (AI) has the potential to revolutionize the automobile industry [15]. This novel technique has various advantages, including increased safety, increased efficiency, and shorter development cycles.

The use of digital twinning technology allows for the development of virtual duplicates of actual cars, allowing for extensive testing in a controlled setting. Developers may assess the performance and capabilities of autonomous driving systems without the requirement for real-world testing by simulating various situations and road conditions [21]. This saves time and costs while also ensuring that the technology is adequately vetted before being implemented on public roadways.

The use of AI into the testing process improves its efficacy even further. AI systems can analyze massive volumes of data generated by the digital twin and give useful insights into the autonomous driving system's performance. AI models may spot trends, optimize decision-making processes, and improve the overall performance and safety of the vehicle by continually learning from data.

One of the major advantages of this method is the capacity to recreate unusual and risky events that are difficult to duplicate in real-world testing [16]. Developers may expose autonomous driving systems to a broad range of complicated events by using the capabilities of digital twinning and AI, such as poor weather conditions, emergency scenarios, and unexpected human behavior. This extensive testing guarantees that the system is strong and capable of dealing with a variety of obstacles, boosting the safety of autonomous cars.

Furthermore, the use of an automated driving automobile test technique based on digital twinning and AI enables quick iteration and improvement. Traditional testing techniques, which rely entirely on physical prototypes and in-person testing, may be time-consuming and expensive. However, using the virtual environment provided by digital twinning, developers may rapidly and efficiently iterate and test multiple settings, algorithms, and scenarios [17]. This agility enables manufacturers to bring autonomous cars to market more quickly while maintaining high levels of safety and dependability.

Furthermore, this strategy has the potential to greatly minimize the environmental effect of autonomous vehicle testing [18]. Real-world testing frequently entails a large amount of miles and fuel use, which results in emissions and resource usage. Developers may reduce the dependency on physical testing by employing digital twinning and AI, therefore lowering the carbon footprint of the development process [19]. However, it is critical to recognize that implementing this strategy involves certain obstacles. To produce accurate test results, the digital twin's precision and fidelity must be assured. Furthermore, constructing AI models that effectively imitate human behavior and decision-making in a variety of settings is a substantial undertaking [20]. Addressing these difficulties will need ongoing study, development, and collaboration among stakeholders such as automobile manufacturers, AI researchers, and others.

References

1. Lv, Z. and Xie, S., Artificial intelligence in the digital twins: State of the art, challenges, and future research topics. *Digital Twin*, 1, 12, 2022.
2. Liu, Q., Leng, J., Yan, D., Zhang, D., Wei, L., Yu, A., Zhao, R., Zhang, H., Chen, X., Digital twin-based designing of the configuration, motion, control, and optimization model of a flow-type smart manufacturing system. *J. Manuf. Syst.*, 58, 52–64, 2021.
3. Lu, Y., Liu, C., Kevin, I., Wang, K., Huang, H., Xu, X., Digital Twin-driven smart manufacturing: Connotation, reference model, applications and research issues. *Robot. Comput. Integr. Manuf.*, 61, 101837, 2020.
4. Dutt, V. and Sharma, S., Artificial intelligence and technology in weather forecasting and renewable energy systems, *Artif. Intell. Renew. Energy Syst.* Elsevier, 189–207, 2022. doi: 10.1016/b978-0-323-90396-7.00009-2.
5. Kumar, A., Kumar, S. A., Dutt, V., Shitharth, S. and Tripathi, E., IoT based arrhythmia classification using the enhanced hunt optimization-based deep learning, *Expert Syst.*, Wiley, 40, 7, Apr. 16, 2023. doi: 10.1111/exsy.13298.
6. Chen, G., Wang, P., Feng, B., Li, Y., Liu, D., The framework design of smart factory in discrete manufacturing industry based on cyber-physical system. *Int. J. Comput. Integr. Manuf.*, 33, 1, 79–101, 2020.
7. Moztarzadeh, O., Jamshidi, M., Sargolzaei, S., Keikhaee, F., Jamshidi, A., Shadroo, S., Hauer, L., Metaverse and medical diagnosis: A blockchain-based digital twinning approach based on MobileNetV2 algorithm for cervical vertebral maturation. *Diagnostics*, 13, 8, 1485, 2023.

8. Anurag, C., Choudhary, J., Thakur, H., Bhardwaj, I.,Haq U. and Rather, A. H., Revolutionizing Wind Energy: A Enhanced Machine Learning Perspective on Wind Turbines Fault Prediction, in: *2023 2nd International Conference on Automation, Computing and Renewable Systems (ICACRS)*, Pudukkottai, India, 2023, pp. 1763–1769, doi: 10.1109/ICACRS58579.2023.10404768.

9. Ebadpour, M., Jamshidi, M., Talla, J., Hashemi-Dezaki, H., Peroutka, Z., A digital twinning approach for the Internet of Unmanned Electric Vehicles (IoUEVs) in the Metaverse. *Electronics*, *12*, 9, 2016, 2023.

10. Kumar, A., Kumar, S. A., Dutt V., Dubey, A. K. and Narang, S., A Hybrid Secure Cloud Platform Maintenance Based on Improved Attribute-Based Encryption Strategies, in: *International Journal of Interactive Multimedia and Artificial Intelligence*, Universidad Internacional de La Rioja, vol. 8, no. 2, p. 150, 2023. doi: 10.9781/ijimai.2021.11.004.

11. Kumar, A., Rathore, P. S., Dubey, A. K., Agrawal, R. and Sharma, K. P., Correction to: LTE-NBP with holistic UWB-WBAN approach for the energy efficient biomedical application, in: *Multimedia Tools and Applications*, Springer Science and Business Media LLC, vol. 82, no. 25, pp. 39813–39813, May 02, 2023. doi: 10.1007/s11042-023-15604-6.

12. Leng, J., Liu, Q., Ye, S., Jing, J., Wang, Y., Zhang, C., Zhang, D., Chen, X., Digital twin-driven rapid reconfiguration of the automated manufacturing system via an open architecture model. *Robot. Comput. Integr. Manuf.*, *63*, 101895, 2020.

13. Chandrasekaran, S., Dutt, V., Vyas, N., Kumar, R., Student Sentiment Analysis Using Various Machine Learning Techniques. *2023 International Conference on Artificial Intelligence and Smart Communication (AISC)*, Greater Noida, India, pp. 104–107, 2023, doi: 10.1109/AISC56616.2023.10085018.

14. Ahmed, M. and Kashem, M.A., IoT Based Risk Level Prediction Model for Maternal Health Care in the Context of Bangladesh, in: *2020 2nd International Conference on Sustainable Technologies for Industry 4.0 (STI)*, pp. 1–6, IEEE, 2020, December.

15. Kumar, S., Rani, S., Jain, A., Verma, C., Raboaca, M.S., Illés, Z., Neagu, B.C., Face spoofing, age, gender and facial expression recognition using advance neural network architecture-based biometric system. *Sensors*, *22*, 14, 5160, 2022.

16. Ilyas, B., Kumar, A., Setitra, M.A., Bensalem, Z.E.A., Lei, H., Prevention of DDoS attacks using an optimized deep learning approach in blockchain technology. *Trans. Emerg. Telecommun. Technol.*, 34, 4, e4729, 2023.

17. Sepasgozar, S.M., Hui, F.K.P., Shirowzhan, S., Foroozanfar, M., Yang, L., Aye, L., Lean practices using building information modeling (Bim) and digital twinning for sustainable construction. *Sustainability*, 13, 1, 161, 2020.

18. Xia, K., Sacco, C., Kirkpatrick, M., Saidy, C., Nguyen, L., Kircaliali, A., Harik, R., A digital twin to train deep reinforcement learning agent for smart manufacturing plants: Environment, interfaces and intelligence. *J. Manuf. Syst.*, 58, 210–230, 2021.

19. Zerouaoui, H. and Idri, A., Reviewing machine learning and image processing based decision-making systems for breast cancer imaging. *J. Med. Syst.*, 45, 1, 8, 2021.

20. Srivastav, A.L., Markandeya, Patel, N. *et al.*, Concepts of circular economy for sustainable management of electronic wastes: Challenges and management options. *Environ. Sci. Pollut. Res.*, 30, 48654–48675, 2023. https://doi. org/10.1007/s11356-023-26052-y.

21. Yun, H. and Park, D., Virtualization of self-driving algorithms by interoperating embedded controllers on a game engine for a digital twining autonomous vehicle. *Electronics*, 10, 17, 2102, 2021.

22. Veledar, O., Damjanovic-Behrendt, V., Macher, G., August. Digital Twins for Dependability Improvement of Autonomous Driving, in: *European Conference on Software Process Improvement*, Cham: Springer International Publishing, pp. 415–426, 2019.

23. Benkhaddra, I., Kumar, A., Setitra, M.A. *et al.*, Design and development of consensus activation function enabled neural network-based smart healthcare using BIoT. *Wirel. Pers. Commun.*, 130, 1549–1574, 2023. https://doi. org/10.1007/s11277-023-10344-0.

24. Uhlenkamp, J.F., Hribernik, K., Wellsandt, S., Thoben, K.D., Digital Twin Applications: A First Systemization of their Dimensions, in: *2019 IEEE International Conference on Engineering, Technology and Innovation (ICE/ITMC)*, 2019, June, IEEE, pp. 1–8.

4

Intelligent Monitoring of Transformer Equipment in Terms of Earlier Fault Diagnosis Based on Digital Twins

Satyabrata Sahoo

Nalla Malla Reddy Engineering College, Hyderabad, India

Abstract

Transformer condition monitoring plays a crucial role in the safe and reliable operation of a power system. The use of digital twin technology in transformer condition monitoring has the capacity to bring about a substantial transformation. Digital twin technology includes creating a virtual model of a physical asset, which is continuously updated with real-time data from sensors. The potential of this technology is able to revolutionize the monitoring process of transformers. In this paper, the use of neural network algorithms for transformer condition monitoring *via* digital twins is proposed. The advantages of exploiting digital twins for transformer monitoring, including the capability to provide an inclusive view of the transformer's condition and to simulate different operating scenarios, are discussed. Then, the use of neural network algorithms for analyzing the data from digital twins to detect and diagnose faults, predict failures, and optimize maintenance schedules is also discussed. Furthermore, the problems related with the implementation of digital twins and neural network algorithms for transformer condition monitoring, including the need for accurate sensor data and appropriate cybersecurity measures, are presented. Lastly, a case study demonstrating the effectiveness of neural network algorithms for transformer condition monitoring through digital twins is provided. The results demonstrate the potential of this approach to improve the accuracy and efficiency of transformer monitoring, reduce costs, and increase the reliability and safety of power systems.

Keywords: Transformer, temperature, fault diagnosis, artificial neural network, digital twins, MATLAB, intelligent monitoring

Email: sahoo.eee@nmrec.edu.in

Abhineet Anand, Anita Sardana, Abhishek Kumar, Srikanta Kumar Mohapatra and Shikha Gupta (eds.) Simulation Techniques of Digital Twin in Real-Time Applications: Design Modeling and Implementation, (87–106) © 2024 Scrivener Publishing LLC

4.1   Introduction

In power systems, transformers play a crucial role in facilitating the efficient transmission and distribution of electricity. However, transformer failures in transmission and distribution systems lead to serious effects, including prolonged power outages with heavy financial losses. In assessing the condition and performance of a distribution transformer, the operational characteristics of transformers such as voltage, current, and temperature play a crucial role. These variables act as crucial indicators and offer intuitive data on the overall condition and functionality of the transformer. Through ongoing monitoring and analysis of these measurements, experts are able to identify possible problems and abnormalities with different states of the transformer. By this, optimal performance is achieved. Generally, the health condition of a transformer deteriorates due to factors like overheating and overloading. These components have a substantial impact on the transformer's health and can cause numerous problems. Overburdening the transformer beyond its capacity places excessive stress on its components, potentially causing damage and reducing overall performance. Similarly, overheating can result in suboptimal operation, affecting efficiency and potentially leading to additional issues. Promptly addressing these factors through monitoring and implementing appropriate measures is crucial to maintaining the transformer's health and extending its lifespan.

Across the ages, a wide range of monitoring technologies and detection strategies has been proposed to accurately identify the faults in transformers [1]. However, an efficient monitoring system plays a vital role in obtaining these objectives. In order to achieve comprehensive monitoring, wired connectivity and one or more sensors are interconnected into the architecture of the transformer. This interconnection enables the sustained monitoring of the transformer's health condition and the collection of crucial status signals. These signals offer meaningful insights into the performance of the transformer, enabling the timely finding of any abnormalities or potential faults.

In the area of monitoring transformer fault diagnosis and predictive maintenance, numerous research works have been proposed by the researcher. For transformer fault diagnosis, a hybrid approach that combines improved gray wolf optimization and least squares support vector machine is proposed in [2]. Different artificial intelligence (AI) algorithms are utilized for transformer fault diagnosis through dissolved gas analysis (DGA) data in [3]. Fuzzy Logic and LabVIEW controller is used to design a system for monitoring transformers of all sizes and ratings, including both dry and oil types in [4]. Finally, in [5], a deep learning-based approach is suggested for transformer failures by means of vibration data.

The utilization of digital twin (DT) technology in the field of transformer condition monitoring [6] is one of the recent notable advancements. For the real-time monitoring and fault diagnosis of transformer equipment, a digital twin has emerged as a highly effective and influential tool over the past few years. By utilizing the capabilities of digital twins, virtual models of physical transformers are created, and facilitating their ability to simulate their behavior correctly predicts the future outcomes. An inclusive illustration of the physical transformer is provided through digital twins by incorporating its operational parameters, design specifications, and historical performance data. This virtual model platform allows for uninterrupted monitoring of the transformer's performance and condition, with enabling early fault detection and timely preventive maintenance actions. Operators are able to gain valuable insights into the equipment's health through analyzing the real-time data from the physical transformer and comparing it with the corresponding digital twin model. By doing so, they are able to identify the potential issues before they escalate into major faults.

With the decreasing costs of computational and storage resources and the widespread acceptance of the Internet of things (IoT) [7], it leads to the growth of the digital twin concept worldwide. Through its innovative approach, a digital twin goes beyond the traditional monitoring and maintenance practices of transformers. It generates an inclusive digital representation of the transformer that truly arrests its complete life cycle after the initial design and manufacturing stages to its operating life. This digital virtual transformer not only replicates the physical features of the transformer but also stores and analyzes the extensive data collected over time.

By the use of different types of sensors in the monitoring system, the sensor data are collected and then aggregated and processed. Furthermore, a precise and realistic model of the physical transformer is generated by using the raw sensor data along with suitable machine learning algorithms [8]. The data which are collected from monitoring sensor devices are precisely examined to detect and extract significant trends and patterns in appropriate features. By utilizing cutting-edge analytics methods like data mining and machine learning, digital twin is able to uncover valuable insights that may otherwise go unnoticed. These insights are able to disclose the transformer's behavior, performance, and health ailment, offering an all-inclusive understanding of its operational dynamics.

The competency of digital twins is spread over far beyond the mere data collection and analysis. Condition monitoring is one of the significant abilities of digital twins, which encompasses the continuous tracking of the transformer's health and performance indices in real time. By equating the behavior predicted by the digital twin and the real-time data, operators are able to quickly identify any deviations or irregularities, allowing for timely intervention and maintenance. Thus, another critical application enabled by digital twins is predictive maintenance. By extracting the gained knowledge from the analysis of historical and real-time data, predictive algorithms are able to estimate potential failures or faults, providing operators with advanced caution to impose preventive actions. By proactively focusing on the maintenance needs, the life cycle of the transformer is to be extended through minimizing downtime and optimizing resource utilization.

The chapter is organized as follows: Section 4.2 presents the proposed methodology for digital twin. It outlines the approach used in this work. In Section 4.3, an overview of machine learning-based predictive maintenance is provided, highlighting its significance. The results and discussion of the proposed work are presented in Section 4.4, offering insights and analysis. Lastly, Section 4.5 concludes the chapter by summarizing the key findings and suggesting future directions for research.

4.2   Methodology

Figure 4.1 explains the schematic block diagram of the complete setup. In this design, sensors are interconnected with the distribution transformer and ESP32 microcontroller. Committed sensors are employed to measure

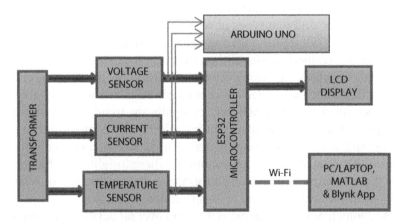

Figure 4.1 Block diagram of transformer condition monitoring.

voltage, current, and temperature, and their outputs are connected to the individual input ports of the ESP32. The ESP32 microcontroller continuously obtains the data from these sensors.

The microcontroller (ESP32) executes all its computations based on the programmed instructions it contains and the received data it collects from the sensors. To process the raw sensor data for extraction of significant information about the transformer's performance and condition, ESP32 utilizes specific algorithms and logic. The ESP32 employs a Wi-Fi connection to transfer the processed data to a Blynk app, after the processing of data is completed. Then, the Blynk app needs to be installed on a personal computer (PC), laptop, or a compatible mobile device for the distribution transformer's parameter monitoring. The app serves as a user interface, catering the real-time visualization and monitoring capabilities. The Blynk app receives the processed data from the ESP32 through Wi-Fi, and it is utilized and presented in a user-friendly format, i.e., the user is able to easily monitor the transformer parameters like voltage, current, and temperature.

In the succeeding paragraphs, the exhaustive descriptions of each major component of the Figure 4.1 block diagram are discussed.

4.2.1 Arduino Uno

When it comes to developing a transformer condition monitoring system, an Arduino microcontroller is an exceptional choice for this due to its unparalleled versatility and extensive pin configuration options. Specifically, one of the most widely used Arduino board is the Arduino Uno, which offers an extensive range of digital and analog input/output (I/O) pins that significantly enhance the system's flexibility and functionality. An Arduino Uno has a total number of 14 digital I/O pins, which includes six pulse-width modulation (PWM) signal generation pins. Due to this, the Arduino Uno enables the precise control and measurement of several components within the monitoring system [9]. This ability proves especially valuable when controlling the parameters such as voltage, current, and temperature, all of which play vital roles in efficiently monitoring transformer conditions. Furthermore, the Arduino Uno boasts six analog input pins, each offering a 10-bit resolution that enables highly precise sensing of analog signals. These analog input pins act as perfect interfaces for linking a wide array of sensors that are vital for monitoring critical transformer parameters and its evaluation.

Additionally, the Arduino Uno presents dedicated power supply pins, including controlled 5- and 3.3-V outputs, as well as ground connections,

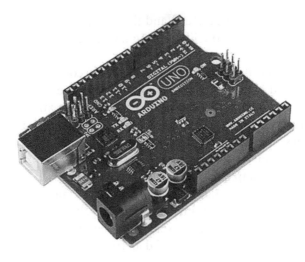

Figure 4.2 Arduino Uno with ATmega328P MC [10].

simplifying the integration of external devices into the monitoring system's network.

This feature-rich pin layout, blended with the Arduino's strong programming capabilities, enables developers to build a comprehensive transformer condition monitoring system that can effortlessly read and acquire data from sensors, efficiently process and analyze that data, and ultimately execute precise control commands to external devices based on the monitored parameters. The Arduino microcontroller, with its unique pin configuration and programmability, offers a highly suitable platform for creating a robust and intelligent transformer condition monitoring system that meets the demanding requirements of modern-day power distribution networks. An Arduino Uno used in this research is shown in Figure 4.2 [10].

4.2.2   ESP32 Microcontroller

In fact, the microcontroller (ESP32) is developed by Espressif Systems. Due to its exceptional versatility and feature-rich design, particularly for Internet of things (IoT) applications, it has gained immense popularity and widespread adoption. One of the most significant features of ESP32 is its dual-core Xtensa 32-bit LX6 microprocessors, which not only improves the overall performance but also enables the simultaneous execution of tasks. This dual-core architecture allows developers to design and execute complicated applications that need efficient multitasking capabilities.

One of the main benefits of the ESP32 is its integrated Wi-Fi (802.11b/g/n) and Bluetooth abilities, which support both Bluetooth 4.2 and Bluetooth Low Energy. This combined arrangement of wireless technologies allows seamless communication and interaction with an enormous variety of devices and networks, enabling the formation of interconnected IoT systems. Another important benefit of the ESP32 is the generous number of GPIO pins that it offers, facilitating easy interfacing with an extensive array of sensors, actuators, and external devices. This GPIO flexibility allows developers to connect and interact with various components, expanding the possibilities for creating IoT applications tailored to specific use cases. Moreover, the ESP32's 12-bit analog-to-digital converter (ADC) is a valuable feature for applications that require precise analog sensor data acquisition. This capability enables accurate and reliable measurement of real-world parameters, such as temperature, humidity, and voltage, enhancing the overall accuracy and performance of IoT systems.

Additionally, the multiple communication interfacing devices such as SPI, I2C, UART, and SD card also support the ESP32 unit. These interfaces offer seamless integration with an extensive range of peripheral devices, facilitating efficient data exchange and enabling the ESP32 to serve as a central hub for connecting and managing various sensors, actuators, and storage devices. The SRAM and Flash memory are the two different memories which are included in the ESP32 microcontroller. This adaptable memory architecture confirms efficient program implementation, allowing developers to create sophisticated applications with ample storage capacity for data and program storage.

Another important feature of the ESP32 is the built-in real-time clock (RTC). This feature confirms accurate timekeeping by maintaining the power consumption that is in minimal value even in deep sleep mode of operation. This capability is specifically valuable in applications that need time-sensitive operations or precise scheduling. Developers may make use of the ESP32's adaptability with widely recognized development environments like the Arduino IDE, which simplifies the programming procedure and delivers a familiar ecosystem for quick prototyping and development. The ESP32 is able to be programmed using the Arduino structure, allowing a varied range of developers to exploit its capabilities without extensive knowledge of low-level hardware programming.

The power efficiency of ESP32 is especially exceptional through utilizing minimal power during operation. This quality of ESP32 is particularly useful for battery-powered IoT purposes. Due to this, the lifespan of the battery is elongated, and the need for regular recharging or replacement is also reduced. The widespread variety of functionalities offered by

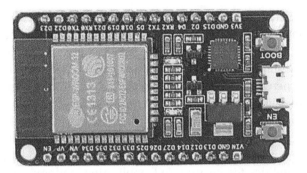

Figure 4.3 ESP32 micro controller [11].

the ESP32, united with its low power consumption, makes it a preferred choice for a varied spectrum of IoT projects. From home automation and industrial surveillance to wearable gadgets and beyond, the ESP32 offers a robust and flexible platform for realizing novel IoT solutions through various domains. The ESP32 micro-controller used in this research is shown in Figure 4.3 [11].

4.2.3 Data Acquisition

To monitor the transformer's condition, three sensors are used to receive the data for voltage, current, and temperature, as shown in Figure 4.1. For the voltage measurement, an AC voltage sensor, i.e., ZMPT101B is used. Similarly, for current and temperature measurement, ACS712 current sensor and PT100 RTD 3 wire temperature sensor is used, respectively. The detailed functionality of these sensors is specified as follows:

Voltage sensor: To measure the alternating current (AC) voltage levels in different applications of an electrical system, an electronic module sensor, i.e., ZMPT101B, is commonly used in various electrical applications. This type of sensor is widely used in smart energy meters, power monitoring systems, and other voltage monitoring applications due to its appropriate design for voltage measurements. By using a built-in step-down transformer, the ZMPT101B sensor transforms the high AC voltage to a lower voltage for appropriate measurement by electronic circuits. The sensor is being designed to function with AC voltages in the range of 0 to 250. By doing so, it is being compatible with usual household and industrial power systems. The sensor unit comprises a primary coil attached in series with the AC power source and a secondary coil that is utilized for voltage measurement. The primary coil is designed to control the high voltage, while the secondary coil offers a proportionate voltage output that is directly related to the measured AC voltage.

To ensure correct voltage measurements, the ZMPT101B sensor module is utilized in two devices, i.e., a precision operational amplifier and a voltage divider circuit. The use of a voltage divider circuit is to separate the output voltage of the secondary coil to an appropriate level for the operational amplifier. The operational amplifier amplifies and filters the signal to generate a precise output voltage that signifies the AC voltage being measured. To acquire the AC voltage measured data from the sensor, the output voltage is usually connected to an ADC or a microcontroller's analog input. Then, the analog input voltage signal is converted into a digital value for further processing or displayed after passing through the ADC or microcontroller. It is also documented that the ZMPT101B sensor offers a scaled-down voltage output, which is proportional to the AC voltage being measured. Therefore, the actual AC voltage value obtained from the sensor is calibrated and appropriately scaled down for a wide range of applications. Through a known AC voltage reference, the calibration of sensors is possible by using a comparison and adjusting the scaling factor accordingly.

In general, for the measurement of AC voltage levels, the AC voltage sensor ZMPT101B is an appropriate choice. Because of this, an electronic module is able to provide accurate and convenient solutions. By integrating

Figure 4.4 AC voltage sensor ZMPT101B [12].

this electronic sensor with microcontrollers or ADCs, the new setup is able to generate with several voltage monitoring systems, making it appropriate for a varied range of applications in power monitoring, energy management, and electrical measurements. The AC voltage sensor used in this research is shown in Figure 4.4 [12].

Current sensor: In a transformer condition monitoring system, the ACS712 current sensor plays a crucial role in accurately measuring the current which passes through the transformer primary and secondary windings. The Hall Effect principle of operation is used here. It is a phenomenon that when the current is passed through a conductor, a magnetic field is generated, and that causes the path of the electrons in a semiconductor material to deflect. In fact, a Hall Effect sensor integrated circuit is used in ACS712 sensor, and that effectively measures the magnetic field and converts it into an electrical signal which is proportional to the monitored current.

The ACS712 current sensor offers significant advantages when it is used in transformer condition monitoring. It is continuously checking the transformer's current flow and permitting the real-time assessment of its operational condition. It is also quickly identifies glitches such as overloading, faults, or phase imbalances. By using the current monitoring system, abnormal operating conditions such as excessive heating or current surges are also identified with the underlying current of the transformer. The ACS712 current sensor enables proactive maintenance and averts unpredicted failures by anticipating probable issues. The collected current data is analyzed by using advanced analytics and algorithms to identify the patterns, trends, and deviations from the natural working conditions. This analysis facilitates predictive maintenance plans through optimizing maintenance effort and cost.

Additionally, the ACS712 current sensor is able to extensively monitor and control systems designed for transformers. To give a comprehensive assessment of the transformer health, this current sensor is able to interface with additional sensors like vibration sensors and temperature sensors. By mingling multiple monitoring parameters of the assessing transformer and finding its status by improving precision and dependability, better-informed decision regarding maintenance and operation is enabled. The ACS712 current sensor used in this research is shown in Figure 4.5 [13].

Temperature sensor: Nowadays, the temperature sensor and its different applications play a crucial role in various industries. One such temperature sensing device is 3wire PT100 RTD (resistance temperature detector), which is highly utilized in the industry due to its reliable and accurate measuring property. The fundamental principle of operation for this device is

Figure 4.5 ACS712 current sensor [13].

the electrical resistance of certain material changes with variations of temperature, In the PT100 RTD, platinum material is utilized with a resistance of 100 ohms at 0°C, and therefore it is named so.

The PT100 RTD is categorically designed to reduce the impact of lead wire resistance on temperature measurements by providing three wire designs in it. Out of three wires, two are connected to the opposite ends of the platinum element, while the third one is connected at the midpoint. To acquire more accurate readings in temperature measurement, this type of architecture is provided in the sensor which compensate the lead wire resistance. Based on the well-established relationship between resistance and temperature, the resistance of the platinum element is going to change in a predictable manner when there is a temperature change taking place. This relationship adheres to a well-established Callendar–Van Dusen equation. The PT100 RTD 3wire temperature sensor is able to provide an accurate indication of the temperature measurement when it is connected across the platinum element to precisely measure the resistance.

Accuracy and stability are the two key advantages of the PT100 RTD temperature sensor. It offers a wide temperature range measurement, i.e., from −200°C to + 600°C with excellent linearity and repeatability. This extensive temperature operating range is utilized in various demanding applications where accurate monitoring of temperature is needed. Therefore, this PT100 RTD 3wire temperature sensor finds extensive application in different areas where temperature control and monitoring are essential like process industries, scientific research, environmental monitoring, HVAC systems etc.

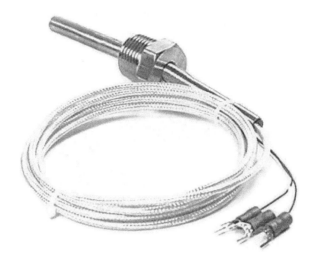

Figure 4.6 PT100 RTD 3 wire temperature sensor [14].

Generally, the PT100 RTD 3 wire temperature sensor is an accurate, reliable, and versatile gadget that plays a crucial role in retaining the optimal temperature control and securing the integrity of different processes and systems in a varied range of industries. The PT100 RTD 3 wire temperature sensor used in this research is shown in Figure 4.6 [14].

4.2.4   Blynk App

Blynk is a popular forum that offers a mobile app and cloud network for designing Internet of things (IoT) applications. It provides an intuitive interface and a wide range of facets to easily connect, control, and visualize the data. As this app is easily compatible with the both iOS and Android devices, it is therefore easily accessible to a wider number of user base. Some of the key features of the Blynk app are listed as follows [15]:

- Gadget synchronization: The Blynk app permits users to connect their IoT gadgets to the Blynk cloud server. This connection can be established *via* Wi-Fi, Ethernet, or other wireless protocols adopted by the IoT gadgets.
- Real-time data display: Blynk app offers an intuitive interface to display real-time data from associated IoT devices. Users are able to generate customizable and interactive dashboards to display sensor readings, control actuators, and monitor numerous parameters.

- Control and activation: With Blynk, operators can distantly control IoT devices and trigger actions through the app. This functionality enables operators to interact with their connected devices from their mobile devices, such as turning on lights, activating motors, or adjusting settings.
- Widgets and customization: A wide range of ready-made widgets are offered by the Blynk. These are buttons, sliders, graphs, gauges, LCD displays, etc., which can be easily added to the app's interface. Users can modify these widgets to display specific data, control device behavior, or offer an intuitive interface for interacting with their IoT projects.
- Virtual pins: Blynk introduces the idea of virtual pins, which are programmable pins that enable bidirectional communication between the app and the IoT device. Virtual pins are easily linked to various widgets or utilized for data synchronization, allowing operators to control multiple devices or display accumulated data on a single screen.
- Notifications and alerts: Push notifications and email alerts are supported by Blynk; it provides timely announcements to users based on predefined conditions. Users are able to set thresholds or rules to trigger alerts when particular events occur, such as beyond temperature limits or detecting motion, etc.
- Data logging and history: Users can log and store historical data from their IoT devices through Blynk. This data is to be displayed in the shape of charts or transferred for further analysis, enabling users to observe trends, recognize patterns, and gain insights into their IoT projects' performance over time.
- Project sharing and collaboration: Blynk offers a platform for distributing IoT projects with others. Users are able to publish their projects, permitting others to access and interact with them, fostering collaboration and knowledge sharing within the Blynk community.

The output of a transformer monitored through a Digital Twin is accurately measured using various sensors. Then, these measured data are virtually displayed on a personal computer through the blink app as shown in the Figure 4.7.

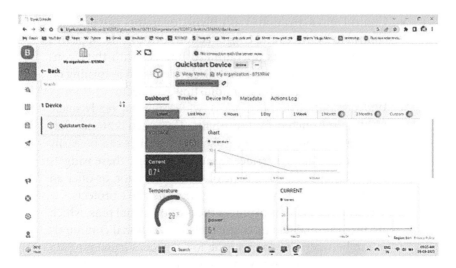

Figure 4.7 Virtual presentation of voltage, current, and temperature.

4.3   Machine Learning-Based Predictive Maintenance

An artificial neural network (ANN) is a key ingredient of artificial intelligence and machine learning systems. It is developed to emulate the behavior of the human brain and is able to learn from data and store information, and based on that knowledge it makes predictions or takes decisions. By utilizing a suitable database, an ANN is able to learn patterns and relationships within the data appropriately and then apply that knowledge in a suitable manner [16].

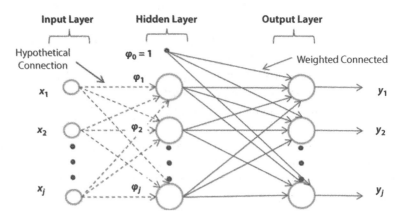

Figure 4.8 A standard RBF neural network structure [17].

The radial basis function network (RBFN) is one of the dominant approaches within the field of artificial neural network. Due to its iconic framework and abilities, the RBFN is validated to be highly effective in different applications. The structure of an RBFN is shown in Figure 4.8, which comprises three essential layers, i.e., input, hidden, and output layers. The input data or vectors are received in the input layers. A wide range of information like images, texts, or numerical data are collected from these input layers. The aim of the input layer is to execute and forward this information to the succeeding layers of the network. In the hidden layer, the layers are hidden from direct interaction with the external environment. Rather, it executes advanced calculations and conversions on the input data and facilitates the network to retrieve meaningful features and representations from the raw input. Inside the hidden layer of RBFN, each neuron corresponds to a radial basis function. These functions are responsible for acquiring and developing the underlying relationships and patterns within the data. The transformed data from the hidden layer is received by the output layer and delivers the final output from the network. Based on the specific problem or task, the RBFN is designed by the presence of number of neurons in the output layer—for example, in a classification problem, every neuron in the output layer is representing a distinct class, and the neuron including the highest activation signifies the predicted class.

To facilitate an effective modeling, the RBFN uses a nonlinear activation function inside each neuron. This function initiates nonlinearity to the computations by aiding the network to learn complex relationships and make sophisticated predictions. By using these activation functions to the transformed data, the RBFN improves its capacity to capture and represent complicated patterns in the input data. By leveraging a variety of functions, the radial basis Gaussian transfer function is employed in this context. From a mathematical standpoint, this function is utilized to achieve the desired computations and transformations within the RBFN. It is given by

$$f(x,b,r) = exp^{\{-(\frac{x-b}{r})^2\}} \tag{4.1}$$

where r is the variance, x is the input, and b is the center. The output of the network at time t is given by

$$y_j(t) = \sum_{k=1}^{n} \omega_{jk} f_j(x,b,r) \tag{4.2}$$

where ω is the weight of the connection string.

Artificial neural network is implemented in a wide range of applications with amazing success. A specialized ANN, i.e., convolutional neural networks (CNNs), is successfully implemented in computer vision for the analysis of visual data. By doing so, it revolutionizes tasks like object detection, image classification, and image segmentation. For sequential data analysis, recurrent neural networks are well suited and make them effective in language processing tasks like machine translation, sentiment analysis and language generation. Moreover, ANNs are also able to show their effectiveness in fraud detection, design of power converter, financial modeling, and many other domains [18].

In view of transformer parameters monitoring, the complex relationship between input variables and transformer parameters is easily correlated through artificial neural network using historical data. Here we are using input variables like voltage, current, and temperature, whereas transformer parameters are like oil quality, winding temperature, and insulation. However, the detailed analysis carried out and presented here is the temperature only. The ANN data training involves a two-step of process. Initially, a training data set is generated by compiling an adequate amount of historical data which contains input variables in proportion to transformer parameters. The generated data set is divided in to two data sets, i.e., training and validation data sets. Based on the input and output patterns, the training data set is used to train the ANN by adopting the weights and biases of the artificial neurons. The validation set is utilized to evaluate the performance of the trained ANN and adjust its parameters to ensure generalization and avoid over-training.

In the process of training, to minimize the error between the predicted transformer parameters and the actual values, the ANN iteratively regulates its internal parameters. This process of training is continued until the desired level of correctness is obtained. After training of the ANN, it is implemented in real-time parameters of monitoring of transformers. By providing the current magnitude of voltage, current, and temperature, the trained ANN is able to forecast the corresponding parameters of transformers with high accuracy. This permits proactive maintenance and timely detection of probable faults or anomalous conditions in the transformer, leading to improved reliability and efficiency.

4.4   Results and Discussion

In this section, by using MATLAB, a digital twin model is generated to simulate the behavior of a transformer based on the predictions of the

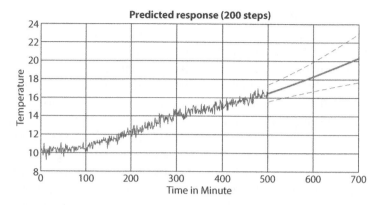

Figure 4.9 Present and predicted temperature monitoring of a transformer.

ANN model. To obtain the best performance from this model, the ANN network is designed accordingly by optimizing its parameters through suitable algorithms. To assess its accuracy and generalization capability, the trained model is validated through a separate dataset. By doing so, the digital twin reflects the current operating conditions by combining sensor data from the transformer and updating that at each interval of time. Early fault detection and its diagnosis are possible by comparing the simulated behavior of the digital twin with the actual measurements. The system, which shows promising outcomes in terms of fault diagnosis accuracy and predictive maintenance, is shown in Figure 4.9.

Figure 4.9 is created by using real-time data acquired from a temperature sensor, which consists of 1,000 samples across a span of 500 min. The model is then trained by utilizing these data. Then, the trained neural network estimates the temperature for an additional 200 minutes. These detailed report/data is able to alert a maintenance person. The plot shows the model's output, with confidence intervals designated by the red-colored dashed plots, which carefully align with the measured values for the validation data. The present and predicted results jointly demonstrate that the model precisely signifies the measured temperature of the transformer. It is to be noted that this output figure will be modified when the input sensor data changes.

4.5   Conclusion and Future Work

In this section, the research manuscript is concluded by summing up the key findings and insights of the study. For condition monitoring of transformers, real-time data like voltage, current, and temperature is collected through sensors. This data is consequently transmitted to a PC. The employment of an ANN-based intelligent monitoring system, using MATLAB and integrated with the hardware to generate digital twins, explains significant potential in improving the accuracy and efficiency of power transformer fault analysis *via* temperature monitoring. Timely detection and diagnosis of faults allow proactive maintenance plans by decreasing downtime and improving the reliability of power systems.

The difficulties confronted in cybersecurity for executing digital twins include ensuring the security of IoT devices, protecting data privacy, securing the network infrastructure, and managing vulnerabilities in devices and systems. The application of an intelligent monitoring system for a power transformer by digital twins for early fault diagnosis is able to help reduce downtime and maintenance costs by recognizing faults early and predicting future failures. The system is able to alert maintenance staffs about possible faults and schedule maintenance activities in advance, which is vital for ensuring uninterrupted power supply. The suggested system can be extended to other sorts of transformer parameter monitoring, such as vibration and oil level, and is also to be used in numerous industries, including power generation, transmission, and distribution.

References

1. Gouda, O.E. and Dein, A.Z.E., Prediction of aged transformer oil and paper insulation. *Electr. Power Compon. Syst.*, 47, 4, 406–419, 2019.
2. Chandrasekaran, S., Dutt, V., Vyas, N., Kumar, R., Student Sentiment Analysis Using Various Machine Learning Techniques. *2023 International Conference on Artificial Intelligence and Smart Communication (AISC)*, Greater Noida, India, pp. 104–107, 2023, doi: 10.1109/AISC56616.2023.10085018.
3. Sharma, N.K., Tiwari, P.K., Sood, Y.R., Review of artificial intelligence techniques application to dissolved gas analysis on power transformer. *Int. J. Comput. Electr. Eng.*3.4, 577–582, 2011.
4. Kumar, A., Kumar, S.A., Dutt, V., Shitharth, S., Tripathi, E., IoT based arrhythmia classification using the enhanced hunt optimization-based deep learning. *Expert Syst.*, 40, 7, e13298, 2023, https://doi.org/10.1111/ exsy.13298.

5. Zhang, C. *et al.*, Transformer fault diagnosis method using IoT based monitoring system and ensemble machine learning. *Future Gener. Comput. Syst.*, 108, 533–545, 2020.

6. Kumar, A., Rathore, P.S., Dubey, A.K. *et al.*, LTE-NBP with holistic UWB- WBAN approach for the energy efficient biomedical application. *Multimed. Tools Appl.*, 82, 39797–39811, 2023, https://doi.org/10.1007/s11042-023-15604-6.

7. Dhanraj, J.A. *et al.*, Design on IoT Based Real Time Transformer Performance Monitoring System for Enhancing the Safety Measures. *IOP Conference Series: Materials Science and Engineering*, vol. 988, pp. 1–5, 2020.

8. Ilyas, B., Kumar, A., Setitra, M.A., Bensalem, Z.E.A., Lei, H., Prevention of DDoS attacks using an optimized deep learning approach in blockchain technology. *Trans. Emerg. Telecommun. Technol.*, 34, 4, e4729, 2023.

9. Dasios, A. *et al.*, Hands-on experiences in deploying cost-effective ambient-assisted living systems. *Sensors*, 15, 14487–14512, 2015.

10. Martin, S. *et al.*, Remote Experimentation Through Arduino-Based Remote Laboratories. *IEEE Rev. Iberoamericana Tecnologias del Aprendizaje*, 16, 2, 180–186, 2021.

11. Srivastav, A.L., Markandeya, Patel, N. *et al.*, Concepts of circular economy for sustainable management of electronic wastes: Challenges and management options. *Environ. Sci. Pollut. Res.*, 30, 48654–48675, 2023, https://doi.org/10.1007/s11356-023-26052-y.

12. Mubarok, H. and Ardiansyah, A., Prototype Design of IoT (Internet of Things)- based Load Monitoring System. *2020 3rd International Seminar on Research of Information Technology and Intelligent Systems (ISRITI)*, Yogyakarta, Indonesia, pp. 377–382, 2020.

13. Fulzele, M. and Umathe, S., PV System With Energy Monitoring to Enhance System Reliability. *2023 International Conference for Advancement in Technology (ICONAT)*, Goa, India, pp. 1–6, 2023.

14. Kumar, A., Kumar, S.A., Dutt, V., Dubey, A.K., Narang, S., A hybrid secure cloud platform maintenance based on improved attribute-based encryption strategies. *Int. J. Interac. Multimed. Artif. Intell.*, 8, 150–157, 2021, http://dx.doi.org/10.9781/ijimai.2021.11.004.

15. Benkhaddra, I., Kumar, A., Setitra, M.A. *et al.*, Design and development of consensus activation function enabled neural network-based smart healthcare using BIoT. *Wirel. Pers. Commun.*, 130, 1549–1574, 2023, https://doi.org/10.1007/s11277-023-10344-0.

16. Bourhis, Y. *et al.*, Explainable neural networks for trait-based multispecies distribution modelling—A case study with butterflies and moths. *Methods Ecol. Evol.*, 14, 1531–1542, 2023.

17. Sahoo, S., Power Control of a Variable Speed Wind Turbine using RBF Neural Network Controller, in: *2022 Intelligent Systems, Lecture Notes in Networks and Systems*, vol. 431, pp. 513–521, Springer, Singapore, 2022.

18. Dutt, V. and Sharma, S., 9 - Artificial intelligence and technology in weather forecasting and renewable energy systems: Emerging techniques and worldwide studies. *Woodhead Publishing Ser. Energy, Artif. Intell. Renew. Energy Syst.*, 1, 189–207, 2022. ISBN 9780323903967, https://doi.org/10.1016/ B978-0-323-90396-7.00009-2.

5

Digital Twin System for Intelligent Construction of Large Span Assembly Type Steel Bridge

Sucheta

Department of Computer Science and Engineering, Chitkara University Institute of Engineering and Technology, Rajpura, Punjab, India

Abstract

There is growing demand for deep learning nowadays. It is a sort of machine learning based on artificial intelligence in which multiple computing layers are used to extract higher level features from data. We do predictions using a single layer, but additional hidden layers can give more accurate and refined results. A computer trains to do classification tasks directly from images, text, or audio sound using deep learning and sometimes gives more accurate results compared to humans. This review covers the colossal information of deep learning under one article. We have also studied different types of deep learning algorithms, types of training, innovation, and architecture applications. In this paper, deep learning algorithms are applied with digital twin technology to improve the efficiency in processing the large amount of sensor data and analyzing data patterns for making accurate predictions. At the present time, digital twin is used in a wide area of domains like in medicare, automotive industry, telecommunication, energy industry, etc. Apart from these areas, digital twin is widely used in the construction field, especially in steel bridges, buildings, construction of tunnels, etc. In this paper, we use an integrated model of deep learning digital twin technology in manufacturing and efficiently optimize the assembly process of steel bridges.

Keywords: Digital twin, deep learning, simulation models and learning techniques

Email: sucheta1036cse.phd22@chitkara.edu.in

Abhineet Anand, Anita Sardana, Abhishek Kumar, Srikanta Kumar Mohapatra and Shikha Gupta (eds.) Simulation Techniques of Digital Twin in Real-Time Applications: Design Modeling and Implementation, (107–122) © 2024 Scrivener Publishing LLC

5.1   Introduction

Digital twin technology works on the basis of digitally copying a physical object virtually, including its features, behavior, and functionality. This real-time digital representation of the object is done by smart sensors which accumulate data from the manufactured product [1]. This paper reviews the literature to understand the benefits of applying deep learning with digital twin technology to improve its efficiency in real-world applications. Deep learning is a sort of machine learning based on artificial intelligence in which multiple computing layers are used to extract higher level features from data [2]. We do predictions using a single layer, but additional hidden layers can give more accurate and refined results. A computer trains to implement categorization tasks directly from images, text, or audios with the help of deep learning. Deep learning is based on neural network, that is the reason it is also called "deep neural networks". It is an advanced and complicated version of neural networks due to its additional layers. Deep learning is much more efficient in performing jobs compared to neural networks, but due to its complex architecture, it requires more time to train.

5.1.1   Digital Twin Technology

It is basically a technique that uses data from real world to make simulations that can foresee how a system or product will perform. Digital twin programs can fuse with artificial intelligence, Internet of things, and software analytic to enrich the output [3]. Digital twin models are mathematical models of physical objects or processes as shown in Figure 5.1. Different mathematical models are improved when combined with deep learning techniques. Digital twin is used to save the cost and computation time for the inspection of a process such as its planning, modeling, execution, monitoring, or improvement.

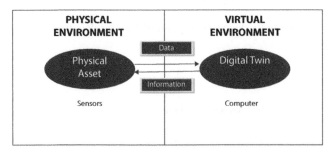

Figure 5.1 Digital twin.

5.1.2   Technologies Used

Digital twin is made up of using four different technologies as shown in Figure 5.2. Internet of things: Internet of things (IoT) sensors allow the constant transmission of data that is used to create a digital replica of a physical object.

Artificial intelligence: Artificial intelligence (AI) is an advanced analytical tool used to analyze data, provide valuable understanding, and make accurate predictions.

Extended reality: Extended reality (XR) is proposed to combine the virtual object with the real world.

Cloud computing: Cloud Computing allows us to store the gathered data that can be accessed from anywhere.

5.1.3   Why Digital Twin?

Digital twins are applied in a wide area of domain. It is used for testing a prototype model, for assessing how a process will perform under different circumstances or situations, and for monitoring the circuition.

The design of digital twin consists of data gathering and designing mathematical models for testing the gathered data, including an interface between the genuine physical entity and the digital model to transmit and accept the information in a real environment [4, 5].

- Gathering the data: Digital twin technology needs the data regarding an entity or a system, for creating a twin model,

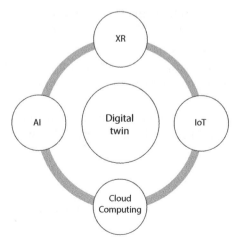

Figure 5.2 Technologies of digital twin.

which represents the states and behaviors of the actual physical object. The data is related to the life process of the actual product, including engineering information, design stipulations, or production processes. It also includes information like parts, equipment, materials, and methods of production. It also carries data associated to action, such as response, historiography, preservation, and documentation. Furthermore, data employed in digital twin technology includes accounting data and end-of-the-line procedures.

- Modeling the data: The gathered data is used to create mathematical logical models to manifest operating outcomes, foretell states, and decide behaviors. The models can advise measures based on statistics, chemistry, physics, deep learning, artificial intelligence, engineering simulations, business rules, or aims, and these models are viewed with three-dimensional graphical objects and elevated modeling in contemplation of aid to understand the verdicts.

- Unification: The results found out from the virtual twins are merged to outline a summary such as by getting the verdicts of the tools twins and applying them to an assembly line twin that can inform an industrial twin. The digital twins are connected in this manner to authorize smart business applications for real-time running evolution and enhancement.

5.1.4 Types of Digital Twins

Digital twins are divided into distinct types controlled by the product magnification size as represented in Figure 5.3. Different twins are applied on different domains. The co-existence of different types of twins [6] within a process or system is also possible. Let us learn the differences between different twins by studying them and how they apply in different areas.

- Asset twins: When the different components are combined together, then an asset twin is formed. By this twin, we are

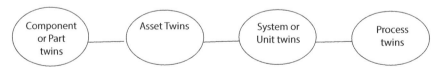

Figure 5.3 Types of digital twin.

able to understand the interaction of the parts that are combined to make an asset and generate tangible actions out of the processing of the examined data.

- System or unit twins: We can analyze the complete process enclosed by operation by the next level of twin called unit or system twins. Basically, the system twins are represented by the combination of different assets to understand the complete functioning system that enables us to observe how distinct assets assemble to structure a whole functioning system. System twins also allow to enhance the performance of the entire system.

- Process twins: The last and the next type of twin is a complete model of digital twin called process twin that reveals the mechanism on how the system works jointly to generate a complete production system in the industry and make the processes more assertive and more efficient.

5.2   Deep Learning

Deep learning is a subarea of machine learning and artificial intelligence that is inspired from the structure of the human biological neuron as depicted in Figure 5.4. Deep learning is basically a neural network which is used to analyze huge amounts of datasets. It is famous for its most important characteristic that is representation learning [8,17]. Deep learning models extract the features from raw input data with its own intelligence. We need not require to feed the features manually.

Deep learning is inspired from the structure of the human brain that is based upon the architecture of neural networks that consist of interconnected neurons.

5.2.1   Types of Deep Neural Networks

There are three types of deep neural networks: *convolution neural network* (CNN), *feed-forward neural networks,* and *recurrent neural networks* (RNNs) [9]. CNN is becoming more popular nowadays due to its vast applications in so many fields. This is composed of convolution, pooling, and fully connected layers to develop a flexible and automatic learning system. *CNN* is used for the analysis of images and recognition of patterns and also used in meteorological departments. In *feed-forward networks,* neurons in one layer are interconnected with neurons in other layers.

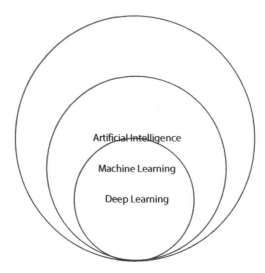

Figure 5.4 Deep learning vs. machine learning.

The input layer accepts the inputs, passes it to the hidden layer, and computes the output from the output layer. This network works in a forward direction, which means that the output is not fed back to the previous layers. *Recurrent neural networks* are developed to overcome the weaknesses of the feed-forward networks. They can process both past and input data and are able to memorize things and use its past experience for the computation of present data. RNNs have been used in weather forecasting, robotics and analysis of time series etc.

5.2.2   Learning or Training in Neural Networks

The artificial neural network (ANN) is completely based on the biological nervous system in the human brain. ANN acquires the more majestic feature of the human brain, i.e., the ability to learn. Learning means to adjust according to changes in the environment. There are three types of training in neural networks: *supervised learning, unsupervised learning,* and *reinforcement learning* [2]. In *supervised learning,* the training process is done under the supervision of a teacher. In this type of training, the target value (desired output) is already known; the input signal passes to the network and generates output. If the actual output is not matched with the target value, an error occurs. An error signifies that the weights need to be adjusted until the output matches with the target value. In *Unsupervised learning,* a target value is not present. Alike inputs are collected together and form a bunch. The output generated for new inputs are based upon the category that matches with the input. *Reinforcement learning* is somewhat similar to supervised learning, but the exact target value is not known. During the training process, the network gets feedback from the environment. The learning process continues until the optimal behavior in an environment is not achieved to obtain maximum reward.

5.3   Simulation vs. Digital Twin Technology

Simulation helps us to know that what may take place in the real world, whereas digital twin allows us to compare and evaluate what may occur besides what is genuinely happening [10].

Both of the digital twin and simulation uses different models to recreate processes and products, but there are inconsistencies between these two terms. The most highlighting difference is that, to study various simulations, digital twin generates a virtual environment including real-time data and bidirectional information flow between the sensors (collects the data) and digital twin. By this, the accuracy of models gets increased, thus providing a better understanding for product monitoring.

5.3.1   Integrating Deep Learning in Simulation Models

There are four types of deep learning simulation models used in digital twin [11]: graph-based modeling, procedural and declarative modeling, discrete and continuous modeling, and object-oriented modeling. These are the models that use the learning techniques of deep learning for its operation and for simulation in digital twin technology.

- Graph-based modeling: In this model, we take a complete system and distill it into subcomponents and connections between them as shown in Figure 5.5. These models need a strong combination of supervised and unsupervised learning techniques.
- Procedural and declarative modeling: These types of models take equations or algorithms as input and convert them into procedures, as represented in Figure 5.6. Solving a series of equations concurrently is one of the examples of this type of modeling. This needs more supervised and less unsupervised learning technique of deep learning for its execution.

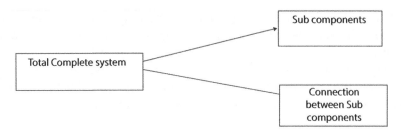

Figure 5.5 Graph-based modeling.

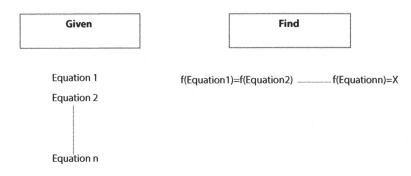

Figure 5.6 Procedural modeling.

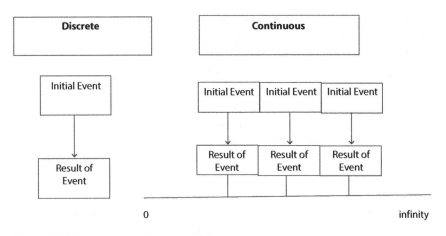

Figure 5.7 Discrete and continuous modeling.

Function: f(Initial model)   f(Initial model) + Minor Differences

Figure 5.8 Object-oriented modeling.

- Discrete and continuous modeling: Discrete simulation solves the result for a single event, and in continuous simulation, it solves the results for many related discrete events in the interval from zero to infinity as displayed in Figure 5.7. This also needs more supervised and less unsupervised deep learning technique for its operation.
- Object-oriented modeling: This type of modeling tells that similar systems have some similarities, in which the characteristics of one type of model is put into other models with some minor differences. In this, the combination of supervised and unsupervised deep learning technique is used. Figure 5.8 shows the diagram of Object oriented modeling.

5.3.2   Benefits of Deep Learning Digital Twin

Digital twin simulation models are improved when integrated with deep learning [12]. Deep learning digitaltwin models have some of the following benefits that show a remarkable impact on industry:

- Comparing costs: Digital twins are used for prototyping of the manufacturing. As deep learning improves the simulation model, a lesser number of prototype iteration is required. As the number of prototypes is reduced, that also reduces the cost of manufacturing.
- Comparing sustainability: The lesser number of prototypes means that a lesser number of materials are used, and therefore less materials are scrapped. To improve the simulation sustainability, we can invest further in cloud computing and use renewable energy for further computation.
- Simpler onboarding: As the simulation gets digitalized, the simulation process can be done on a computer more

efficiently, and simulation results that are very simple and easy to understand by humans are generated very quickly.
- Unsupervised learning: With the use of unsupervised learning, we can create new fields of research that are never being observed and are very difficult to explore as new experiments without deep learning.

5.3.3   Applications of Digital Twin Technology

The integration of digital twin with deep learning technology is applied in various industrial sectors like construction, aerospace, automotive industry, energy, telecommunication, healthcare, and manufacturing.

- Architecture, engineering, and construction: Digital twin with deep learning is applied in construction [13] and structural designs by creating a virtual representation of infrastructure and building before it is built. It allows architects and engineers to simulate the scenarios and identify the problems in the infrastructure and provide a real-time view of the infrastructure; thus, we can visualize the buildings remotely. It also allows real-time monitoring and analyzing the building when the construction part is complete, helps to optimize energy consumption, and reduces the need of carbon footprints of building [29]. As we analyze the issues before the construction begins, we resolve the issues prior to building construction, and automatically it reduces the cost of maintenance. Deep learning digital twin model is also used in the construction of large span assembly type steel bridges. Construction with steelreduces industrial noise, dust, and wastage during construction, thus with less damage in the environment.
- Aerospace: Digital twin uses deep learning technology to improve the performance of the aviation industry [14, 15]. Digital twin models are used in aircraft and spacecraft to predict major issues, optimize the performance, and make decisions about maintenance, servicing, fixing, and product life cycle management. It also helps aerospace companies to reduce costs, enhance the performance and safety factors, and improve the efficiency for customers.
- Automotive industry: In the automotive industry, digital twins are used [16] in running simulations. It is cheaper and

easier to perform destructive testing in order to ensure safe design standards compared to physical vehicles. With the use of deep learning, the digital twin also helps in identifying issues before they occur on the physical object [30, 32]. It makes possible to fix those issues before they appear in real physical objects. Self-driving cars are the most important example of digital twin deep learning (DTDL) models.

- Energy industry: In the energy industry, this includes perhaps a wind farm, a traditional coal plant, or a nuclear facility [31]. The digital twin deep learning model uses data from physical objects to generate maximum profits and minimize maintenance risks and costs. A digital replica of a wind turbine is one of the examples in the energy industry where the data is obtained from a motor of a turbine to analyze the efficiency, current scenario, and its condition. Operators are able to predict the increase or decrease in the speed of wind from the simulation experiments and utilize the data to generate optimal results and maximum profits with minimum maintenance cost.

- Telecommunication: The most improbable digital replica invention in telecommunication is a network digital twin. It allows companies to examine the network operations in live and predict any of the events that may occur to preclude downtime. Entrepreneurs generate various digital twins to direct networks appropriately. In this manner, each replica has a minimal burden and allows functioning with the actual parts of a network competently.

- Healthcare: Digital twin was initially limited to a component or a single device, but with the arrival of deep learning technology, digital twin now gets improved and able to represent a complete complex structure, process, system, or place. The digital twin of several hospital systems helps in improving and optimizing the entire ecological community [19]. It designs a lot of configurations of hospital resources along with the movement of patients, doctors, and instruments with real-time monitoring of people, assets, and systems. Deep learning convolution neural networks are used for the simulation of real-time data images gathered from a hospital and classify those images for the diagnosis of various diseases that will help the doctors make accurate decision and enhance the quality of life of patients in a short period of time with optimal utilization of resources.

- Manufacturing: Digital twins are modeled for assets, assembly line production, finished products, and further real world statistics throughout the production process. Digital twin allows smart operators to prognosticate the quality of the finished product and help them to make more accurate decisions about matters such as material upgrade and process betterment [7]—for instance, a digital twin is used to track and examine data from many sensors such as pressure and temperature to identify possible issues with instruments before they become ultra-critical. This will help manufacturing companies in making plans for maintenance and repairs and increasing the productivity [18].

5.4 Literature Review

For the literature survey, the papers published from 2019 to 2023 were focused on. The papers which focused mainly on integrated models of digital twin deep learning were selected. Table 5.1 summarizes the findings of theresearch papers studied during this literature survey. In Table 5.1, a total 10 papers were considered for review. The research papers are based on the existing literature review of improving the performance of digital twin with deep learning technology in a wide area of applications.

Table 5.1 Digital twin deep learning model for wide applications.

S. no.	Authors	Year of publication	Methodology	Findings
1	Mergen Kor, Ibrahim Yitmen, Sepehr Alizadehsalehi	2023	Qualitative and quantitative analysis, questionnaire, decision-support system for process optimization	DL-integrated DT model for validating and facilitating Construction 4.0 specially for decision making
2	SaadRazzaq, Babar Shah, Farkhund Iqbal, Muhamm ad Ilyas, Fahad Maqbool, and Alv aro Rocha [22]	2023	RFID readers, high-edge computing devices, RFID server	Digital twin framework

(Continued)

Table 5.1 Digital twin deep learning model for wide applications. (*Continued*)

S. no.	Authors	Year of publication	Methodology	Findings
3	Imran Ahmed, Misbah Ahmad, Gwanggil Jeon [21]	2022	Cascade RCNN architecture	Detection architecture and smart healthcare system based on digital twin model
4	Jinkang Guo, Zhihan Lv [23]	2022	DT technology, PLM model	Reality and virtual existence
5	Zaheer Allam, David S. Jones [25]	2021	Internet of things (IoT)	6G technology, smart, digital, and sustainable cities
6	Aidan Fuller, Zhong Fan, Charles, and Chris Barlow [20]	2020	Industry 4.0 facilitated digital twin growth, artificial intelligence, internet of things (IoT)	Digital twins model along with IoT, IoT for data analytics
7	Gray Bachelor Eugenio Brusa, Davide Ferretto, Andreas Mitschke [24]	2020	Model-based design (MBD), model-based systems engineering	Maintaining the trace of dependence and changes
8	Ahmadi-	2020	Creating a live model for	Participation and continuous
	Assalemi G, Al- Khateeb H, Maple C *et al.* [27]		Healthcare services	monitoring system, cyber-security challenges along with ethical implications
9	Bouzguenda S, Alalouch C, Fava N [26]	2019	Critical content analysis	Contribution to social sustainability
10	Laaki H, Miche Y, Tammi K [28]	2019	Network manipulation module	DT architecture and development

5.5   Conclusion

We provided an in-depth overview of the integrated models of deep learning digital twin technology in this article. We have analyzed the types of digital twin and how learning techniques of deep learning are used in different simulation models for improving the digital twin technology. We have studied recent miscellaneous papers in which deep learning is used for improving the performance of digital twin models. It is an excellent chance for making use of digital twin deep learning models and, in addition, investigation of other optimization methods in the early detection of potential issues for manufacturing a new product. This paper gives the researchers a better understanding of DTDL models and the possible benefits of DTDL models in a wide area of domain like in manufacturing, medicare, automotive industry, 3D construction of buildings, large span assembly line steel bridges, etc. The future scope of DTDL models is virtually limitless on the account of the continually increasing number of empirical power concerning their use. Thus, digital twin deep learning models are continuously acquiring new skills and expertise, which means that they are capable of constantly generating new insights required to build superior products and extra-efficacious processes.

References

1. Fuller, A., Fan, Z., Day, C., Barlow, C., Digital twin: Enabling technologies, challenges and OpenResearch. *IEEE Access*, 8, 108952–108971, 2021.
2. I.H. and Sarker, Deep learning: A comprehensive overview on techniques, taxonomy applications and research directions. *SN Comput. Sci.*, 2, 1–20, 2021.
3. Rathore, M.U., The Role of AI, Machine learning, and big data in digital twinning: A systematic literature review, challenges, and opportunities. *IEEE Access*, 9, 32031–32052, 2021.
4. Segovia, M. and Garcia-Alfaro, J., Design, modeling and implementation of digital twins. *Sensors*, 22, 5396, 2022.
5. Minerva, R., Lee, G.M., Crespi, N., Digital Twin in the IoT context: A survey on technical features, scenarios, and architectural models. *Proc. IEEE*, 108, 1785–1824, 2020.
6. Valk, H., Habe, H., Moller, F., Archetypes of digital twins. *Bus. Inf. Syst. Eng.*, 64, 375–391, 2022.
7. Ma, X., Tao, F., Zhang, M., Wang, T., Zuo, Y., Digital twin enhanced human-machine interaction in product lifecycle. *Proc. CIRP*, 83, 789–793, 2019.

8. Benkhaddra, I., Kumar, A., Setitra, M.A. *et al.*, Design and development of consensus activation function enabled neural network-based smart healthcare using BIoT. *Wirel. Pers. Commun.*, 130, 1549–1574, 2023. https://doi.org/10.1007/s11277-023-10344-0.

9. Frank, E.S., Zhen, Y., Han, F., Shailesh, T., Matthias, D., An Introductory review of deep learning for prediction models with big data. *Front. Artif. Intell.*, 3, 1–22, 2020.

10. Wright, L. and Davidson, S., How to tell the difference between a model and a digital twin. *Adv. Model. Simul. Eng. Sci.*, 7, 13, 2020.

11. Arcucci, R., Zhu, J., Hu, S., Guo, Y., Deep data assimilation: Integrating deep learning with data assimilation. *Appl. Sci.*, 11, 1114, 2021.

12. Lv, Z. and Xie, S., Artificial intelligence in the digital twins: State of the art, challenges, and future research topics. *Digital Twin*, 1, 12, 2022.

13. Srivastav, A.L., Markandeya, Patel, N. *et al.*, Concepts of circular economy for sustainable management of electronic wastes: Challenges and management options. *Environ. Sci. Pollut. Res.*, 30, 48654–48675, 2023. https://doi.org/10.1007/s11356-023-26052-y.

14. Xiong, M. and Wang, H., Digital twin applications in aviation industry: A review. *Int. J. Adv. Manuf. Technol.*, 121, 5677–5692, 2022.

15. Aydemir, H., Zengin, U., Durak, U., The digital twin paradigm for aircraft review and outlook, in: *AIAA Sci Tech, Forum*, p. 0553, 2020.

16. Piromalis, D. and Kantaros, A., Digital twins in the automotive industry: The road toward physical-digital convergence. *Appl. Syst. Innov.*, 5, 65, 2022.

17. Ilyas, B., Kumar, A., Setitra, M.A., Bensalem, Z.E.A., Lei, H., Prevention of DDoS attacks using an optimized deep learning approach in blockchain technology. *Trans. Emerg. Telecommun. Technol.*, 34, 4, e47290, 2023.

18. Lee, J. and Singh, J., Integration of digital twin and deep learning in cyber-physical systems: Towards smart manufacturing. *IET Collab. Intell. Manuf.*, 2, 34–36, 2020.

19. Sun, T., He, X., Li, Z., Digital twin in healthcare: Recent updates and challenges. *Digit. Health*, 9, 1–13, 2020.

20. Fuller, A., Fan, Z., Charles, Barlow, C., *Digital Twin: Enabling Technologies, Challenges and Open Research*, IEEE Xplore, IEEE Access, 2020.

21. Ahmed, P., Ahmad, M., Jeon, G., Integrating Digital Twins and Deep Learningfor Medical Image Analysis in the era of COVID-19, Author links open overlay. *Virtual Real. Intell. Hardw.*, 4, 4, 292–305, 2022.

22. Razzaq, S., Shah, B., Iqbal, F., Ilyas, M., Maqbool, F., Rocha, A., Deep Classrooms: a deep learning based digital twin framework for on-campus class rooms. *Neural Comput. Appl.*, 35, 8017–8026, 2023.

23. Guo, J. and Lv, Z., Application of Digital Twins in multiple fields. *Multimed. Tools. Appl.*, 81, 26941–26967, 2022.

24. Gray, B., Brusa, E., Ferretto, D., Mitschke, A., Model-based design of complex aeronautical systems through digital twins and thread concepts. *IEEE Syst. J.*, 14, 2, 1568–1579, 2020.

25. Allam, Z. and Jones, D.S., Future (post-COVID) digital, smart and sustainable cities in the wake of 6G: Digital twins, immersive realities and new urban economies. *Sci. Direct*, 101, 1–26, 2021.

26. Bouzguenda, S., Alalouch, C., Fava, N., Towards smart sustainable cities: A review of the role digital citizen participation could play in advancing social sustainability. *Sustain. Cities Soc.*, 50, 101627, 2019.

27. Ahmadi-Assalemi, G., Al-Khateeb, H., Maple, C. *et al.*, Digital twins for precision healthcare, in: *Cyber defence in the Age of AI, Smart Societies and Augmented Humanity. Advanced Sciences and Technologies for Security Applications*, pp. 133–158, Springer, Cham, 2020.

28. Laaki, H., Miche, Y., Tammi, K., Prototyping a digital twin for real time remote control over Mobile networks: application of remote surgery. *IEEE Access*, 7, 20325–20336, 2019.

29. Angjeliu, G., Coronelli, D., Cardani, G., Development of the simulation model for Digital Twin applications in historical masonry buildings: The integration between numerical and experimental reality. *Comput. Struct.*, 238, 106282, 2020.

30. Barbie, A., Pech, N., Hasselbring, W., Flogel, S., Wenzhofer, F., Walter, M., Shchekinova, E., Busse, M., Turk, M., Hofbauer, M., Developing an Underwater Network of Ocean Observation Systems with Digital Twin Prototypes—A Field Report from the Baltic Sea. *IEEE Internet Comput.*, 26, 33–42, 2021.

31. Moghadam, F.K. and Nejad, A.R., Online condition monitoring of floating wind turbines drive train by means of digital twin. *Mech. Syst. Signal Process.*, 162, 108087, 2022.

32. Pylianidis, C., Snow, V., Overweg, H., Osinga, S., Kean, J., Athanasiadis, I.N., Simulation-assisted machine learning for operational digital twins. *Environ. Model. Softw.*, 148, 105274, 2022.

Digital Twin Application on System Identification and Control

Rakesh Kumar Pattanaik and Mihir Narayan Mohanty*

Siksha 'O' Anusandhan (Deemed to be University), Bhubaneswar, Odisha, India

Abstract

Digital twin technology is a virtual representation of a real world along its function ability. It is the building block for different industries for system identification and control under the Industry 4.0 paradigm. System identification is the initial step in model-based control design which uses observed input–output data to develop mathematical models of the given dynamic systems. Once the dynamic system model's parameters have been determined, an appropriate control model should be developed for the nonlinear plant. An advanced virtual representation of physical object or process is modeled and presented in this work. The model has the ability to learn and adapt according to the real environment data. Furthermore, it can validate and simulate the current and future behavior of the actual process. In most of the plant works on real-time data, a virtual process control system must be designed. The model shall be used in the application of prediction, monitoring, and controlling of nonlinear plant. Digital twin is a relatively new form of technology, and its application is becoming increasingly prevalent in a variety of fields, including manufacturing, automobiles, medicine, smart cities, and other areas. This study aims to provide a comprehensive view of digital twin technology, including its implementation challenges and limitations, as they pertain to the most important fields of engineering and beyond. In this work, a nonlinear SISO plant is used to identify the superiority of the proposed machine learning model. Initially, a deep-RVFLN model is designed to identify the parameters of the SISO plant. A comparison study is presented between the performance of the proposed model and earlier models.

*Corresponding author: mihir.n.mohanty@gmail.com

Abhineet Anand, Anita Sardana, Abhishek Kumar, Srikanta Kumar Mohapatra and Shikha Gupta (eds.) Simulation Techniques of Digital Twin in Real-Time Applications: Design Modeling and Implementation, (123–162) © 2024 Scrivener Publishing LLC

Keywords: Digital twin technology, system identification, nonlinear dynamic systems, machine learning, random vector functional link neural network

6.1 Introduction

In the era of fourth Industrial Revolution or Industry 4.0, an utmost automated system is needed. One of the major challenges is parameter estimation and control when the system changes over time. In such a case, the parameter is estimated using online system identification techniques. Model or system data can be utilized once for an estimate in an offline identification procedure. Real-time model identification is needed when parameters change over time. Online estimating algorithms are able to create predictions about a model's parameters and states whenever fresh data becomes available during the operation of the underlying physical system. These predictions may be made at any time. Online state estimate is mostly accomplished with system identification algorithm or Toolbox by employing linear extended and unscented Kalman filter or particle filter techniques. In most cases, a recursive algorithm is used to carry out the process of the online parameter estimate. Recursive algorithms make use of the most recent measurements in addition to the estimations of the parameter values that were calculated in earlier iterations. Therefore, recursive algorithms are effective in terms of the amount of memory that they need. In addition to this, the computational requirements for recursive algorithms are lower. An online identification model that closely mimics the real plant has the same characteristics as the real plant, and because of this, an online model may be used at any time to evaluate predicted changes in operations, for the purpose of either control or optimization. It can be utilized as real-time monitoring, de-bottlenecking, plant redesign, and other operational tasks.

Digital twin or virtual model technology is growing in popularity for its online identification capabilities. It is a model of a real digital system that can be used for simulation, integration, testing, monitoring, and maintenance. Similar to system identification, to forecast future states and optimize/adapt/control, the physical processes are measured and compared to a virtual model. There are several real-world applications for DT. One of the applications include electric vehicles. In order to accurately predict and optimize the performance of a vehicle and increase vehicle safety, DT can simulate a real-world driving environment. DT can also optimize manufacturing processes, energy management, real-time condition monitoring (at all levels and in all powertrain components), component reuse, and recycling processes. The review demonstrated that data-driven DTs can manage complicated systems better than model-based ones [1]. DT may also be used for the control of faults in gas turbines, which is another application [2]. First, integrating the mechanism model and measurement data to simulate the gas turbine's effect is presented. Second, the relative accuracy of the model parameters is controlled. A model with an error module can be modeled faster. The third approach employs the DT model to self-learn the features. The results of the comparisons demonstrate the clear advantage of the proposed approach over existing approaches to providing early warning of performance issues in gas turbines.

A brief survey was performed and is reported in this article, which will help in future multidisciplinary research. An example of on online system identification is also considered for virtual model design for DT technology.

The chapter is organized as follows: Section 6.2 describes the DT technology and its application. Section 6.3 summarizes the earlier work. Section 6.4 describes the methodology of the proposed work. Section 6.5 provides the application on system modeling and result discussion. Finally, Section 6.6 concludes the technical article.

6.2   Digital Twin Technology and Its Application

6.2.1   Related Work on Digital Twin

Digital twin (DT) refers to the digital replica in terms of a dynamic virtual model of any physical system, both of which are connected intermits through the real-time data. Exchanging task as a result of the implementation of a wide variety of equipment in industrial process, with the presence of complicated structures and the presence of several operating conditions, could result in an increase in the frequency of accidents and the difficulty of performing maintenance. The digital twin monitor systems and processes in real time and analyzes data to detect problems. It also provides scheduled preventive maintenance to reduce downtimes. A digital twin system for control application use in automated process industry, featuring a cooperative design for the integration of virtual modeling, process tracking and diagnostics, and optimized management, is presented in [3]. Closed-loop virtual systems and residual signals have been proposed to be modeled using adaptive system identification with error-free case data to handle uncertain model parameters. Hence, intelligent tracking and control systems are needed to make practical security choices in industrial automation production [4, 5]. By adapting digital twin method in various industries, nonlinear complex and dynamic plants, it allows the user to monitor the production process automatically and evaluate deviations in the virtual environment. Furthermore, it allows the automation process to run accurately with a suitable control model [6, 7]. Traditional model-based approaches to describing the state-space of complicated systems are impractical due to the exponential increase of process data. To create digital twins for process industries, data-driven technology has emerged as a viable option.

In the beginning, multivariate statistical analysis shows how well data-driven tools work. Most linked works on multivariate statistics are about tracking conditions and diagnosing systems [8]. The GLR, PCA, and PLS methods for data-driven systems are well explained in [9].

Techniques based on data for diagnosing and designing digital systems, such as FDA and SVM, are presented in [10, 11]. Subspace identification method (SIM) creates a state-space matrix MIMO system-simulated mirror [12]. The SIM is created in [13] together with an observer-based algorithm to handle the process tracking systems' data-driven architecture. However, it is challenging to build available virtual models for complicated closed-loop systems using the current SIMs. Because of this, the identification performance of digital twins needs to be improved through the improvement of an adaptable SIM [14]. Using linear–quadratic (LQ) control, a method that implemented an adaptive failure compensation strategy for DTS with unknown parameters is presented in [15]. In [16], LQ control with model matching is integrated to solve the issue of dispersed configuration when faulty controllers are removed. In contrast, conventional control methods rely on fixed reconstruction gains to boost control performance but are unable to dynamically adapt their gains in response to changes in the results of a process diagnostic. The digital twin model can be represented with four types of dimensions as geometry physics, behavior, and regulation in virtual space, depending on the characteristics of the physical object being modeled [17]. The geometric model explains the assembly relationships of the physical object as well as the geometric structure that it has. The physical model is meant to represent the physical attributes, characteristics, and constraints of the object that is being modeled. The behavioral model is a representation of the dynamic behavior that the physical object demonstrates as a reaction to the internal and exterior mechanisms. The digital twin model is better because the rule model takes into account past data and can use implicit knowledge. The multidimensional digital doppelganger model can make predictions, optimize performance, and exercise control in the virtual world because it incorporates information from multiple fields. Effective digital twin models, however, require the integration of a number of different digital twin modeling components.

In order to fully understand digital twin modeling, a theoretical framework that breaks it down into its component parts and then examines them individually is proposed [18]. Various current studies on the definitions of the digital twin and analysis on the difference between them have been descried in [19]. However, the current evaluation works only look at the surface-level functional depiction of the digital twin model, ignoring the deep-level analysis of the model attributes and features that actually form the digital twin model.

There are three main uses for digital twins, as listed in parenthesis: simulation [20], monitoring [21], and control [22]. The use of digital twins allows for the assignment of numerous functions to a single instance. The purpose of simulation includes applications in which the behavior of real-world objects can be replicated in a virtual environment. Because of this, it is possible to plan optimized products for various plant physical systems. The objective of monitoring in all applications concentrate on the representation of the current state and its interpretation of a physical object. Digital twins manage products or industrial assets in control applications.

6.2.2 DT Application

In addition to the various levels of success that have been accomplished in the area of engineering, the digital twin framework in the field of healthcare is receiving an increasing amount of attention [23]. As a result of the digital twin technology's "best-fit" characteristic, the implementation of digital twin models in healthcare settings will represent a change from previously accepted care approaches. In 2021, 25% of healthcare leaders tried the digital twin, and 66% said they would spend more in it over the next 3 years [11]. Different applications of DT are presented in Table 6.1.

The application includes aircraft, city, and healthcare. Table 6.1 displays their hierarchical distribution. In aircraft, the term "system of systems" (SoS) refers to the entire aeroplane. The term "system" refers to the subsystems that together make up the flying vehicle. One example of this would be the propulsion system. The term "unit" refers to the component of the subsystem that is responsible for carrying out the subsystem's responsibilities. In particular, new system-level models need to be developed and thoroughly studied. When it comes to the study of cities, a single individual municipal construction is considered to be the unit. The building complex,

Table 6.1 Application of digital twin model in other fields.

Field of application	Service unit	Process	SoS
Aerospace	Model for aircraft tire [4]	N/A	UAV [14, 16]
	Model for air rudder [5, 6]		Spacecraft [15]
	Model for aero-engine bearing [7]		Rocket [16]
	Model for aircraft cabin section [8]		
	Model for hydraulic valve for aircrafts [9]		
	Model for air bearing for aircrafts [10]		
	Model for turbofan for aircraft [11]		
City	Model for utility pole in the city [17]	Campus [26]	City [27–30]
	Model for all the bridges in the city [18–20]		
	Model for building infrastructures of the city [21–25]		
Healthcare	Model for coronary heat vessels [31]	Cardiovascular system [33]	N/A
	Model for heart test-related equipment [32]		

which may include a commercial estate as well as residential sections, is located at the system level. Lastly, the elevation of the entire city has been raised to SoS. The city-focused digital twin models are primarily dispersed at the unit and SoS levels. Different levels of a DT model are presented in Table 6.2.

Table 6.2 List of levels of DT technology.

Different levels	Types of model	Initial model or physical twin modeling	Data acquisition	Performance evaluation of basic machine learning operators	System environment for machine learning
Pre-digital twin	Virtual system	No	NA	No	No
Digital twin	Physical twin	Yes	Update and maintenance of health status	No	No
Adaptive digital twin	Adaptive UI	Yes	Update and maintenance of health status	Yes	No
Intelligent digital twin	All of the above with reinforcement learning	Yes	Update and maintenance of health status	Yes	Yes

6.2.3   Different Levels of DT Models

6.2.3.1   Pre-Digital Twin

Level 1 provides assistance for decision-making during the concept design as well as the preliminary design. For most systems, the first step before building a real prototype is to construct a virtual prototype, which is a model of the system in its generic executable form. It reduces technical risks and identifies early engineering issues. This virtual prototype is known as pre-digital twin. In the early stages of the design process, virtual prototyping includes the creation of a model of the system, similar to the majority of model-driven techniques. The virtual prototype, however, is not necessary for the final system. As an illustration, consider the testing, planning, and decision-making processes involved in, say, trajectory control in lane-changing driverless cars.

6.2.3.2 Model Design

In the next level of the model is created when the virtual system model is able to incorporate data from the physical system regarding its performance, health, and support. The data are then given back to the digital twin, which modifies its model to reflect the new information. This also affects the maintenance schedule for the actual system. During real-time operation, the physical twins acquire knowledge from one or more digital twins, which enhances the performance of the physical systems due to the advantage of bidirectional communication between physical and digital twins.

6.2.3.3 Adaptive Model with DT Technology

An adaptive DT is the third level. It makes the physical and digital twins adaptable and user-friendly (in the style of a smart product model). The adaptive user interface responds to user/operator choices and objectives. This stage requires learning human operator preferences and goals in various contexts [33]. An approach for supervised machine learning based on neural networks is used, and the collection of these attributes falls under the purview of this algorithm. During both the operations and support phases, this digital twin is useful for supporting real-time planning and decision-making.

6.2.3.4 The Process of Intelligent DT

The intelligent digital twin has reached level 4 of development. It possesses all of the characteristics of a level 3 digital twin, including an approach that incorporates supervised machine learning because it is capable of unsupervised machine learning. It is able to distinguish items and patterns that are present in the environment in which it is being used.

6.2.4 Dynamic Model

As practical plants are nonlinear and dynamic in nature, they contain high-dimensional data which can cause significant computational overheads and memory problems. The plant is first dissected into significant sections linked with a physical entity using the multi-block PLS procedure [34]. Each plant component is modeled as a discrete-time multivariable state-space in order to create the simulated system or virtual system.

$$T(m+1) = \alpha T(m) + \beta k(m) + \partial(m)$$
$$P(m) = \delta T(m) + \gamma k(m) + M(m)$$

(6.1)

where $T(m) \in R^n, P(m) \in R^s, k(m) \in R^i$ signify scalars that serve as state variables vector, outputs of the process, and inputs to the system, respectively. $\partial(m) \in R^n$ and $k(m) \in R^n$ represent distributions of noise with a zero mean. Matrix elements α, β, δ and γ represent states. For real-time application, a plant model can be observed and controlled. Furthermore, the virtual system can be modified for real-time application. The given state-space matrix A is deemed steady and non-derogatory [35]. Complex nonlinear features can be modeled using nonlinear state-spaces [36, 37]. While monitoring large data, a variable selection method [38] is required to reduce redundant data and irrelevant variables. Creating DTs for nonlinear dynamic systems is difficult due to the existence of two distinct time scales. Residual signals are used to characterize system features using system identification methods. For MIMO systems, a single residual signal results in poor tracking performance [39]. Conventional system identification methods would have difficulty determining appropriate parameters in order to achieve satisfactory residual outcomes because of unknown system orders and closed-loop interferences. As a result, with the help of earlier research [40–42], a multiple adaptive SIM to simulate appealing virtual reflections for the processing system is proposed in this work. The Hankel structures P_f, P_n, T_f, T_n were initially constructed where the closed-loop output data is denoted as P and input data is denoted as k to generate the past Hankel matrix:

$$Q_p = [P_n^l, k_n^l]^l$$

(6.2)

$$P_f = \begin{bmatrix} P(m) & \cdots & P(l+N-1) \\ \vdots & \ddots & \vdots \\ P(m+s) & \cdots & P(m+s+N-1) \end{bmatrix}$$

$$P_n = \begin{bmatrix} P(m-s-1) & \cdots & P(m-s+N-2) \\ \vdots & \ddots & \vdots \\ P(m+1) & \cdots & P(m+N-2) \end{bmatrix}$$

$$k_f = \begin{bmatrix} k(m) & \cdots & k(m+N-1) \\ \vdots & \ddots & \vdots \\ k(m+s) & \cdots & k(m+s+N-1) \end{bmatrix}$$

$$k_n = \begin{bmatrix} k(m-s-1) & \cdots & k(m-s+N-2) \\ \vdots & \ddots & \vdots \\ k(m+1) & \cdots & k(m+N-2) \end{bmatrix} \tag{6.3}$$

where N stands for the total amount of data that was selected, n stands for the data that was collected in the "past," and f stands for the data that will be collected in the "future." The order of the observers is denoted by the numeral s as $s \geq n$.

The dynamic model calculates from:

$$P_f = B_s T_m + H_{Us} k_f + H_{ws} w_f + \vartheta_f$$
$$T_m = [T_m + T_{m+N-1}] \tag{6.4}$$

where $H_{ws} w_f + \vartheta_f$ represents the output vector of the process. B_s, H_{Us}, and H_{ws} are represented as quasi-standard forms. The residual signal $res(k)$ is needed to assess the model–real process difference. Residual signal analysis is based on building many residual generators that are fed by all process input factors and a single sensor signal. The one-to-one connection between the ith output and the parity-value-based residual generator [43] defines a parity value where $\alpha_{si} = [\alpha_{s,i,0}, \ldots, \alpha_{s,i,s_i}] \in R^{s_i} + 1$ is defined and $\beta_{si} = \alpha_{si} H_{kSI}$. Thus, the ith residual correlation matrix as $a_{zi}, b_{zi}, c_{zi}, d_{zi}, L_{zi}$ are calculated corresponding to the α_{si} and β_{si}.

$$a_{zi} = \begin{bmatrix} 0 & 0 & 0 \\ 1 & 0 & 0 \\ 0 & 1 & 0 \end{bmatrix} \in R^{s_i \times s_i}$$

$$L_{zi} = -\begin{bmatrix} -_{s,i,0} \\ -_{s,i,1} \\ -_{s,i,-1} \end{bmatrix} \in R^{s_i \times 1}, \tag{6.5}$$

$$b_{zi} = -\begin{bmatrix} \beta_{s,i,0} \\ \beta_{s,i,1} \\ \beta_{s,i,-1} \end{bmatrix} \in R^{s_i \times 1},$$

$$c_{z,i} = [0 \ldots\ldots 0 \ 1] \in R^{1 \times s_i}$$

$$d_{zi} = \beta_{s,i,-1} \in R^{1 \times 1}$$

where $Z(m) = O \times T(m)$ along with a transform matrix $O \in R^{s_i \times n}$.

The residual value $res(k)$ can be modeled by combining the outputs of m adaptive residual generators and using the appropriate value of $L_{0,i}$ for each residual generator, and the final representation is presented as:

$$Z(l+1) = a_z z(l) + b_z k(l) + L_2 O(l) - L_0 r(l) \in R^s$$
$$res(l) = O(l) - c_z z(l) - d_z k(l) \in R^m \tag{6.6}$$

6.2.5   Digital Twin and Machine Learning

Applications are considered to be simple if they have a small number of variables and a straight relationship that can be determined with relative ease between the inputs and the outputs. Such applications do not require machine learning approach. However, machine learning and analytics can help most real-world systems make sense of multiple data streams. In this context, the term "machine learning" refers to the application of any algorithm to a data source in order to find or discover patterns that can subsequently be utilized in a variety of ways. Machine learning approach has the ability to compute complex real-time data and find a feasible solution. It is able to evaluate data in real time, make adjustments to behavior with only a minimum amount of supervision, and increase the probability of desired results. Additionally, machine learning has the potential to contribute to the production of meaningful insights, which can lead to cost reductions. The applications of machine learning capabilities in the digital twin are presented in [44, 45]. Many different types of learning approaches been used for various digital twin models. The learning process includes supervised learning using neural network. The process include simulation and controlled experimentation of testbench [46]. In case of unsupervised learning, the model learns the object and patterns. A typical example includes clustering techniques virtually [47, 48]. The third type of learning is reinforcement learning of a system under uncertain conditions. A user can partially observe the operations of the external environment [49, 50].

6.3   Control and Identification: A Survey

The identification of a black box is a system—the "art" of constructing dynamical mathematical models using data collected from any dynamical system. A dynamical system is a state of system in which the system behavior varies over time. To identify any given system, the characteristics of both signal and the system and their properties are required. It is important to study fundamental parameters during identification, including the system's impulse response, the frequency components of a signal (Fourier series, Fourier transformations), and the distribution of power and energy across frequencies. The technique starts from measuring the system's behavior and external effects (inputs, output) and tries to find a mathematical link between them without diving into specifics of what is occurring inside the system. Input and output data are both used in system identification methods; however, the latter can also use exclusively output data (e.g., frequency domain decomposition). In most cases, an input–output method would provide more accurate results; however, the input data is not always readily available. In order to select an equivalent model from a collection of provided models for the system under test, it was believed that identification should be based on the input and output data [51, 52]. L. Ljung in [53] presented a more precise definition of identification in 1978; according to this definition, identification has three components— data, models, and standards. Lastly, we pick one model out of several that best matches the data. Ding Feng [54] defines system identification as generating an input signal, using experimental input and output data, picking a class of models, constructing an error criterion function, and optimizing a model to fit the data. Black-box and white-box engineering system models are the basic techniques [55]. In white-box modeling, the model is based on first-principles physical model. When the model and test results are compared, it is frequently realized that the nominal model does not give sufficient precision to predict the structural response to an excitation. This is mostly due to (i) modeling mistakes caused by model simplification, discretization, and so on, (ii) parameter errors caused by incorrectly specifying model parameters, and (iii) measurement inaccuracies caused by noise and measurement errors. To address (ii) and (iii) mistakes, a hybrid category of modeling known as gray-box modeling should be used. The area of system identification focuses on parameter estimation. Throughout the procedure, it is also possible to estimate the degree of uncertainty that is associated with the parameters that is estimated as error. This calculation of uncertainty may be seen as overlapping both the system identification and the uncertainty quantification processes. The linear models are easy to compute and have simple input–output relationships that most of the time give a good enough view of how a system works. However, even during normal operation, many dynamic systems exhibit some nonlinear behavior. If strong nonlinear properties are identified during the testing of the model, a nonlinear model must be replaced with a linear model. Many strategies for constructing a mathematical model with minimum user participation have been developed for black-box system identification [56–58]. Compared to a linear model, identifying a nonlinear system usually requires a lot more parameters because the model needs to be able to represent the real behavior of the structure much better. The black-box model requires selecting a model structure and estimating its parameters from test data. Most of the approaches, however, were neither quick nor robust; they required user input and relied on high-dimensional optimization algorithms [59–61]. If the model exhibits linear time invariant (LTI) behavior, the problem is reduced to selecting an appropriate model order. The gray-box models have known structures but unknown parameters. The gray-box system identification attempts to estimate these parameters using test data. The gray-box models that approximate reality have been developed over decades in several application sectors. They are huge, intricate, and sophisticated, making simulation time-consuming. These models include parameterized finite element models. Most of their parameters have physical implications, such as the following:

- Parameters that describe the geometry of the system, such as the length and cross-section area of structural members.
- Some parameters, such as Young's modulus, yield stress, and Poison's ratio, describe the way a material behaves.

- Parameters like applied pressure and forced ground motion that describe how the systems are loaded.

Identifying linear systems was a priority at first, but nonlinear systems have been getting increasing attention in recent years. Typically, there are two types of models used to describe dynamical systems: linear and nonlinear. Traditional identification methods [62–64] identify the system model framework and error criteria function.

Traditional linear system identification methods include least squares, gradient correction, maximum likelihood, and others. Some limitations are listed as, in the least squares approach, the input signal must be known and change substantially. Some dynamic systems cannot satisfy these criteria. It is not possible to synchronize the structure identification process with the parameter identification process. On the other hand, the vast majority of systems that are actually used in the real world are nonlinear. Transfer functions, which relate the input to the output of linear systems, are constant at all excitation levels. Hence, the mathematical model generated by identification at one operating point may be subsequently used to predict another operating point. The model selection according to the characteristic of the given plant for a DT model can be done according to Figure 6.1.

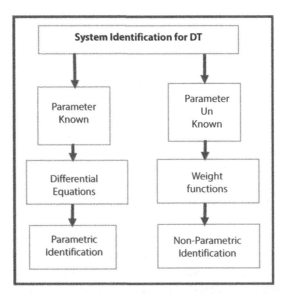

Figure 6.1 Block diagram of the system identification process for the digital twin model.

6.3.1   Hierarchy of System Identification Methods

6.3.1.1   Parametric Methods

If there is some previous knowledge about an appropriate model of the system, a parametric model may be used to produce a set of parameters for defining the input–output behavior of the system. These parameters can then be used to make predictions about the system. In linear systems, modal analysis goes one step farther than traditional analysis by compressing the parameters in the mathematical model into a minimal set of modal parameters. These parameters include the modal frequencies, modal vectors, and modal scaling. Modeling systems using parameters is an example of a parametric modeling approach. One example of this approach is direct parameter estimation.

6.3.1.2   Nonparametric Methods

In this indirect method, impulse response, step response, and frequency response functions are used to simulate a set of linear dynamical systems. Step response is also included in this method. The non-parametric shapes are subsequently fitted using continuous-time parametric models. Only parametric models may be properly referred to as "continuous-time models." The identification of non-parametric models can be accomplished through the use of a variety of techniques. Figure 6.2 presents the parametric and nonparametric models for DT.

6.3.2   Machine Learning Approach

The nonlinear system modeling theory and application have evolved significantly in recent years. The non-linear autoregressive moving average with exogenous inputs (NARMAX) model is recognized to describe a broad class of discrete-time non-linear systems [65–69]. Non-linear functional expansion of delayed inputs, outputs, and prediction error explains the NARMAX model. Modeling a real-world system is difficult since its mathematical function is complex and unknown, so neural networks can be studied as an alternative. Layers of these units are organized in such a way that data is inputted into the system at the input layer, then moves through either one or several intermediary layers, and finally arrives at the output layer. During the supervised learning process, the network is trained by making adjustments to the connection strengths between the nodes based on the prediction error, which is the difference between the

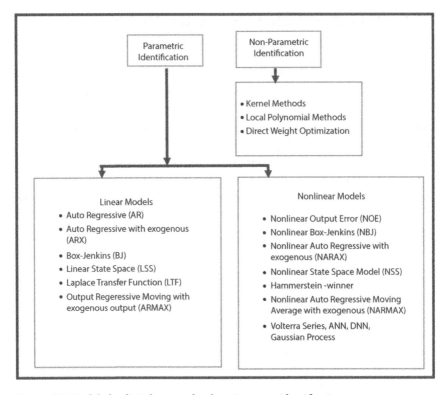

Figure 6.2 Models for digital twin technology in system identification.

actual output of the network and the output that the network was designed to generate. Weights are adjusted incrementally until the output error is close to the actual error. These models, which include neural networks with multiple layers and linear dynamics, can be viewed as generalized neural networks. The linear and nonlinear autoregressive moving average (ARMA) model is proposed in [70]. The result demonstrates that ARMA/NARMA models can be derived from ANN models by changing the activation function to a polynomial. According to the findings of the simulations, the suggested parameter estimators perform better than the already used estimators for time-varying ARMA (AR, MA) models in terms of accuracy and/or numerical efficiency [71]. Consistent work on improving autoregression had been done and is shown in [72–78].

A parameter estimation method had been proposed with static and dynamic back-propagation method to estimate the parameters of static and dynamic systems [79]. The disadvantage of the BP algorithm is that the computational complexity of the network is very high. In addition, it takes more time to train the model. A modified artificial neural network (MANN) is presented, and its related backpropagation (BP) learning method is created, in which the activation function (AF) is introduced before the linking weights of each artificial neuron. In addition, the normally fixed slope of AF is modified during training to improve and speed up multi-layer artificial neural network (MANN) training [80–83]. Methods that are based on neuro-fuzzy models are rapidly becoming established as one of the more common nonlinear identification approaches, and this is happening not just in the academic world but also in applications that are used in industries. The concept of neuro-fuzzy modeling may be thought of as a gray-box approach that sits on the cusp of the intersection between neural networks and qualitative fuzzy models. Neural network, pattern recognition, and regression analysis methods are used to develop neuro-fuzzy models. This work discusses neuro-fuzzy modeling strategies for nonlinear system identification, focusing on accuracy vs. interpretability [84].

A recurrent self-organizing neural fuzzy inference network (RSONFIN) is designed as a nonlinear model to identify nonlinear dynamic systems [85]. The RSONFIN is a recurrent multi-layered connectionist network that is built from a set of dynamic fuzzy rules. In order to create the temporal links within the network, a feedforward neural fuzzy network is modified by adding some feedback connections to symbolize the memory components. In general, there are no hidden nodes in the RSONFIN. This means that there are no membership functions and fuzzy rules. The proposed model is constructed with structure learning and parameter learning capabilities which offer a powerful dynamic neural fuzzy identification model. For nonlinear dynamic system identification, a computationally efficient Legendre neural network (LeNN) is presented in [86]. The LeNN's single-layer architecture reduces the computational cost compared to an MLP.

A nonlinear system identification approach employing suitable learning algorithm with multi-layered perceptron (MLP) is presented in [87]. This research offers a biogeography-based optimization (BBO)-based MLP architecture for nonlinear system identification. The suggested MLP architecture with BBO learning provides a promising approach for the identification of nonlinear systems since it combines the two different types of learning strategies. Multilayer and recurrent networks are linked in new configurations in the proposed model. The objective of the proposed models is to design a method for the dynamic adjustment of the parameters based on backpropagation. For dynamic processes with nonlinear features, a guided nonlinear dynamic system (NDS) based on variational autoencoder (VAE) is given [88]. In order to identify Takagi–Sugeno (TS) fuzzy models in real time, this work provides two cutting-edge learning methods based on the Kalman filter [89]. The unscented Kalman filter (UKF) and dual estimation form the basis of the proposed methods. Therefore, TS models can use nondifferentiable membership functions. Compared to earlier studies on the same topic, the presented methods may be used for the online parameter estimation of a larger class of TS models. The proposed techniques can approximate nonlinear systems because the UKF can handle several nonlinear dynamics. Numerical and practical examples demonstrate the proposed methods' benefits. Other development works on Kalman filer are presented in [90–91]. The successful modeling of dynamic systems has been accomplished using randomized algorithms.

The CNN model is analyzed in the frequency domain because the convolution operation, which is a crucial feature of the dynamic system, is transformed into the product in the frequency domain. To begin, the CNN model is represented both the input and output sequences. Then, the frequency domain analysis is determined as the effect of CNN's random weights. From the result, there are optimal weights, and the modeling precision using those weights was compared with those chosen at random. The proposed method was theoretically evaluated with a two-stage training technique to the popular random weight algorithm that is presented in [92]. The context layered locally recurrent neural network (CLLRNN) was created to identify dynamic systems [93]. To improve the RNN network performance, the fractional backpropagation through time (FBPTT) technique was devised [94]. The fractional calculus-based gradient descent approach might be used to derive the FBPTT algorithm. The FBPTT approach outperforms the typical backpropagation through time methodology on three estimation problems: pattern classification nonlinear dynamic system identification and Mackey–Glass chaotic time series prediction. From the simulation analysis, the superiority of the model is verified.

RNNs include long–short term memory (LSTM). It employs recurrent processes and gates to process information sequences. LSTM outperforms feedforward and recurrent NNs in audio and video time series modeling. In order to make use of all the benefits that come with combining LSTM with NN, this research employs a hybrid approach [95]. A multilayer perceptron and hierarchical recurrent network makes up the innovative neural model. The learning algorithm incorporates backpropagation through time training approaches [96].

Functional link ANN (FLANN) is an alternative ANN structure that employs the well-known backpropagation method to identify nonlinear dynamic systems [97]. With the correct functional extension, a FLANN may recognize nonlinear systems as well as the MLP structure sometimes better. Furthermore, the FLANN architecture is adjoined with a supervised learning algorithm to estimate the weights of the network [98]. Discussions on more development activities on FLANN may be found in [99, 100]. The identification of nonlinear dynamic systems utilizing RBF networks that have been selected using many criteria is taken into serious consideration [101]. RBF networks are frequently utilized as a framework for modeling nonlinear systems due to their versatility. System identification begins with the determination of its structure, which is the number of basis functions, and there is a trade-off between model complexity and accuracy in this challenge. Discussions on more development activities on RBF may be found in [102–107].

Extreme learning machines (ELM) are recently gaining popularity in machine learning to solve problems like parameter estimation, regression, classification, clustering, and feature selection due to their fast training, accurate classification, and good generalization/universal approximation. ELM evolves as a feed-forward neural network incorporated into its framework [108, 109]. The input matrix and hidden neuron weights are randomly assigned. The least-squares approach calculates output weights after tuning the ELM hidden neuron layers. Thus, the least-squares technique performs better and quicker than quadratic programming in ordinary SVM or gradient methods in classic BP-based NNs. In addition to ELM, [110] introduces the random vector functional link network (RVFLN) and offers a version on this network. RVFLN's input and output layers are directly coupled, a feature that greatly improves the network's generalization performance. One advantage of RVFLN over ELM is that it reduces the model complexity [111–115].

A kernel is a technique in machine learning that maps non-linear input into a higher-dimensional space in a way that does not need us to see or comprehend that higher-dimensional region. The kernel function has been employed as a solution in the area of system identification [115–121].

Deep learning is getting a lot of popularity owing to the fact that it is superior to traditional machine learning methods in terms of accuracy when it is trained with a huge quantity of data. With small data, standard machine learning techniques are best. The method of supervised learning is used in deep learning. Supervised learning's strength is its ability to rapidly expand the number of hidden layers for computation in response to a large data collection. While this method does add complexity to the model, it ultimately produces more precise results in less time.

6.3.3 Deep Neural Network Approach

For frequency-domain adaptive system identification, a unique end-to-end deep learning-based adaptation control technique is proposed and presented in [122]. The approach that is being presented makes use of a deep neural network in order to map observable signal properties to corresponding step-sizes that regulate the modification of the filter. By minimizing the average normalized system distance of the adaptive filter, the network's parameters are optimized in an end-to-end way in order to get the best possible results. Model-based adaptation control requires explicit signal power spectral density estimates and additional techniques to deal with model imperfections. Furthermore, a hybrid model, deep reconstruction models (DRMs), that combine deep learning and Elman neural networks (ENNs) is presented in [123]. To accelerate modeling convergence, restricted Boltzmann machines (RBMs) are used to layer-wise initialize model parameters. In order to describe and regulate nonlinear (NL) system behavior, the linear parameter-varying (LPV) framework is used [124, 125].

Next-generation system identification must create flexible models and estimators to simulate complicated systems. Nonlinearity makes this work harder [126]. In many practical applications, output feedback stability issues can adversely impact long-term predictor performance. Deep networks, which are successful at classification challenges, have not yet cross-fertilized with system identification. Deep prediction networks, based on a hierarchical design, are presented in [127] as an effective deep learning algorithm. Its kernel-based technique controls complexity in layers that enhance long-term predictions. A real-time deep neural network (DNN) that approximates unknown nonlinear system dynamics is presented in [128]. The framework's weight update technique is based on multi-message concurrent learning, which results in continuous updates to the DNN's output layer weights but discrete, batch-like updates to the DNN's internal features.

Due to its superior learning ability, DBN is becoming increasingly prominent in nonlinear system modeling and identification. Unfortunately, gradient-based weight optimization for DBN always results in a poor training outcome and a local optimum [129]. This research proposes a DBN with PLSR-DBN for nonlinear system modeling to optimize DBN weights using PLSR. Weight initialization uses unsupervised contrastive divergence (CD) technique. In addition, layer-by-layer PLSR modeling optimizes CD algorithm weights from top to bottom. Instead of gradient approach, PLSR-DBN may establish optimal weights using many PLSR models, thus improving performance. Then, convergence is theoretically analyzed to prove that the PLSR-DBN model works. In addition to the previous work, a model is proposed using a self-organizing deep belief network (SODBN) with pruning and growth algorithms [130]. Experimental data reveal that SODBN outperforms several neural networks. Further development work on the model is discussed in [131, 132]. For the purpose of nonlinear system identification, deep recurrent neural networks are presented in [133]. It has been demonstrated that state-space models can be converted into recurrent neural networks and *vice versa*.

Deep Boltzmann machine (DBM) has proved effective in classification, regression, and time series modeling. DBM's input feature extraction and noise tolerance should make it a better neural network for nonlinear system modeling [134]. In this study, a DBM is used to simulate nonlinear systems by estimating input and output probability distributions. Modeling accuracy is achieved when binary vectors or conditional probability transformations encode the system's output and input. Maximizing the input–output conditional distribution trains the DBM. The findings of the simulation indicate that the accuracy of the modeling has been increased.

The proposed CNN improves real structure response estimation. The CNN is better than the MLP algorithm since it is easier to understand the mechanism during training [135–137]. For nonlinear system identification, denoising autoencoders' deep learning methods are adjusted [138]. When compared to MLPs, deep neural networks feature fewer hidden nodes and more hidden layers, making them a more suitable alternative model for the identification of nonlinear systems. More works on autoencoders are presented in [139].

In machine learning, recurrent neural networks are popular study topics. LSTM is one of several novel RNN topologies and concepts. A novel LSTM idea to discover and govern dynamic systems is presented in [140]. Convex-based LSTM networks will be used for quick learning as a deep learning model for dynamic system identification. Simulations show that the novel LSTM structure outperforms standard RNN and single LSTM networks [141]. For nonlinear systems whose dynamics are unknown, we introduce differentiable predictive control (DPC) as a deep learning-based replacement for explicit model predictive control (MPC). A neural state-space model is learned from system dynamics time-series observations in the DPC framework. The closed-loop system dynamics model differentiates the MPC loss function to optimize the neural control strategy using stochastic gradient descent. Random hidden weights and pseudo-inverse computation for output weights improve regression and classification algorithms [142]. Furthermore, a nonlinear auto-regressive complex benchmark system is analyzed using a multi-layer ELM (ML-ELM) model. The model provides better performance result than traditional ELM. Similarly, a speech signal is identified as an application of system identification by using the deep LSTM model [143].

From Section 6.2, the related works on DT and system identification are discussed. From the discussion, it was analyzed that system identification can be represented as an online identification model or DT model. To solve the system identification problem, three techniques were used. As online system identification deals with complex and huge data, it requires fast and accurate a deep learning identification model. In this survey, a SISO nonlinear and dynamic plant is used for identification and control purposes. Hence, a DT model as identification and control model for the proposed deep learning model is presented in Section 6.6.

6.4 Proposed Methodology

From previous discussions, the authors have found that machine learning approach is an efficient approach to handle nonlinear and complex real-time systems.

6.4.1 DT Technology Application in Identification and Control

RVFLN is similar in structure to a single-hidden-layer feedforward neural network (SLFN), but it adds a direct link between the input and output layers, while SLFN does not. Random weights are used to connect the hidden layer nodes to the input nodes, and the total weight vector of the direct linkages and the hidden layer or enhancement nodes is estimated using generalized least squares. RVFLN's input–output connection regularizes the network. It boosts randomized RVFLN generalization [144]. RVFLN is simpler than ELM due to the direct connection [145]. RVFLN can minimize training error and output weight norms. Parameter estimation and control models require quick convergence and generalization, which this architecture provides. Given samples of Z where $\{T = \left((T_P P_P) | T_p \in R^a \right), P_P \in R^b, p = 1, \ldots G\}$, where T_P, P_P each are element of samples that carries $T_P = [T_p^1, T_p^2 \ldots T_p^a]^T$ is denoted as a dimensional input vector and $T_P = [T_p^1, T_p^2 \ldots T_p^b]^T$ is a, b dimensional output vector. The traditional RVFLn enhancement node A is represented by:

$$H_0{}^{\beta 0} = P(m)$$

The output weight matrix is represented by the symbol β_0. H_0 is a matrix that is formed by arbitrarily mapped features that are connected from the hidden nodes and input features. Isolated from one another, this matrix can be expressed as:

$$H_0 = \begin{bmatrix} T_1 \\ \vdots \\ T_G \end{bmatrix} = \begin{bmatrix} h_1(T_1) & \cdots & h_r(T_1) \\ \vdots & \ddots & \vdots \\ h_1(T_G) & \cdots & h_r(T_G) \end{bmatrix}_{G*r}$$

$$T = \begin{bmatrix} T_1^1 & \cdots & T^c \\ \vdots & \ddots & \vdots \\ T_G^1 & \cdots & T_G^c \end{bmatrix}_{G*c}$$

$$H = \begin{bmatrix} h_1(T_1) & \cdots & h_r(T_1) \, T_1^1 & \cdots & T_1^c \\ \vdots & \ddots & \vdots & \vdots & \ddots & \vdots \\ h_1(T_z) & \cdots & h_r(T_G) T_G^1 & \cdots & T_G^c \end{bmatrix}_{G*(r+c)}$$

$$\beta^0 = \begin{bmatrix} \beta^0{}_1{}^T \\ \vdots \\ \beta^0{}_{r+c}{}^T \end{bmatrix}_{(r+c)*d}$$

$$P = \begin{bmatrix} P_1^T \\ \vdots \\ P_G^T \end{bmatrix}_{G*d}$$

$h_1(T_1) = \dot{\varphi}(w_1^h * T + \alpha_1), h_r T) = \dot{\varphi}(w_r^h * T + \alpha_r)$ *and* $\dot{\varphi}(.)$ *donates the non-linear activation function.* w_1^h represents the random weight, and α_1 represents the bias that is allocated to the layer that connects the input and hidden layers. Now, the output weight β^0 calculated as:

$$\beta^0 = H^+ P$$

$$\beta^0 = H^T (HH^T + \frac{i}{S})^{-1} P$$

Following the RVFLn algorithm, model training is ideal, takes less time, and performs well. Further additional development has been done to improve the model performance, such as learning speed. This procedure is based on the concept of training in a supervised manner without fine-tuning the training parameters, and it takes the shape of a stack. An orthogonal feature of the input data is mapped and then passed to the hidden layers, where the output weight is computed analytically using the proposed method. The proposed method consists of three hidden layers, with the output layer represented as a SoftMax layer. The outcome of the hidden layers can be determined by using the formulas as follows:

$$H_i = \dot{\omega}\left(H_{i-1} * \beta_i^{0T}\right); 1 \le i \le 1$$

where the nonlinear activation function is represented by the symbol $\dot{\varphi}$ (.). At layer 1, the hidden output matrix is represented by the symbol H_i, whereas the training output weight is indicated by the notation β_i^0. The deep-RVFLN final output is calculated as:

$$T^\beta = H^T (HH^T + \frac{i}{S})^{-1} P \tag{6.7}$$

or

$$T^\beta = \left(H^T H + \frac{i}{S}\right)^{-1} H^T P \tag{6.8}$$

where $H = [H_k T']$, and H_k is the last hidden layer output. From Figure 6.2, T is the input data set, y is the output, the first output matrix is β_0^0, and the last output matrix weight is β_0^k or the kth layer.

In Figure 6.3(a), the block diagram of the proposed model is depicted. In Figure 6.3(b), the block diagram of a DT model to identify the SISO plant is shown. From the block diagram input to the actual plant is $T(m)$, and the actual plant is denoted as $G(m)$. The proposed model is denoted as $P(m)$. $\breve{P}(m), \breve{G}(m)$ are the approximate models of their original body. The main goal of the identification is to find the difference/error between two approximate models. The proposed model should contain the same parameter as the actual model.

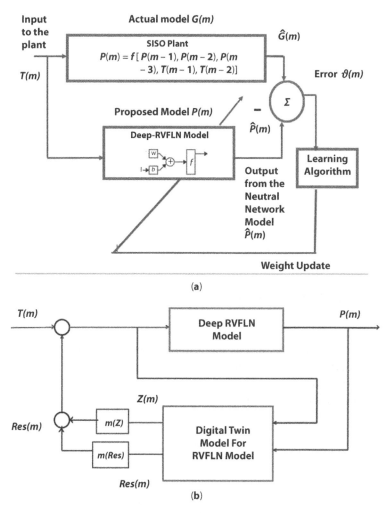

Figure 6.3 (a) Proposed machine learning model for control application, (b) Digital twin control model for the machine learning model.

The architecture of the proposed deep-RRVFLN model is depicted in Figure 6.4. From the figure, it can be seen that the model has one input layer, three hidden layers, and an output layer. There is a direct connection between the input layer and output layer that makes this method unique as it provides better computational accuracy. As the layers are increased, the model performance also increases.

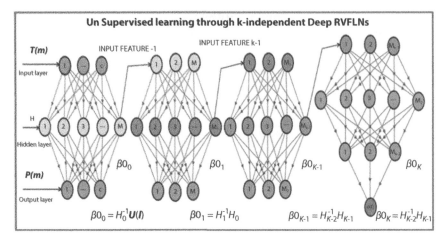

Figure 6.4 Architecture of the proposed DT model.

6.5   Result Analysis and Discussion

In this section, a nonlinear dynamic model is verified, and the performance is compared to that of the proposed model and the basic RVFLN model. Furthermore, by using the following methods, the error values can be converted into two performance indices: mean absolute error (MAE) and mean square error (MSE).

$$
\text{MSE} = \frac{1}{N} \sum_{i=1}^{N} (X_i - p_i)^2
$$

$$
\text{MAE} = \sqrt{\frac{\sum |X - Pd|}{P}}
$$

(6.9)

where X_i is the desired outcome, p_i is the expected outcome, and N is the overall number of samples.

6.5.1   Case Study: Control Application

An example of a SISO system that has been taken into consideration in this article and the mathematical expression that is driving the incoming signal is explained below:

$$P(m) = f[P(m-1), P(m-2), P(m-3), T(m-1), T(m-2)]$$

The nonlinear plant is dependent on the three previous outputs and the two previous inputs. A random function and a sinusoid function are used to generate the 1,000 input signals that are used in the training process. This training is carried out by collecting the signals as they are generated. The first 350 input signals are generated with a regular distribution within [2, 2], and the remaining 550 signals are generated with sin(2k/250). After the training procedure has been finished, the effectiveness of the identification model is evaluated using the input signals that are described in more detail below:

$$f[T_1, T_2, T_3, T_4, T_5] = \frac{T_1, T_2, T_3, T_5(T_3 - 1), T_4}{1 + T_2^2 + T_3^2} \tag{6.10}$$

$$T_1 = P(m-1), T_2 = P(m-2), T_3 = P(m-3), T_4 = P(m), T_5 = P(m-1) \tag{6.11}$$

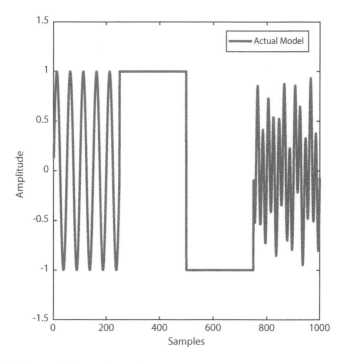

Figure 6.5 Output of the actual signal.

The actual SISO plant output is seen from Figure 6.5; it has 1,000 samples. The corresponding plant has to be identified. Initially, uniformly distributed random signals are used as a trial-and-error method. The random signals used are [-0.5 to 0.5], [-1 to 1], and [-1.5 to 1.5], but the tracking results were unsatisfactory. The error between the models is more. Hence, the standard benchmark coefficients were used, and the results were analyzed.

Figure 6.6 shows the output of the controller model. Control parameter estimation of the plant is required after getting the initial output. The main idea is to minimize the error with a suitable learning algorithm. The feedback controller is named as residual controller. In Figure 6.7 the output of the proposed model is depicted. The proposed model is verified along with basic RVFLN, ELM, and AAERVFN.

From Table 6.3, the performance of the proposed model is verified. The proposed deep-RVFLN archives 0.0056 MSE and 0.00354 MAE. Compared to other models, it archives the best result. Hence, it is a good

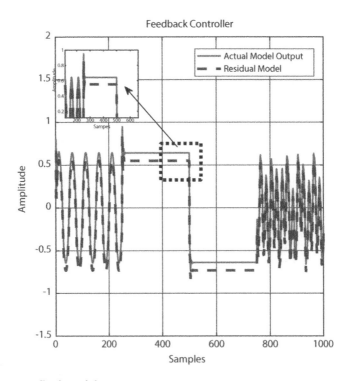

Figure 6.6 Feedback module output.

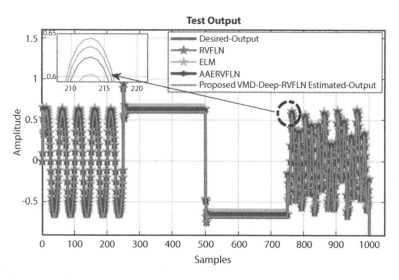

Figure 6.7 Proposed VMD-based deep-RVFLN estimated output.

Table 6.3 Performance measure of nonlinear systems.

Methods used	MSE error	MAE error	Method type
WRFNN	0.098	-	Non-iterative randomized method (N-Iter-rand)
RSONFIN	0.078	-	Iteration
NFIS-DN	0.0	-	Iteration
ANFIS	0.683	0.0581	Iteration
CFLANN-DRLS	0.802	0.0634	Iteration
TAKAGI-SUGENO	0.0683	0.0581	Iteration
RVFLN	0.0566	0.0491	Iteration
ELM	0.0868	0.0584	N-Iteration-rand
AAERVFLN	0.0525	0.0397	N-Iteration-rand
Proposed deep-RVFLN	0.0056	0.00354	N-Iteration-rand

identification model and can be used as a DT control model for the non-linear and dynamic plant.

6.6 Conclusion and Future Work

At a conceptual level, the focus of this article is on the methodologies of virtual modeling or online system identification. The application of digital twins (DT) in dynamical systems has an enormous amount of potential—for example, it may be used for active control, health monitoring, diagnosis, and prognosis as well as the computation of remaining usable life. However, the implementation of this technology in real time has been slower than was anticipated, notably due to a lack of information that are relevant to the application being used.

Hence, the main goal of this work is to make a DT detection and control model that can process data quickly and give correct results. Therefore, it may be used in online system identification. In order to identify the SISO plant, a nonlinear identification model in the form of a VMD-deep RVFL neural network has been presented. Afterwards, the DT model is developed into a controller. Table 6.3 shows that the proposed VMD-deep RVFLN has a lower MSE than the classic RVFLN, ELM, and AAERVFN. Improving the model's efficiency requires adding more hidden layers.

References

1. Ibrahim, M., Rjabtšikov, V., Gilbert, R., Overview of digital twin platforms for EV applications. *Sensors*, 23, 3, 1414, 2023.
2. Minghui, H., Ya, H., Xinzhi, L., Ziyuan, L., Jiang, Z., Bo, M.A., Digital twin model of gas turbine and its application in warning of performance fault. *Chin. J. Aeronaut.*, 36, 3, 449–470, 2023.
3. He, R., Chen, G., Dong, C., Sun, S., Shen, X., Data-driven digital twin technology for optimized control in process systems. *ISA Trans.*, 95, 221–234, 2019.
4. Jain, P., Chakraborty, A., Pistikopoulos, E.N., Mannan, M.S., Resilience-based process upset event prediction analysis for uncertainty management using Bayesian deep learning: Application to a polyvinyl chloride process system. *Ind. Eng. Chem. Res.*, 57, 14822–36, 2018.
5. Dai, Y.Y., Wang, H.Z., Khan, F., Zhao, J., Abnormal situation management for smart chemical process operation. *Curr. Opin. Chem. Eng.*, 14, 49–55, 2016.

6. Eckhart, M. and Ekelhart, A., Towards Security-Aware Virtual Environments for Digital Twins, in: *Proceedings of the 4th ACM Workshop on Cyber-Physical System Security*, pp. 61–72, 2018.

7. Patterson, E.A., Taylor, R.J., Bankhead, M., A framework for an integrated nuclear digital environment. *Prog. Nucl. Energy*, 87, 97–103, 2016.

8. Yin, S., Li, X., Gao, H., Kaynak, O., Data-based techniques focused on modern industry: An overview. *IEEE Trans. Ind. Electron*, 62, 1, 657–67, 2015.

9. Severson, K., Chaiwatanodom, P., Braatz, R.D., Perspectives on process monitoring of industrial systems. *Annu. Rev. Control*, 42, 190–200, 2016.

10. Ding, S.X., Zhang, P., Jeinsch, T., Ding, E.L., Engel, P., Gui, W., A Survey of the Application of Basic Data-driven and Model-based Methods in Process Monitoring and Fault Diagnosis, in: *Preprints of the 18th IFAC world congress*, pp. 12380–8, 2011.

11. Yin, S., Ding, S.X., Haghani, A., Hao, H., Zhang, P., A comparison study of basic data-driven fault diagnosis and process monitoring methods on the benchmark tennessee eastman process. *J. Process Control*, 22, 9, 1567–81, 2012.

12. Qin, S.J., An overview of subspace identification. *Comput. Chem. Eng*, 30, 10–12, 1502–13, 2006.

13. Ding, S.X., Zhang, P., Naik, A., Ding, E.L., Huang, B., Subspace method aided datadriven design of fault detection and isolation systems. *J. Process Control*, 19, 9, 1496–510, 2009.

14. Zhao, B., Liu, D., Li, Y., Observer based adaptive dynamic programming for fault tolerant control of a class of nonlinear systems. *Inf Sci.*, 384, 21–33, 2017.

15. Wen, L., Tao, G., Yang, H., Chen, F., Adaptive LQ control-based actuator failure compensation, in: *American Control Conference*, pp. 2011–6, 2016.

16. Tao, F., Liu, W., Zhang, M., Hu, T., Qi, Q., Zhang, H. *et al.*, Five-dimension digital twin model and its ten applications. *CIMS*, 25, 01, 1–18, 2019.

17. Tao, F., Zhang, H., Qi, Q., Xu, J., Sun, Z., Hu, T. *et al.*, Theory of digital twin modelling and its application. *CIMS*, 27, 1, 1–16, 2021.

18. Barricelli, B.R., Casiraghi, E., Fogli, D.A., Survey on digital twin: Definitions, characteristics, applications, and design implications. *IEEE Access*, 7, 167653–71, 2019.

19. Corral-Acero, J., Margara, F., Marciniak, M., Rodero, C., Loncaric, F., Feng, Y. *et al.*, The 'Digital Twin' to enable the vision of precision cardiology. *Eur. Heart J.*, 41, 48, 4556–64, 2020.

20. Wagg, D. J., Worden, K., Barthorpe, R. J., Gardner, P., Digital twins: State-of-the-art and future directions for modelling and simulation in engineering dynamics applications. *ASCE-ASME J. Risk Uncert. Eng. Syst. Part B Mech. Eng.*, 6, 3, 030901, 2020.

21. Kourti, T. and MacGregor, J.F., Process analysis, monitoring and diagnosis, using multivariate projection methods. *Chemom. Intell. Lab. Syst.*, 28, 1, 3–21, 1995.

22. Mercère, G. and Bako, L., Parameterization and identification of multivariable state-space systems: A canonical approach. *Automatica*, 47, 8, 1547–55, 2011.

23. Chen, H., Tiňo, P., Yao, X., Cognitive fault diagnosis in tennessee eastman process using learning in the model space. *Comput. Chem. Eng*, 67, 33–42, 2014.

24. Benkhaddra, I., Kumar, A., Setitra, M.A. *et al.*, Design and development of consensus activation function enabled neural network-based smart healthcare using BIoT. *Wireless Pers. Commun.*, 130, 1549–1574, 2023, https://doi.org/10.1007/s11277-023-10344-0.

25. Duan, C., Fei, Z., Li, J., A variable selection aided residual generator design approach for process control and monitoring. *Neurocomputing*, 171, 1013–20, 2016.

26. Ding, S.X., Wang, Y., Yin, S., Zang, P., Yang, Y., Ding, E.L., Data-Driven Design of Fault-Tolerant Control Systems, in: *Proceedings of 8th IFAC Symposium on Fault Detection, Supervision and Safety of Technical Processes*, pp. 1323–8, 2012.

27. Wang, J., Moreira, J., Cao, Y., Gopaluni, R. B., Neural network and Sparse identification of Nonlinear Dynamics Integrated Algorithm for Digital Twin identification. *IFAC-Papers On Line*, 56, 6921–6926, 2023.

28. Li, C., Huang, Z., Huang, Z., Wang, Y., Jiang, H., Digital twins in engineering dynamics: Variational equation identification, feedback control design and their rapid update. *Nonlinear Dyn.*, 11, 5, 4485–4500, 2023.

29. Ding, S.X., Yin, S., Wang, Y., Yang, Y., Ni, B., Data-driven design of observers and its applications A review on basic data-driven approaches for industrial process monitoring. *IEEE Trans. Ind. Electron*, 61, 11, 6418–28, 2014.

30. Ketzler, B., Naserentin, V., Latino, F., Zangelidis, C., Thuvander, L., Logg, A., Digital twins for cities: A state of the art review. *Built Environ.*, 46, 4, 547–573, 2020.

31. Madni, A.M., Madni C.C. and Lucero, S.D., Leveraging digital twin technology in model-based systems engineering. *Systems*, 7, 1, 1–13, 2019.

32. Srivastav, A.L., Markandeya, Patel, N. *et al.*, Concepts of circular economy for sustainable management of electronic wastes: Challenges and management option. *Environ. Sci. Pollut. Res.*, 30, 48654–48675, 2023, https://doi.org/10.1007/s11356-023-26052-y.

33. Madni, A.M., Sievers, M., Erwin, D., Madni, A., Ordoukhanian, E., Pouya, P., Formal Modeling of Complex Resilient Networked Systems, in: *Proceedings of the AIAA Science and Technology Forum*, San Diego, CA, USA, 7–11 January 2019.

34. Madni, A.M., Sievers, M., Ordoukhanian, E., Pouya, P., Madni, A., Extending Formal Modeling for Resilient Systems, in: *Proceedings of the 2018 INCOSE International Symposium*, Washington, DC, USA, 7–12 July 2018.

35. Madni, A.M., Next Generation Adaptive Cyber-Physical Systems, in: *Proceedings of the 21st Annual Systems Engineering Conference*, Tampa, FL, USA, 22–24 October 2018.

36. Madni, A.M., Madni, C.C., Sievers, M., Adaptive Cyber-Physical-Human Systems, in: *Proceedings of the 2018 INCOSE International Symposium*, Washington, DC, USA, 7–12 July 2018.

37. Madni, A.M., Samet, M.G., Freedy, A.A., Trainable on-line model of the human operator in information acquisition tasks. *IEEE Trans. Syst. Man Cybern.*, 12, 504–511, 1982.

38. Angjeliu, G., Coronelli, D., Cardani, G., Development of the simulation model for digital twin applications in historical masonry buildings: the integration between numerical and experimental reality. *Comput. Struct.*, 238, 106282, 2020.

39. Santagati, C. and Russa, F.M.L., Historical sentient – building information model: A digital twin for the management of museum collections in historical architectures. The International Archives of the Photogrammetry. *Remote Sens. Spat. Inf. Sci.*, XLIII-B4, 775–762, 2020.

40. Wang, P., Yang, M., Zhu, J., Ju, R., Li, G., Dynamic data driven modeling and simulation method for digital twin. *J. Syst. Eng. Electron*, 42, 12, 2779–86, 2020.

41. Liu, Y., Xu, H., Liu, D., Wang, L., A digital twin-based sim-to-real transfer for deep reinforcement learning-enabled industrial robot grasping. *Robot. Comput.-Integr. Manuf.*, 78, 102365, 2022.

42. Elkarii, M., Bouallou, C., Ratnani, A., Towards modelling a diphasic flow using the CFD technique to achieve a digital twin of a phosphate slurry piping process. *Chem. Eng. Trans.*, 81, 757–62, 2020.

43. Khakimov, R.A. and Shcherbo, N.S., Development and creation a model of a digital twin of the cubepart rectification installation for the separation of a binary wateralcohol mixture. *IOP Conf. Ser.: Mater. Sci. Eng.*, 450, 062006, 2018.

44. Aversano, G., Ferrarotti, M., Parente, A., Digital twin of a combustion furnace operating in flameless conditions: Reduced-order model development from CFD simulations. *Proc. Combust. Inst.*, 2021, 5373–5381, 2021.

45. Ilyas, B., Kumar, A., Setitra, M.A., Bensalem, Z.E.A., Lei, H., Prevention of DDoS attacks using an optimized deep learning approach in blockchain technology. *Trans. Emerg. Telecommun. Technol.*, 34, 4, e4729, 2023.

46. Liu, S., Bao, J., Lu, Y., Li, J., Lu, S., Sun, X., Digital twin modelling method based on biomimicry for machining aerospace components. *J. Manuf. Syst.*, 58, 180–95, 2021.

47. Liu, S., Lu, Y., Li, J., Song, D., Sun, X., Bao, J., Multi-scale evolution mechanism and knowledge construction of a digital twin mimic model. *Robot CIM-Int. Manuf.*, 71, 102123, 2021.

48. Liu, Z., Chen, W., Zhang, C., Data super-network fault prediction model and maintenance strategy for mechanical product based on digital twin. *IEEE Access*, 7, 177284–96, 2019.

49. Laukotka Hanna, F., Schwede, M., Dieter Krause, L., Use of digital twins overarching life cycle phases: Model-based product family development using the aircraft cabins as example. *Z für Wirtsch Fabr.*, 115, 101–4, 2020.

50. Bare, Z., Gaertig, E., Krebs, J., Arndt, C., Gensel A. A note on leakage jet forces: application in the modelling of digital twins of hydraulic valves. *Int. J. Fluid Power*, 22, 1, 113–46, 2021.

51. Zadeh, L., From circuit theory to system theory. *Proc. IRE*, 50, 5, 856–865, May 1962.

52. Li, M., & Liu, X., Maximum likelihood least squares based iterative estimation for a class of bilinear systems using the data filtering technique. *Int. J. Control Autom. Syst.*, 18, 6, 1581–1592, 2020.

53. Ljung, L., Convergence analysis of parametric identification methods. *IEEE Trans. Automat. Contr.*, 23, 5, 770–783, Oct. 1978.

54. Ding, F., System identification, Part A: Introduction to the identification. *J. Nanjing Univ. Inf. Sci. Technol.: Nat. Sci. Edition*, 3, 1, 1–22, 2011.

55. Nelles, O., *Nonlinear System Identification: From Classical Approaches to Neural Networks and Fuzzy Models*, Springer, Berlin, 2001.

56. McKelvey, T., Akçay, H., Ljung, L., Subspace-based multivariable system identification from frequency response data. *IEEE Trans. Autom. Control*, 41, 960–979, 1996.

57. Peeters, B., Van der Auweraer, H., Guillaume, P., Leuridan, J., The PolyMAX frequency domain method: A new standard for modal parameter estimation? *Shock. Vib.*, 11, 395–409, 2004.

58. Van Overschee, P. and De Moor, B., N4SID: Subspace algorithms for the identification of combined deterministic-stochastic systems. *Automatica*, 30, 75–93, 1994.

59. Reynders, E., Houbrechts, J., De Roeck, G., Fully automated (operational) modal analysis. *Mech. Syst. Signal Pr.*, 29, 228–250, 2012.

60. Kumar, A., Rathore, P.S., Dubey, A.K. *et al.*, LTE-NBP with holistic UWB- WBAN approach for the energy efficient biomedical application. *Multimed. Tools Appl.*, 82, 39797–39811, 2023, https://doi.org/10.1007/s11042-023-15604-6.

61. Verboven, P., Parloo, E., Guillaume, P., Van Overmeire, M., Autonomous structural health monitoring—part I: Modal parameter estimation and tracking. *Mech. Syst. Signal Pr.*, 16, 637–657, 2002.

62. VanDerHorn, E., and Mahadevan, S., Digital Twin: Generalization, characterization and implementation. *Decis. Support Syst.*, 145, 113524, 2021.

63. Pang, Z. and Cui, H., *MATLAB Simulation of System Identification and Adaptive Control*, National Defense Industry Press, Beijing, 2009.

64. Liu, D., *System Identification Methods and Applications*, National Defense Industry Press, Beijing, 2010.
65. Araújo, Í. B., Guimarães, J.P., Fontes, A., II, Linhares, L.L., Martins, A.M., Araújo, F.M., NARX model identification using correntropy criterion in the presence of non-Gaussian noise. *J. Control. Autom. Electr. Syst.*, 30, 453–464, 2019.
66. Guo, Y., Wang, L., Li, Y., Luo, J., Wang, K., Billings, S.A., Guo, L., Neural activity inspired asymmetric basis function TV-NARX model for the identification of time-varying dynamic systems. *Neurocomputing*, 357, 188–202, 357, 2019.
67. Sepahvand, S., Abedi, M., Pourgholi, M., A Modification on Stochastic Approximation Algorithm with Expanding Truncations For Estimation of NARX Systems, in: *2019 27th Iranian Conference on Electrical Engineering (ICEE)*, 2019, April, IEEE, pp. 925–928.
68. Chon, K.H. and Cohen, R.J., Linear and nonlinear ARMA model parameter estimation using an artificial neural network. *IEEE Trans. Biomed. Eng.*, 44, 3, 168–174, 1997.
69. Jachan, M., Matz, G., Hlawatsch, F., Time-frequency ARMA models and parameter estimators for underspread nonstationary random processes. *IEEE Trans. Signal Process.*, 55, 9, 4366–4381, 2007.
70. Wang, J., Liang, J., Che, J., Sun, D., ARMA model identification using particle swarm optimization algorithm, in: *2008 International Conference on Computer Science and Information Technology*, 2008, August, IEEE, pp. 223–227.
71. Stadnytska, T., Braun, S., Werner, J., Comparison of automated procedures for ARMA model identification. *Behav. Res. Methods*, 40, 250–262, 2008.
72. Jami'in, M.A., Sutrisno, I., Hu, J., Deep searching for parameter estimation of the linear time invariant (LTI) system by using quasi-ARX neural network, in: *The 2013 International Joint Conference on Neural Networks (IJCNN)*, 2013, August, pp. 1–5, IEEE.
73. Jin, G.D., Lu, L.B., Zhu, X.F., A method of order determination for ARX and ARMA models based on nonnegative garrote. *Appl. Mech. Mater.*, 721, 496–499), 2015.
74. Kumar, A., Kumar, S.A., Dutt, V., Shitharth, S., Tripathi, E., IoT based arrhythmia classification using the enhanced hunt optimization-based deep learning. *Expert Syst.*, 40, 7, e13298, 2023, https://doi.org/10.1111/ exsy.13298.
75. Hossain, M.B., Moon, J., Chon, K.H., Estimation of ARMA model order via artificial neural network for modeling physiological systems. *IEEE Access*, 8, 186813–186820, 2020.
76. Berardengo, M., Rossi, G.B., Crenna, F., Sea spectral estimation using ARMA models. *Sensors*, 21, 13, 4280, 2021.
77. Kumpati, S.N. and Kannan, P., Identification and control of dynamical systems using neural networks. *IEEE Trans. Neural Netw.*, 1, 1, 4–27, 1990.

78. Fujita, T., Xi, T., Ikeda, R., Kehne, S., Fey, M., Brecher, C., Identification of a practical digital twin for simulation of machine tools. *Int. J. Autom. Technol.*, 16, 3, 261–268, 2022.

79. Patra, J.C., Pal, R.N., Chatterji, B.N., Panda, G., Identification of nonlinear dynamic systems using functional link artificial neural networks. *IEEE Trans. Syst., Man, Cybernetics, Part B (Cybernetics)*, 29, 2, 254–262, 1999.

80. Babuška, R. and Verbruggen, H., Neuro-fuzzy methods for nonlinear system identification. *Annu. Rev. Control*, 27, 1, 73–85, 2003.

81. Lin, C.J. and Chin, C.C., Prediction and identification using wavelet-based recurrent fuzzy neural networks. *IEEE Trans. Syst., Man, Cybernetics, Part B (Cybernetics)*, 34, 5, 2144–2154, 2004.

82. Lin, Y.Y., Chang, J.Y., Lin, C.T., Identification and prediction of dynamic systems using an interactively recurrent self-evolving fuzzy neural network. *IEEE Trans. Neural Netw. Learn. Syst.*, 24, 2, 310–321, 2012.

83. Samanta, S., Suresh, S., Senthilnath, J., Sundararajan, N., A new neuro-fuzzy inference system with dynamic neurons (nfis-dn) for system identification and time series forecasting. *Appl. Soft Comput.*, 82, 105567, 2019.

84. Wu, X., Han, H., Liu, Z., Qiao, J., Data-knowledge-based fuzzy neural network for nonlinear system identification. *IEEE Trans. Fuzzy Syst.*, 28, 9, 2209–2221, 2019.

85. Juang, C.F. and Lin, C.T., A recurrent self-organizing neural fuzzy inference network. *IEEE Trans. Neural Netw.*, 10, 4, 828–845, 1999.

86. Patra, J.C. and Bornand, C., Nonlinear dynamic system identification using Legendre neural network, in: *The 2010 International Joint Conference on Neural Networks (IJCNN)*, pp. 1–7. IEEE, 2010, July.

87. Mao, W.L., Hung, C.W., Chang, T.W., Nonlinear system identification using BBO-based multilayer perceptron network method. *Microsyst. Technol.*, 27, 4, 1497–1506, 2021.

88. Shen, B. and Ge, Z., Supervised nonlinear dynamic system for soft sensor application aided by variational auto-encoder. *IEEE Trans. Instrum. Meas.*, 69, 9, 6132–6142, 2020.

89. Vafamand, N., Arefi, M.M., Khayatian, A., Nonlinear system identification based on Takagi-Sugeno fuzzy modeling and unscented Kalman filter. *ISA Trans.*, 74, 134–143, 2018.

90. Lei, Y., Xia, D., Erazo, K., Nagarajaiah, S., A novel unscented Kalman filter for recursive state-input-system identification of nonlinear systems. *Mech. Syst. Signal Process.*, 127, 120–135, 2019.

91. Janjanam, L., Saha, S.K., Kar, R., Mandal, D., An efficient identification approach for highly complex non-linear systems using the evolutionary computing method based Kalman filter. *AEU-Int. J. Electron. Commun.*, 138, 153890, 2021.

92. Yu, W. and Pacheco, M., Impact of random weights on nonlinear system identification using convolutional neural networks. *Inf. Sci.*, 477, 1–14, 2019.

93. Khan, S., Ahmad, J., Naseem, I., Moinuddin, M., A novel fractional gradient-based learning algorithm for recurrent neural networks. *Circ. Syst., Signal Process.*, 37, 593–612, 2018.

94. Coban, R., A context layered locally recurrent neural network for dynamic system identification. *Eng. Appl. Artif. Intell.*, 26, 1, 241–250, 2013.

95. Gonzalez, J. and Yu, W., Non-linear system modeling using LSTM neural networks. *IFAC-PapersOnLine*, 51, 13, 485–489, 2018.

96. Yuan, X., Li, L., Wang, Y., Nonlinear dynamic soft sensor modeling with supervised long short-term memory network. *IEEE Trans. Ind. Inf.*, 16, 5, 3168–3176, 2019.

97. Nanda, S.J., Panda, G., Majhi, B., Tah, P., Improved identification of nonlinear MIMO plants using new hybrid FLANN-AIS model, in: *2009 IEEE International Advance Computing Conference*, 2009, March, IEEE, pp. 141–146.

98. Patra, J.C. and Kot, A.C., Nonlinear dynamic system identification using Chebyshev functional link artificial neural networks. *IEEE Trans. Syst., Man, Cybernetics, Part B (Cybernetics)*, 32, 4, 505–511, 2002.

99. Rossi, A., Moretti, M., Senin, N., Neural networks and NARXs to replicate extrusion simulation in digital twins for fused filament fabrication. *J. Manuf. Process.*, 84, 64–76, 2022.

100. Bhattacharjee, S.S. and George, N.V., Nonlinear system identification using exact and approximate improved adaptive exponential functional link networks. *IEEE Trans. Circuits Syst. II: Express Briefs*, 67, 12, 3542–3546, 2020.

101. Kondo, N., Hatanaka, T., Uosaki, K., Nonlinear dynamic system identification based on multiobjectively selected RBF networks, in: *2007 IEEE Symposium on Computational Intelligence in Multi-Criteria Decision-Making*, pp. 122–127, IEEE, 2007, April.

102. Peng, H., Ozaki, T., Toyoda, Y., Oda, K., Nonlinear system identification using radial basis function-based signal-dependent ARX model. *IFAC Proc. Volumes*, 34, 6, 675–680, 2001.

103. Qiao, J.F. and Han, H.G., Identification and modeling of nonlinear dynamical systems using a novel self-organizing RBF-based approach. *Automatica*, 48, 8, 1729–1734, 2012.

104. Ayala, H.V.H. and dos Santos Coelho, L., Cascaded evolutionary algorithm for nonlinear system identification based on correlation functions and radial basis functions neural networks. *Mech. Syst. Signal Process.*, 68, 378–393, 2016.

105. Ayala, H.V.H., Habineza, D., Rakotondrabe, M., dos Santos Coelho, L., Nonlinear black-box system identification through coevolutionary algorithms and radial basis function artificial neural networks. *Appl. Soft Comput.*, 87, 105990, 2020.

106. Zhou, Y. and Ding, F., Modeling nonlinear processes using the radial basis function-based state-dependent autoregressive models. *IEEE Signal Process. Lett.*, 27, 1600–1604, 2020.

107. Pattanaik, R.K. and Mohanty, M.N., Nonlinear system identification for speech model using linear predictive coefficients based radial basis function. *J. Inf. Optim. Sci.*, 43, 5, 1139–1150, 2022.
108. Mishra, S., Satapathy, P., Tripathy, L., Dash, P.K., A VMD Based Extreme Learning Machine Approach for Nonlinear System Identification, in: *2019 International Conference on Information Technology (ICIT)*, pp. 143–148, IEEE, 2019, December.
109. Köktürk-Güzel, B.E. and Beyhan, S., Symbolic regression based extreme learning machine models for system identification. *Neural Process. Lett.*, 53, 2, 1565–1578, 2021.
110. Nimmy, S.F., Hussain, O.K., Chakrabortty, R.K., Hussain, F.K., Saberi, M., Explainability in supply chain operational risk management: A systematic literature review. *Knowl.-Based Syst.*, 235, 107587, 2022.
111. Zhang, L. and Suganthan, P.N., A comprehensive evaluation of random vector functional link networks. *Inf. Sci.*, 367, 1094–1105, 2016.
112. Pratama, M., Angelov, P.P., Lughofer, E., Er, M.J., Parsimonious random vector functional link network for data streams. *Inf. Sci.*, 430, 519–537, 2018.
113. Shi, Q., Katuwal, R., Suganthan, P., Tanveer, M., Random vector functional link neural network-based ensemble deep learning. *Pattern Recognit.*, 117, 107–978, 2021.
114. Luk, R.P. and Damper, R., II, Non-parametric linear time-invariant system identification by discrete wavelet transforms. *Digit. Signal Process.*, 16, 3, 303–319, 2006.
115. Kumar, A., Kumar, S.A., Dutt, V., Dubey, A.K., Narang, S., A hybrid secure cloud platform maintenance based on improved attribute-based encryption strategies. *Int. J. Interac. Multimed. Artif. Intell.*, 8, 150–157, 2021. http://dx. doi.org/10.9781/ijimai.2021.11.004.
116. Pillonetto, G., Dinuzzo, F., Chen, T., De Nicolao, G., Ljung, L., Kernel methods in system identification, machine learning and function estimation: A survey. *Automatica*, 50, 3, 657–682, 2014.
117. Chandrasekaran, S., Dutt, V., Vyas, N., Kumar, R., Student Sentiment Analysis Using Various Machine Learning Techniques, in: *2023 International Conference on Artificial Intelligence and Smart Communication (AISC)*, Greater Noida, India, pp. 104–107, 2023.
118. Jain, S. and Majhi, S., Zero-Attracting Kernel Maximum Versoria Criterion Algorithm for Nonlinear Sparse System Identification. *IEEE Signal Process. Lett.*, 29, 1546–1550, 2022.
119. Pattanaik, R.K., Mohanty, M.D., Mohanty, M.N., Identification and Control of Nonlinear System using Kernel-RVFLN, in: *2022 2nd Odisha International Conference on Electrical Power Engineering, Communication and Computing Technology (ODICON)*, pp. 1–6, IEEE, 2022, November.
120. Pattanaik, R.K. and Mohanty, M.N., *Nonlinear System Identification Using Robust Fusion Kernel-Based Radial basis function Neural Network2022*

International Conference on Emerging Smart Computing and Informatics (ESCI), pp. 1–5, 2022, March.

121. Haubner, T., Brendel, A., Kellermann, W., End-to-End Deep Learning-Based Adaptation Control for Frequency-Domain Adaptive System Identification, in: *ICASSP 2022-2022 IEEE International Conference on Acoustics, Speech and Signal Processing (ICASSP)*, pp. 766–770, IEEE, 2022, May.

122. Jin, X., Shao, J., Zhang, X., An, W., Malekian, R., Modeling of non-linear system based on deep learning framework. *Nonlinear Dyn.*, 84, 1327–1340, 2016.

123. Anh, H.P.H. and Van Kien, C., Robust control of uncertain nonlinear systems using adaptive regressive Neural-based deep learning technique. *Expert Syst. Appl.*, 214, 119084, 2023.

124. Verhoek, C., Beintema, G., II, Haesaert, S., Schoukens, M., Tóth, R., Deep-Learning-Based Identification of LPV Models for Nonlinear Systems, in: *2022 IEEE 61st Conference on Decision and Control (CDC)*, pp. 3274–3280, IEEE, 2022, December.

125. Dalla Libera, A. and Pillonetto, G., Deep prediction networks. *Neurocomputing*, 469, 321–329, 2022.

126. Zancato, L. and Chiuso, A., A novel deep neural network architecture for non-linear system identification. *IFAC-PapersOnLine*, 54, 7, 186–191, 2021.

127. Greene, M.L., Bell, Z., II, Nivison, S., Dixon, W.E., Deep neural network-based approximate optimal tracking for unknown nonlinear systems. *IEEE Trans. Automat. Contr.*, 68, 3171–3177, 2023.

128. Qiao, J., Wang, G., Li, W., Li, X., A deep belief network with PLSR for nonlinear system modeling. *Neural Netw.*, 104, 68–79, 2018.

129. Qiao, J., Wang, G., Li, X., Li, W., A self-organizing deep belief network for nonlinear system modeling. *Appl. Soft Comput.*, 65, 170–183, 2018.

130. Man, Y., Ding, L., Xiaoguo, Z., Nonlinear System Identification Method Based on Improved Deep Belief Network, in: *2018 Chinese Automation Congress (CAC)*, pp. 2379–2383, IEEE, 2018, November.

131. Wenjing, L., Junfei, Q., Guandi, W., Nonlinear System Identification Using Deep Belief Network Based on PLSR, in: *2017 36th Chinese Control Conference (CCC)*, pp. 10807–10812, IEEE, 2017, July.

132. Schüssler, M., Münker, T., Nelles, O., Deep Recurrent Neural Networks for Nonlinear System Identification, in: *2019 IEEE Symposium Series on Computational Intelligence (SSCI)*, pp. 448–454, IEEE, 2019, December.

133. Zaki, A.M., El-Nagar, A.M., El-Bardini, M., Soliman, F.A.S., Deep learning controller for nonlinear system based on Lyapunov stability criterion. *Neural Comput. Appl.*, 33, 1515–1531, 2021.

134. Wu, R.T. and Jahanshahi, M.R., Deep convolutional neural network for structural dynamic response estimation and system identification. *J. Eng. Mech.*, 145, 1, 04018125, 2019.

135. Andersson, C., Ribeiro, A.H., Tiels, K., Wahlström, N., Schön, T.B., Deep Convolutional Networks in System Identification, in: *2019 IEEE 58th*

conference on decision and control (CDC), pp. 3670–3676, IEEE, 2019, December.

136. Lopez-Pacheco, M. and Yu, W., Complex valued deep neural networks for nonlinear system modeling. *Neural Process. Lett.*, 54, 1, 559–580, 2022.

137. Alwan, N.A. and Hussain, Z.M., Deep learning for robust adaptive inverse control of nonlinear dynamic systems: Improved settling time with an auto-encoder. *Sensors*, 22, 16, 5935, 2022.

138. De la Rosa, E., Yu, W., Li, X., Nonlinear System Modeling with Deep Neural Networks and Autoencoders Algorithm, in: *2016 IEEE International Conference on Systems, Man, and Cybernetics (SMC)*, pp. 002157–002162, IEEE, 2016, October.

139. Wang, Y., A New Concept Using LSTM Neural Networks for Dynamic System Identification, in: *2017 American Control Conference (ACC)*, pp. 5324–5329, IEEE, 2017, May.

140. Sahoo, A.K., Pandey, R.N., Mishra, S.K., Dash, P.P., Identification of real-time maglev plant using long-short term memory network based deep learning technique, *J. Sci. Ind. Res.*, 79, 1101–1105, 2020.

141. Akyol, K., Comparing of deep neural networks and extreme learning machines based on growing and pruning approach. *Expert Syst. Appl.*, 140, 112875, 2020.

142. Pattanaik, R.K., Pattanayak, B.K., Mohanty, M.N., Use of multilayer recursive model for non-linear dynamic system identification. *J. Stat. Manage. Syst.*, 25, 6, 1479–1490, 2022.

143. Lian, C., Zhu, L., Zeng, Z., Su, Y., Yao, W., Tang, H., Constructing prediction intervals for landslide displacement using bootstrapping random vector functional link networks selective ensemble with neural networks switched. *Neurocomputing*, 291, 1–10, 2018.

144. Thon, C., Röhl, M., Hosseinhashemi, S., Kwade, A., Schilde, C., Artificial intelligence and evolutionary approaches in particle technology. *KONA Powder Part. J.*, 41, 3–25, 2024.

145. Samal, D., Dash, P.K., Bisoi, R., Modified added activation function based exponential robust random vector functional link network with expanded version for nonlinear system identification. *Appl. Intell.*, 52, 5, 56575683, 2022.

Part 2

REAL TIME APPLICATIONS OF DIGITAL TWIN

7

Digital Twinning-Based Autonomous Take-Off, Landing, and Cruising for Unmanned Aerial Vehicles

Kiran Deep Singh[1], Prabhdeep Singh[2] and Mohit Angurala[3*]

[1]*Chitkara University Institute of Engineering and Technology, Chitkara University, Rajpura, Punjab, India*
[2]*Department of Computer Science and Engineering, Graphic Era Deemed to be University, Dehradun, Uttarakhand, India*
[3]*Apex Institute of Technology (CSE), Chandigarh University, Mohali, Punjab, India*

Abstract

Drones, or unmanned aerial vehicles (UAVs), have altered many sectors, most notably the security, transportation, and maintenance sectors. Autonomy in UAV operations remains a major research challenge, especially in high-stake flying phases like take-off, landing, and cruising. This research investigates the feasibility of using digital twin-based methods to improve UAV autonomy during certain flight stages. The study aims to learn more about digital twinning, how it works, what problems it solves, how it may be implemented, and what advantages and disadvantages it has over existing systems. The study begins by explaining digital twins and how they might be used in crewless aerial vehicles. It focuses on how digital twinning uses real-time data capture, sensor fusion, and environmental analysis to realize UAV autonomy. Next, we look at the difficulties and restrictions of today's techniques for autonomous take-off, landing, and flight. Digital twinning-based systems are discussed regarding the gaps they intend to fill, such as the over-reliance on pre-programmed flight paths and the restricted flexibility they now offer. An architecture is provided for implementing digital twin technology in UAVs. The framework specifies the hardware, software, algorithms, and data for fully autonomous flights. It highlights the importance of having a physical UAV and its digital twin that sync regarding sensor technology, compute capacity,

Corresponding author: drmohitangurala@gmail.com

Abhineet Anand, Anita Sardana, Abhishek Kumar, Srikanta Kumar Mohapatra and Shikha Gupta (eds.) Simulation Techniques of Digital Twin in Real-Time Applications: Design Modeling and Implementation, (165–182) © 2024 Scrivener Publishing LLC

and synchronization. Possible advantages of methods based on digital twins are mentioned, such as increased flexibility, quicker reaction times, and greater protection. Sensor optimization, processing needs, and data security are also discussed as examples of feasibility issues. By looking ahead, we can fully realize the benefits of digital twinning-based autonomous operations for UAVs, ushering in a new era of highly effective, highly flexible, and highly secure UAV missions.

Keywords: Unmanned aerial vehicles (UAVs), autonomous take-off, landing, and cruising, digital twins, cloud computing

7.1   Introduction

Drones, or unmanned aerial vehicles (UAVs), are becoming increasingly popular and useful for various applications, such as surveillance, logistics, agricultural, and infrastructure assessment. Improving UAVs' capabilities, efficiency, and safety through autonomous operation has become an important field of study. Using digital twins is a possible method for making UAVs fully autonomous. The review by [1] highlights the growing importance of vision systems in unmanned aerial vehicles (UAVs), emphasizing their critical role in various applications and the need for advancements in automatic visual data understanding to drive future UAV vision research and applications.

UAVs' utility and autonomy can be greatly improved by using digital twinning, which includes making a digital replica or simulation of a physical object or system. Researchers and engineers can gain superior control and decision-making abilities by developing a digital twin of an UAV and simulating its behavior, performance, and responsiveness in various settings. [2] provide an UAV-assisted sparse sensing technique to address the high energy consumption problem in wireless sensor networks (WSNs), providing effective data collecting and lower energy consumption using compressive sensing and optimization methodologies.

When applied to unmanned aerial vehicles (UAVs), digital twinning-based autonomous take-off, landing, and cruising have enormous potential to revolutionize these crucial flight stages. As a result of manual control or pre-programming, take-off and landing processes have been less flexible and efficient. Using digital twinning, UAVs can optimize their take-off and landing operations in real time based on autonomous assessments of parameters, including wind, runway, and payload weight. Safe and effective operations can be guaranteed with the help of this technology, which enables exact trajectory planning, power calculations, and control inputs.

[3] describe a federated deep learning approach for privacy-preserving and resource-efficient aerial image classification using Internet-connected UAVs for disaster site identification, highlighting its benefits in terms of privacy, energy efficiency, and data communication requirements.

UAVs can now have fully autonomous flight thanks to digital twinning. UAVs with digital twins can constantly monitor and evaluate flight characteristics, sensor data, and ambient factors throughout the cruising phase. Flight patterns, speeds, altitudes, and power consumption can all be optimized by dynamic adjustments made possible by this real-time analysis, leading to maximum efficiency and productivity. Using digital twinning-based methods, UAVs can avoid obstacles, optimize flight paths, and adjust to new airspace regulations. [4] said that combining Unity and ROS, enabling real-time inspection and interaction between the robot entity and virtual environment, including path planning and training, creates a virtual–real control system that improves staff safety and job efficiency.

Autonomous operations for UAVs based on digital twins provide many advantages. Because it allows for instantaneous analysis and decision-making based on precise virtual representations of the UAV and its environment. This technology greatly improves the safety of UAV operations. Minimizing the incidence of accidents and collisions enables identifying and reducing potential dangers. In addition, UAVs are better able to do difficult tasks and missions thanks to digital twinning's capacity to give adaptation and flexibility. [5] analyzes the effectiveness of UV communication for uplink connection in UAV networks, stressing the advantages of UV communication in non-line-of-sight outdoor environments and addressing interference impacts on system performance.

It is critical, however, to recognize the difficulties and restrictions of digital twinning-based autonomy for UAVs. Extensive data gathering, calibration, and validation processes are needed to generate accurate and reliable digital twins. Technical challenges also arise when trying to keep the real UAV in sync with its digital double in real time. There may also be limits to the UAV's local processing power due to the computational demands of executing digital twins in real-time.

7.1.1   Problem Statement

There are still challenges to be solved, especially in take-off, landing, and cruising, even though UAVs have made great progress in autonomous flying. Due to their inflexibility, manual control or predetermined flight paths are used in conventional approaches. Therefore, cutting-edge methods are required to let UAVs independently handle these crucial flight stages.

Several restrictions are imposed by the present methods for launching and landing UAVs and taking them on a cruise. Both competent pilots and the possibility of human mistakes are added complications when taking off and landing manually. However, environmental factors such as wind speed, runway availability, and nearby objects cannot be considered while planning a predetermined flight path. The UAV is constrained in its ability to optimize flying efficiency and safety by these constraints.

Furthermore, the scalability and deployment of UAVs may be constrained by the need for manual control or pre-programmed flight paths, especially in complicated situations. The ability of unmanned aerial vehicles (UAVs) to take off, land, and cruise autonomously is becoming increasingly important as their applications grow in urban distribution, emergency response, and infrastructure inspection. The environments in which UAVs operate, such as congested airspace, difficult terrain, or rapidly changing weather, are inherently dynamic and unpredictable. Therefore, there is an urgent need to create cutting-edge methods that let UAVs carry out these vital flight phases independently, with autonomy and intelligence.

To overcome the drawbacks of conventional technologies for autonomous take-off, landing, and cruising, digital twinning-based systems present a possible option. Digital twinning facilitates real-time monitoring, analysis, and optimization of flight operations by constructing a virtual replica or simulation of the UAV, including its physical structure, components, and behavior. The UAV's performance can be simulated and predicted using the digital twin, accounting for data from onboard sensors, weather forecasts, and environmental inputs.

During take-off and landing, UAVs that employ digital twinning can make real-time adjustments to their flight characteristics like trajectory, speed, and control inputs. They may adjust their flight patterns according to the weather, increasing efficiency and reducing risk. In addition, digital twinning allows UAVs to adjust their flight plans and behavior depending on real-time feedback and data collected while they are in the cruising phase. It improves their capabilities in navigating challenging airspace, avoiding obstructions, and selecting the most efficient flight paths.

However, various obstacles must be overcome before autonomous take-off, landing, and cruise UAVs can be implemented successfully using digital twins. Developers must employ stringent calibration and validation procedures for digital twins to depict the real UAV accurately. Technical hurdles must be cleared to achieve real-time synchronization between the UAV and its digital duplicate. Furthermore, it may be necessary to have robust onboard processing capabilities to meet the computational demands of running digital twins in real time.

Even though unmanned aerial vehicles (UAVs) have made great strides in autonomous flying, take-off, landing, and cruise areas remain problematic. The UAV's inability to respond to changing conditions results from its dependence on human pilots and predetermined flight plans. To improve the UAVs' autonomy, adaptability, and safety during these crucial flight phases, digital twinning-based technologies present a possible alternative. Suppose the technical hurdles of adopting digital twinning-based autonomy can be surmounted. In that case, UAV operations can become more streamlined and insightful, opening the door to wider adoption across industries and uses. Even though unmanned aerial vehicles (UAVs) have made great strides in autonomous flying, they still face obstacles during take-off, landing, and sustained flight. Due to their inflexibility, manual control or predetermined flight paths are used in conventional approaches. Therefore, cutting-edge methods are required to let UAVs independently handle these crucial flight stages.

7.1.2   Research Objectives

The primary goal of this chapter is to investigate and assess the feasibility of digital twinning-based methods for enabling autonomous take-off, landing, and flight in unmanned aerial vehicles. Among the specific aims are the following:

Looking into digital twins and how they can help with UAVs: To achieve this goal, we must investigate digital twin technology, learn its concepts, and consider its possible uses for unmanned aerial vehicles (UAVs). This chapter will present a high-level overview of the concept and its importance in improving the autonomy of UAVs during take-off, landing, and cruising by evaluating existing literature and research. The difficulties and restrictions of today's autonomous take-off, landing, and flight systems are analyzed. This study aims to determine the strengths and weaknesses of current methods for launching, landing, and navigating UAVs. This chapter will show why new methods, such as digital twinning-based approaches, are needed by critiquing present methods like human control and pre-programmed flight courses.

To improve UAV autonomy during these stages of flight, we propose a framework for using digital twinning technology.

This goal entails developing a comprehensive framework for incorporating digital twinning technology into UAV systems, which requires expanding upon the existing knowledge of digital twinning and its application to UAVs. The framework will include all the parts, algorithms, and procedures needed for fully autonomous flight. For better UAV autonomy, it will consider things like real-time data integration, sensor fusion, decision-making algorithms, and control systems, among other things.

Examining digital twinning-based approaches to UAV operations in terms of their use, practicability, and potential disadvantages: This study assesses the viability of implementing autonomous take-off, landing, and cruise in UAV operations using digital twinning. It will look at the possible benefits of digital twinning, such as greater safety, adaptability, and efficiency. Potential pitfalls and difficulties in deploying digital twinning technology, including computing demands, data synchronization, and calibration procedures, will also be covered in this chapter.

The chapter aims to add to the body of research on autonomous UAV operations and explore the possibility of digital twinning-based methods by exploring these questions. This study's results will educate researchers, engineers, and industry professionals on the benefits, drawbacks, and prospects of using digital twinning technology to enable unmanned aerial vehicles to perform autonomous take-offs, landings, and cruises. Ultimately, this study aspires to pave the path for more effective and intelligent UAV operations across various areas by driving advancements in UAV autonomy.

7.2   Digital Twinning for UAV Autonomy

Digital twinning as a concept and its possible UAV applications will be covered in this section. It will focus on how digital twinning can facilitate autonomous UAVs during important flight phases like take-off, landing, and cruising. "Digital twinning" is described as making a computer-generated copy or simulation of a real-world object or system down to its smallest detail. To "digitally twin" an unmanned aerial vehicle (UAV) means creating a computer model replicating the real UAV in every respect, including the design, specs, sensor inputs, and control mechanisms. [6] presents a reactive constrained navigation scheme for UAVs that uses a nonlinear model predictive controller (NMPC) and onboard 2-D LiDAR for obstacle avoidance, with efficient computation using OpEn and PANOC, making it a versatile framework for fast nonlinear control and obstacle avoidance in obstacle-dense environments.

Digital twinning has many uses in unmanned aerial vehicles, including improving autonomous take-off, landing, and flight. The digital twin can simulate and predict the UAV's performance in different situations using real-time data from onboard sensors, weather forecasts, and environmental inputs. As a result, the UAV can assess its surroundings, gather relevant data, and adjust its flight parameters accordingly. The digital twin helps the UAV optimize its take-off trajectory, thrust, and control inputs by providing information on wind speed, runway conditions, and aircraft weight. The digital twin can change the take-off plan dynamically for factors like runway length, obstacle presence, and wind direction, resulting in a safe and controlled ascent. The digital twin also helps with precision navigation and control during the landing phase by considering things like wind speed, runway conditions, and the proximity of obstructions. To land safely and precisely in difficult conditions, the UAV can make real-time adjustments to its approach angle, descent rate, and control inputs based on data from the digital twin.

Additionally, digital twinning improves the cruising phase by letting the UAV optimize its flight path, adjust to varying conditions, and react to events as they happen in real time. The UAV can make calculated decisions about course correction, altitude change, and collision avoidance because of the digital twin's ability to track traffic in the air, the weather, and the locations of other nearby aircrafts. It assures safe navigation, reduces the potential for accidents, and generally boosts operations' efficiency. The fidelity of the digital twin to the physical counterpart must be ensured through precise calibration and validation processes if digital twinning is to be successfully implemented for UAV autonomy. [8] presents an effective way for enhancing information dissemination in intelligent transportation systems (ITSs) utilizing unmanned aerial vehicles (UAVs), addressing difficulties such as catastrophes, power outages, and traffic congestion, with simulation results proving higher performance over comparative alternatives. The UAV and its digital counterpart must perfectly sync for real-time monitoring, analysis, and decision-making. To facilitate this connection between the UAV and its digital twin, combining cutting-edge sensor fusion techniques, data processing algorithms, and communication systems may be necessary.

To sum up, digital twinning has a lot of potential to help us get to the point when UAVs can take off, land, and fly. Digital twinning allows unmanned aerial vehicles (UAVs) to adjust flight settings, optimize trajectories, and make well-informed judgments during crucial flight stages by constructing a virtual duplicate that matches the physical UAV and incorporates real-time data and environmental inputs. Surveillance, logistics, agriculture, and infrastructure inspection applications could benefit greatly from digital twinning-based techniques since they increase UAV operations' autonomy, adaptability, and safety. According to [7], drones, also known as unmanned aerial vehicles (UAVs), are gaining popularity and use in the commercial, nonprofit, military, and disaster relief sectors due to their versatility in jobs such as surveying, disaster relief, and military operations.

7.3   Challenges and Limitations

The difficulties and restrictions of the currently used techniques for autonomous take-off, landing, and cruising will be discussed. In this part, we will discuss the deficiencies that methods based on digital twinning hope to fix, as shown in Figure 7.1.

7.3.1   Manual Control and Pre-Programmed Flight Paths

UAVs traditionally rely on manual control or pre-programmed flight paths for autonomous flying. When responding to constant, unpredictable changes, these methods fall short. The need for frequent human intervention with manual control compromises the scalability and efficiency of UAV operations. Predetermined flight paths are not adaptable to changes in the terrain or the weather. By empowering UAVs to independently assess and react to real-time data, digital twinning-based techniques hope to circumvent these restrictions and enable more nuanced and dynamic flight control.

7.3.2   Limited Adaptability to Dynamic Environments

Autonomous systems' take-off, landing, and flying have difficulties adjusting to dynamic situations. Regarding the efficiency and security of UAV operations, variables like wind speed, runway conditions, obstacles, and

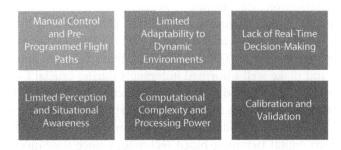

Figure 7.1 Challenges and limitations.

weather can make a huge difference. Integrating real-time data and adjusting flight settings might be difficult with conventional methods. Methods based on digital twinning use digital twin capabilities to model and foresee the UAV's actions in complex settings. UAVs can dynamically adapt their performance to changing conditions by considering real-time data inputs and environmental elements.

7.3.3   Lack of Real-Time Decision-Making

Autonomous UAVs must analyze sensor data and external inputs in real time. Onboard, real-time decision-making is a common limitation of current approaches. Delays in making decisions, especially during crucial flight stages, might jeopardize the safety and efficiency of UAV operations. Approaches based on digital twinning make it possible for UAVs to use real-time data processing and predictive modeling. UAVs can become more self-sufficient and efficient in their operations by incorporating digital twin technology, allowing them to constantly analyze sensor data, evaluate the surrounding environment, and make real-time decisions. [8] presents a digital twin-based smart manufacturing system focused on value co-creation, optimizing production capacity, and leveraging population intelligence algorithms, demonstrating a 13.26% increase in overall system profit and improved resource efficiency for collaborative manufacturing enterprises in the Industry 4.0 era.

7.3.4   Limited Perception and Situational Awareness

Perception and situational awareness are essential for autonomous and risk-free UAV flights. Traditional approaches may not account for modern perception technologies because they rely on limited sensor inputs [9]. Obstacles, terrain differences, and nearby aircraft may be harder to spot and react to accurately. By utilizing sensor fusion methods and cutting-edge perception algorithms, systems based on digital twinning improve perception and situational awareness. More accurate navigation, obstacle avoidance, and collision detection are all made possible for UAVs by combining data from many sensors using the digital twin concept.

7.3.5   Computational Complexity and Processing Power

Digital twinning-based techniques necessitate substantial computational resources and processing capacity to provide real-time data analysis and decision-making. Challenges in hardware needs and scalability can arise from the difficulty of recreating the physical UAV in a digital twin and the computational demands of processing sensor data in real time. Digital twinning-based approaches to UAV autonomy rely heavily on efficient and streamlined computational operations.

7.3.6 Calibration and Validation

The digital twin model must undergo extensive calibration and validation to represent the actual UAV accurately. Inaccurate forecasts and degraded autonomous operations might result from discrepancies between the digital twin and the physical system. Careful calibration processes, data fusion techniques, and validation methodologies are required to provide exact synchronization and calibration between the UAV and its digital twin. Successful implementation requires attention to the difficulties of keeping the digital twin in sync with the physical UAV and ensuring accurate data. To improve the independence, flexibility, and security of UAV operations across the whole flight cycle (launch, landing, and cruising), digital twinning-based methods work to overcome these obstacles and restrictions. UAVs can transcend the limitations of conventional approaches and adapt to changing situations by using real-time data processing, predictive modeling, and improved perceptual techniques gained through digital twinning. Unmanned aerial system (UAS) capabilities in several fields could be dramatically improved by adopting digital twinning-based techniques for autonomy. These fields include surveillance, logistics, agriculture, and infrastructure inspection.

7.4 Proposed Framework

A proposed framework, shown in Figure 7.2, for incorporating digital twinning technology into UAVs will be provided in this section. The framework will detail the necessary components and data to facilitate autonomous take-off, landing, and cruise. The proposed design for incorporating digital twinning technology into UAVs provides a promising method for realizing autonomous take-off, landing, and cruise. UAVs can respond to changing conditions, fine-tune their flights for maximum safety and efficiency, and create a digital duplicate of themselves through real-time sensor data, environmental analysis, decision-making algorithms, and synchronization. The framework lays out a course for further study and development of digital twinning-based autonomy for unmanned aerial vehicles, opening new doors for use in various sectors.

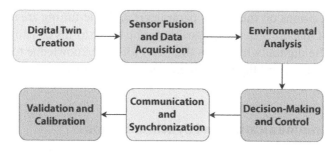

Figure 7.2 Proposed framework.

7.4.1   Digital Twin Creation

The initial stage of the proposed architecture is the development of a digital twin that faithfully resembles the actual UAV. The process entails creating a digital replica of the UAV's physical form, parts, and technical specs. The digital twin should also include relevant sensor inputs, control mechanisms, and environmental data for accurate simulation and analysis.

7.4.2   Sensor Fusion and Data Acquisition

The digital twin must receive real-time sensor data from the physical UAV to enable autonomous operation during take-off, landing, and cruising. It incorporates data collected by in-vehicle sensors such as global positioning systems, altimeters, accelerometers, and gyroscopes. The UAV's surroundings are represented in great detail and accuracy because of the use of sensor fusion algorithms, which integrate and combine data from many sensors.

7.4.3   Environmental Analysis

The digital twin evaluates external elements, including wind speed, weather, runway conditions, and obstacles, to establish the best possible take-off, landing, and cruise settings. The sensor data and environmental inputs are processed by sophisticated algorithms, allowing the UAV to make real-time course corrections.

7.4.4   Decision-Making and Control

The UAV can make decisions and take actions without human intervention thanks to the digital twin's analysis of data in real time and environmental inputs. Decisions on the flight's parameters and fine-tuning are made with the help of machine learning algorithms and other forms of artificial intelligence. The digital twin equips the UAV with the knowledge to optimize launch, landing, and flight parameters such as trajectory, thrust, and control inputs.

7.4.5 Communication and Synchronization

Communication and synchronization are essential in facilitating a natural interaction between the physical UAV and its digital duplicate. The framework's sophisticated data exchange methods and communication protocols connect the UAV to its digital duplicate in real time. By doing so, the UAV can share its sensor data and flying status with its digital counterpart and receive up-to-date instructions and guidance.

7.4.6 Validation and Calibration

Precise calibration and validation are required to ensure that the digital twin is accurate to the real UAV. To accomplish this, real-world flight data must be compared to the digital twin's behavior and performance. To guarantee that the simulation faithfully reflects the UAV's actual behavior, calibration procedures synchronize the digital twin with the physical UAV.

7.4.7 Iterative Improvement

The proposed structure fosters continuous development by incorporating feedback loops and data-driven analysis into the design process. Data from the UAV's flights can be continuously collected and compared with the predictions generated by the digital twin to fine-tune the algorithms, models, and control techniques. The efficiency, flexibility, and precision of the digital twin-based autonomy system are all improved through this iterative process.

Real-time data analysis and decision-making pose significant challenges that can only be met with the advanced computational capabilities and processing power the proposed framework assumes. Data security and privacy concerns must also be addressed to safeguard the UAV's operations and stop unwanted access to the digital twin.

7.5 Benefits and Feasibility

Here we will examine the possible advantages and practicality of digital twinning-based techniques for autonomous take-off, landing, and cruise in unmanned aerial vehicles (UAVs). The benefits of increased adaptability, real-time decision-making, and increased safety will be analyzed alongside the difficulties and restrictions of implementing these features. The merits and practicality of digital twinning-based approaches to accomplishing autonomous take-off, landing, and cruise in UAVs are discussed and shown in Figure 7.3. UAV operations are bolstered by digital twinning's greater agility, real-time decision-making, and increased safety. Implementing digital twinning-based systems is becoming possible as sensor technologies, processing requirements, synchronization, and data security improve. More research, development, and testing are required to fully achieve the potential of digital twinning-based autonomy in UAVs and unleash their vast applications in various industries. [11] describes a three-step process for greatly extending the lifetime of wireless sensor nodes, including topology selection, UAV-assisted data collecting, and high-rate recharging, exceeding previous strategies with a doubled throughput and six times greater energy savings.

7.5.1 Improved Adaptability

Digital twinning-based methods improve UAVs' adaptability at pivotal points in flight, which is a major advantage. Manual or predetermined flight paths are common in conventional approaches, limiting the UAV's ability to adapt to changing conditions. UAVs may adapt their flight characteristics, trajectory, and control inputs in real time with the help of digital twinning, which uses real-time data collecting, sensor fusion, and environmental analysis. Because of this flexibility, UAVs can fly over rough

Figure 7.3 Benefits and feasibility.

terrain, avoid collisions with unforeseen obstructions, and maximize fuel efficiency.

7.5.2   Real-Time Decision-Making

UAVs can now make real-time decisions thanks to techniques based on digital twinning. The UAV's digital twin constantly monitors sensor data and environmental inputs to make flight, landing, and cruise decisions based on the best available information. The UAV can make timely course corrections and control input adjustments thanks to this on-the-fly decision-making, maximizing flight safety and efficiency. UAV autonomy is improved by the ability to adjust to changing conditions, requiring less human intervention dynamically.

7.5.3   Enhanced Safety

Take-off, landing, and flight of unmanned aerial vehicles (UAVs) all present unique safety challenges. Approaches based on digital twinning can significantly increase safety by simulating flight conditions before they are put into practice. The digital twin allows testing out what-if scenarios, spotting dangers, and fine-tuning avoidance procedures. Potential dangers can be recognized and handled by modeling crucial flight stages in a virtual environment, lowering the likelihood of mishaps or collisions during actual operations.

7.5.4   Feasibility Considerations

Several aspects affect whether or not autonomous take-off, landing, and cruise can be implemented using digital twinning-based systems. Obtaining real-time data from the UAV and its surroundings calls on cutting-edge sensor technology and data acquisition systems. These sensors must be trustworthy and precise so that environmental analysis and choices can be made confidently.

Furthermore, it is difficult because of the computational needs of processing real-time data and performing complicated algorithms. High-performance computing and sufficient processing power are necessary to analyze and make real-time choices. Edge computing and cloud-based solutions are two examples of recent developments in computing that can help overcome these obstacles. [10] introduces an interactive digital twin visualization framework for large electromechanical equipment, featuring offline pre-rasterization and cloud-end fusion rendering and effectively addressing complexity challenges, demonstrated through a heavy truck case study.

In addition, for efficient autonomous operations, it is essential to maintain sync between the actual UAV and its digital counterpart. Maintaining a constant data flow between the UAV and the digital twin calls for dependable communication technologies and data exchange protocols. By coordinating this way, the UAV's flight parameters may be guided and monitored in real time, allowing smooth, hands-free autonomy.

Finally, concerns about data privacy and security must be taken into account. The digital twin is a secure repository for private data about the UAV, its operations, and its surroundings. To keep the digital twin safe from being hacked or altered in any way, strong cybersecurity precautions are required.

7.6   Conclusion and Future Directions

Digital twinning-based techniques have great potential for accomplishing autonomous take-off, landing, and cruise in UAVs. The results of this study add to the existing body of information on UAV autonomy and bring to light the necessity for additional study in this area. Unlocking the full potential of digital twinning-based autonomous operations and radically altering their use across industries and sectors require overcoming the difficulties and investigating the future paths described.

In this study chapter, we looked into the feasibility of using digital twinning-based methods for fully autonomous UAVs, including take-off, landing, and flight. The primary results emphasize the advantages of digital twinning, including its increased versatility, real-time decision-making, and improved safety in UAV operations. UAVs can improve the efficiency and dependability of their operations through real-time data collecting, sensor fusion, and environmental analysis to make instantaneous adjustments to flight parameters and control inputs. While digital twinning-based approaches to UAV autonomy show promise, they have several obstacles and restrictions that must be overcome before they can be widely adopted. These include data security concerns, synchronization between the physical UAV and its digital duplicate, and cutting-edge sensor technologies. Future studies should focus on stronger and more dependable sensor systems, optimized processing capacities, enhanced communication protocols, and bolstered cybersecurity protections. Future studies into digital twinning-based autonomous operations for UAVs can go in several interesting ways. First, using the digital twin's data to investigate the feasibility of integrating machine learning and artificial intelligence approaches can further improve the decision-making capabilities of UAVs. It has the potential to result in autonomous systems that are smarter and more flexible.

It is also important to look into how well digital twin-based methods scale. It will be crucial to scale digital twin models to support many UAVs flying in tandem as UAV technology develops and its applications spread. Future research should also focus on the human–machine interface in digital twinning-based UAV autonomy, improving the effectiveness and safety of UAV missions by learning how humans may work with UAVs in autonomous operations, such as through creating user-friendly interfaces and communication protocols. Finally, it is important to investigate the potential influence of digital twinning-based autonomous operations on UAV policies and regulations. Increases in UAV autonomy highlight the need for updated legal frameworks to facilitate the appropriate and secure introduction of UAVs into airspace.

References

1. Han, Y., Liu, H., Wang, Y., Liu, C., A comprehensive review for typical applications based upon unmanned aerial vehicle platform. *IEEE J. Sel. Top. Appl. Earth Obs. Remote Sens.*, 15, 9654–9666, 2022.
2. Cuicui, L., Yu, R., Xiangming, L., Peijin, W., Zenbin, D., Guoxin, M., Haokun, C., Unmanned aerial vehicle-assisted sparse sensing in wireless sensor networks. *IEEE Wirel. Commun. Lett.*, 12, 977–981, 2023, doi: 10.1109/LWC.2023.3254580.
3. Khullar, V. and Singh, H.P., Privacy protected internet of unmanned aerial vehicles for disastrous site identification. *Concurr. Comput.*, 639, 119017, 2023.
4. Li, J., Liu, M., Wang, W., Hu, C., Inspection robot based on offline digital twin synchronization architecture. *IEEE J. Radio Freq. Identif.*, 6, 943–947, 2022.
5. Tadayyoni, H., Ardakani, M.H., Heidarpour, A.R., Uysal, M., Ultraviolet communications for unmanned aerial vehicle networks. *IEEE Wirel. Commun. Lett.*, 11, 1, 178–182, 2021.
6. Lindqvist, B., Mansouri, S.S., Haluška, J., Nikolakopoulos, G., Reactive navigation of an unmanned aerial vehicle with perception-based obstacle avoidance constraints. *IEEE Trans. Control Syst. Technol.*, 30, 1847–1862, 2021.
7. Jaiswal, S. and Sidhanta, S., Toward a smart multi-unmanned aerial vehicle system. *IEEE Potentials*, 41, 22–25, 2021.

8. Kawamoto, Y., Mitsuhashi, T., Kato, N., UAV-aided information diffusion for Vehicle-to-vehicle (V2V) in disaster scenarios. *IEEE Trans. Emerg. Topics Comput.*, 10, 1909–1917, 2021.

9. Tang, Q., Wu, B., Chen, W., Yue, J., A digital twin-assisted collaborative capability optimization model for smart manufacturing system based on Elman-IVIF-TOPSIS. *IEEE Access*, 11, 40540–40564, 2023.

10. Yuxi, Z., Jing., T., Xue, Y., Wenshu, X., Li, J., Gang, X., Hongxin, Z., Digital twins visualization of large electromechanical equipment. *IEEE J. Radio Freq. Identif.*, 6, 993–997, 2022.

11. Angurala, M., Bala, M., Bamber, S.S., Wireless battery recharging through UAV in wireless sensor networks. *Egypt. Inform. J.*, 23, 21–31, 2022.

8

Execution of Fully Automated Coal Mining Face With Transparent Digital Twin Self-Adaptive Mining System

Bharat Tripathi[1], Nidhi Srivastava[2] and Amod Kumar Tiwari[3*]

[1]*Department of AIT-CSE, Chandigarh University, Mohali, Punjab, India*
[2]*Department of AIIT, Amity University, Lucknow, Uttar Pradesh, India*
[3]*Department of Computer Science, Rajkiya Engineering College Sonbhadra, Sonbhadra, Uttar Pradesh, India*

Abstract

Digital twin technology is used to simulate and forecast the behavior of physical systems in a very effective manner. Several industries, including manufacturing, energy, healthcare, transportation, mining, and construction, can benefit from the deployment of digital twins. They can aid businesses in streamlining operations, cutting expenses, boosting productivity, and raising product quality with very less human effort. With the use of digital twin technology, the performance of a physical system, process, or object may be tracked, analyzed, and improved in real time. It builds a digital representation of a physical object that may be used to model behavior and forecast performance and of coal mining operations using sensors, data analytics, and simulation. There are only a few simulation methods that can be applied to develop digital twins. The particular system being modeled and the simulation's objectives will determine the technique to use. In this chapter, various types of digital twin simulation methods are discussed. Finite element analysis, computational fluid dynamics, multi-body dynamics, discrete event simulation, and agent-based modeling are discussed with their key finding, and novel simulation to automate coal mining using digital twin technology is also proposed. It entails breaking the structure or system down into smaller components and then simulating the behavior of each component using mathematical models.

Corresponding author: amodtiwari@gmail.com

Abhineet Anand, Anita Sardana, Abhishek Kumar, Srikanta Kumar Mohapatra and Shikha Gupta (eds.) Simulation Techniques of Digital Twin in Real-Time Applications: Design Modeling and Implementation, (183–194) © 2024 Scrivener Publishing LLC

Keywords: Finite element analysis, computational fluid dynamics, multi-body dynamics, discrete event simulation, agent-based modeling, coal mining

8.1 Introduction

Implementing cutting-edge technology and procedures to optimize coal extraction operations is necessary for a fully automated coal mining face with a transparent digital twin self-adaptive mining system. The use of robots and other technology to carry out different mining activities without overt human involvement is referred to as a fully automated coal mining face. This covers coal-related operations such drilling, blasting, cutting, loading, and transportation [1]. A virtual copy or simulation of a real asset or system is known as a "digital twin" [4, 18–21]. In the context of coal mining, a transparent digital twin is a precise, real-time representation of the mining face that incorporates information on the geology, machinery, environmental factors, and other pertinent factors.

A variety of sensor technologies are used to construct a transparent digital twin and allow self-adaptive capabilities. These sensors record information on environmental variables, worker safety, gas levels, equipment performance, and geotechnical conditions. The information is put into the digital twin, which offers a thorough view of the mining face and its activities. Real-time monitoring and control of the mining face are made possible by the digital twin and self-adaptive mining system. Operators and engineers may remotely follow progress, spot possible problems, and make choices using the digital twin interface [6]. Based on the analyzed data, the system generates alerts and suggestions that enable for proactive maintenance and optimization.

There are various advantages to operating a fully automated coal mining face with a transparent digital twin self-adaptive mining system. By limiting the amount of time that workers are exposed to dangerous situations, it improves safety. By adjusting operations based on real-time data and predictive analytics, it boosts productivity and efficiency. It also makes cost-cutting, environmental sustainability, and remote operating capabilities possible.

8.2 Simulation Methods in Digital Twins

8.2.1 Computational Fluid Dynamics

Using numerical analysis and data structures, the field of computational fluid dynamics (CFD) studies and resolves issues involving fluid flows.

The computations necessary to simulate the fluid's free-stream flow and its interactions with surfaces constrained by boundary conditions (both liquids and gases) are done on computers. The principles of CFD are founded on the laws of mass, momentum, and energy that govern fluid motion [16]. CFD can be used to study various phenomena such as turbulence, heat transfer, and multiphase flow. CFD is being widely used in engineering, science, and industry for design, optimization, and analysis purposes.

8.2.1.1   *Software Tools That are Being Used in Today's Domain for CFD*

- Ansys Fluent and CFX: Ansys offers a comprehensive suite of CFD products that can handle complex and multiphysics problems. Ansys Fluent is a solver that can handle a wide range of applications, such as aerodynamics, combustion, multiphase flow, heat transfer, etc. Ansys CFX is another solver that is specialized for turbomachinery and rotating machinery applications.
- STAR-CCM+: STAR-CCM+ is a CFD software from Siemens that can handle complex geometries and physics. It has features such as adaptive mesh refinement, overset mesh, polyhedral meshing, etc. [10]. It can also integrate with other Siemens products for multidisciplinary simulations.
- COMSOL Metaphysics: COMSOL Metaphysics is a software platform that can perform simulations of various physical phenomena, such as fluid flow, heat transfer, electromagnetics, acoustics, etc. [11]. It has a user-friendly interface and a powerful equation-based modeling capability.
- OpenFOAM: OpenFOAM is a free, open-source software for CFD that is widely used by researchers and practitioners. It has a large library of solvers and utilities for various applications, such as incompressible and compressible flow, turbulence modeling, multiphase flow, etc. It also allows users to customize and extend the code according to their needs.
- CAD-integrated tools: Some CAD software also offer CFD capabilities within their platforms, such as SolidWorks Flow Simulation and Autodesk CFD [13]. These tools are useful for performing basic fluid flow and heat transfer analysis on CAD models without leaving the CAD environment.

8.2.1.1.1   Steps to Perform CFD

- Formulate the flow problem: Define the objectives, assumptions, and simplifications of the problem. Identify the physical phenomena and governing equations involved. Choose the appropriate turbulence model, numerical scheme, and solver settings.
- Model the geometry and flow domain: Create or import the CAD model of the body and the surrounding fluid region. Define the dimensions, scale, and orientation of the model. Apply any necessary simplifications or modifications to the geometry.
- Establish the boundary and initial conditions: Specify the type and value of the physical quantities at the boundaries of the flow domain, such as pressure, velocity, temperature, etc. Specify the initial values of the physical quantities in the interior of the flow domain.
- Generate the grid: Divide the flow domain into a finite number of cells or elements using a meshing tool. Choose the appropriate mesh type, size, quality, and refinement level for each region of the domain. Check and validate the mesh for any errors or inconsistencies.
- Establish the simulation strategy: Choose the type of simulation (steady-state or transient), the convergence criteria, the time step size (if transient), and the output parameters. Set up any monitors, probes, or plots to track the simulation progress and results.
- Establish the input parameters and files: Prepare and organize all the input files and parameters required by the CFD solver. Check for any missing or incorrect data. Save and backup your files before running the simulation.
- Perform the simulation: Run the CFD solver on your computer or on a cloud platform. Monitor the simulation progress and check for any errors or warnings. Stop or pause the simulation if necessary. Save and backup your result files after completion.
- Post-process and analyze the results: Visualize and explore the results using a post-processing tool. Generate plots, graphs, contours, vectors, animations, etc., to display the physical quantities of interest. Compare and validate your

results with experimental data or analytical solutions. Interpret and report your findings and conclusions [8].

8.2.1.2   Real-World Applications of CFD

CFD has many applications in various fields of study and industries, such as the following:

- By mimicking the development of vapor bubbles within a liquid, cavitation in propellers, nozzles, turbines, spillways, and valves can be avoided.
- Calculating the dynamic rotor force that causes instability in rotating machinery such as compressors, steam pumps, gas turbines, and turbo-expanders.
- Employing turbulence models to research laminar and turbulent flow and foresee how turbulence would affect a CAD-engineered design.
- Aerodynamics and aerospace analysis by simulating the flow of air around aircrafts, rockets, satellites, etc., and optimizing their performance and design.
- Weather simulation by modeling the atmospheric dynamics and predicting the weather patterns and climate change [2].
- Natural science and environmental engineering by simulating the flow of water, air, pollutants, etc., in natural and man-made systems.
- Industrial system design and analysis by optimizing the fluid flow and heat transfer in various processes and equipment such as pipes, valves, pumps, and heat exchangers.
- Biological engineering by modeling the blood flow, respiratory system, drug delivery, etc., in living organisms [9].
- Engine and combustion analysis by simulating the fuel injection, ignition, combustion, and emissions in internal combustion engines.
- Visual effects for film and games by creating realistic animations of fluids such as water, fire, smoke, etc.

8.2.2   Multibody Dynamics

Multibody dynamics is a study of the complex behavior of mechanical machines that contain flexible rigid and/or bodies connected using joints [23]. The systems can go under both translational and rotational motions due to applied forces and torque. Different multibody simulations enable us to perform multibody dynamics simulations for complex systems, such as vehicle equipment, aircraft landing gear, etc. We can specify forces like gravity, torque, and motion to simulate the responses of our model.

Joints and constraints libraries are used to specify the degree of freedom between a pair of bodies, e.g., to model the constraint between a roller coaster car and the track, point on curve constraint block can be used. Force and torque libraries are used to model forces and torques that act on bodies, such as using spatial contact force to model constraint to simulate forces between a pair of bodies.

These systems are presented as a discrete mathematical representation of actual mechanical systems, leading to a collection of ordinary differential equations that can be resolved using numerical techniques [12]. A dynamist must therefore possess a thorough understanding of theoretical mechanics and practical mathematics.

8.2.3   Kinematics for Multibody Systems

Figure 8.1 includes actively driven servomotors without inertia as well as springs, dampers, and rigid structures with inertia, which are all examples of multibody systems [5]. Rigid bearings or other devices join the bodies together at any extra applied forces and torques as well as subject to any other type of support.

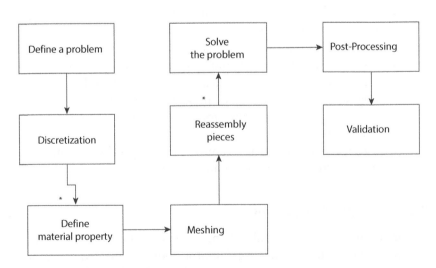

Figure 8.1 Steps to perform a novel finite element analysis.

Therefore, the multibody systems modeling approach is well suited for simulating mechanical systems with complex geometries and significant stiffness variations [7], which typically lead to motions with frequencies under 50 Hz.

8.3   Literature Review

This section reviews the existing literature on automated mining systems, digital twin technology, and self-adaptive mining algorithms. It highlights successful case studies and identifies the gaps that this research aims to fill. The finite element method (FEM), a numerical approach, is used in Finite Element Analysis (FEA), which simulates any given physical phenomenon for estimating solutions to partial differential equations' boundary value issues. In simple words, it divides the complex problems into sub-problems and converts each sub-problem to a mathematical representation. Consider dissecting the brackets holding up the air conditioner (or another substantial support). Predicting the stress, strain, and displacement within the brackets is the aim of a static analysis at this point. In order to maintain balance over any volume of the body, internal tensions develop within a body. We can use the idea of equilibrium to determine displacement [7]. It will be challenging to apply the idea of equilibrium because the bracket has a 2D shape. The finite element method approaches this issue by breaking down the body into numerous little elements that are all connected at nodes. The collection of tiny elements created by the aforementioned procedure is known as a mesh. Mesh could be a surface element like a square, triangle, etc., for 2D bodies and solid element like pyramid and cube for 3D bodies. Apart from this, we can use second-order elements as well, as they are comparatively more accurate and easier to use as they have additional mid-side nodes or midpoints. However, for the abovementioned bracket, we could use solid element or line element. In finite element analysis, we mainly calculate displacement [23, 24], which helps us further in calculating stress and strain. For each small element, we define a vector {u} which contains all the possible displacements for the node of an element, also known as vector of element nodal displacement.

8.3.1   Classification of MBD Simulations

- Kinematic simulation: Kinematic simulation is defined as a model with no DOF. Through a purely geometric investigation, it assesses position, velocity, and acceleration.

- Dynamic simulation: It examines how a system moves as a result of applied forces and inertia forces [25]. It works with models that have one or more DOF. Improving product function and quality across a wide range of industries is the basic application of dynamic simulation.
- Quasi-static simulation: It examines the equilibrium conditions of a system that is moving slowly. The most common applications used for quasi-static simulation are design of the suspension, tilt-table stability analysis, and steady-state simulations [26].
- Linear simulation: It is a study of a system's vibrational modes at any operational point. It is evaluation of the system transfer function at any specified operating point. The applications for linear simulation are stability analysis, NVH, and plant models for control system design.

8.3.2 Finite Element Analysis

In finite element analysis, we mainly calculate displacement [23, 24], which helps us further in calculating stress and strain. For each small element, we define a vector {u} which contains all the possible displacements for a node of an element, also known as vector of element nodal displacement.

For example, for a 2D beam element: {u} = {u1, v1, w1, u2, v2, w2}
Degrees of freedom per node = 3
Therefore, the general equation for FEA is as follows:

$$\{f\} = [k] \{u\} \tag{8.1}$$

8.4 Proposed Work

In proposed work, we improved the finite element analysis simulation for the execution of a fully automated coal mining face using self-adaptive advanced digital twins [17]. The advanced FEM is a numerical approach used in FEA to improve the efficiency of the current finite element system, which simulates any given physical phenomenon for estimating solutions to partial differential equations' boundary value issues. In simple words, it divides the complex problems into sub-problems and converts each sub-problem to a mathematical representation [22]. Table 8.1 shows the list of findings from different simulation methods.

Table 8.1 Evaluation of the approaches' accuracy for various simulation methods [6].

Study title	Authors	Year	Methodology	Key findings
Study 1	G. N. Schroeder, C. Steinmetz, R. N. Rodrigues	2021	Multibody dynamics	Result accuracy is independent of mesh size
Study 2	T. Riedelsheimer, S. Gogineni, and R. Stark	2021	Multibody dynamics	System reusable collection of modeling entities
Study 3	M. S. Ibrahim	2020	Finite element analysis	Result accuracy is proportional to mesh size
Study 4	A. Burger, C. Cichiwskyj, S. Schmeißer, and G. Schiele	2020	Finite element analysis	System coordinate systems
Study 5	Cronrath, A. R. Aderiani, and B. Lennartson	2019	Finite element analysis	Result accuracy is proportional to mesh size

$$\{f\} = \{f_x1, f_y1, m1, f_x2, f_y2, m2\} \tag{8.2}$$

$$\{u\} = \{u1, v1, w1, u2, v2, w2\} \tag{8.3}$$

$$[k] = \begin{bmatrix} k11 & \cdots & k16 \\ \vdots & \ddots & \vdots \\ k61 & \cdots & k66 \end{bmatrix} \tag{8.4}$$

where

$\{f\}$ = vector of nodal forces and moments
$\{u\}$ = vector of nodal displacement
$[k]$ = stiffness matrix of element

For the above-mentioned beam element, consider dissecting the brackets holding up the air conditioner (or another substantial support). Predicting the stress, strain, and displacement within the brackets is the aim of a static analysis at this point [15]. In order to maintain balance over any volume of the body, internal tensions develop within a body. We can use the idea of equilibrium to determine displacement [9]. It will be challenging to apply the idea of equilibrium because the bracket has a 2D shape [14]. The finite element method approaches this issue by breaking down the body into numerous little elements that are all connected at nodes. The collection of tiny elements created by the aforementioned procedure is known as a mesh [2]. A mesh could be a surface element like square, triangle, etc., for 2D bodies and a solid element like pyramid and cube for 3D bodies. Apart from this, we can use a second-order element as well, as they are comparatively more accurate and easier to use as they have additional mid-side nodes or midpoints [3]. However, for the abovementioned bracket, we could use solid element or line element [2].

$[k]$ is a global sparse and banded matrix known as stiffness matrix.

8.5   Conclusion

In conclusion, the adoption of such a system transforms coal mining operations by utilizing automation, digital twins, and AI-powered algorithms to maximize productivity, safety, and sustainability in the mining sector. Overall, the DT is moving forward with full force, and its almost limitless potential makes it a crucial and more well-liked participant in the race. The advancement of its enabling technologies, which are always changing, puts us one step closer to the creation of actual DTs. The number of attempts to construct the DT has increased as scientific interest in it grows, yet several persistent and prevalent challenges remain. In the age of AI, the emphasis is on the data, and the DT finds itself in the center of an information loop: it requires well-researched data to fuel its sophisticated ML algorithms, and then it further enables a deeper comprehension of that data *via* its interactive and predictive accomplishments, including some difficult riddles.

References

1. Schroeder, G.N., Steinmetz, C., Rodrigues, R.N., Henriques, R.V.B., Rettberg, A., Pereira, C.E., A methodology for digital twin modeling and deployment for industry 4.0. *Proc. IEEE*, 109, 4, 556–567, 2021.

2. Riedelsheimer, T., Gogineni, S., Stark, R., Methodology to develop-digital twins for energy efficient customizable IoT-products. *Proc. CIRP*, 98, 258–263, 2021.

3. Tao, F., Zhang, M., Nee, A.Y.C., *Digital Twin Driven Smart Manufacturing*, Academic, London, U.K., 2019.

4. "What is a digital twin?" IBM. Accessed, 2022. [Online]. Available: https://www.ibm.com/uk-en/topics/what-is-a-digital-twin.

5. Kaur, M., Gupta, S., Kumar, D., Verma, C., Neagu, B.-C., Raboaca, M.S., Delegated proof of accessibility (DPoAC): A novel consensus protocol for blockchain systems. *Mathematics*, 10, 2336, 2022. https://doi.org/10.3390/math10132336

6. Chakraborty, S. and Adhikari, S., Machine learning based digital twin for dynamical systems with multiple time-scales. *Comput. Struct.*, 243, 106410, 2021.

7. Ali, M.A., Guan, Q., Umer, R., Cantwell, W.J., Zhang, T., Deep learning based semantic segmentation of µCT images for creating digital material twins of fibrous reinforcements. *Compos. Part A Appl. Sci. Manuf.*, 139, 106131, 2020.

8. Maschler, B., Braun, D., Jazdi, N., Weyrich, M., Transfer learning as an enabler of the intelligent digital twin. *Proc. CIRP*, 100, 127–132, Jan. 2021.

9. Wang, Z. *et al.*, A digital twin paradigm: Vehicle-to-cloud based advanced driver assistance systems, in: *Proc. IEEE 91st Veh. Technol. Conf. (VTC-Spring)*, pp. 1–6, 2020.

10. Kaur, M. and Gupta, S., Blockchain consensus protocols: State-of-the-art and future directions, in: *2021 International Conference on Technological Advancements and Innovations (ICTAI)*, Tashkent, Uzbekistan, pp. 446–453, 2021, doi: 10.1109/ICTAI53825.2021.9673260.

11. Revetria, R., Tonelli, F., Damiani, L., Demartini, M., Bisio, F., Peruzzo, N., A real-time mechanical structures monitoring system based on digital twin, IoT and augmented reality, in: *Proc. IEEE Spring Simulat. Conf. (SpringSim)*, pp. 1–10, 2019.

12. Kumar, D., Verma, C., Dahiya, S., Singh, P.K., Raboaca, M.S., Illés, Z., Bakariya, B., Cardiac diagnostic feature and demographic identification (CDF-DI): An IoT enabled healthcare framework using machine learning. *Sensors*, 21, 19, 6584, 2021. https://doi.org/10.3390/s21196584

13. Burger, A., Cichiwskyj, C., Schmeißer, S., Schiele, G., The elastic Internet of Things—A platform for self-integrating and self-adaptive IoT-systems with support for embedded adaptive hardware. *Future Gener. Comput. Syst.*, 113, 607–619, 2020.

14. Gupta, S. and Saini, A.K., An artificial intelligence based approach for managing risk of IT systems in adopting cloud. *Int. J. Inf. Technol.*, 13, 2515–2523, 2021. https://doi.org/10.1007/s41870-018-0204-2

15. Mitchell, M., Why AI is harder than we think. *arXiv*, 2104, 12871, 2021.

16. Ibrahim, M.S. *et al.*, Machine learning and digital twin driven diagnostics and Prognostics of light-emitting diodes. *Laser Photon. Rev.*, 14, 12, 2000254, 2020.

17. Gupta, S. and Saini, A. K., Information system security and risk management: Issues and impact on organizations. *Glob. J. Enterp. Inf. Syst.*, 5, 1, 31–35, 2013.

18. Alexopoulos, K., Nikolakis, N., Chryssolouris, G., Digital twindriven supervised machine learning for the development of artificial intelligence applications in manufacturing. *Int. J. Comput. Integr. Manuf.*, 33, 5, 429–439, 2020.

19. Xue, F., Lu, W., Chen, Z., Webster, C.J., From LiDAR point cloud towards digital twin city: Clustering city objects based on gestalt principles. *ISPRS J. Photogramm. Remote Sens.*, 167, 418–431, 2020.

20. Farhat, M.H., Chiementin, X., Chaari, F., Bolaers, F., Haddar, M., Digital twin-driven machine learning: Ball bearings fault severity classification. *Meas. Sci. Technol.*, 32, 4, 044006, 2021.

21. Samnejad, M., Shirangi, M.G., Ettehadi, R., A Digital Twin of Drilling Fluids Rheology for Real-Time Rig Operations, in: *Proceedings of Offshore Technology Conference*, p. 18, 2020.

22. Cronrath, C., Aderiani, A.R., Lennartson, B., Enhancing digital twins through reinforcement learning". *Proceedings of IEEE 15th International Conference Automation Science and Engineering (CASE)*, pp. 293–298, 2019.

23. Ilyas, B., Kumar, A., Setitra, M.A., Abidine Bensalem, Z.E., Lei, H., Prevention of DDoS attacks using an optimized deep learning approach in blockchain technology. *Trans. Emerg. Telecomm. Technol.*, 34, 4, e4729, 2023.

24. Mitra, D., Gupta, S., Kaur, P., An algorithmic approach to machine learning techniques for fraud detection: A comparative analysis, in: *2021 International Conference on Intelligent Technology, System and Service for Internet of Everything (ITSS-IoE)*, Sana'a, Yemen, pp. 1–4, 2021, doi:10.1109/ITSS-IoE53029.2021.9615349.

25. Vargas, H.F. and Vivas, O.A., Gesture recognition system for surgical robot's manipulation, in: *Proceedings of IEEE XIX Symposium on Image, Signal Processing and Artificial Vision*, pp. 1–5, 2014.

26. Benkhaddra, I., Kumar, A., Setitra, M.A. *et al.*, Design and development of consensus activation function enabled neural network-based smart healthcare using BIoT. *Wirel. Pers. Commun.*, 130, 1549–1574, 2023. https://doi.org/10.1007/s11277-023-10344-0.

9

MGF-Based BER and Channel Capacity Analysis of Fisher Snedecor Composite Fading Model

Hari Shankar* and Yogesh

Department of Computer Science and Engineering, Chitkara University Institute of Engineering and Technology, Chitkara University, Rajpura, Punjab, India

Abstract

This chapter introduces the moment generating function (MGF)-based performance for Fisher Snedecor (F) fading model over device-to-device (D2D) communication channels. At first, the probability density function (PDF) of this new fading model is presented, and then the corresponding expression of MGF is obtained. Using MGF, the average bit error rate (ABER) expressions for binary and multilevel signaling are derived. We further derive the channel capacity expressions under various transmission protocols like optimal rate adaption (ORA) and channel inversion with fixed rate (CIFR). The numerical results are presented as the function of average signal-to-noise ratio (SNR) with different fading parameters and compared with the Monte Carlo simulation results for validation purposes. The result shows that error rate and channel capacity have better performance for higher fading severity.

Keywords: Composite fading, shadowing, ABER, channel capacity, moment generating function

9.1 Introduction

In a wireless communication system, the received signal is generally characterized by both multipath fading and shadowing effects. Multipath fading

---

Corresponding author: hari.shankar55@gmail.com

Abhineet Anand, Anita Sardana, Abhishek Kumar, Srikanta Kumar Mohapatra and Shikha Gupta (eds.) Simulation Techniques of Digital Twin in Real-Time Applications: Design Modeling and Implementation, (195–214) © 2024 Scrivener Publishing LLC

or small-scale fading occurs due to reflection, refraction, and scattering from surrounding objects like tree, building, mountain, etc., whereas shadowing occurs due to obstructions between the transmitter and the receiver [1]. Thus, it is necessary for system designers to have a statistical model that is suitable for a composite fading environment. In [2], the Fisher Snedecor model has been proposed, which is suitable for device-to-device or wearable communication systems [2]. Research on wearable communication is not only interesting but also important because it has various applications in the field of communication, military, medical, sports, etc. [3, 4].

ABER and channel capacity are both the most important performance analysis parameters in the design of a digital communication system over a wireless fading channel. The BER performance depends on the applied signaling schemes, diversity techniques, and SNR [1]. However, channel capacity provides the information about maximum data transmission through the wireless channel [1]. It should be noted that the maximum data rate is always less than the capacity of the channel. The channel capacity for different adaptive policies has become interesting from the last decades. Various adaptive transmission policies have been used to find the capacity, such as OPRA, ORA, CIFR, and truncated CIFR (TIFR) [5].

For different scenarios, the error rates have been derived using MGF method in [6–8]. The capacity analysis using MGF method were presented in [9, 10]. It should be noted that the MGF-based analysis given in [9, 10] are mathematically efficient and simple to use if and only if the MGF is written in a simple closed form.

The MGF of κ-μ and η-μ fading were derived in [11], which were used to compute the error rate including special cases. In [12], the MGF expression of α-μ distribution was obtained. After that, the ABER for different coherent modulation schemes and the outage probability using MGF approach were calculated [12]. The derived expressions can be reduced to Nakagami-m, Rayleigh, and Weibull distribution as special cases. In [13], the MGF-based unified expression for error rate and capacity for maximum ratio combining (MRC) diversity of Nakagami-m/gamma channels was proposed. The author in [13] further derived a unified hyper-Fox's H fading as a generalized model for some exiting well-known fading distribution. Some numerical results were obtained for various fading environments that show a good agreement with the simulation result. In [14], the MGF of a generalized K fading channel was proposed for arbitrary values. The MGF expression of a generalized two-ray fading model was computed in [15]. The MGF and truncated MGF expressions of a Rayleigh Gamma-shadowed fading model was derived in [16].

The composite fading model given in [2] is functionally equal to the Fisher Snedecor distribution [1]. In [2], the D2D measurement at 5.8 GHz was performed in both outdoor and indoor open environments. The empirical values were best fitted to theoretical values of the proposed composite fading model. The author in [2] further analyzed the performance measures like MGF, outage probability (OP), CDF, AF, and BEP for basic binary signaling schemes using the derived MGF expression. In [17], the error probability for M-ary signaling and average channel capacity analysis was performed for F channels. In the work of [18], the exact and high SNR capacities for several methods using a PDF-based approach were computed for the F fading model. The capacity analyses over the F channels for different power and rate adaptive methods using a PDF-based approach were also illustrated in [19, 20]. The exact and approximate upper-bound error rate expressions for M-ary signaling over F fading were computed in [21].

The ABER expression using binary and multilevel modulation schemes, except BPSK and DPSK, had not been elaborated therein using MGF-based approach. Moreover, the expression for channel capacity using MGF method is also not presented in [2]. The derived MGF is presented in the form of the sum of two expressions (using Kummer confluent hypergeometric function). Therefore, it is difficult and lengthy to further make an analysis of performance parameters like ABER and capacity using MGF approach. The given MGF in [2] is also valid only with condition, $m + m_s \neq N, m_s \neq N$.

In this chapter, we derive the MGF expression for both integer and non-integer values, which will be helpful to compute the error rate and capacity expressions. The analysis of ABER is provided for several signaling schemes. Furthermore, the capacity analysis is illustrated for the ORA and CIFR schemes. The result of the presented work reduces to classical multipath fading models as special cases.

9.2   Fisher Snedecor Composite Fading Model

The envelope PDF for random variable r is represented as [2, Eq. 3],

$$f_R(r) = \frac{2m^m \cdot (m_s \Omega)^{m_s} r^{2m-1}}{B(m, m_s)(mr^2 + m_s \Omega)^{m+m_s}} \tag{9.1}$$

where $B(\cdot, \cdot)$ is the beta function [22]. m and m_s is the fading severity and shadowing parameter, respectively. As $m_s \to 0$, the rms signal power undergoes heavy shadowing, and with $m_s \rightarrow \infty$, light shadowing or no shadowing of rms signal power occurs. Thus, (9.1) reduces to PDF of Nakagami-m distribution [2]. $\Omega = E[r^2]$ is the mean square value of the envelope signal.

Hence, the PDF of SNR is given by [2, Eq. 5]:

$$f_\gamma(\gamma) = \frac{m^m \cdot \gamma^{m-1}(m_s\bar{\gamma})^{m_s}}{B(m,m_s)(m\gamma + m_s\bar{\gamma})^{m+m_s}} \qquad (9.2)$$

where instantaneous SNR (γ) is defined as $\gamma = \bar{\gamma} \cdot R^2 / \Omega$ and $\bar{\gamma} = E[\gamma]$ represents the average SNR.

Now, the MGF can be defined as [1]:

$$M_\gamma(s) = \int_0^\infty \exp(-s\gamma) f_\gamma(\gamma) d\gamma \qquad (9.3)$$

Putting (9.2) into (9.3),

$$M_\gamma(s) = \int_0^\infty \exp(-s\gamma) \frac{\gamma^{m-1} m^m (m_s\bar{\gamma})^{m_s}}{(m\gamma + m_s\bar{\gamma})^{m+m_s} B(m,m_s)} \qquad (9.4)$$

As we know the following relations [1, Eq. 4.268]:

$$\exp(-s\gamma) = G_{0,1}^{1,0}\left(s\gamma \,\middle|\, \begin{matrix} - \\ 0 \end{matrix} \right) \qquad (9.5)$$

By substituting (9.5) in (9.4), we get

$$M_\gamma(s) = \frac{(m_s\bar{\gamma})^{m_s}}{B(m,m_s)m^{m_s}} \int_0^\infty G_{0,1}^{1,0}\left(s\gamma \,\middle|\, \begin{matrix} - \\ 0 \end{matrix} \right) \frac{\gamma^{m-1}}{(\gamma + m_s\bar{\gamma}/m)^{m+ms}} d\gamma \qquad (9.6)$$

Using [22, page no. 852, Eq. 7.811.5] and after algebraic calculation, the above expression becomes

$$M_\gamma(s) = \frac{1}{\Gamma(m+m_s)B(m,m_s)} G_{1,2}^{2,1}\left(\frac{sm_s\bar{\gamma}}{m} \left| \begin{matrix} 1-m \\ m_s \quad 0 \end{matrix} \right.\right) \quad (9.7)$$

where $\Gamma(\cdot)$ is the Gamma function [22].

9.3 Performance Analysis Using MGF

Analysis based on the MGF tool is very easy since it does not require numerical integration in most of the cases. It is also not needed to solve double integration to derive the ABER expression. Using MGF technique, the expression of BER for coherent and non-coherent signaling, and adaptive capacity for F fading model will derive an illustration.

9.3.1 ABER

BER is the most important performance analysis matrix for wireless communication system designs. However, it is not easy task to derive the error probability expression in a closed form. The MGF method is an easy way to evaluate the BER for different modulation schemes. The ABER expression can be obtained by averaging the BER of AWGN over that of the fading model [1, 6]:

$$P_e(E) = \int_0^\infty P_e(E/\gamma)f_\gamma(\gamma)d\gamma \quad (9.8)$$

9.3.1.1 BDPSK and NBFSK

The ABER for BDPSK ($a = 1$) and NBFSK ($a = 0.5$) can be obtained by directly using the MGF expression [23]:

$$P_b(E) = 0.5 \cdot M_\gamma(a) \quad (9.9)$$

By using (9.7) and (9.9), we get

$$P_b(E) = \frac{0.5}{B(m,m_s)\Gamma(m+m_s)} G_{1,2}^{2,1}\left(\frac{am_s\bar{\gamma}}{m}\left|\begin{array}{cc} 1-m & \\ m_s & 0 \end{array}\right.\right) \qquad (9.10)$$

9.3.1.2 BPSK and BFSK

The BER for BPSK and BFSK can be obtained as follows [23]:

$$P_b(E) = \frac{1}{\pi}\int_0^{\pi/2} M_\gamma\left(\frac{b}{\sin^2(\theta)}\right)d\theta \qquad (9.11)$$

By using (9.7), we get

$$P_b(E) = \frac{0.5}{\pi \cdot B(m,m_s)\Gamma(m+m_s)} \underbrace{\int_0^{\pi/2} G_{1,2}^{2,1}\left(\frac{bm_s\bar{\gamma}}{m\sin^2\theta}\left|\begin{array}{cc} 1-m & \\ m_s & 0 \end{array}\right.\right)d\theta}_{I}$$

$$(9.12)$$

where b is the constant, which is associated with various modulation schemes, i.e., for BPSK, we put $b = 1$; for BFSK, we set $b = 0.5$; and for BFSK with minimum correlation, we set $b = 0.715$. Let $\sin^2(\theta) = x$, so the integral term (I) in (9.12) can be written as

$$I = \frac{1}{2}\int_0^1 G_{1,2}^{2,1}\left(\frac{bm_s\bar{\gamma}}{mx}\left|\begin{array}{cc} 1-m & \\ m_s & 0 \end{array}\right.\right)x^{-1/2}\cdot(1-x)^{-1/2}dx \qquad (9.13)$$

By using the property of Meijer G function and [22, Eq. 7.811.2], we get the above expression as follows:

$$I = \frac{1}{2}\Gamma(0.5)G_{3,2}^{1,3}\left(\frac{m}{bm_s\bar{\gamma}}\left|\begin{array}{ccc} 0.5 & 1-m_s & 1 \\ m & 0 & \end{array}\right.\right) \qquad (9.14)$$

By substituting the value of I in (9.12),

$$P_b(E) = \frac{\Gamma(0.5)}{2\pi \cdot B(m,m_s)\Gamma(m+m_s)} G_{3,2}^{1,3} \left(\frac{m}{bm_s\bar{\gamma}} \left| \begin{array}{ccc} 0.5 & 1-m_s & 1 \\ m & 0 & \end{array} \right. \right)$$

(9.15)

9.3.1.3 MAM

BER for MAM is given as follows [23]:

$$P_b(E) = \frac{2(M-1)}{M\pi \log_2(M)} \int_0^{\pi/2} M_\gamma \left(\frac{g_{AM}}{\sin^2(\theta)} \right) d\theta$$

(9.16)

where $g_{AM} = 3\log_2(M)/(M^2-1)$ and M = 2, 4, 6, 8.....
By plugging (9.7) in (9.16), we obtain

$$P_b(E) = \frac{2(M-1)}{M\pi \log_2(M) \cdot B(m,m_s)\Gamma(m+m_s)} \int_0^{\pi/2} G_{1,2}^{2,1} \left(\frac{g_{AM}m_s\bar{\gamma}}{m\sin^2\theta} \left| \begin{array}{cc} 1-m & \\ m_s & 0 \end{array} \right. \right) d\theta$$

(9.17)

The integration in (9.17) is identical to (9.11) that we have already solved, so the solution of (9.17) becomes

$$P_b(E) = \frac{(M-1)\Gamma(0.5)}{\pi M \log_2(M) \cdot \Gamma(m+m_s)B(m,m_s)} G_{3,2}^{1,3} \left(\frac{m}{g_{AM}m_s\bar{\gamma}} \left| \begin{array}{ccc} 0.5 & 1-m_s & 1 \\ m & 0 & \end{array} \right. \right)$$

(9.18)

9.3.1.4 Square MQAM

The error rate for square MQAM is defined as follows [23]:

$$P_b(E) = \frac{4}{\pi \log_2(M)} \left\{ \left(1 - \frac{1}{\sqrt{M}}\right) \int_0^{\pi/2} M_\gamma \left(\frac{g_{MQAM}}{\sin^2(\theta)} \right) d\theta - \left(1 - \frac{1}{\sqrt{M}}\right)^2 \int_0^{\pi/4} M_\gamma \left(\frac{g_{MQAM}}{\sin^2(\theta)} \right) d\theta \right\}$$

(9.19)

where $g_{MQAM} = 3\log_2(M)/2(M-1)$
   As we know that [24, Eq. 19]

$$\int_0^{\pi/2} M_\gamma\left(\frac{g_{MQAM}}{\sin^2(\theta)}\right)d\theta = \frac{1}{12}M_\gamma\left(g_{MQAM}\right) + \frac{1}{4}M_\gamma\left(\frac{4}{3}g_{MQAM}\right) \quad (9.20)$$

$$\int_0^{\pi/4} M_\gamma\left(\frac{g_{MQAM}}{\sin^2(\theta)}\right)d\theta = \frac{1}{8}M_\gamma\left(2g_{MQAM}\right) \quad (9.21)$$

By putting the value of (9.20) and (9.21) in (9.19), we get

$$P_b(E) = \frac{4}{\pi\log_2(M)}\left[\left(1-\frac{1}{\sqrt{M}}\right)\left\{\frac{1}{12}M_\gamma\left(g_{MQAM}\right) + \frac{1}{4}M_\gamma\left(\frac{4}{3}g_{MQAM}\right)\right\} - \left(1-\frac{1}{\sqrt{M}}\right)^2\left\{\frac{1}{8}M_\gamma\left(2g_{MQAM}\right)\right\}\right]$$

$$(9.22)$$

By substituting (9.7) in (9.22), we get

$$P_b(E) = \frac{4}{\pi\log_2(M)B(m,m_s)\Gamma(m+m_s)}\left[\left(1-\frac{1}{\sqrt{M}}\right)\left\{\frac{1}{12}G_{1,2}^{2,1}\left(\frac{g_{MQAM}m_s\bar{\gamma}}{m}\left|\begin{matrix}1-m\\m_s\quad 0\end{matrix}\right.\right)\right.\right.$$

$$\left.\left. + \frac{1}{4}G_{1,2}^{2,1}\left(\frac{4g_{MQAM}m_s\bar{\gamma}}{3m}\left|\begin{matrix}1-m\\m_s\quad 0\end{matrix}\right.\right)\right\} - \left(1-\frac{1}{\sqrt{M}}\right)^2\left\{\frac{1}{8}G_{1,2}^{2,1}\left(\frac{2g_{MQAM}m_s\bar{\gamma}}{m}\left|\begin{matrix}1-m\\m_s\quad 0\end{matrix}\right.\right)\right\}\right]$$

$$(9.23)$$

9.3.1.5   MPSK

The symbol error rate (SER) for coherent MPSK is as follows [23]:

$$P_S(E) = \frac{1}{\pi}\int_0^{\pi-\pi/M} M_\gamma\left(\frac{g_{MPSK}}{\sin^2(\theta)}\right)d\theta \quad (9.24)$$

where $g_{MPSK} = \sin^2(\pi/M)$

Equation (9.24) can be solved as follows [24, Eq. 16]:

$$P_S(E) = \left(\frac{\Theta}{2\pi} - \frac{1}{6}\right) M_\gamma\left(g_{MPSK}\right) + \frac{1}{4} M_\gamma\left(\frac{4}{3} g_{MPSK}\right) + \left(\frac{\Theta}{2\pi} - \frac{1}{4}\right) M_\gamma\left(\frac{g_{MPSK}}{\sin^2 \Theta}\right)$$

(9.25)

where $\Theta = \pi - \pi / M$

Putting (9.7) in (9.25), we get

$$P_S(E) = \frac{1}{B(m, m_s)\Gamma(m + m_s)}\left[\left(\frac{\Theta}{2\pi} - \frac{1}{6}\right)G_{1,2}^{2,1}\left(\frac{g_{MPSK}m_s\bar{\gamma}}{m}\bigg|\begin{matrix}1 - m\\m_s \quad 0\end{matrix}\right) + \frac{1}{4}G_{1,2}^{2,1}\left(\frac{4g_{MPSK}m_s\bar{\gamma}}{3m}\bigg|\begin{matrix}1 - m\\m_s \quad 0\end{matrix}\right)\right.$$
$$\left. + \left(\frac{\Theta}{2\pi} - \frac{1}{4}\right)G_{1,2}^{2,1}\left(\frac{g_{MPSK}m_s\bar{\gamma}}{m\sin^2 \Theta}\bigg|\begin{matrix}1 - m\\m_s \quad 0\end{matrix}\right)\right]$$

(9.26)

9.3.2 NMFSK

The conditional symbol error rate for non-coherent MSFK is as follows [25, Eq. 7]:

$$P_s\left(E / \gamma\right) = \frac{1}{M}\sum_{i=2}^{M}(-1)^i\binom{M}{i}\exp\left(-\left(1 - \frac{1}{i}\right)\gamma\right)$$

(9.27)

The error probability for NMFSK is as follows [25, Eq. 2]:

$$P_s\left(E\right) = \frac{1}{M}\sum_{i=2}^{M}(-1)^i\binom{M}{i}\int_0^\infty \exp\left(-\left(1 - \frac{1}{i}\right)\gamma\right)f_\gamma(\gamma)d\gamma$$

(9.28)

Equation (9.28) can also be written as follows:

$$P_s\left(E\right) = \frac{1}{M}\sum_{i=2}^{M}(-1)^i\binom{M}{i}M_\gamma\left(\left(1 - \frac{1}{i}\right)\right)$$

(9.29)

Now, by using (9.7), we get the SEP for non-coherent MFSK of F composite fading model as follows:

$$
P_s(E) = \frac{1}{M} \sum_{i=2}^{M} (-1)^i \binom{M}{i} \frac{1}{B(m, m_s)\Gamma(m+m_s)} G_{1,2}^{2,1}\left(\left(1 - \frac{1}{i}\right) \frac{m_s \bar{\gamma}}{m} \middle| \begin{matrix} 1-m \\ m_s \end{matrix} \quad 0 \right)
$$

(9.30)

9.3.3   Adaptive Channel Capacity

9.3.3.1   ORA

The computation of capacity for ORA using MGF is a well-known and simple method. In this, we take the derivative of MGF $M'_\gamma(s)$,s multiplying the exponential integral function $E_i(.)$ [22], and then take the integration. Thus, the capacity for ORA is given as follows [10, Eq. 7]:

$$
C_{ORA} = \frac{1}{\ln(2)} \int_0^\infty E_i(-s) M'_\gamma(s) ds
$$

(9.31)

Thus, $M'_\gamma(s)$ is expressed as follows:

$$
M'_\gamma(s) = \frac{d}{ds} M_\gamma(s)
$$

(9.32)

By putting the expression of MGF from (9.7) into (9.32), we obtain

$$
M'_\gamma(s) = \frac{1}{\Gamma(m+m_s)B(m, m_s)} \frac{d}{ds} G_{1,2}^{2,1}\left(\frac{sm_s \bar{\gamma}}{m} \middle| \begin{matrix} 1-m \\ m_s \end{matrix} \quad 0 \right)
$$

(9.33)

Using [26],

$$
M'_\gamma(s) = \frac{-1}{\Gamma(m+m_s)B(m, m_s) \cdot s} G_{2,3}^{3,1}\left(\frac{sm_s \bar{\gamma}}{m} \middle| \begin{matrix} 1-m & 0 \\ 1 & m_s \end{matrix} \quad 0 \right)
$$

(9.34)

By substituting (9.34) in (9.31), we obtained

$$C_{ORA} = \frac{-1}{\ln(2)} \int_0^\infty E_i(-s) \frac{1}{\Gamma(m+m_s)B(m,m_s)\cdot s} G_{2,3}^{3,1}\left(sm_s\bar{\gamma} \left|\begin{array}{ccc} 1-m & 0 & \\ m & 1 & m_s \end{array}\right. \begin{array}{c} \\ 0 \end{array} \right) ds$$

(9.35)

As we know the following relations [26, Eq. 8.4.11.1],

$$E_i(-s) = -G_{1,2}^{2,0}\left(s \left|\begin{array}{cc} 1 & \\ 0 & 0 \end{array}\right. \right)$$

(9.36)

By putting (9.36) into (9.35),

$$C_{ORA} = \frac{1}{\ln(2)B(m,m_s)\Gamma(m+m_s)} \int_0^\infty \frac{1}{s} G_{1,2}^{2,0}\left(s \left|\begin{array}{cc} 1 & \\ 0 & 0 \end{array}\right. \right) G_{2,3}^{3,1}\left(sm_s\bar{\gamma} \left|\begin{array}{ccc} 1-m & 0 & \\ m & 1 & m_s \end{array} \begin{array}{c} \\ 0 \end{array}\right. \right) ds$$

(9.37)

Using [26, Eq. 2.24.1.1], we get

$$C_{ORA} = \frac{1}{\ln(2)B(m,m_s)\Gamma(m+m_s)} G_{4,4}^{3,3}\left(sm_s\bar{\gamma} \left|\begin{array}{cccc} 1-m & 1 & 1 & 0 \\ m & 1 & m_s & 0 \end{array}\right. \right)$$

(9.38)

9.3.3.2   CIFR

The C_{CIFR} using MGF method can be defined as follows [10, Eq. 18]:

$$C_{CIFR} = \log_2\left(1 + \frac{1}{\underbrace{\int_0^\infty M_\gamma(s)ds}_{I}} \right)$$

(9.39)

The integral term presented in (9.39) is given as follows:

$$I = \int_0^\infty M_\gamma(s)ds = \frac{1}{\Gamma(m+m_s)B(m,m_s)} \int_0^\infty G_{1,2}^{2,1}\left(\frac{sm_s\bar{\gamma}}{m} \left| \begin{matrix} 1-m \\ m_s \end{matrix} \right. \begin{matrix} \\ 0 \end{matrix} \right)ds$$

(9.40)

Using [22, Eq. 7.811.4], we get the solution of (9.40) as follows:

$$I = \frac{\Gamma(m_s+1)\Gamma(m-1)m}{\Gamma(m+m_s)B(m,m_s)m_s\bar{\gamma}}$$

(9.41)

Putting (9.41) into (9.39), we get C_{CIFR} as follows:

$$C_{CIFR} = \log_2\left(1 + \frac{\Gamma(m+m_s)B(m,m_s)m_s\bar{\gamma}}{\Gamma(m_s+1)\Gamma(m-1)m} \right)$$

(9.42)

9.4 Numerical Results

In this section, we present the MGF-based result for various performance measures of F fading. The result of BER/SER is obtained for binary signaling, such as BDPSK, NBFSK, BPSK, BFSK, and MSK and for multilevel signaling like MAM, MPSK, square MQAM, and NMFSK.

Figure 9.1 represents the ABER for BDPSK and NBFSK. From Figure 9.1, it is observed that BDPSK has better BER performance compared to NBFSK for any values of fading severity (m) parameter under heavy shadowing ($m_s = 1$).

Figure 9.2 represent the ABER using BPSK schemes of F composite fading model (continuous line) for various m with light shadowing or no shadowing ($m_s = 20$). The result is compared with BER (BPSK) of existing fading models. By considering light shadowing, for $m = 1$, ABER (BPSK) of the F composite model (9.15) coincides with ABER of Rayleigh fading [1, Eq. 4.134], and $m = 2.5$, (9.15) coincides with ABER of Nakagami-m [1, Eq. 4.138]. In Figure 9.2, by varying m while the shadowing parameter was kept constant ($m_s = 20$), the error rate performance improves.

The numerical result of ABER *versus* average SNR using BFSK and BPSK, as given in (9.15), signaling for different values of fading severity

$(m = 2, 8)$ and fixed m_s, is illustrated in Figure 9.3. As the fading severity parameter increases while m_s was kept constant (under heavy shadowing), the BER gets decreased for any modulation schemes. In Figure 9.3, the BPSK has minimum error for any value of m and m_s. Moreover, it was also

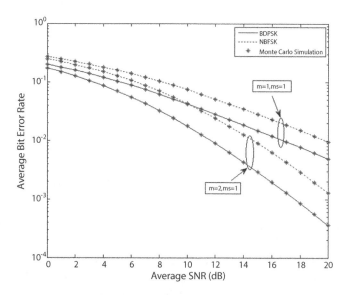

Figure 9.1 ABER *versus* $\bar{\gamma}$ for BDPSK and NBFSK.

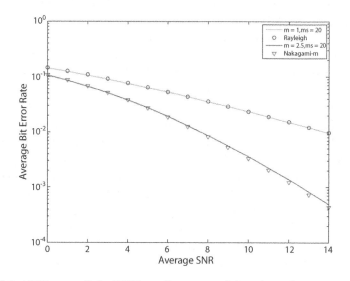

Figure 9.2 ABER *versus* $\bar{\gamma}$ for BPSK over F composite fading channel.

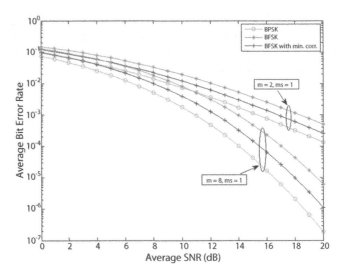

Figure 9.3 ABER for BPSK and BFSK over F composite fading channel.

observed that BFSK has worst error rate performance compared to two others (BPSK and MSK).

Figure 9.4 depicts the ABER using MAM schemes (9.18) for $M = 4, 8$, 16, and 32 with $m = 2$ and $m_s = 1$. On increasing M from 4 to 32, the BER performance gets degraded as expected. Figure 9.5 illustrates the plot of average BER *versus* average SNR for square MQAM modulation schemes (9.23) with $M = 4, 8, 16$, and 32 for different m (1 and 4) and fixed m_s. On increasing M, the ABER gets increased for any value of m and m_s, as shown in Figure 9.5. Moreover, on increasing m for any value of M while the shadowing parameter was kept constant ($m_s = 1$), the ABER gets decreased.

Figure 9.6 shows ABER for MPSK (9.26) for $M = 2, 4, 8$, and 16 with $m = 2$ and $m_s = 1$. The numerical result shows an accurate match with the simulation result that validated the derived expression of ABER for the MPSK modulation schemes given in (9.26). On increasing M (2 to 16), the BER performance gets decreased, as illustrated in Figure 9.6. With $M = 2$, we obtained the ABER for BPSK which is also present in Figure 9. 2.

Figure 9.7 shows the error rate for NMFSK (9.30) with a different signaling level. We have used different m (2 and 8) with heavy shadowing ($m_s = 1$) and light shadowing ($m_s = 15$) to plot the error rate graph. The fading severity with light shadowing (no shadowing) represents better BER performance compared to fading severity with heavy shadowing. Under heavy shadowing, on increasing the m, the BER also gets decreased for any value

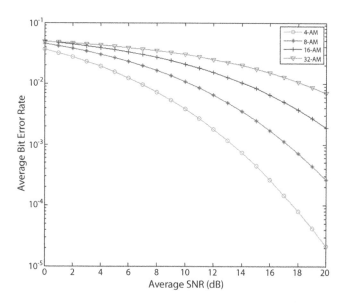

Figure 9.4 ABER using M-ary AM with various *M*.

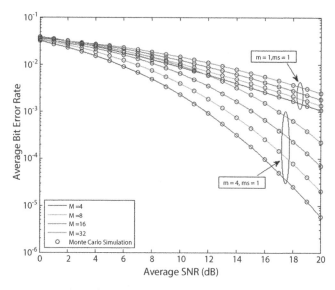

Figure 9.5 Average BER *versus* average SNR $(\bar{\gamma})$ for square MQAM with $M = 4, 8, 16,$ and 32 over F composite fading channel.

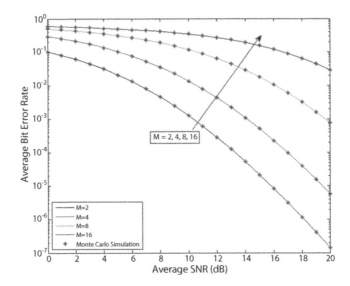

Figure 9.6 Average BER *versus* average SNR ($\overline{\gamma}$) for MPSK with various signaling level (M) with $m = 5$ and $m_s = 5$ over F composite fading channel.

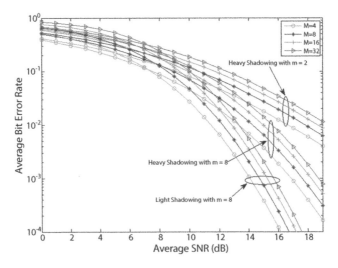

Figure 9.7 Average BER *versus* average SNR ($\overline{\gamma}$) for NMFSK with $M = 4, 8, 16$, and 32 over F composite fading channel.

of M. Moreover, the BER gets increased on increasing M from 4 to 32 for a fixed value of m and m_s, respectively.

Figure 9.8 depicts the C_{ORA} (9.38) for various m (1 and 2.5) with light shadowing ($m_s = 20$). In this figure, the result of channel capacity, as given in (9.38), is compared with the capacity of classical fading models that

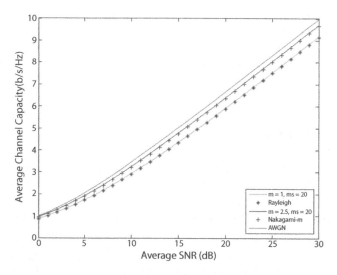

Figure 9.8 Capacity for ORA for different m and its comparison.

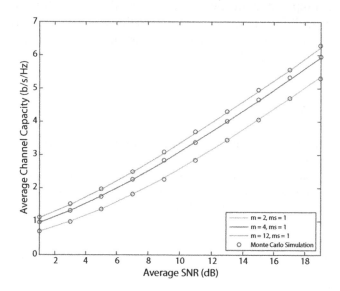

Figure 9.9 Capacity using CIFR with different m and $m_s = 1$.

show a good agreement. For $m_s = 20$, (9.38) coincides with the C_{ORA} of Rayleigh (at $m = 1$) [5, Eq. 36] and Nakagami-m model (at $m = 2.5$) [1, Eq. 4.207]. In Figure 9.8, the capacity increases as m becomes higher but not above the capacity of the AWGN channel. The result shows that we can get more data transmission over F channels with an increase in the value of m.

The result of capacity under CIFR policy (9.42) for different m under heavy shadowing ($m_s = 1$) is presented in Figure 9.9. In Figure 9.9, on increasing m between 2 and 12 with $m_s = 1$, the capacity gets increased. The numerical result of C_{CIFR} shows a good match with the simulation result that validated the proposed expression for channel capacity using CIFR schemes.

9.5 Conclusion

In this chapter, we have studied the performance of F model using MGF. First of all, the expression for MGF is derived. By using the proposed MGF, we have derived the expression for BER using several signaling schemes like BDPSK, NBFSK, BPSK, BFSK, MSK, MAM, square MQAM, MPSK, and NMFSK. Furthermore, the capacity expressions for ORA and CIFR are computed. The accuracy of the result has been checked through the results of special cases and Monte Carlo simulations. The study shows that the higher fading severity parameter has better BER and channel capacity performance compared to the lower one. The MGF-based analysis can also be studied using different diversity techniques that are widely used to combat the fading effect. The analysis can also be obtained with inference-limited scenarios in the practical design of digital communication systems.

References

1. Shankar, P.M., *Fading and shadowing in wireless system*, Springer, New York, NY, 2012.
2. Yoo, S.K., Cotton, S.L., Sofotasios, P.C., Matthaiou, M., Valkama, M., Karagiannidis, G.K., The Fisher-Snedecor F distribution: A Simple and Accurate Composite Fading Model. *IEEE Commun. Lett.*, 21, 1661–1664, 2017.
3. Bhatia, H., Panda, S.N., Nagpal, D., Internet of Things and its applications in healthcare-A survey. In: *IEEE International Conference on Reliability, Infocom Technologies and Optimization (Trends and Future Directions), (ICRITO)*, pp. 305–310, 2020.

4. Gill, K.S., Sharma, A., Anand, V., Sharma, K., Gupta, R., Human action detection using EfficientNetB3 model. In *IEEE International Conference on Computing Methodologies and Communication (ICCMC)*, pp. 745–750, 2023.

5. Alouini, M.S. and Goldsmith, A., Capacity of Rayleigh fading channels under different adaptive transmission and diversity combining techniques. *IEEE Tran. Veh. Technol.*, 48, 1165–1181, 1999.

6. Simon, M.K. and Alouini, M.S., *Digital Communication over Fading Channels*, 2nd ed. John Wiley & Sons, 2005.

7. Simon, M.K. and Alouini, M.S., A unified approach to the performance analysis of digital communication over generalized fading channels. *Proc. IEEE*, 86, 1860–1877, 1998.

8. Alouini, M.S. and Goldsmith, A.J., A unified approach for calculating error rates of linearly modulated signals over generalized fading channels. *IEEE Trans. Commun.*, 47, 1324–1334, 1999.

9. Hamdi, K.A., Capacity of MRC on correlated Rician fading channels. *IEEE Trans. Commun.*, 56, 708–711, 2008.

10. Renzo, M.D., Graziosi, F., Santucci, F., Channel capacity over generalized fading channels: A novel MGF-based approach for performance analysis and design of wireless communication systems. *IEEE Trans. Veh. Technol.*, 59, 1, 127–149, 2010.

11. Da Costa, D.B. and Yacoub, M.D., Moment generating functions of generalized fading distributions and applications. *IEEE Commun. Lett.*, 12, 112–114, 2008.

12. Magableh, A.M. and Matalgah, M.M., Moment generating function of the generalized α-μ distribution with applications. *IEEE Commun. Lett.*, 13, 411–413, 2009.

13. Ferkan, F. and Alouini, M.S., A novel unified expression for the capacity and bit error probability of wireless communication systems over generalized fading channels. *IEEE Trans. Commun.*, 60, 7, 1862–1876, 2012.

14. Efthymoglou, G.P. On the performance analysis of digital modulations in generalized-K fading channels. *Wirel. Pers. Commun.*, 65, 3, 643–651, 2012.

15. Rao, M., Lopez-Martinez, F.J., Alouini, M.S., Goldsmith, A., MGF approach to the analysis of generalized two-ray fading models. *IEEE Trans. Wireless Commun.*, 14, 5, 2548–2561.

16. Hamed, A., Alsharef, M., Rao, R.K., MGF based performance analysis of digital wireless system in urban shadowing environment. *Proceedings of the World Congress on Engineering and Computer Science*, 2015.

17. Aldalgamouni, T., Ilter, M.C., Badarneh, O.S. *et al.*, Performance analysis of Fisher–Snedecor F composite fading channels. *Proc. IEEE Middle East and North Africa Communications Conf. (MENACOMM)*, Jounieh, Lebanon, pp. 140–144, 2018.

18. Zhao, H., Yang, L., Salem, A.S., Alouini, M., Ergodic capacity under power adaption over Fisher-Snedecor F fading channels. *IEEE Commun. Lett.*, 23, 546–549, 2019.

19. Yoo, S.K., Sofotasios, P.C., Cotton, S.L., Muhaidat, S., Lopez-Martinez, F.J., Romero-Jerez, J.M., Karagiannidis, G.K., A comprehensive analysis of the achievable channel capacity in F composite fading channels. *IEEE Access*, 2019.
20. Kapucu, N. and Bilim, M., Analysis of analytical capacity for Fisher-Snedecor F fading channels with different transmission schemes. *Electron. Lett.*, 55, 283–285, 2019.
21. Kapucu, N., Error performance of digital modulations over Fisher-Snedecor F fading channels. *AEU-Int. J. Electron. Commun.*, 108, 73–78, 2019.
22. Gradshteyn, I.S. and Ryzhik, I.M., *Table of Integrals, Series, and Products*, 7th ed, Academic Press, London, 2007.
23. Peppas, K.P., Nistazakis, H.E., Tombras, G.S., An overview of the physical insight and the various performance metrics of fading channels in wireless communication systems. *Adv. Trends Wirel. Commun.*, 2011.
24. Singh, S.P. and Kumar, S., Closed form expressions for ABER and capacity over EGK fading channel in presence of CCI. *Int. J. Electron.*, 104, 3, 513–527, 2017.
25. Sun, J. and Reed, I.S., Performance of MDPSK, MPSK, and noncoherent MFSK in wireless Rician fading channels. *IEEE Trans. Commun.*, 47, 813–816, 1999.
26. Brychkov, Y.A., Marichev, O., II, Prudnikov, A.P., *Integrals and Series, vol 3:more special functions*, Gordon and Breach Science Publishers, New York-London, 1986.

10

Precision Agriculture: An Augmented Datasets and CNN Model-Based Approach to Diagnose Diseases in Fruits and Vegetable Crops

Sparsh Mehta*, Gurwinder Singh and Yogiraj Anil Bhale

Department of AIT-CSE, Chandigarh University, Punjab, Mohali, India

Abstract

Pests and diseases pose significant threats to the fruit and vegetable industry, leading to yield reductions, compromised produce quality, and financial losses for growers. An accurate diagnosis of diseases is challenging due to similar symptoms and the possibility of multiple diseases occurring simultaneously. This study proposes a deep learning-based approach using a convolutional neural network (CNN) model to classify and identify diseases in fruits and vegetables by modeling various scenarios and treatments in the digital twin environment. This enables resource optimization and the creation of more potent disease control strategies. The approach involves creating a dataset of disease images, augmenting it with scaling and rotation techniques, and training the CNN model for disease recognition. The proposed model achieves high values for evaluation metrics such as accuracy, precision, recall, specificity, and F1-score, ranging from 96.85% to 99.3%. It effectively identifies individuals with diseases and healthy leaves, outperforming other models such as InceptionNet and EfficientNetB0. However, accurately diagnosing Marssonina leaf blotch (MLB) remains a challenge due to similarities with other diseases. Additionally, an extended experiment with the ResNet18 model demonstrates promising results, utilizing techniques like cyclical learning rate (CLR) optimization. The study suggests further research to improve accuracy for challenging diseases like MLB, enhance generalization to new data, explore other deep learning architectures and techniques, and investigate transfer learning for better classification performance.

*Corresponding author: sipsmehta@gmail.com

Abhineet Anand, Anita Sardana, Abhishek Kumar, Srikanta Kumar Mohapatra and Shikha Gupta (eds.) Simulation Techniques of Digital Twin in Real-Time Applications: Design Modeling and Implementation, (215–242) © 2024 Scrivener Publishing LLC

Keywords: Crop diseases, deep learning, prediction accuracy, data augmentation, precision agriculture, computer vision, agricultural sustainability

10.1   Introduction

Precision agriculture has emerged as a transformative approach to optimize agricultural practices and improve crop yields. One of the key challenges faced by farmers is the accurate and timely diagnosis of diseases in fruits and vegetable crops. Disease outbreaks can lead to significant crop losses, impacting food production and economic stability. Traditional disease diagnosis methods often rely on visual assessment by agricultural professionals, which is laborious, subjective, and susceptible to human errors. With the advancements in computer vision and machine learning techniques, automated disease diagnosis systems have shown great potential in addressing these challenges.

The fruit and vegetable industry is an essential sector of the agriculture industry, playing a crucial role in promoting healthy and nutritious food for the population. It encompasses the production, processing, and marketing of various fruits and vegetables, including berries, citrus, melons, tree fruits, and vegetables such as tomatoes, peppers, and leafy greens. The industry's importance lies in its significant contribution to global food security, economic growth, and job creation. The industry generates substantial revenue, provides employment opportunities for millions of people worldwide, and plays a crucial role in addressing the growing need for fresh and healthy produce.

However, the fruit and vegetable industry faces several challenges, with pests and diseases being one of the most significant issues. Pests and diseases have a severe impact on the industry, causing output to decrease, quality to decline, and production expenses to rise. In addition, pests and diseases have caused significant financial losses for growers and impact the supply and demand dynamics of the industry. Accurately diagnosing different diseases can be a challenge for farmers, as the symptoms can be similar, and multiple diseases can occur simultaneously.

In this chapter, we introduce an innovative approach to diagnose diseases in fruits and vegetable crops using augmented datasets and a convolutional neural network (CNN) model. Augmented datasets, which include a comprehensive representation of diseases prevalent in fruits and vegetable crops, are employed to train a robust disease classification model. By incorporating augmented datasets, our approach aims to improve the model's capacity to generalize and precisely classify diseases under different conditions. This connection to the concept of digital twin (DT) or simulation of DT can be made by using the augmented datasets to simulate and represent the virtual environment of the crops, allowing for the model training and evaluation of the CNN model in a digital representation of the real-world agricultural scenario.

The core component of our approach is the CNN model, a deep learning architecture specifically designed for image classification tasks. CNNs have shown remarkable performance in various computer vision applications, including disease diagnosis in agriculture. By leveraging the inherent capabilities of CNNs to extract complex features and learn hierarchical representations from images, our model can capture subtle disease patterns that may not be easily discernible to the human eye. The CNN model is trained on the augmented datasets to learn discriminative features and develop a robust disease classification framework. The connection between the CNN model and the concept of digital twin (DT) or simulation of DT can be established by considering the CNN model as a digital representation of the disease diagnosis system, capable of simulating the decision-making process based on the input images of crops. This digital representation can then be integrated with the real-world agricultural systems to enhance disease diagnosis and management practices.

A. Problem formulation

Conventional methods of plant disease diagnostics entail examining samples visually and analyzing them manually. However, these methods are often time consuming, subjective, and prone to errors. Thus, there is a need for more accurate and efficient methods for disease diagnosis. Embracing the synergistic potential of computer vision and machine learning techniques pioneering deep learning methodologies, including the CNN model that we propose, possesses the transformative capability to conquer the hurdles encountered in disease diagnosis. This connection to the concept of Digital Twin (DT) or simulation of DT can be made by considering the CNN model as a digital representation of the disease diagnosis system, capable of simulating the decision-making process based on the input images of crops in a virtual environment.

A cutting-edge convolutional neural network (CNN) model can be proficiently trained to achieve precise classification and identification of various diseases by discerning intricate patterns and extracting distinctive features from the images. The use of deep learning-based approaches can significantly improve the accuracy of disease diagnosis, allowing farmers to make informed decisions about how to manage their crops.

Accurate diagnosis can lead to the implementation of appropriate and effective treatments, reducing the spread of diseases and minimizing the impact on yields, quality, and revenue. Moreover, the use of deep learning-based approaches can help reduce the environmental impact of using pesticides and other chemicals, as farmers can use the right amount of pesticides and fungicides based on accurate disease diagnosis.

B. Objectives

The problem addressed in this chapter is the accurate and timely diagnosis of diseases in fruits and vegetable crops in the context of precision agriculture. The goal is to develop a robust and efficient approach that utilizes augmented datasets and a convolutional neural network (CNN) model to accurately classify and diagnose diseases in crops. This approach aims to leverage the concept of digital twin (DT) or simulation of DT by using the augmented datasets to simulate and represent the virtual environment of the crops, allowing for the training and evaluation of the CNN model in a digital representation of the real-world agricultural scenario.

The specific challenges include the identification of diseases based on visual symptoms, the need for accurate and automated classification in real-world scenarios, and the requirement for timely interventions to mitigate the impact of diseases on agricultural productivity. The paper aims to propose a solution that improves the accuracy of disease diagnosis, enables a quick response by farmers, and enhances the overall crop management practices in the field of precision agriculture.

The objectives of this chapter are as follows:

- To develop an intelligent automated setup utilizing computer vision and machine learning-based techniques to enable the early detection and diagnosis of crop diseases
- To assess the efficacy of various machine learning algorithms in disease classification and detection, emphasizing the strengths inherent in CNNs
- To compare the effectiveness of traditional feature extraction methods and deep learning techniques, such as CNNs, in crop disease identification and classification, emphasizing the benefits of CNNs in capturing complex features
- To demonstrate the potential of an autonomous disease identification and diagnosis system, utilizing the CNN model and augmented datasets, in improving crop yield and

reducing the economic and environmental impact of crop diseases

- To contribute to the body of research on computer vision and machine learning to detect and categorize crop diseases and provide insights for further development and improvement of these methods, including their integration with digital twin (DT) or simulation of DT concepts.

C. Significance

The proposed deep learning-oriented approach for diagnosing ailments in fruits and vegetables has significant implications for the efficiency and sustainability of the industry as well as for reducing the use of harmful chemicals and enhancing food security. Firstly, accurately diagnosing diseases can help farmers make informed decisions about how to manage their crops, leading to improved yields and higher revenues. By using the proposed deep learning-based approach, farmers can take appropriate measures, such as using the right pesticides or fungicides and controlling the spread of the disease. This can reduce the need for overuse of pesticides and other chemicals, which may have unfavorable effects on nature and human health. The integration of this approach with the concept of digital twin (DT) or simulation of DT can provide farmers with a virtual representation of their crops, allowing for simulations and predictions to optimize disease management strategies.

Secondly, the proposed approach can help enhance food security by improving the quality and quantity of produce. Accurate disease diagnosis enables timely interventions and treatments, reducing crop losses and ensuring a steady supply of healthy fruits and vegetables. This is especially crucial in meeting the increasing demand for fresh and nutritious produce. By leveraging deep learning-based approaches and the concept of digital twin (DT) or simulation of DT, farmers can optimize their crop management practices, leading to better resource allocation, reduced production costs, and improved overall agricultural sustainability.

Furthermore, the proposed approach of using a CNN model with augmented datasets for disease diagnosis in fruits and vegetables, in conjunction with the concept of digital twin (DT) or simulation of DT, has the potential to revolutionize the fruit and vegetable industry. By improving the accuracy and efficiency of disease diagnosis, this approach can enhance the management practices, reduce the use of harmful chemicals, and contribute to the goal of achieving sustainable and secure food production.

10.2　Literature Review

However, experts agree that insects, crop illnesses, pests, a lack of good disease monitoring and forecasting systems, and crop diseases are major contributors to low yield. The apple industry loses a lot of money every year due to diseases and pests [1]. In July 2013, the valley's apple orchards were hit by a fungus called *Alternaria*. More than 70% of the cultivators were infected, and the illness spread rapidly in the Baramulla and Bandipora regions. Many fruits were lost due to the disease, which, in turn, impacted fruit production [2]. Experts in the field claim that the lack of an effective mechanism for disease forecasting and identification contributed significantly to the rapid spread of this devastating pandemic [2]. If there had been a fast detection system, the damage could have been avoided through early identification of the illness and prompt action.

A workable solution to alleviate the labor-intensive and expensive approach would be an autonomous system that can diagnose diseases at an early stage and give applicable remedies and ideas in a timely manner. As the farmers' "knight in shining armor," this technology has the potential to sustainably increase crop yields by significant margins.

To get over the drawbacks of using manual, time-consuming, and expensive methods, many researchers have sought to expedite the process of disease diagnosis using photographs of leaves. These methods are geared toward early disease detection, with the goal of swiftly administering effective treatment. The vast majority of these techniques use computer vision and machine learning to classify images into a number of categories. Machine learning describes a group of algorithms that can get smarter as they absorb more data. Several popular machine learning algorithms are commonly used for classification tasks, such as decision trees, k-nearest neighbors (kNN), artificial neural networks (ANN), and support vector machines (SVM). Mokhtar *et al.* employed an SVM-based approach to diagnose tomato ailment [3], where SVM seeks to maximize the margin between different categories. The widely recognized approach developed by Dubey and Jalal [4] involved the application of K-means defect segmentation clustering and subsequent defect classification using multi-class SVM. Dandawate and Kokare [5] and Raza *et al.* [6] have also utilized SVM-based techniques for plant disease categorization.

In recent years, there has been a significant shift toward utilizing deep learning techniques, specifically utilizing convolutional neural networks (CNNs) to automatically learn features for computer vision tasks [7]. In contrast to traditional feature extraction methods, which rely on hand-crafted features, CNNs directly learn feature representations from raw input data, such as images. These networks consist of several layers of processing units, where each layer performs a convolution operation to glean characteristics from raw data. The extracted features are then refined by passing through additional layers of processing units that perform operations such as pooling and non-linear activation.

Furthermore, deep learning models can be trained end to end, optimizing the categorization and feature extraction steps jointly and resulting in superior performance compared to traditional methods where feature extraction and classification are treated separately. Several studies have shown the effectiveness of these approaches in various computer vision tasks, such as plant disease detection [8], image classification [9], automatic diagnosis of medical images [10], and more [11]. These results are due to feature extraction capabilities that are more highly discriminatory and tolerant of imperfect input data. Recently, there has been a significant shift toward using automatic feature discovery using deep learning methods in computer vision tasks [7], and it has contributed significantly to the feature extraction and classification tasks which are optimized jointly, resulting in better performance than traditional approaches. It has also outperformed the traditional manually designed features in many computer vision tasks due to their ability to learn features that are more discriminative and robust to changes in the image, etc., such as [8] and [9] focus on tomato diseases, discussing classification and symptom visualization. [10] provides an overview and recommendations for using deep learning in plant disease diagnosis. [11] proposes an automatic leaf disease detection approach. [12] has introduced a framework for pest classification in tomato plants using transfer learning techniques. In their study, Prakash et al. [13] proposed an optimized convolutional neural network approach for detecting and classifying crop diseases, whereas Pradhan et al. [14] conducted a comparative analysis of deep convolutional neural network models to differentiate between apple leaf diseases. [15] pays attention to a neural ensemble trained with transfer learning for identifying plant leaf diseases. [16] presents a transfer learning approach for multi-crop leaf disease classification. Narmadha et al. [17] introduced a deep transfer learning-based model specifically for rice plant disease detection. Additionally, Saeed et al. [18] used convolutional neural networks trained with transfer learning to identify illnesses in tomato leaves intelligently. The studies by J. Wan et al. [19], K. He et al. [20], and Benkhaddra et al. [21] cover deep learning for content-based image retrieval, deep residual learning for image recognition, and the design of a consensus activation function-enabled neural network for smart healthcare using BIoT.

A. Gap analysis

Conducting a gap analysis is crucial in research and problem-solving as it helps identify disparities between the current state and desired goals,

Table 10.1 Gap analysis.

The apple industry suffers significant financial losses each year due to diseases and pests.
The lack of a good disease monitoring and forecasting system contributes to the rapid spread of diseases like Alternaria.
Manual and time-consuming methods for disease identification are not efficient. An autonomous system for early disease diagnosis and timely remedies is needed.
Traditional machine learning algorithms (SVM, kNN, ANN, and decision trees) have been used for disease classification, but there is a shift towards deep learning techniques.
Deep learning models, specifically convolutional neural networks (CNNs), have shown superior performance in feature extraction and classification tasks compared to traditional methods.
CNNs learn features automatically from raw input data, eliminating the need for hand-crafted features. Deep learning models can optimize feature extraction and classification jointly, leading to better performance.
CNNs have shown promising results in various computer vision tasks, including plant disease detection.

highlighting areas requiring improvement or advancement as mentioned in Table 10.1.

These gaps indicate the need for an improved and automated system for disease identification and monitoring in the agricultural industry. The shift toward deep learning techniques, particularly CNNs, highlights their potential to address by overcoming the limitations of traditional methods. CNNs enhance both the accuracy and efficiency of disease diagnosis.

10.3 Major Fruit Diseases in the Valley

Pests and diseases pose a major challenge to horticulture in Kashmir, specifically:

- Bacterial apple scab attacks not only the leaves but also the fruit and results in round, corky areas on the skin of the fruit that are gray or brown in color. Severely damaged leaves could turn yellow and drop.
- Alternaria, another bacterial illness, causes brown, round spots to the surface of affected leaves.

- Sooty blotch, a fungus, leads to the formation of marks on the surface of fruits that are green, sooty, or foggy.
- Flyspeck, another fungus, results in glossy spherical spots on the fruit's surface that resemble the excrement of flies. These spots are elevated and appear in clusters. Powdery mildew, a fungus that manifests as a white or gray powder on the undersides of leaves, results in tiny and malformed fruits.
- Apple mosaic (ApMV), a viral illness that is widespread in India, appears as dazzling cream patches on springtime leaves that can later develop necrotic in the summer.
- Marssonina leaf blotch (MLB), an infectious fungal disease, primarily affects the upper surface of leaves. It manifests as circular areas with a dark green coloration, which progressively transforms into a brown hue.

10.4 Methodology

As shown in Figure 10.1, the operational procedure for the proposed method may be broken down into three distinct phases as follows:

1) Data preparation: This is a crucial aspect of deep learning, as it provides the necessary input for these models to learn from. However, for this particular chapter, there is no pre-existing dataset of sufficient size that can be used. Thus, it is essential to generate a new dataset for the chapter. This involves collecting and organizing images of leaves and fruits from different types of apples that have been damaged or affected by various diseases.

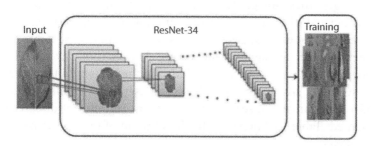

Figure 10.1 Overview of the proposed methodology [23].

2) Model training: This is where we use a convolutional neural network (CNN) to classify illnesses in apples. The most significant ability of deep learning models is to learn from data automatically, without any human involvement. The training-learned features of the model are more precise and useful than the manually created features. To train our model, we employ transfer learning to initialize the model's parameters, followed by fine-tuning using the dataset.

3) Classification: This is when the finalized version of the deep learning model is used. The algorithm can determine the sort of disease that has damaged a plant based on an illustration of a sickened leaf, captured and uploaded by the user.

A. Dataset preparation

For this chapter, we focused on three types of illnesses, namely, Alternaria, Marssonina leaf blotch (MLB), and powdery mildew, out of the eight that are common in the valley, along with seven apple varieties as sample data given in Figure 10.2. Our primary source of information was the Himachal Pradesh Horticulture Department, which cultivates various fruit types for scientific and educational purposes. We collected a dataset of nearly 6,000 pictures of diseased as well as healthy leaves, with the data mostly collected during June–August as sample data given in Figure 10.3, when plant diseases are prevalent. We used various mobile phone brands and digital cameras to capture each photo manually. To ensure a robust generalization of our model to unseen data, we included images with varying illumination and quality in our dataset. We want our model to be applicable in real-world scenarios having blurry, low-light photos. That is why having the same source data for both the training and testing sets is so important. Our dataset comprises a total of 70,295 images, which are categorized into 38 different classes within the training class as mentioned in Figure 10.4. The testing class consists of 8,795 images, while the validation class contains 8,777 images. These images represent a diverse range of plant species and their associated diseases. Images of many different kinds of plants, such as tomatoes, grapes, oranges, soybeans, squash, potatoes, maize (corn), strawberries, peaches, apples, blueberries, cherries (both sweet and sour), bell peppers, and raspberries, are included in the dataset. In total, there are 14 unique plant species included in the dataset. Additionally, the dataset covers a wide range of diseases, with a total of 26 different diseases being represented. Table 10.2 presents the distribution of images across the different classes.

Figure 10.2 Dataset from each class: (a) Alternaria, (b) powdery mildew, (c) Marsonina.

(*Continued*)

(d) Healthy

Figure 10.2 (Continued) Dataset from each class: (d) healthy.

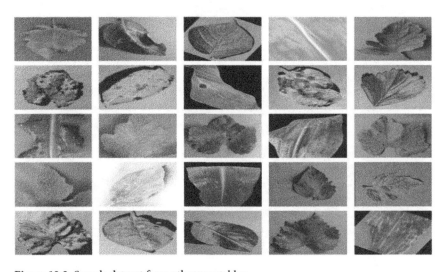

Figure 10.3 Sample dataset from other vegetables.

B. Model development

In the context of model development, this section focuses on the construction and fine-tuning of a convolutional neural network (CNN) for image classification tasks. CNNs are chosen for their ability to learn intricate

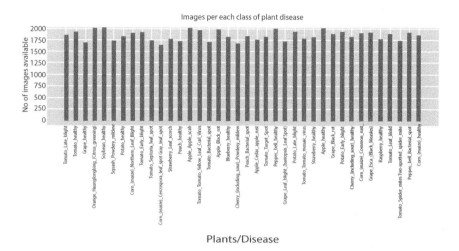

Figure 10.4 Total count for each class.

features in visual data, making them suitable for pattern recognition challenges such as object identification and picture classification [19].

For this study, we utilize a pre-trained version of the CNN known as ResNet-34, developed by Microsoft Research Asia [20]. Pre-trained models are preferred because they reduce the training time and enhance the accuracy, especially when working with limited training data [22]. In this chapter, we delve into the architecture of ResNet-34, consisting of 16 residual blocks, and its application to our target dataset as mentioned in Figure 10.5.

The training process aims to minimize loss and achieve high accuracy, with our suggested model reaching an accuracy of 97% after 50 iterations. Additionally, we detail the implementation of the ResNet18 model, a highly effective CNN for image classification, and the incorporation of a custom Channel Attention layer for improved feature extraction.

The ResNet18 model is constructed by combining ResNet blocks, which consist of convolutional layers, batch normalization, ReLU activation, and shortcut connections. This model's architecture includes global average pooling and a fully connected layer with softmax activation for classification.

The training process involves TensorFlow, optimization techniques, loss functions, and data preprocessing. Our methodology leverages the ResNet18 architecture, channel attention, and well-established building

Table 10.2 Plant disease dataset.

Name	Tomato late blight	Tomato healthy	Grape healthy	Orange Haunglongbing (Citrus greening)	Soybean healthy	Squash powdery mildew
No. of images	1,851	1,926	1,692	2,010	2,022	1,736
Name	Apple Apple scab	Tomato Tomato Yellow Leaf Curl Virus	Tomato Bacterial spot	Apple Black rot	Blueberry healthy	Cherry (including sour) Powdery mildew
No. of images	2,016	1,961	1,702	1,987	1,816	1,683
Name	Potato healthy	Corn (maize) Northern Leaf Blight	Tomato Early blight	Tomato Septoria leaf spot	Corn (maize) Cercospora leaf spot Gray leaf spot	Strawberry Leaf scorch
No. of images	1,824	1,908	1,920	1,745	1,642	1,774
Name	Peach Bacterial spot	Apple Cedar apple rust	Tomato Target Spot	Pepper, bell healthy	Grape Leaf blight (Isariopsis Leaf Spot)	Potato Late blight
No. of images	1,838	1,760	1,827	1,988	1,722	1,939

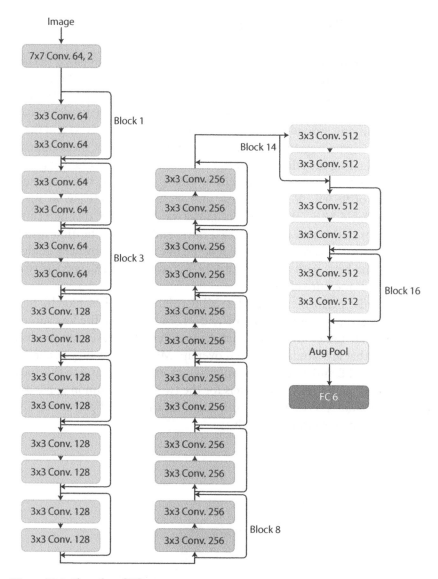

Figure 10.5 Flow chart [23].

blocks to achieve robust and effective results for image classification tasks. The subsequent sections will elaborate on the experimental setup, results, and discussions, highlighting the ResNet18 model's performance and contributions to our research objectives.

10.5   Results and Discussion

The suggested model's classification performance on our prepared dataset is noted and given in Figure 10.6 as a confusion matrix. In the context of disease diagnosis, accuracy, recall, specificity, precision, and F-measure have been used to evaluate the performance of a predictive model in correctly identifying individuals who have a disease (true positives) and those who do not (true negatives). Performance metrics are the most important for evaluating the efficacy of categorization algorithms. Our suggested model has attained accuracy as precision, recall, specificity, and F-measure (F1-score) of 96.9%, 96.85%, 99.3%, and 96.85%, respectively, as mentioned in Table 10.3. There are straightforward ways for distinguishing healthy (normal) leaves from diseased ones, and the classification results for the healthy class are favorable. Out of the five diseases, powdery mildew performs the best, with accuracy of 99.1%, recall of 99.2%, specificity of 99.8%, and F-measure of 98.9%.

Our model performed worst for MLB (Marssonina leaf blotch) than any other category, with only 93.3% and 94.3% accuracy. The low success rate can be attributed to the fact that many different diseases can produce symptoms that are similar and even overlap. Misdiagnosis may occur, for instance, if MLB and scab share similar symptoms. According to this focal point, the PPV and sensitivity levels for the two most common apple diseases (scab and Alterneria) are both high. In a positive light, fewer FNs occur when the recall value is high.

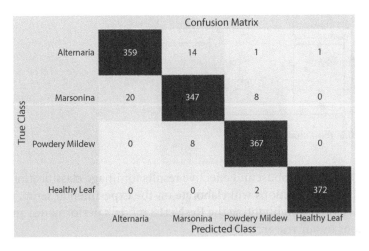

Figure 10.6 Confusion matrix.

Table 10.3 Performance metrics for the proposed model.

Metrics	Formula	Value
Accuracy	$\dfrac{\text{Number of correctly classified samples}}{\text{Total number of samples}}$	97.2%
Precision	$\dfrac{\text{Number of true positive samples}}{\text{Number of true positive samples + number of false positive samples}}$	96.9%
Recall	$\dfrac{\text{Number of true positive samples}}{\text{Number of true positive samples + number of false negative samples}}$	96.85%
F-measure	$\dfrac{2 \times \text{precision} \times \text{recall}}{\text{Precision + recall}}$	96.85%

A. Comparison with other models

InceptionNet, a deep convolutional neural network (CNN) architecture, is intended to collect characteristics at various spatial scales by utilizing multiple convolutional filters with variable kernel sizes. The stacking of many modules to form InceptionNet's architecture is what gives it its distinctive look. Each module comprises of numerous parallel convolutional layers with various kernel sizes, followed by a pooling layer and a concatenation layer that joins the results from the parallel routes. By doing so, the network is able to gather characteristics at various spatial resolutions and combine them into a single representation that can be applied to classification.

The training and validation accuracy for a 17-epoch InceptionNet model are displayed in Figure 10.7. The model's excellent training accuracy of 98.99% showed that it could successfully fit the training set of data. The model may have overfit the training data and failed to generalize effectively to new data because the validation accuracy was lower at 81.88%. The model's inability to effectively learn from the validation data is further supported by the significant validation loss values observed in later epochs.

EfficientNetB0: This is a neural network design that combines a variety of effective building pieces, such as squeeze-and-excitation blocks and depthwise separable convolutions, to minimize the amount of parameters and calculations needed while retaining high accuracy. EfficientNetB0 is employed for many computer vision applications, such as picture classification and object recognition, etc.

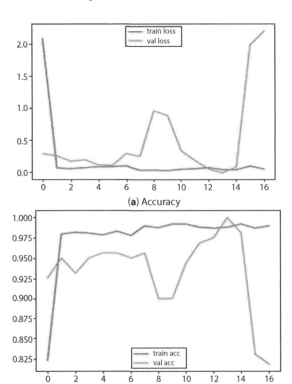

Figure 10.7 Accuracy and loss curve for InceptionNet.

The model's training process consisted of 17 epochs, as evident from the provided training results. At the end of each epoch, the model's performance was evaluated on a separate validation set, and the corresponding loss and accuracy values were recorded (refer to Figures 10.8a and 10.8b). The loss value indicates the dissimilarity between the model's predictions and the actual values, with lower values indicating better performance. In this case, the initial loss was 1.69 and gradually decreased to 1.39 by the fourth epoch. Subsequently, the loss fluctuated between 1.36 and 1.46 for the remaining epochs.

A model's accuracy is measured by the proportion of times its predictions are spot on, with higher values indicating better performance. In this instance, the initial accuracy was 0.34 and varied between 0.36 and 0.39 for the subsequent epochs.

The model was tested on a validation set to determine how well it can perform with novel, unseen data. The results indicate that the model achieved a relatively modest maximum validation accuracy of 0.3125.

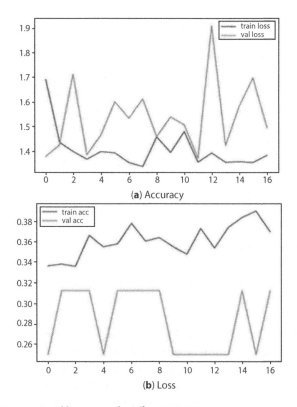

Figure 10.8 Accuracy and loss curve for efficient net B0.

This suggests that the model might not have effectively generalized to fresh data. It is important to note that optimizing the model's performance could involve adjusting the hyperparameters, augmenting the training data, or applying transfer learning techniques.

Table 10.4 Comparison table for different models.

Model name	Train accuracy	Validation accuracy	Train loss	Validation loss
Proposed model	0.9687	0.9511	1.1423	1.1249
InceptionNet	0.9899	0.8188	0.0615	2.2035
EfficientNet B0	0.3901	0.25	1.3585	0.25

It can be demonstrated that the proposed model outperformed the other two models in terms of both accuracy and loss during training and validation. A high training accuracy of 0.9687 and a high validation accuracy of 0.9511 show that the proposed model successfully classifies the images in the dataset. Further evidence that the suggested model generalizes well to new data is its low training loss of 1.1423 as well as its low validation loss of 1.1249. Alternatively, InceptionNet showed overfitting to the training data by achieving a high training accuracy of 0.9899 but a much lower validation accuracy of 0.8188. With a training accuracy of 0.3901 and a validation accuracy of 0.2500, EfficientNetB0 performed poorly, as summarized in Table 10.4.

10.6   Extended Experiment

Furthermore, ResNet18 with same additional features is trained and tested on the same dataset and explained as follows:

A. Model architecture: ResNet18 with channel attention
We present the architecture of our implemented ResNet18 model, which has been designed for image classification tasks. The model has various layers, such as a fully connected layer, a batch normalization layer, and a convolutional layer. The summary of the model, obtained through TensorFlow, is provided in Table 10.5.

The architecture comprises the following key components:

- Conv2D layer: The initial convolutional layer (conv2d) takes the input image and applies a 2D convolution operation, producing feature maps.
- Batch normalization layer: In order to increase training stability and convergence, the batch normalization layer standardizes the activations from the preceding layer.
- ResNet Blocks: The ResNet18 model consists of a sequence of eight ResnetBlock layers (*resnet$_b$lock, resnet$_b$lock$_1$*, ..., *resnet$_b$lock$_7$*). Each ResnetBlock is responsible for extracting and refining features. The blocks include convolutional layers, batch normalization, ReLU activation, and a shortcut Global average pooling: Following the ResNet blocks, a global average pooling 2d layer is applied to reduce spatial dimensions by computing the average value of each feature map. This step aggregates spatial information into a vector.

Table 10.5 Summary of the ResNet18 model architecture.

Layer (type)	Output shape	Parameter number
conv2d (Conv2D)	Multiple	1,792
Batch normalization (BatchNorm)	Multiple	256
resnet block	Multiple	74,948
resnet block 1	Multiple	74,948
resnet block 2	Multiple	233,480
resnet block 3	Multiple	298,376
resnet block 4	Multiple	929,808
resnet block 5	Multiple	1,190,672
resnet block 6	Multiple	3,711,008
resnet block 7	Multiple	4,757,024
Global average pooling 2d (GAP)	Multiple	0
Dense	Multiple	19,494
Total parameters		11,291,806
Trainable parameters		11,282,206
Non-trainable parameters		9,600

- Dense layer: The final dense layer is a fully connected layer that performs the classification task. It maps the extracted features to the desired number of classes using the softmax activation function.

The model contains a total of 11,291,806 parameters, with 11,282,206 parameters being trainable. The non-trainable parameters are associated with the batch normalization layers.

The presented ResNet18 architecture provides a powerful and effective framework for image classification tasks, combining the advantages of deep convolutional networks with residual connections. In the following sections, we will describe the training process, evaluation metrics, and experimental results achieved using this model architecture.

B. Model compilation and optimization

To optimize our ResNet18 model, we employed the cyclical learning rate (CLR) technique, which allows for the dynamic adjustment of the learning rate during training. We initialized the cyclical learning rate object with the following parameters:

- initial learning rate: the initial learning rate at the start of training.
- maximal learning rate: the maximum learning rate that the cycle reaches.
- step size: the total number of training steps (epochs) in one cycle. In this case, we set it to the length of the training set.
- scale fn: A scaling function that determines the learning rate schedule within a cycle. Here we used a scale function that decreases the learning rate by half for each successive cycle.
- scale mode: The mode for scaling the learning rate. In this case, we set it to "cycle" to ensure the learning rate scales back to the initial value at the end of each cycle.

Next, we configured the Adam optimizer with the learning rate set to the cyclical learning rate object. Additionally, we specified a clip value of 0.1 to limit the magnitude of gradient updates.

Finally, we compiled the model using the "categorical cross-entropy" loss function, which is suitable for multi-class classification tasks. The optimizer and evaluation metric (accuracy) were also specified during the compilation process.

By employing the cyclical learning rate technique and configuring the Adam optimizer, we aimed to enhance the training process and improve the model's ability to converge to an optimal solution. The model is now ready for training and evaluation using the compiled settings. The model was compiled with the Adam optimizer, which used the cyclical learning rate as the learning rate and a clip value of 0.1. The loss function used was categorical cross-entropy, and the accuracy metric was used for evaluation. During training, the model's loss decreased, and its accuracy increased with each epoch. The model achieved a high validation accuracy of 98.56% after 10 epochs, indicating good performance on unseen data as depicted in Figure 10.6.

The training results show the performance of the model during the training process. Let us analyze the key observations from the training results:

- Loss and accuracy trends: The loss values consistently decreased from epoch to epoch, indicating that the model was learning and improving its predictions over time. This is supported by the increasing trend in accuracy, where the model's ability to correctly classify images improved with each epoch.

- Validation performance: To test the model's capacity to generalize to new data, we tracked the validation loss and accuracy. The validation loss decreased significantly throughout the training, indicating that the model was not overfitting and was able to generalize well. The validation accuracy also improved over time, reaching a high of 98.56% accuracy in the final epoch.

- Comparison between training and validation: The training accuracy (98.06% in the last epoch) was slightly higher than the validation accuracy (98.56% in the last epoch), suggesting that the model might have slightly overfit the training data. However, the difference is relatively small, indicating that the model's generalization performance was still good.

- High accuracy: The achieved accuracy of 98.56% on the validation set is quite impressive, indicating that the model can effectively classify plant diseases based on the given dataset. This high accuracy suggests that the model has learned meaningful patterns and features from the images to distinguish between different plant diseases.

- Early stopping point: It is worth noting that the training could have been stopped earlier as the validation accuracy started to plateau around the sixth epoch. This could have saved computational resources while still achieving a similar level of performance.

Overall, the training results demonstrate that the model, trained using a cyclical learning rate and the Adam optimizer, was successful in learning to classify plant diseases with high accuracy. The model's performance suggests its potential usefulness in practical applications for diagnosing and monitoring plant health.

C. Attainment

This table presents a summary of key metrics used to evaluate the performance of a model. These metrics provide insights into the model's effectiveness in classification tasks, particularly in identifying diseased plants. The table includes metrics such as loss, recall, precision, true positives, true negatives, false negatives, false positives, specificity, sensitivity, accuracy, and the F1 score. These values are essential for assessing the model's performance in tasks related to plant disease detection and classification.

Based on the evaluation metrics, as mentioned in Table 10.6 the model exhibits exceptional performance in multiple aspects. The low loss value indicates that, on average, the model's predictions deviate only slightly from the true values, demonstrating its robust predictive capability. Additionally, the model achieves high scores in recall, precision, and specificity. The recall score signifies its effectiveness in correctly identifying positive samples (diseased plants) among the actual positives, while the precision score reflects its accuracy in predicting positive samples without misclassifying healthy plants. The high specificity score indicates its proficiency in identifying negative samples (healthy plants) accurately. Plot of accuracy and loss curve is shown in Figure 10.9. Model evaluation metrics are shown in Table 10.6.

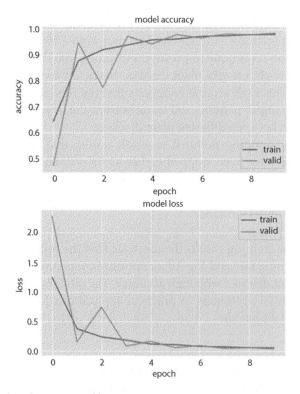

Figure 10.9 Plot of accuracy and loss curve.

Table 10.6 Model evaluation metrics.

Metric	Value
Loss	0.0384
Recall	0.9867
Precision	0.9898
True positive (TP)	8678
True negative (TN)	325326
False negative (FN)	117
False positive (FP)	89
Specificity (SPE)	1.0
Sensitivity (SEN)	0.9998
Accuracy	0.9878
F1 score	0.9883

10.7   Concluding Remarks

Based on the results presented, the proposed model achieved promising classification performance on the prepared dataset. It demonstrated high accuracy, precision, recall, specificity, and F1-score, with values ranging from 96.85% to 99.3%. The results indicate that the model is effective in correctly identifying individuals with the disease (true positives) and those without (true negatives). The classification results for the healthy class were favorable, indicating that the model can accurately distinguish healthy (normal) leaves from diseased ones. However, the accuracy for Marssonina leaf blotch (MLB) was lower compared to other classes, suggesting that there may be challenges in accurately diagnosing this disease due to similar symptoms with other diseases. In terms of model comparison, the proposed model outperformed InceptionNet and EfficientNetB0 in terms of accuracy, training loss, validation loss, and generalization to new data. While InceptionNet achieved high training accuracy, it suffered from overfitting, as evidenced by the lower validation accuracy. EfficientNetB0 demonstrated poor performance with low training and validation accuracy.

The extended experiment with the ResNet18 model showed promising results as well. The model architecture, consisting of convolutional layers, batch normalization, ResNet blocks, global average pooling, and a dense layer, proved effective for image classification tasks. The model had over 11 million trainable parameters and achieved good results. To optimize the ResNet18 model, the cyclical learning rate (CLR) technique was employed, allowing for a dynamic adjustment of the learning rate during training. The Adam optimizer was used with a clip value of 0.1 to limit gradient updates. The model was compiled with the categorical cross-entropy loss function and achieved good accuracy. Based on these results, the proposed model and the ResNet18 model with CLR optimization show promise for disease diagnosis based on leaf images. Further research can focus on enhancing the accuracy for challenging diseases like Marssonina leaf blotch (MLB) and exploring techniques to improve generalization to new data. Additionally, investigating other deep learning architectures and techniques, such as transfer learning, can be valuable for further improving the classification performance.

For future scope, a model may involve developing a disease detection and recommendation system that can provide information about illnesses, localize affected areas, and contribute data for studying diseases, analyzing fruit yields, and predicting outbreaks. Such a system would have the potential to support agricultural professionals and empower farmers in effectively managing crop diseases.

References

1. Beigh, M., Peer, Q.J.A., Kher, S., Ganai, N., Disease and pest management in apple: Farmers' perception and adoption in J&K state. *J. Appl. Natural Sci.*, 7, 1, 293–297, 2015.
2. Bhat, K., Peerzada, S., Ali, A. *et al.*, Alternaria epidemic of apple in Kashmir. *Afr. J. Microbiol. Res.*, 9, 12, 831–837, 2015.
3. Kumar, A., Kumar, S.A., Dutt, V., Shitharth, S., Tripathi, E., IoT based arrhythmia classification using the enhanced hunt optimization-based deep learning. *Expert Syst.*, 40, 7, e13298, 2023. https://doi.org/10.1111/ exsy.13298.
4. Dubey, S.R. and Jalal, A.S., Detection and classification of apple fruit diseases using complete local binary patterns, in: *2012 Third International Conference on Computer and Communication Technology*, IEEE, pp. 346–351, 2012.
5. Dandawate, Y. and Kokare, R., An automated approach for classification of plant diseases towards development of futuristic decision support system in indian perspective, in: *2015 International conference on advances in computing, communications and informatics (ICACCI)*, pp. 794–799, IEEE, 2015.

6. Chandrasekaran, S., Dutt, V., Vyas, N., Kumar, R., Student Sentiment Analysis Using Various Machine Learning Techniques. *2023 International Conference on Artificial Intelligence and Smart Communication (AISC)*, Greater Noida, India, pp. 104–107, 2023, doi: 10.1109/AISC56616.2023.10085018.

7. Kumar, A., Rathore, P.S., Dubey, A.K. *et al.*, LTE-NBP with holistic UWB-WBAN approach for the energy efficient biomedical application. *Multimed Tools Appl.*, 82, 25, 39797–811, 2023 Oct.

8. Saleem, M.H., Potgieter, J., Arif, K.M., Plant disease detection and classification by deep learning. *Plants*, 8, 11, 468, 2019.

9. Kumar, A., Swarn., A., Dutt., V., Sitharth., S., Triapthi., E., IoT based Arrhythmia Classification Using the Enhanced Hunt Optimization based Deep Learning, Expert Systems. *J. Knowl. Eng.*, 40, 7, e13298, 2023 Aug. ISSN:1468-0394.s.

10. Ilyas, B., Kumar, A., Setitra, M.A., Bensalem, Z.E.A., Lei, H., Prevention of DDoS attacks using an optimized deep learning approach in blockchain technology. *Trans. Emerging. Telecommun. Technol.*, 34, 4, e4729, 2023.

11. Chowdhury, M.E., Rahman, T., Khandakar, A., Ayari, M.A., Khan, A.U., Khan, M.S., Al-Emadi, N., Reaz, M.B., II, Islam, M.T., Ali, S.H.M., Automatic and reliable leaf disease detection using deep learning techniques. *AgriEngineering*, 3, 2, 294–312, 2021.

12. Pattnaik, G., Shrivastava, V.K., Parvathi, K., Transfer learning-based framework for classification of pest in tomato plants. *Appl. Artif. Intell.*, 34, 13, 981–993, 2020.

13. Dutt, V. and Sharma, S., 9 - Artificial intelligence and technology in weather forecasting and renewable energy systems: emerging techniques and worldwide studies, in: *Woodhead Publishing Series in Energy, Artificial Intelligence for Renewable Energy Systems*, pp. 189–207, Woodhead Publishing, 2022, ISBN 9780323903967, https://doi.org/10.1016/ B978-0-323-90396-7.00009-2.

14. Pradhan, P., Kumar, B., Mohan, S., Comparison of various deep convolutional neural network models to discriminate apple leaf diseases using transfer learning. *J. Plant Dis. Prot.*, 129, 6, 1461–1473, 2022.

15. Srivastav, A.L., Markandeya, Patel, N. *et al.*, Concepts of circular economy for sustainable management of electronic wastes: challenges and management options. *Environ. Sci. Pollut. Res.*, 30, 48654–48675, 2023. https://doi.org/10.1007/s11356-023-26052-y.

16. Paymode, A.S. and Malode, V.B., Transfer learning for multi-crop leaf disease image classification using convolutional neural network vgg. *Artif. Intell. Agric.*, 6, 23–33, 2022.

17. Narmadha, R., Sengottaiyan, N., Kavitha, R., Deep transfer learning based rice plant disease detection model. *Intell. Autom. Soft Comput.*, 31, 2, 2022 Feb 1.

18. Kumar, A., Kumar, S.A., Dutt, V., Dubey, A.K., Narang, S., A Hybrid Secure Cloud Platform Maintenance Based on Improved Attribute-Based

Encryption Strategies. *Int. J. Interact. Multimed. Artif. Intell. IJIMAI,* 8, 2, 150–157, 2023.

19. Wan, J., Wang, D., Hoi, S.C.H., Wu, P., Zhu, J., Zhang, Y., Li, J., Deep learning for content-based image retrieval: A comprehensive study, in: *Proceedings of the 22nd ACM international conference on Multimedia,* pp. 157–166, 2014.

20. He, K., Zhang, X., Ren, S., Sun, J., Deep residual learning for image recognition, in: *Proceedings of the IEEE Conference on Computer Vision and Pattern Recognition,* pp. 770–778, 2016.

21. Benkhaddra, I., Kumar, A., Setitra, M.A. *et al.,* Design and Development of Consensus Activation Function Enabled Neural Network-Based Smart Healthcare Using BIoT. *Wirel. Pers. Commun.,* 130, 1549–1574, 2023. https://doi.org/10.1007/s11277-023-10344-0.

22. Wani, M.A., Bhat, F.A., Afzal, S., Khan, A.I., Training supervised deep learning networks, in: *Advances in Deep Learning,* pp. 31–52, Springer, Singapore, 2020.

23. Khan, A.I., Quadri, S.M.K., Banday, S., Deep learning for apple diseases: classification and identification. *Int. J. Comput. Intell. Stud.,* 10, 1, 1–12, 2021.

11

A Simulation-Based Study of a Digital Twin Model of the Air Purifier System in Chandigarh Using LabVIEW

Jyoti Verma[1], Monika Sethi[2]*, Vidhu Baggan[2], Manish Snehi[1] and Jatin Arora[2]

[1]Punjabi University Patiala, Patiala, Punjab, India
[2]Chitkara University Institute of Engineering and Technology, Chitkara University, Patiala, Punjab, India

Abstract

Digital Twin's popularity is growing in the past few years due to its great potential in manufacturing, healthcare, and other electronic infrastructures. A digital twin presents a replica of physical processes, plants, objects, and systems and hence helps in easy analysis, optimization, and real-time monitoring. Digital twin technology has the potential to efficiently innovate digital systems to reduce cost and increase safety. Due to the rise in computational power and availability of data, its importance is growing in decision making, problem solving, and system development. Digital twin technology creates virtual duplicates of physical systems for real-time simulation and analysis. In this chapter, the authors have presented LabVIEW's potential to provide a digital twin simulator model for Chandigarh's air purifier system. The chapter starts with an overview of Chandigarh's air pollution statistics and digital twin technology's role in air quality monitoring. After a literature analysis on pollutants in the air and the quality of air monitoring, LabVIEW and its digital twin model for simulation capabilities are introduced. The methodology section discusses Chandigarh's air purification system, LabVIEW simulation model components, data gathering, and analysis methods to design a digital twin. The chapter further presents simulation results and comparisons to real-world data. The research discusses the research findings and the LabVIEW simulation model's applications and drawbacks. The research findings help create efficient air quality monitoring systems that can inform Chandigarh's air quality strategy.

Corresponding author: monika.sethi@chitkara.edu.in

Abhineet Anand, Anita Sardana, Abhishek Kumar, Srikanta Kumar Mohapatra and Shikha Gupta (eds.) Simulation Techniques of Digital Twin in Real-Time Applications: Design Modeling and Implementation, (243–260) © 2024 Scrivener Publishing LLC

The report concludes with a research summary and future research ideas. The study shows how LabVIEW can generate simulation representations of digital twins and solve real-world problems like air pollution monitoring.

Keywords: Digital twin, LabVIEW, air quality, Chandigarh, India, simulation

11.1 Introduction

Computer engineering, mathematics, and data analytics have helped digital twin technology evolve. They accurately model physical systems that take time, resources, and skill. High-performance computers, machine learning, and artificially intelligent systems make the digital twin generation more accessible and faster [1]. Digital twins simulate physical scenarios in real time. Data from sensors that are modeling and other sources is used to build an exact and comprehensive system model. The model can analyze a system's behavior and anticipate its performance. Digital twins have many advantages. It can optimize industrial production by detecting shortcomings and development opportunities [2]. The use of digital twins is becoming essential for making choices and solving issues as physical systems generate more data. Due to their real-time simulation and analysis of complex systems, digital twins will transform the design, building, and functioning of physical structures in many industries. Substantial automobiles, industrial pollution, and car emissions have degraded Chandigarh City's air quality (although it is a least polluted city compared to other cities of India). Particulate matters, nitrogen monoxides, sulfur compounds, monoxide compounds, and dust pollute the air. Indoors and outside, these pollutants come from different sources. Air pollution restrictions vary by source, country, and additional variables [3]. In Tribune Chowk, Sector 26, the Chandigarh pollution control committee established India's tallest air purifier tower, which covers 500 m. The air purification system must be monitored and evaluated to improve the air quality. Digital twin technologies and LabVIEW can be used to build a Chandigarh air purifier digital twin simulator model. This study evaluates how well the LabVIEW simulation framework simulates the air purifier system's performance. This study aims to propose a digital twin to improve air quality monitoring and development in Chandigarh and elsewhere [4].

11.1.1   Background Information on Chandigarh's Air Pollution Problem

Industrial, vehicular, and stubble burning in northern India's states and Chandigarh have caused serious air pollution around the city. The city's PM2.5 and other pollution levels consistently exceed WHO guidelines. The COVID-19 lockdown temporarily improved the air quality in the city, but long-term solutions are needed to address the problem. Digital twin technology allows real-time air purifier system monitoring and modeling. This study suggests LabVIEW's capacity to simulate Chandigarh's air purification system as a digital twin. Air quality monitors measure both inside and outside air contaminants. It can detect PM2.5, PM10, CO, CO_2, ozone (O_3), NO_2, SO_2, formaldehyde (HCHO), and total volatile organic compounds (TVOCs) [5]. The monitor detects and displays these contaminants in real time. Air quality sensors can help analyze and manage air pollution in homes, companies, educational institutions, and other indoor locations. Sensors measure indoor and outdoor air pollution. These sensors detect particulate pollution, ozone, sulfurous oxides, nitrous oxide, and other harmful compounds. A digital twin can give real-time air quality data to municipality and environmental specialists, helping them improve the air quality. Air quality control devices use many types of sensors. Particulate matter sensors assess air pollution, which can harm human health. Carbon monoxide sensors detect deadly gas [6]. Ozone sensors measure the toxic gas that may trigger respiratory and other health issues. Nitrogen oxide sensors measure combustion engine-produced nitrogen oxides, which pollute the air. Air quality sensors are expensive and hard to get. Technology has made sensors more affordable and accessible, making air quality monitoring easier for people and groups. This allows more widespread and reliable air quality monitoring, which can assist in identifying issues and influencing policy. Air pollution sensors are essential for environmental research. They can track air quality trends, detect pollution sources, and evaluate pollution controls. Sensor data helps pollution control board and environmental specialists enhance the air quality and public health. Figure 11.1 shows the air purification sensors, and their details are discussed as follows [7]:

1. Carbon monoxide sensors: These sensors detect the incomplete combustion of gas, oil, and wood that produced toxic carbon monoxide.

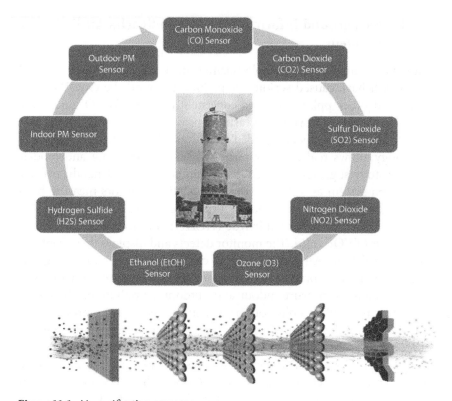

Figure 11.1 Air purification sensors.

2. Carbon dioxide sensors: These sensors monitor airborne CO_2. CO_2 sensors monitor air quality and operate ventilation systems. They can monitor environmental air quality and industrial CO_2 leakage.

3. Sulfur dioxide sensors: Fossil fuel burning produces sulfur dioxide, a severe air pollutant. Industrial SO_2 sensors detect power plants and other pollutant outputs.

4. Nitrogen dioxide sensors: Automobiles and power plants emit NO_2, a major air pollutant. Nitrogen dioxide sensors measure atmospheric nitrogen dioxide concentrations. Indoor and outdoor NO_2 sensors monitor the condition of the air and warn of unsafe amounts.

5. Ozone sensors: These sensors monitor ultraviolet rays and air pollutants that create ozone. Ozone causes smog and respiratory issues. Indoor and outdoor ozone sensors monitor the condition of the air and warn of unsafe amounts.

6. Ethanol sensors: Ethanol, a volatile organic molecule created by sugar fermentation, is used to fuel cars and make alcohol. Industrial ethanol sensors detect ethanol production emissions.

7. Hydrogen sulfide sensors: Organic matter decays to produce hydrogen sulfide, which can be observed in wastewater treatment facilities and other industrial environments. Hydrogen sulfide sensors monitor the condition of the air and warn of unsafe hydrogen sulfide levels.

8. Indoor particulate matter sensors: These sensors measure airborne particulate matter. Indoor air pollution is caused by particulate matter.

9. Outdoor particulate matter sensors: These sensors measure outdoor particulate matter concentration. Urban particulate matter sensors track air quality and warn of unsafe particulate matter levels. They can also track long-distance pollution transport and industrial air quality.

Air quality sensors measure air pollution in a given location. They can be deployed indoors or outside in homes, offices, manufacturing facilities, and other places. Air quality monitors inform the public's wellness, urban planning, and environmental policy. Air quality monitoring tools use electronic printed circuit board (PCBs). PCBs can accurately monitor and evaluate particulates, carbon monoxide, nitrogen oxides, and ozone. Figure 11.2 shows environmental PCBs.

Air purifiers clean the air by removing impurities. Air purifiers do this differently depending on the type. This filter collects allergens such as pollen, dust, and pet dander. HEPA filters contain particles as small as 0.3 μm in air purifiers. Activated carbon filters eliminate pollutants and smell. Ionizers or precipitators of electrostatic charge can also purify air. These appliances charge airborne particles, making them stick to surfaces and each other for easier removal. Air purifiers with filters and ionizers work best. Air purifiers clean the air, improving air quality and maybe health. Electrostatic air purifiers pass air *via* a charged filter. The filter implicated in the opposite direction surface captures charged particles as air goes through. Electrostatic filters collect dust, pollen, and other airborne particles with charged plates or fibers, and ionization chamber air purifiers release negatively charged ions. Airborne particles like pollen, dust, and other pollutants become heavier and fall due to these ions. Negative-ion-producing filaments or needles make up the ionization chamber. Regulated air purifiers filter particles, pollen, smoke, and other particles with the help

Figure 11.2 Air quality PCBs [34].

of activated carbon, HEPA, and pre-filters. The air purifier regulates filter flow to maximize efficiency. Photocatalytic air purifiers circulate air through a catalyst chamber, usually titanium dioxide. When subjected to ultraviolet light, the catalyst material releases free radicals that kill airborne pathogens, viruses, and mold colonies. Photocatalytic disinfection is often used with HEPA filters to purify air [8, 9].

11.1.2   Digital Twin Technology and Its Relevance to Air Quality Monitoring

Digital twins can mimic, monitor, and optimize physical systems and objects. A digital twin embodiment of the air purification system can be used for continuous performance tracking and air quality monitoring situations. This helps identify potential issues, optimize system performance, and create effective air quality control strategies. LabVIEW, a prominent graphical programming language, can simulate complicated systems built on their digital counterparts. It affects air quality surveillance systems with specific data collecting, processing, and visualization interfaces. A digital twin representation of an air purifying system often has numerous levels representing system components. Figure 11.3 shows the evidence of

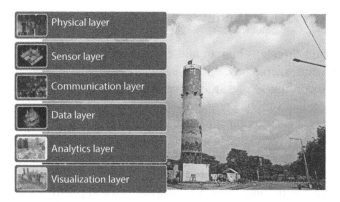

Figure 11.3 Layers in digital twin models for air purification systems [11].

different layers for air purification. The standard air purification digital twin modeling levels are described as follows [10]:

1. Physical layer: Filters, fans, and conduits comprise this layer. The digital twin design simulates system behavior on the physical layer.
2. Control layer: This layer includes air purification system control systems. Algorithms may control the control layer's fan speed, filter settings, and air quality.
3. Data layer: This layer collects and monitor air purification system data. Air quality, flow and pressure sensors may be in the data layer.
4. Analytics layer: This layer analyzes air purification system data. Machine learning simulations may be in the analytics layer for filter lifespan, maintenance difficulties, and system performance.
5. Visualisation layer: The visualization layer may contain 2D or 3D air purification system representations and real-time data visualization tools for system performance monitoring. It consists of the digital twin model's GUI.

These layers provide an air purification system's digital replica, allowing users to mimic and optimize its performance in real time. A digital twin model can increase air quality and energy efficiency by revealing air purification system operations by merging these layers.

11.2   Literature Review

Air pollution threatens human and environmental health worldwide. Air pollution causes, impacts, and control methods have been extensively studied. According to one study, massive transit vehicles, pollution from factories, and automobile emissions contribute to Chandigarh's air pollution. Winter vegetation burning also contributes.

LabVIEW is widely used in data collecting, control systems, and automation. Its interface makes building digital instruments, analyzing information, and interfacing with hardware devices easy. LabVIEW's modularity and flexibility with many programming options and platforms make it perfect for digital twin simulation models. LabVIEW may be used to create digital twin simulations for air purification systems that accurately mimic their behavior. LabVIEW can simulate an air purifier system using sensor and instrument data. The model can anticipate system performance, optimize the system's layout, and evaluate control options. LabVIEW's modularity makes it perfect for design iteration and testing. The simulation model's connectivity with hardware devices lets it interface with sensors and actuators for real-time data collecting and control. LabVIEW simulates digital dual air purifier systems well.

Urban air pollution and its health and environmental effects have been studied extensively recently. Chandigarh has high PM2.5, PM10, sulfur, and nitrogen oxide levels. Digital twin technology is promising for measuring and simulating air quality. A digital replica of a physical system allows controlled simulation and testing. Manufacturing, the aerospace industry, and healthcare have used this technology, and air quality monitoring is being researched. Engineering and science use LabVIEW for data collecting, analysis, control, and simulation. It has been used to build digital twins of wastewater treatment facilities, turbines for wind power, and microgrids. LabVIEW may build the Chandigarh purification system's digital twin simulation model. This study will assess the simulation model's air quality predictions for Chandigarh. Researchers have used digital twins to monitor air quality and manage pollution. Kritzinger et al. [11] suggested a digital twin solution to maximize urban air pollution management techniques using real-time information and simulation models. Ilyas et al. [12] created a digital twin framework for indoor pollution monitoring that models air flow and contaminant diffusion in real time using data from several sensors. Leser et al. [13] used LabVIEW to sample and analyze PM2.5 and PM10 pollutants in real time. Longo et al. [14] used LabVIEW to create a low-cost urban air quality surveillance system, including CO, nitrogen dioxide, and O_3 sensors. These studies show how digital twins and LabVIEW can monitor air quality and regulate pollution. However, more studies are needed to determine these systems' usefulness and scalability in real-world applications, especially in outdoor pollution in the atmosphere [15].

11.3   Methodology

A typical air purifier system includes a mist chamber, water reservoir, sewage tube, and particle filters. The air-cleaning system uses vapor and filtration to remove particles, sulfur, nitrogen, and other hazardous oxides. The mist chamber draws contaminated air and employs a water mist to catch the big particles collected and dump them into a water container [16]. Particulate filters clean the air before releasing it into the environment. The system covers the entire city to monitor and improve air quality. An air filtration system is essential to fighting air pollution and improving the residents' health [17].

The LabVIEW simulation of an air purification system could contain the components listed as follows [18–23]:

1. User interfaces: LabVIEW allows users to interact with the simulation model. This program lets users enter parameters and view simulation results.
2. Data acquisition: LabVIEW's data gathering module collects data from air purifier sensors and devices. The data includes humidity, pressure, temperature, and air quality.
3. Controller: LabVIEW's control module controls air purification. Data and user preferences are used to adjust the configuration methods.
4. Simulation engine: LabVIEW's simulation engine creates an electronic environment purification system. It executes a model of the system's behavior based on input data and control algorithms.
5. Visualization: The LabVIEW visualization module displays simulation results. It shows how the air filtration system works and affects air quality *via* graphics.
6. Data analysis component: LabVIEW analyzes air purification system data. The user can identify data patterns and trends and decide on the study.

When combined, these components might simulate an air purification system extensively. This model could evaluate the system's performance and optimize its operation to improve air quality. Figure 11.4 depicts this study's data collection and processing steps. Air quality sensors can be deployed at many locations to collect data on air pollutants. The data included suspended particulate matter, waste with a width of 10 mm, oxides of nitrogen-containing compounds, and SO_2. LabVIEW simulated the air filtration system using sensor-collected data [24–28].

The acquired data calibrated and validated the LabVIEW simulator model. The model used for the simulation was adjusted to match the air purifier equipment. These changes ensured accuracy. After that, the modeling framework was used to forecast the air purification system's performance under various situations, such as air pollution changes [29–32]. The simulation model was validated by comparing its results to real-world data. The LabVIEW simulation framework's ability to predict the air purification system's performance was tested by comparing its results to other simulation methods. LabVIEW requires data collection and analysis to create a digital twin of a purifying system. These technologies would record the system's actions and create an electronic replica. Sensors simplify air quality, humidity, temperature, and pressure data collection. Coupling these

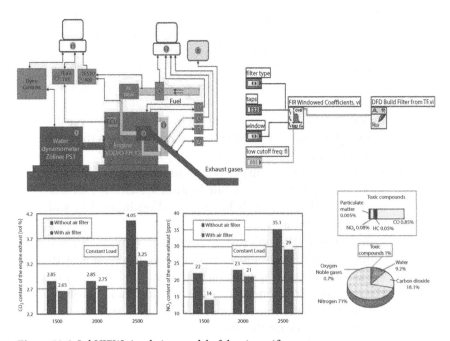

Figure 11.4 LabVIEW simulation model of the air purifier system.

sensors to a microprocessor or data acquisition equipment collects data. LabVIEW can record data from sensors over time [35–37]. This will create a large dataset for digital twin simulation. LabVIEW statistical analysis can analyze data. Correlation, regression, and outlier detection may be included. Machine learning algorithms can be used to find patterns in the data.

Air flow pressure and flow in the air filtration system using CFD can provide a complete digital counterpart of the system's physical attributes [38]. System identification methods can help you find the computational framework that best describes the air purifier system's operation. State-space modeling, response impulse analysis, and response frequency analysis are approaches that can be used to implement machine learning algorithms. The project's aims and requirements will influence the data collection and research methods used to create a purifying system's digital twin [39]. Integrating these approaches can provide a precise and in-depth digital replica model for simulations, evaluation, and optimization [40].

A LabVIEW digital replica of an air purifying system often has numerous components that imitate its operation. The quality of air sensors offers input to the digital replica. A LabVIEW twin may replicate air quality data by creating random or specified moisture, temperature, and air pressure readings. LabVIEW digital twin control algorithms imitate the air purification system functioning. They can replicate air filters, ionizers, and UV lamps. Based on sensor air quality data, computers can mimic components on/off. LabVIEW digital twins for air purification systems need HMIs. Users can communicate with the digital twin, assess air quality, and manage the system. LabVIEW can be used to design the HMI's switches, controls, and graphs. The LabVIEW digital twin's data collection and logging component stores air quality sensors and other system data and analyzes, diagnoses, and optimizes this data. A LabVIEW digital replica can store data in a database or file format for easy access and analysis. LabVIEW digital twins visualize air quality metrics and other system characteristics. This lets users quickly spot data trends and make informed system decisions. LabVIEW offers statistical tools and signal processing methods alongside graphical representations.

11.4   Results

Simulation findings allow a digital twin model's behavior to be compared to accurate data and validate it. The simulation findings' accuracy depends on the digital twin model's assumptions and data quality and quantity.

It can measure the air purification system's behavior under different operating settings to evaluate simulation results to accurate data. Sensors on the system can measure air flow rate, temperature drop, and air quality. Data from the real world can be compared to digital twin model simulations. To ensure simulation fidelity, the digital twin model must be validated under various operating situations and system configurations. The model may be tested under different air circulation rates, filtration types, and surroundings and compared to accurate data. In conclusion, a digital twin model's simulation results depend on its data quality and assumptions. Simulation findings must be compared to real-world data to verify model fidelity and identify errors. System configuration, operational circumstances, and model assumptions affect the simulation results. As demonstrated in Figure 11.5, creating simulation results requires a thorough grasp of the system, modeling approach, and input parameters.

The air purifier system reduces PM2.5 particles by 90% in simulations but only 85% in real life. Simulation and data from the real world differ for several reasons. Data collected from a real-world system under various operating conditions could be added to the digital twin model to improve its accuracy. Laboratory testing could be used to validate the model.

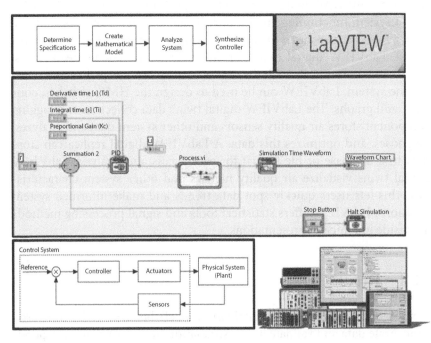

Figure 11.5 Simulation using Labview [33].

LabVIEW's graphical designing interface lets non-programmers develop and edit simulation models. Its pre-built modules and functions make simulating sophisticated mathematical models and algorithms easy. LabVIEW may communicate with real-world detectors and data collection equipment to monitor and analyze real-time data from the simulated system, programmable logic controllers, PLCs, and microcontrollers to create models that closely simulate real-world scenarios. Air purification system simulation is not limited to LabVIEW. Computational fluid dynamics (CFD), finite element analysis (FEA), and agent-based models (ABM) are also popular. The application and systems being modeled determine the modeling technique. LabVIEW is ideal for simulation systems with physical and operational components, while CFD and FEA are better for fluid or solid dynamics and ABM for social and behavioral techniques.

11.5 Discussion

LabVIEW digital twin simulation of air purification systems has far-reaching effects. Air purifiers can reduce the health risks of air pollution in many countries. Digital twin systems can tune air purification systems to remove contaminants and purify the air. Air purifiers are energy-intensive, especially at high flow rates or with inadequate filtering. Digital twin models help optimize air purifier systems to save energy and improve air quality. Digital twin versions optimize air purifier performance, lowering the maintenance and running expenses. Digital twin simulations can analyze air purifier system layouts to find the most efficient and effective ones. This can result in more customized air purifier systems. LabVIEW-based digital twin simulation of air purification systems can lead to novel simulation and modeling methods and applications. This can boost air purification technology innovation and benefit society.

The LabVIEW simulator offers many purifications of air and other applications, but it has several drawbacks. The LabVIEW simulator can optimize air purification systems by studying how different parameters affect system performance. The LabVIEW simulator may not fully represent an air purification system. The model's assumptions and input data determine LabVIEW's precision. The LabVIEW simulator lets engineers test and design novel air purification systems before building them. The LabVIEW simulator allows students and apprentices to learn about purification systems safely. Researchers can use the LabVIEW simulation model to test innovative air purification concepts and applications.

11.6   Conclusion

The LabVIEW simulation model predicts air purifier system performance in air quality, energy consumption, and cost-effectiveness. Optimizing air purifier systems with the digital twin concept can boost efficiency, efficacy, and cost-effectiveness. The digital twin approach can analyze air purifier system layouts to find the most successful and cost-effective ones. The digital twin model may mimic how contaminants affect air quality and air purification systems. Research could improve air quality, energy efficiency, affordability, and air purification innovation. LabVIEW digital twin simulation for Chandigarh City air purification systems is thus suggested as it may optimize efficiency, enhance air quality, and reduce the health and environmental impacts of pollutants in the air. Validating the LabVIEW simulator against accurate data can improve its accuracy. Future research could include environmental elements, behavior among people, and building architecture in the LabVIEW simulator to affect the air purification system's performance. Digital twin models of air purification systems may improve the indoor air quality in homes, transportation networks, and other enclosed places. Hybrid models that blend digital and physical twin simulations can replicate air purification systems better. Future studies can examine the long-term consequences of air filtration systems on human health, the environment, and the indoor microbiome. By addressing these study topics, digital twin simulation for air purification systems can be developed and applied more effectively and efficiently, improving the well-being of humans and the environment.

References

1. Arora, J. and Ramkumar, K.R., Difference computation using change identification techniques for structured web documents'. *IOP Conference Series: Materials Science and Engineering*, vol. 1022, no. 1, 2021, doi: 10.1088/1757-899X/1022/1/012054.
2. Dröder, K. *et al.*, A machine learning-enhanced digital twin approach for human-robot-collaboration'. *Proc. CIRP*, 76, 187–192, March 2018, doi: 10.1016/j.procir.2018.02.010.
3. Fikar, M. *et al.*, Proceedings of the 2017 21st International Conference on Process Control (PC), Hotel Sorea Trigan Baník, Štrbské Pleso, Slovakia, pp. 258–262, 2017.

4. Fuller, A. *et al.*, Digital Twin: Enabling Technologies, Challenges and Open Research. *IEEE Access*, 8, 108952–108971, 2020, doi: 10.1109/ ACCESS.2020.2998358.

5. Ghosh, A.K. *et al.*, Developing sensor signal-based digital twins for intelligent machine tools. *J. Ind. Inf. Integr.*, 24, 100242, 2021, doi: 10.1016/j. jii.2021.100242.

6. Huang, S. *et al.*, Blockchain-based data management for digital twin of product. *J. Manuf. Syst.*, 54, 361–371, August 2019, doi: 10.1016/j.jmsy.2020.01.009.

7. Jiang, Z., Guo, Y., Wang, Z., Digital twin to improve the virtual-real integration of industrial IoT. *J. Ind. Inf. Integr.*, 22, 100196, January 2021, doi: 10.1016/j.jii.2020.100196.

8. Jones, D. *et al.*, Characterising the Digital Twin: A systematic literature review. *CIRP J. Manuf. Sci. Technol.*, 29, 36–52, 2020, doi: 10.1016/j. cirpj.2020.02.002.

9. Kansal, I. *et al.*, Digital Image Processing and IoT in Smart Health Care -A review, in: *2022 International Conference on Emerging Smart Computing and Informatics (ESCI)*, IEEE, pp. 1–6, 2022, doi: 10.1109/ ESCI53509.2022.9758227.

10. Kiritsis, D., Closed-loop PLM for intelligent products in the era of the Internet of things. *Comput. Aided Des.*, 43, 5, 479–501, 2011, doi: 10.1016/j. cad.2010.03.002.

11. Kritzinger, W. *et al.*, Digital Twin in manufacturing: A categorical literature review and classification. *IFAC-PapersOnLine*, 51, 11, 1016–1022, 2018, doi: 10.1016/j.ifacol.2018.08.474.

12. Ilyas, B., Kumar, A., Setitra, M.A., Bensalem, Z.E.A., Lei, H., Prevention of DDoS attacks using an optimized deep learning approach in blockchain technology. *Trans. Emerging. Telecommun. Technol.*, 34, 4, e4729, 2023.

13. Leser, P.E. *et al.*, A digital twin feasibility study (Part II): Non-deterministic predictions of fatigue life using *in-situ* diagnostics and prognostics. *Eng. Fract. Mech.*, 229, 106903, 2020, doi: 10.1016/j. engfracmech.2020.106903.

14. Longo, F., Nicoletti, L., Padovano, A., Ubiquitous knowledge empowers the Smart Factory: The impacts of a Service-oriented Digital Twin on enterprises' performance. *Annu. Rev. Control*, 47, 221–236, 2019, doi: 10.1016/j. arcontrol.2019.01.001.

15. Chandrasekaran, S., Dutt, V., Vyas, N., Kumar, R., Student Sentiment Analysis Using Various Machine Learning Techniques. *2023 International Conference on Artificial Intelligence and Smart Communication (AISC)*, Greater Noida, India, pp. 104–107, 2023, doi: 10.1109/AISC56616.2023.10085018.

16. McFarlane, D. *et al.*, The intelligent product in manufacturing control and management. *IFAC Proceedings Volumes (IFAC-PapersOnline)*, IFAC, 2002, doi: 10.3182/20020721-6-es-1901.00011.

17. Melesse, T.Y., Di Pasquale, V., Riemma, S., Digital twin models in industrial operations: A systematic literature review. *Proc. Manuf.*, 42, 2019, 267–272, 2020, doi: 10.1016/j.promfg.2020.02.084.

18. Min, Q. *et al.*, Machine Learning based Digital Twin Framework for Production Optimization in Petrochemical Industry. *Int. J. Inf. Manage.*, 49, 502–519, 2019, doi: 10.1016/j.ijinfomgt.2019.05.020.

19. Srivastav, A.L., Markandeya, Patel, N. *et al.*, Concepts of circular economy for sustainable management of electronic wastes: challenges and management options. *Environ. Sci. Pollut. Res.*, 30, 48654–48675, 2023, https://doi.org/10.1007/s11356-023-26052-y.

20. Prana Air Air Quality Sensors, 2023. Available at: https://www.pranaair.com/air-quality-sensor/.

21. Qi, Q. *et al.*, Enabling technologies and tools for digital twin. *J. Manuf. Syst.*, 58, 3–21, August 2021, doi: 10.1016/j. jmsy.2019.10.001.

22. Rosen, R. *et al.*, About the importance of autonomy and digital twins for the future of manufacturing. *IFAC-PapersOnLine*, 28, 3, 567–572, 2015, doi: 10.1016/j.ifacol.2015.06.141.

23. Roy, R. *et al.*, Continuous maintenance and the future – Foundations and technological challenges. *CIRP Ann. Manuf. Technol.*, 65, 2, 667–688, 2016, doi: 10.1016/j.cirp.2016.06.006.

24. Ruppert, T. and Abonyi, J., Integration of real-time locating systems into digital twins. *J. Ind. Inf. Integr.*, 20, 100174, October 2020, doi: 10.1016/j.jii.2020.100174.

25. Ruzsa, C., Digital twin technology-external data resources in creating the model and classification of different digital twin types in manufacturing.' *Proc. Manuf.*, 54, 209–215, Dec 2020, doi: 10.1016/j. promfg.2021.07.032.

26. Semeraro, C. *et al.*, Digital twin paradigm: A systematic literature review. *Comput. Ind.*, 130, 76, 2021, doi: 10.1016/j.compind.2021.103469.

27. Sierla, S. *et al.*, Roadmap to semi-automatic generation of digital twins for brownfield process plants. *J. Ind. Inf. Integr.*, 27, 100282, August 2021, 2022, doi: 10.1016/j.jii.2021.100282.

28. Kumar, A., Kumar, S.A., Dutt, V., Dubey, A.K., Narang, S., A Hybrid Secure Cloud Platform Maintenance Based on Improved Attribute-Based Encryption Strategies. *Int. J. Interact. Multimed. Artif. Intell.*, 8, 2, 2021. http://dx.doi.org/10.9781/ijimai.2021.11.004.

29. Kumar, A., Rathore, P.S., Dubey, A.K. *et al.*, LTE-NBP with holistic UWB- WBAN approach for the energy efficient biomedical application. *Multimed Tools Appl.*, 82, 39797–39811, 2023. https://doi.org/10.1007/s11042-023-15604-6.

30. Bhola, J., Shabaz, M., Dhiman, G., Vimal, S., Subbulakshmi, P., Soni, S.K., Performance evaluation of multilayer clustering network using distributed energy efficient clustering with enhanced threshold protocol. *Wirel. Pers. Commun.*, 26, 3, 2175–2189, 2022.

31. Suhail, S. *et al.*, Towards situational aware cyber-physical systems: A security-enhancing use case of blockchain-based digital twins. *Comput. Ind.*, 141, 16, 2022, doi: 10.1016/j.compind.2022.103699.

32. Dutt, V. and Sharma, S., 9 - Artificial intelligence and technology in weather forecasting and renewable energy systems: emerging techniques and worldwide studies, in: *Woodhead Publishing Series in Energy, Artificial Intelligence for Renewable Energy Systems*, pp. 189–207, Woodhead Publishing, UK, 2022, ISBN 9780323903967, https://doi.org/10.1016/B978-0-323-90396-7.00009-2.

33. Valckenaers, P. *et al.*, Intelligent products: Agere versus Essere. *Comput. Ind.*, 60, 3, 217–228, 2009, doi: 10.1016/j.compind.2008.12.008.

34. Verma, J., Bhandari, A., Singh, G., iNIDS: SWOT Analysis and TOWS Inferences of State-of-the-Art NIDS solutions for the development of Intelligent Network Intrusion Detection System. *Comput. Commun.*, 195, 227–246, August 2022, doi: 10.1016/j.comcom.2022.08.022.

35. Kumar, A., Kumar, S.A., Dutt, V., Shitharth, S., Tripathi, E., IoT based arrhythmia classification using the enhanced hunt optimization-based deep learning. *Expert Syst.*, 40, 7, e13298, 2023. https://doi.org/10.1111/exsy.13298.

36. What Is LabVIEW, 2023. Available at: http://www.ni.com/labview/.

37. Xu, X., From cloud computing to cloud manufacturing. *Robot. Comput. Integr. Manuf.*, 28, 1, 75–86, 2012, doi: 10.1016/j. rcim.2011.07.002.

38. Yao, J.F. *et al.*, Systematic review of digital twin technology and applications. *Vis. Comput. Ind. Biomed. Art*, 6, 1, 2, 2023, doi: 10.1186/ s42492-023-00137-4.

39. Yeratapally, S.R. *et al.*, A digital twin feasibility study (Part I): Non- deterministic predictions of fatigue life in aluminum alloy 7075-T651 using a microstructure-based multi-scale model. *Eng. Fract. Mech.*, 228, 106888, 2020, doi: 10.1016/j.engfracmech.2020.106888.

40. Kumar, A., Swarn., A., Dutt., V., Sitharth., S., Triapthi., E., IoT based Arrhythmia Classification Using the Enhanced Hunt Optimization based Deep Learning, Expert Systems. *J. Knowl. Eng.*, 40, e13298, 2023, ISSN:1468-0394.

12

Use of Digital Twin in Predicting the Life of Aircraft Main Bearing

Urvashi Kumari[1]* and Pooja Malhotra[2]†

*[1]School of Hospitality and Tourism, GD Goenka University,
Gurugram, Haryana, India
[2]Visiting Faculty, Department of Computer Engineering, Netaji Subhash University
of Technology, Dwarka, New Delhi, India*

Abstract

The idea of a digital twin (DT) has grown in popularity as a way to keep track of product-related data throughout the product's life cycle. Health monitoring systems are one of the manufacturing system areas where the digital twin (DT) has been proposed and deployed. To continuously monitor wear, anomalies, deformation, and the manufacturing system's overall reliability, these systems employ digital twin technology. The use of digital twin technology to predict the life of aircraft main bearings is examined in this chapter. The main bearing is a vital component whose failure can have catastrophic consequences in the aircraft propulsion system. Using the capabilities of digital twin technology, engineers may create virtual replicas of the main bearing and monitor its performance in real time. Because preventive maintenance techniques are made possible by this predictive capability, downtime is decreased and bearing lifespan is increased. This chapter covers the crucial stages of developing a digital twin for an aircraft's primary bearings, including data collection, model creation, and predictive analytics. Additionally, it examines the challenges and potential advantages of using digital twin technology for aircraft maintenance.

Keywords: Digital twin (DT), aircraft main bearing, random forest (RF), sensors, machine learning

*Corresponding author: urvashi.kumari@gdgu.org
†Corresponding author: poojajind@gmail.com

Abhineet Anand, Anita Sardana, Abhishek Kumar, Srikanta Kumar Mohapatra and Shikha Gupta (eds.) *Simulation Techniques of Digital Twin in Real-Time Applications: Design Modeling and Implementation*, (261–288) © 2024 Scrivener Publishing LLC

12.1 Introduction

12.1.1 Background

The safe and effective operation of aircrafts is essential to the aviation sector, and any failure in crucial components can have serious repercussions. An essential element in the aircraft's propulsion system is the main bearing, serving a crucial function. The main bearing's primary function is to provide support to the rotating shaft, ensuring that the engine operates smoothly and reliably. In the event of an aircraft main bearing failure, catastrophic consequences can occur, such as engine malfunctions, loss of control, or even complete engine failure. To enhance safety and operational efficiency significantly, it is of utmost importance to accurately predict the main bearing's lifespan and conduct proactive maintenance before any potential failure arises [5]. In the aviation industry, maintenance practices have traditionally depended on scheduled inspections and replacements, following predetermined time intervals or flight hours. However, this method can prove inefficient and costly, as components might be replaced prematurely, resulting in unnecessary downtime and higher maintenance expenses.

Aviation maintenance procedures have been revolutionized by the development of digital twin technology [1]. A digital twin is a virtual representation of a real-time imitation of the behavior, features, and performance of a physical asset or system. Digital twins provide real-time monitoring, predictive analysis, and optimization of maintenance plans by combining sensor data, advanced analytics, and machine learning algorithms [2]. Engineers and maintenance staff can continuously check the condition of the main bearings of aircrafts by using digital twin technology. The digital twin gathers information on temperature, vibration, and lubrication levels from sensors that are integrated into the bearing. This information is then examined to look for irregularities, forecast possible failures, and calculate the bearing's remaining useful life (RUL) [6].

There are various benefits of employing digital twin technology to predict the life of aircraft main bearings [3]. First off, proactive maintenance is made possible, allowing for the performance of maintenance tasks based on the actual state and expected health of the bearing rather than predetermined periods. This method decreases unplanned downtime and improves aircraft availability. Second, maintenance strategies can be optimized thanks to digital twin technology. Maintenance tasks can be scheduled more successfully and expenses associated with premature replacements or emergency repairs can be decreased by precisely forecasting the life of the main bearing [7]. The performance and behavior of the primary bearing can also be better understood thanks to digital twins. Engineers can examine the gathered data and spot patterns or trends that might point to possible problems or window of opportunity for design enhancements.

There are issues that need to be resolved despite the many advantages of employing digital twin technology to forecast the life of aircraft main bearings. These difficulties include assuring data availability and quality, verifying the precision of predictive models, integrating digital twin systems with current maintenance infrastructure, and resolving privacy and security issues related to the collection and analysis of sensitive data [8]. However, the aviation sector stands to gain much from the use of digital twin technology. The technology is anticipated to significantly contribute to improving aircraft safety, optimizing maintenance procedures, and cutting operational costs as it continues to develop and mature.

12.1.2   Importance of Predictive Maintenance

Predictive maintenance is a maintenance approach that leverages advanced technologies and data analysis to predictequipment failures and determine the optimal timing for maintenance actions. It plays a crucial role in various industries, including aviation, and offers several significant benefits as follows:

a. Minimizing unplanned downtime: Unplanned equipment failures can lead to costly downtime, disrupt operations, and result in significant financial losses. By implementing predictive maintenance, potential failures can be identified in advance, allowing for proactive maintenance actions to be taken [9]. This minimizes unplanned downtime by addressing issues before they cause equipment breakdowns or failures.

b. Cost reduction: Predictive maintenance helps optimize maintenance activities and reduces unnecessary maintenance tasks. Instead of following fixed schedules or performing preventive maintenance based on general time or usage intervals, predictive maintenance focuses on performing maintenance actions when they are truly needed. This approach avoids unnecessary replacements or repairs, optimizing the use of resources and reducing maintenance costs [10].

c. Increased equipment reliability: By continuously monitoring equipment health and analyzing data, predictive maintenance allows for the early detection of potential issues or degradation. This early detection enables timely intervention, preventing minor problems from escalating into major failures [11]. As a result, the reliability and performance of equipment are improved, ensuring smooth and uninterrupted operations.

d. Extended equipment lifespan: Regular and timely maintenance based on predictive insights helps to extend the lifespan of equipment. By identifying and addressing issues at an early stage, the root causes of failures can be mitigated, reducing wear and tear and prolonging the operational life of the equipment [12, 13]. This leads to cost savings by avoiding premature replacements and investments in new equipment.

e. Enhanced safety: In industries where equipment failure can pose safety risks, such as aviation, predictive maintenance plays a critical role in ensuring the safety of operations. By identifying and addressing potential failures in advance, the risk of accidents or incidents caused by equipment malfunctions is significantly reduced [14]. This enhances safety for personnel, passengers, and the overall environment.

f. Optimized maintenance planning: Predictive maintenance provides valuable insights into the health and performance of equipment. By analyzing data trends and patterns, maintenance activities can be planned and scheduled more effectively. This optimization of maintenance planning allows for the efficient allocation of resources, minimizing operational disruptions and maximizing productivity [15].

g. Improved data-driven decision-making: Predictive maintenance relies on advanced analytics and data-driven insights. By collecting and analyzing equipment data, maintenance teams gain a deeper understanding of the operational conditions, usage patterns, and failure modes [16, 17]. This data-driven decision-making approach enables more informed choices regarding maintenance strategies, spare parts management, and operational optimization.

In summary, predictive maintenance is essential for industries seeking to optimize maintenance practices, improve equipment reliability, and reduce costs associated with unplanned downtime and unnecessary maintenance activities. By harnessing the power of advanced technologies and data analysis, organizations can achieve higher operational efficiency, increased safety, and extended equipment lifespan.

12.1.3   Challenges in Aircraft Main Bearing Life Prediction

Predicting the life of aircraft main bearings poses several challenges due to the complex operating conditions and the critical nature of these components. Some of the key challenges in aircraft main bearing life prediction include the following [11–14, 16, 17]:

1. Limited data availability: Obtaining comprehensive and high-quality data related to the operating conditions, loads, and stresses experienced by aircraft main bearings can be challenging. The limited availability of data may hinder accurate life prediction models and require extrapolation or assumptions.

2. Multifactorial degradation: The life of aircraft main bearings is influenced by multiple factors, including cyclic loading, temperature variations, lubrication conditions, and operational environment. Accounting for the combined effect of these factors and their interaction presents a significant challenge.

3. Lack of failure data: Aircraft main bearings are designed to have a long operational life, and failures are relatively rare events. The scarcity of failure data makes it difficult to establish statistically significant failure patterns, which can impact the accuracy of life prediction models.

4. Complex loading conditions: Aircraft main bearings are subjected to varying and complex loading conditions during operation. These conditions include different thrust loads, rotational speeds, and oscillations, making it challenging to accurately simulate and predict the fatigue life of the bearings.

5. Material variability and aging: Main bearing materials may exhibit variability in properties and performance, even within the same production batch. Additionally, the aging and degradation of materials over time can impact the bearing's fatigue life and increase the uncertainty in life prediction models.

6. Insufficient understanding of failure mechanisms: While extensive research has been conducted on bearing failure mechanisms, there may still be gaps in the understanding of failure modes specific to aircraft main bearings. The complexity of the bearing's internal structure and the interaction between different components make it challenging to identify and model failure mechanisms accurately.

7. Incomplete knowledge of operational conditions: Obtaining accurate and detailed information regarding the operational conditions and usage history of aircraft main bearings can be challenging. The incomplete knowledge of operational parameters, such as loading history and operating temperature ranges, can affect the accuracy of life prediction models.

8. Validation and verification: Validating and verifying the accuracy of life prediction models for aircraft main bearings is a significant challenge. Conducting extensive testing and monitoring over long durations to collect failure data for validation purposes can be costly and time-consuming.

Addressing these challenges requires a multidisciplinary approach, combining expertise in materials science, mechanical engineering, data analytics, and domain knowledge of aircraft systems. Collaboration between manufacturers, operators, and researchers is crucial to collect and share data, develop accurate models, and validate predictions for aircraft main bearing life. Advances in digital twin technology and the integration of real-time monitoring systems can help overcome some of these challenges by providing more comprehensive data and enabling predictive maintenance strategies.

12.1.4 Digital Twin Technology in Aviation

Digital twin technology has emerged as a game-changer in the aviation industry, revolutionizing various aspects of aircraft operations, maintenance, and safety. Digital twins make it possible to monitor, analyze, and optimize actual assets or systems in real time by building their virtual counterparts. These are used in aviation for design and development, enabling simulations, virtual prototyping, and iterative design improvements. They enhance manufacturing processes by optimizing production, reducing errors, and enabling predictive maintenance. During operations, digital twins provide real-time monitoring of aircraft systems, enabling performance optimization,predictive analytics, and data-driven decision-making.

In maintenance and asset management, digital twins support proactive maintenance strategies, remote monitoring, and diagnostics, improving efficiency and reducing downtime. Furthermore, digital twins enhance safety, compliance, and risk analysis by continuously monitoring aircraft performance and ensuring regulatory adherence [18, 19]. With its transformative capabilities, digital twin technology is driving innovation, efficiency, and safety in the aviation industry. In addition, digital twin technologies help in achieving the said aspects.

12.2   Fundamentals of Digital Twin Technology

At its core, digital twin technology involves creating virtual replicas of physical assets or systems to monitor, analyze, and optimize their performance. The fundamentals of digital twin technology revolve around three key components. Firstly, there is the physical asset itself, which could be an aircraft, engine, or any other complex system. Secondly, there is the virtual representation or model of the asset, which captures its geometry, behavior, and characteristics. Several data sources, including sensor data, design requirements, and performance data from the past, are used to generate this virtual model. The real-time link, which enables two-way communication between the physical asset and its digital twin, is the last step. Continuous data exchange made possible by this connection makes monitoring, analysis, and control easier. The digital twin acts as a living, breathing replica of the physical asset, offering helpful information for decision-making, predictive analytics, and optimization. Industries may achieve new levels of productivity, dependability, and performance in their operations by utilizing the basics of digital twin technology.

12.2.1   Components of a Digital Twin

The virtual representation, monitoring, analysis, and optimization of a physical asset or system are all made possible by a digital twin, which is made up of a number of essential components [20]. As shown in Figure 12.1, the essential elements of a digital twin are as follows:

- Physical asset: The physical asset refers to the actual object or system in the physical world that the digital twin represents. It can be an aircraft, a manufacturing plant, a power plant, or any other complex entity.

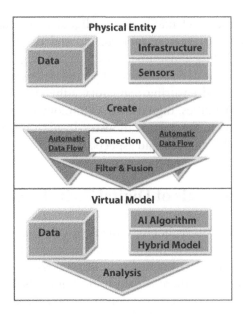

Figure 12.1 Virtualization of the physical system.

- Virtual model: The virtual model is the digital counterpart of the physical asset. It is a detailed and dynamic representation that encompasses the asset's geometry, structure, behavior, and attributes. The virtual model is created using various data sources, including design specifications, sensor data, historical records, and simulations.
- Sensor data and IoT connectivity: Sensors play a crucial role in capturing real-time data from the physical asset. These sensors collect information on parameters such as temperature, pressure, vibration, and location. The sensor data is transmitted through the Internet of Things (IoT) connectivity, allowing for continuous monitoring and updating of the digital twin [4].
- Data integration and analytics: Data integration involves aggregating and processing data from multiple sources, including sensors, operational systems, and external databases. Advanced analytics techniques, such as machine learning and statistical analysis, are applied to the integrated data to derive meaningful insights and identify patterns, trends, anomalies, or potential issues.

- Real-time monitoring and control: Real-time monitoring involves the continuous collection, analysis, and visualization of data from the physical asset and its virtual model. It enables operators and engineers to monitor the asset's performance, health condition, and operational parameters in real time. This component allows for timely intervention, decision-making, and control actions.
- Simulation and prediction: The simulation component of a digital twin enables the creation of virtual scenarios and what-if analyses. It allows for the testing and validation of different operating conditions, configurations, or maintenance strategies without affecting the physical asset. Prediction capabilities utilize historical data and analytics to forecast the future behavior, performance, or maintenance needs of the asset, aiding in proactive decision-making.
- Human–machine interface: The human–machine interface provides a user-friendly platform or dashboard for interacting with the digital twin. It allows operators, engineers, and other stakeholders to access real-time data, visualizations, alerts, and performance indicators. The interface enables effective communication, collaboration, and decision-making based on the insights derived from the digital twin.

A digital twin creates a complete, real-time, and dynamic representation of a physical object by combining these elements. It makes it possible to monitor, analyze, optimize, and make decisions for better performance, upkeep, and efficiency across a range of sectors.

12.2.2   Enabling Technologies for Digital Twin

The development and operation of digital twin technology are greatly facilitated by the Internet of Things (IoT). Sensor networks are used by IoT to gather real-time data from physical assets. These sensors are capable of tracking a wide range of variables, including temperature, pressure, vibration, humidity, and more. The fundamental data for digital twins is provided by sensor networks, allowing for real-time monitoring and the capture of the behavior and performance of the physical asset. IoT relies on robust connectivity solutions to transmit data from sensors to the digital twin system. Technologies such as wireless protocols (e.g., Wi-Fi, Bluetooth, Zigbee), cellular networks (e.g., 4G, 5G), and wiredconnections (e.g., Ethernet) ensure seamless and reliable data transmission.

Connectivity solutions provide the means for real-time data exchange, enabling continuous updates and synchronization between the physical asset and its digital twin.

Cloud computing plays a vital role in supporting the storage, processing, and analysis of massive amounts of data generated by IoT devices. Cloud platforms provide scalable and flexible infrastructure to handle the computational requirements of digital twin systems. They enable real-time data processing, complex analytics, and the ability to store historical data for trend analysis and predictive modeling. Edge computing brings computational capabilities closer to the data source, reducing latency and enabling real-time processing and decision-making at the network edge. By processing data locally on edge devices or gateways, edge computing minimizes the need for transmitting large volumes of raw data to the cloud. This reduces network congestion, enhances real-time responsiveness, and improves data privacy and security.

Effective data visualization and user interfaces are essential for understanding and interacting with the digital twin system. Visualization tools present real-time and historical data in a meaningful and intuitive manner, enabling users to monitor the physical asset's status, analyze trends, and make informed decisions. User interfaces provide controls and interaction capabilities to operate and manipulate the digital twin system.

By leveraging these enabling technologies within the IoT ecosystem, digital twin systems can collect, process, and analyze real-time data from physical assets, enabling accurate representation, monitoring, and simulation of the asset's behavior. The IoT infrastructure provides the foundation for building and operating digital twins, supporting their integration with various domains, including manufacturing, infrastructure, healthcare, and transportation.

12.3   Benefits of Digital Twin Technology

Digital twin technology offers a wide range of benefits across industries. Here are some key advantages:

- Enhanced product design and development: Digital twins enable virtual prototyping and simulations, allowing for design optimization, performance testing, and validation before physical production. This leads to improved product quality, reduced development time, and cost savings.

- Improved operational efficiency: Digital twins provide real-time monitoring and analysis of assets, allowing for data-driven insights to optimize operations. This includes optimizing energy consumption, streamlining processes, reducing waste, and improving overall efficiency.
- Proactive maintenance and reduced downtime: By continuously monitoring asset health and performance, digital twins enable predictive maintenance. They can detect anomalies, predict failures, and trigger maintenance actions before breakdowns occur. This reduces unplanned downtime, extends asset lifespan, and avoids costly emergency repairs.
- Increased safety and risk mitigation: Digital twins facilitate the real-time monitoring of asset behavior and condition, allowing for the early identification of potential safety risks. This enables proactive risk mitigation measures, enhances operational safety, and minimizes the likelihood of accidents or failures.
- Optimal resource utilization: Digital twins provide insights into asset utilization, performance, and efficiency, enabling organizations to optimize resource allocation. This includes managing inventory, scheduling maintenance activities, and allocating workforce based on actual needs, leading to cost savings and improved resource utilization.
- Enhanced decision-making and planning: Digital twins offer data-driven insights and simulations, enabling informed decision-making and scenario planning. This includes optimizing production schedules, predicting equipment performance, and evaluating the impact of changes or interventions before implementation.
- Improved customer experience: With real-time monitoring and analysis, digital twins enable organizations to provide better customer support and service. They can proactively address customer needs, anticipate issues, and offer personalized recommendations or solutions, resulting in improved customer satisfaction and loyalty.
- Accelerated innovation and iterative improvements: Digital twins facilitate continuous data collection and analysis, enabling organizations to gain insights and feedback for iterative improvements. This supports innovation, product

enhancement, and optimization of processes, ultimately driving competitiveness in the market.

- Training and simulation: Digital twins can be utilized for training purposes, creating virtual environments to simulate complex scenarios or operational conditions. This enables effective training, skill development, and decision-making in a safe and controlled setting.
- Sustainability and environmental benefits: By optimizing resource utilization, reducing waste, and improving efficiency, digital twins contribute to sustainability efforts. They help organizations identify opportunities for energy savings, emission reductions, and environmentally friendly practices.

Overall, digital twin technology offers significant benefits, including improved productivity, reduced costs, enhanced safety, and better decision-making. It empowers organizations to unlock new levels of efficiency, innovation, and competitiveness in today's rapidly evolving business landscape.

12.3.1   Aircraft Main Bearings: Structure and Failure Modes

When it comes to sustaining and enabling the rotation of different rotating parts, such engine shafts, propellers, or rotor systems, aircraft main bearings are essential. The typical purpose of these bearings is to support heavy loads, provide smooth rotation, and protect the stability and integrity of the aircraft's propulsion or power transmission system. The structure of aircraft main bearings can vary depending on the specific application and aircraft type, but they commonly consist of the following components as shown in Figure 12.2.

The stationary outer ring which is also called the outer race of the main bearing provides the assembly of the bearing. The inner race is used to provide the track for the rolling elements and is mounted on the rotating shaft. For the proper functioning and smooth rotation of the shaft, the rolling element is placed in between the inner and the outer race, respectively, to balance and transmit the load between them. To ensure the appropriate distribution of load and least friction, the retainer or cage is used to place the rolling element such that it is evenly spaced.

There are many factors affecting the failure of aircraft main bearings, which include one or more of attributes like operational environment, degradation of materials, maintenance routine and manufacturing defects. Following are few of the very common failures:

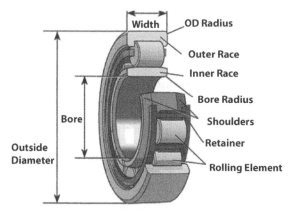

Figure 12.2 Roller bearing.

- Fatigue failure: The main bearing can fail due to fatigue caused by repeated loading and unloading cycles. Fatigue failure can also be caused by excessive loads, lack of lubrication which increases the risk of crack development, high-speed rotation, spilling, or pitting on the surface of the main bearing [21].
- Wear: A very common cause of failure is due to continuous friction and contact between the rolling elements, causing the races to wear. With time, this wear can lead to a reduction in performance of the bearing and a probability of failure.
- Contamination: Bearings can get contaminated from their working environment and elements like dust particles and debris, causing bearing damage and, subsequently, bearing failure. This type of contamination can lead to abrasion and surface defects compromising the integrity of the bearing, hence speeding up the wearing process.
- Lubrication issues: Lubrication maintains the film thickness between the rolling elements and races, and improper lubrication will result in an increase in friction, overheating, wear, and subsequent failure.
- Overloading: The plastic deformation and catastrophic failure of components of bearing due to the excessive force caused by load that is more than the permitted load capacity of the bearing can cause overload failure.
- Misalignment: If the shaft between the mating components are misaligned, then it can impose additional pressure on

the bearing and can lead to increased friction, uneven loading, and accelerated wear.

- Corrosion: The structural integrity of the bearing can be
  compromised due to the corrosion caused by environmental
  factors or lack of protection. Corrosion can lead to surface
  pitting, deterioration of material, and eventually the failure
  of the bearing.

To implement effective monitoring techniques, maintenance strategies,
reliability, and safety of all operations of aircrafts, it is essential to understand the structure and modes of aircraft main bearing failure [22]. For
the prevention of failure and optimal performance of the critical components of aircraft, it is essential to perform inspection regularly, maintain
the proper lubrication, and strictly follow the recommended practices for
maintenance. For the safe operations of aircrafts, it is crucial to promptly
address any damage, sign of wearing, or abnormalities so as to prevent a
possible failure. The main bearings of the aircraft are the important and
vital components for efficiently rotating the critical systems of aircraft. Due
to its importance in the aviation environment, diligent design, manufacturing, and maintenance practices are imposed to ensure their durability,
performance, and safety [23].

12.4   Developing a Digital Twin for Aircraft Main Bearings

The importance of aircraft main bearings has motivated the development
of a digital twin for it. The process of developing a digital twin includes
various steps starting from the virtualization of physical bearings and integrating it with real-time data from different relevant sources and IOT sensors. The key steps in developing a digital twin for aircraft main bearings
are:

1. Data acquisition: In the first step, the data of the physical main
   bearing is being collected. Data acquisition is done by collecting data about specifications, design information, material properties, and operational parameters. Furthermore, to
   collect real-time data about temperature, lubrication, load,
   and vibration, different sensors can be installed on the main
   bearing and its surrounding components.

2. Model creation: With the help of collected and acquired data for aircraft main bearings, a digital model of the aircraft main bearing is developed. This virtual model depicts the exact physical characteristic of the bearing like its behavior in the actual world, geometry, and material properties. To create the bearing structure virtually, computer-aided design (CAD) tools can be used to simulate its mechanical behavior and finite element analysis (FEA) techniques can be used.

3. Sensor integration: The main idea behind digital twin is to link the real-time data which is collected from sensors installed on components or on the physical bearings. These sensors continuously transmit data for the digital twin to analyze and provide an accurate representation about the operating condition of the main bearing.

4. Analytics and algorithms: The next step is to extract meaningful insight from the collected data using machine learning techniques and analytical algorithms. These algorithms are used to scan and identify patterns, anomalies (if any), and indicators of potential failures for predictive analysis and proactive maintenance.

5. Performance monitoring: The digital twin then monitors the performance continuously, and it keeps track of the main bearing's physical health using the real-time data transmitted by the sensors. The detection of potential issues is being analyzed by comparing the deviations from actual operating conditions with the expected or optimal conditions.

6. Predictive maintenance: The remaining useful life of the main bearing, the potential failure, and the maintenance schedule recommendations can be forecasted by the digital twin with the help of predictive algorithms and data analysis. This proactive approach helps reduce maintenance cost, minimize downtime, and maximize the lifespan of the aircraft bearings.

7. Simulation and what-if scenarios: To conduct virtual tests and to evaluate different scenarios, simulation can be done with the help of the digital twin. This helps in identifying potential performance improvements, design optimization, and the effect on the performance of the bearing in case of operational changes.

8. Visualization and user interface: To visualize the digital twin and data related to it, a user-friendly interface is developed.

With the help of a user-friendly interface, operators, maintenance personnel, and engineers can easily interact with the digital twin to access information and make informed decisions.

9. Continuous improvement: Based on the feedback from the real-time performance of the physical main bearing, the digital twin is updated and improved continuously. The accuracy and effectiveness of the digital twin is further enhanced with the help of algorithm refinement, integration of additional data sources, and validation against actual performance.

By developing a digital twin for aircraft main bearings, operators and maintenance personnel can gain valuable insights into the bearings' condition, performance, and remaining useful life.

12.5   Predictive Analytics for Main Bearing Life Prediction

To forecast the life of aircraft main bearings, it is crucial to use predictive analysis. Predictive analysis techniques analyze real-time and historical data to provide insight on the remaining useful life of aircraft main bearings. It provides an option of proactive maintenance, repair, and replacement strategies. Figure 12.3 shows the predictive model for aircraft main bearing with digital twin. The following key steps are involved in predictive analytics for main bearing life prediction:

I. Data collection: The first step of predictive analysis is to gather relevant data for the main bearings. This includes operational data such as load, temperature, lubrication condition, vibration, and maintenance schedule records. Data collected from operational data of similar bearings from past or fleet-wide data are also very valuable for predictive models' accuracy.

II. Data preprocessing: In data preprocessing, there is a need to clean the collected data, interpolate the missing values, remove outliers, and normalize the data to convert it into a desired format for analysis.

III. Feature selection: The third step is to identify the most relevant features or variables that impact the life of the main bearings with the help of automatic feature selection algorithms, domain expertise, or statistical techniques. Selecting the right features helps in building accurate predictive models.

IV. Model development: Statistical techniques or machine learning techniques are used to build predictive models to predict the remaining useful life of the main bearings. Deep learning models, regression, support vector machines, and random forests are a few algorithms that can be implemented depending on the desired accuracy and data complexity.

V. Training and validation: With the help of historical data about the bearing life information, the predictive models are trained and validated using altogether separate data. The validation process helps to evaluate their performance and reliability. The model is assessed to ensure that it works well on unseen data.

VI. Predictive analytics: After the training and validation of the models, they can be employed to predict the remaining useful life of the aircraft main bearings based on periodic or real-time data collected from the sensors on bearings. The model takes considerations of many factors including maintenance practices, operating conditions, and environment-related factors to predict the remaining life of main bearings.

VII. Maintenance strategies: The predictive analysis model provides predictions that are helpful in developing strategies for proactive maintenance. The digital twin model can identify the risk of bearing failure, and hence maintenance activities can be scheduled for inspections, replacement activities, or lubrication to avoid unplanned downtime and also reduce the cost of maintenance.

VIII. Continuous improvement: The predictive digital models and machine learning algorithms should be continuously improved and updated based on the feedback regarding the performance of the bearing in real time. In this way, the predictive model is refined, aiming to enhance the accuracy and incorporate additional factors or trends affecting bearing life.

With the capabilities of main bearing life prediction predictive analytics, aircraft operation-related maintenance can be scheduled effectively, unscheduled downtime will be reduced, and overall maintenance costs will be minimized. The proactive approach enables maintenance, replacement,

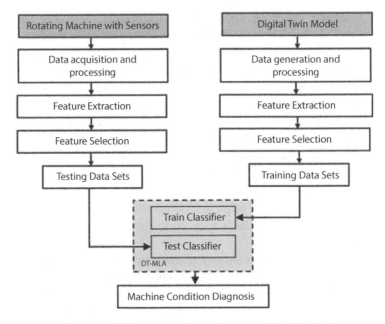

Figure 12.3 Predictive model for an aircraft main bearing with a digital twin.

and timely interventions to ensure the liability and longevity of the components in bearings while optimizing the operational efficiency.

12.5.1   Machine Learning Algorithms for Predictive Modeling

In analyzing historical data patterns with the help of predictive modeling, classification, and making predictions, machine learning algorithms play an essential role. Here are machine learning algorithms that are commonly used for predictive modeling:

I. Linear regression: Linear regression is a powerful but simple algorithm used for regression analysis to establish a linear relationship between the target variable and the input variables. It allows the prediction of continuous numerical values [24].

II. Decision trees (DT): Decision trees are versatile algorithms that can be implemented for both classification and regression tasks. They create a tree-like model where features are represented with internal nodes, decision rules are represented by each branch, and the outcome is represented by leaf nodes. Decision trees can handle both categorical and numerical data and are well known for their interpretability [25–27].

III. Random forest (RF): Random forest is an assembly learning algorithm that combines several decision trees to formulate predictions. It works on combining results, where each sub-tree of the forest is trained on a random subset of the features and data. Random forest provides strong predictions and moderate over-fitting [28].

IV. Gradient boosting: Another ensemble learning technique is gradient boosting which combines weak learner decision trees in a sequential order. An improvement in predictive accuracy is achieved by training each new learner to correct the mistakes on the basis of the mistakes made by the previous learners. XG Boost and Light GBM are popular implementations of gradient boosting.

V. Support vector machines (SVM): SVM is a very powerful algorithm used for both tasks of classification and regression. It creates an optimal hyper-plane that maximally separates dissimilar classes or predicts continuous values. SVM can handle both linear and nonlinear relationships through the use of kernel functions [24].

VI. Neural networks: Neural networks have gained popularity due to their ability to learn intricate patterns and identify relationships from data, specifically with deep learning models. They consist of interrelated layers of artificial neurons that imitate the brain structure of humans. Deep learning models, like recurrent neural networks (RNNs) and convolutional neural networks (CNNs), have proven significant performance in natural language processing, image analysis, and time-series prediction tasks.

VII. Naïve Bayes: Naïve Bayes is a probabilistic algorithm based on Bayes' theorem. The algorithm assumes that the features are not dependent on each other, simplifying the processing and calculations. Naïve Bayes is commonly used for the classification of tasks and works very well with large feature sets [29].

VIII. K-nearest neighbors (KNN): KNN is a simple but effective algorithm to classify new data points on the basis of majority votes of their nearest neighbors in the feature space. It is particularly useful when the data show local patterns and does not need training as it uses the complete training dataset for prediction [30].

IX. Ensemble methods: Ensemble methods merge multiple models to improve the accuracy and robustness of prediction. Examples include bagging, where several models are trained on diverse subsets of the data, and stacking, where the predictions of multiple models are combined using a meta-model.

A suitable machine learning algorithm is selected on the basis of the specific problem, the specific performance criteria, and the nature of the data. However, experimenting with multiple algorithms and comparing their outcome to identify the appropriate algorithm is always beneficial for a given task of a predictive model.

For aircraft maintenance, digital twin technology serves various advantages, such as enhanced efficiency, predictive maintenance, and minimum downtime. However, implementing and utilizing digital twin for the maintenance process of aircraft main bearings also imposes some challenges.

12.5.2   Challenges of Digital Twin for Aircraft Health

1. Data integration and quality [32]: The accurate representation of aircraft main bearings into digital twin technology relies heavily on the quality and integrity of data collected from different sources like sensor data, historical data, and records from maintenance. Creating a digital model by integrating and consolidating data from these different sources can be challenging. Moreover, ensuring the accuracy, quality, and consistency of the data is critical to generate significant insights and predictions.

2. Connectivity and data transfer: Ensuring uninterrupted connectivity for real-time data transfer from the physical main bearing of the aircraft and the digital twin can be complex due to the different geographical locations of the aircrafts. There must be a secure and reliable communication system established to transmit data from systems and sensors on the aircraft to the digital twin model environment. The effectiveness of the digital twin model in monitoring and predicting behavior will reduce the downtime for maintenance needs and ensure a seamless network connectivity [32].

3. Model calibration and validation: The validation and calibration of the created digital twin models need to be

checked for the actual representation of the physical aircraft condition and behavior. This involves developing correlations between the aircraft main bearing sensor data and the actual maintenance requirements. Calibration and validation are time-consuming processes as they require extensive data analysis, finding difference with real-world observations, and domain expertise. In making decisions related to the maintenance of aircraft main bearings, the accuracy and reliability of the digital twin model are very crucial.

4. Complexity and scale: Due to the highly complex and several interconnected components and subsystems, it is challenging to create and simulate the intricacy of the complete aircraft system into an accurate digital twin model. Various aspects like avionics, mechanical, electrical, and structural systems must be incorporated in developing the digital twin model. Ensuring the real-time performance of the digital twin model in managing the complexity and scale is a significant challenge.

5. Security and data privacy: For aircraft system maintenance, digital twin technology is dependent on sensitive data collection analysis. The utmost importance is about the privacy and security of data. Strong measures of cyber security need to be implemented to protect the infrastructure of the digital twin from potential cyber threats. Additionally, regulations or data privacy compliance and enforcement of appropriate data access controls are required to maintain confidentiality.

6. Integration with existing maintenance processes: The integration of digital twin technology implementation within the process of existing aircraft maintenance also causes challenges. There will be a need for the organization to modify the workflow for maintenance, train employees, and ensure the smooth integration of preexisting maintenance management systems with the digital twin model. Careful planning and coordination of infrastructure and existing workflow are required to align with the digital twin technology.

7. Cost and return on investment: The organization needs to invest in software, hardware, data storage, connectivity, security, and skilled personnel to implement and maintain aircraft maintenance and digital twin infrastructure. Although the long-term benefit of a digital twin is very promising, the investment at the initial stage and the recurrent maintenance

costs must be considered and carefully assessed by organizations through a cost–benefit analysis to evaluate a possible return on investment.

8. Data volume and velocity: The digital twin system should be implemented to handle and scale up with the large amount of data generated from various sensors and the systems of aircrafts. The digital twin systems must process real-time high-volume data sent by different sensors and ensure to analyze and monitor them in a timely manner. To implement real-time processing of a large volume of data generated by the aircraft system, efficient data storage, communication mechanisms, and processing are required.

9. Computational power: To analyze the complex data of aircrafts, digital twin systems often require considerable computational capabilities and efficiency. This can be achieved through simulation, executing advanced analytics algorithms, and creating real-time insights. The digital twin system's computational capabilities demand proper computing infrastructure, such as cloud services and resources and powerful servers.

10. Latency and responsiveness: Aircraft maintenance operations is very crucial and time sensitive as it requires monitoring and decision-making in a real-time environment; hence, slow data processing or delay in data transmission can affect the digital twin system's effectiveness. Efficient data transmission protocols and optimized speed for data processing can minimize the delay and ensure in-time responsive feedback from the aircraft digital twin.

11. Integration with legacy systems: Maintaining aircrafts involves integration with existing operational systems like enterprise resource planning system (ERP), equipment monitoring systems, and maintenance databases. For uninterrupted integration and interoperability among these legacy systems, the digital twin is very critical for holistic maintenance insights. Factors like data synchronization and compatibility must be taken cared of to make a smooth integration.

12.5.3   Security Threats of the Digital Twin in Aircraft Virtualization

Although aircraft maintenance, with the help of the digital twin, offers a number of benefits, it also poses a risk on data security and privacy concerns [33]. Following are few key security and privacy considerations related to aircraft maintenance using digital twin technology:

- Data privacy: The digital twin model works by collecting large amounts of sensitive data of the aircraft's sensors and systems, operational data, and maintenance record. It is very important to implement strong data privacy measures to guard these data and information from unauthorized access, misuse, and disclosure. This requires implementing access controls, encryption, secure data storage, and
- Digital twins rely on collecting and processing vast amounts of data, including sensitive information about the aircraft's systems, maintenance records, and operational data. It is crucial to implement robust data privacy measures to protect this information from unauthorized access, disclosure, or misuse. This requires implementing access controls, encryption and secure data storage.
- Cybersecurity: Digital twins are susceptible to cyber attacks, data breaches, unauthorized access, and cyber attacks to the infrastructure of the digital twin and its connected systems. For prevention from cyber threats, strong cyber security measures, such as intrusion detection system, network security protocols, and regular security assessments, are important to protect the systems and subsystems of the digital twin.
- Authentication and access control: Users accessing the digital twin system must be authenticated, and their integrity must be checked to ensure the safety of the digital twin system. Implementing strong authentication techniques, such as role-based access control and multi-factor authentication, can be helpful in preventing unauthorized access and securing sensitive maintenance data.
- Secure communication: A protocol for secure communication protocols should be implemented to protect data transfer between the other maintenance systems and the digital twin. Transport layer security (TLS)/secure socket layer (SSL) protocols, virtual private networks (VPNs),

and encryption techniques can help ensure the privacy and integrity of the data exchanged.

- Vulnerability management: To manage vulnerabilities, regular assessments and space management are necessary to recognize and address possible security vulnerabilities in the digital twin system. Keeping up-to-date software and firmware, monitoring for security patches and updates, and addressing any identified vulnerabilities on time can keep the digital twin secured.

- Data integrity and trustworthiness: It is essential to keep the data utilized in the digital twin honest and reliable. Making use of data quality controls, data validation and verification methods, and data reconciliation procedures can assist to guarantee that the digital twin operates with accurate and trustworthy data.

- Supply chain security: Consider the security of the entire digital twin ecosystem's supply chain. Included in this are the security procedures used by the vendors, suppliers, and contractors engaged in the design, implementation, and upkeep of the digital twin system. Security obligations and requirements should be covered by proper due diligence and contractual agreements.

- Regulatory compliance: Observe pertinent data protection and privacy laws, including the General Data Protection Regulation (GDPR) and laws that are specific to your sector. To preserve user privacy and avoid legal and compliance problems, make sure that data collecting, processing, and storage procedures adhere to all applicable laws and regulations.

- Create an incident response strategy to deal with security issues or breaches in an efficient manner: Procedures for incident identification, reaction, containment, communication, and recovery should be part of this strategy. Test and update the plan frequently to account for changing security threats. Taking care of these security and privacy issues involves a multifaceted strategy incorporating technology and regulation procedures and staff awareness. To ensure the effective protection of sensitive aircraft maintenance data, cyber security and privacy professionals must be included in the design, deployment, and maintenance of digital twin systems.

12.6   Future Prospects and Conclusion of Digital Twin for Aircraft Health

With the potential to completely change the way maintenance is carried out, the future of digital twin technology for aviation maintenance seems bright. As they develop, digital twins will offer more precise and sophisticated preventive maintenance capabilities. Digital twins can predict probable faults or maintenance requirements by evaluating real-time data from the aircraft's sensors and systems. This proactive method contributes to the improvement of aircraft availability and reliability while reducing unscheduled downtime and optimizing maintenance schedules. The prediction capacities of digital twins will be improved by the combination of digital twin technology with artificial intelligence (AI) and machine learning (ML) techniques. Based on historical data, operational conditions, and maintenance records, AI and ML can evaluate enormous volumes of data, find patterns, and make predictions [31]. Through this integration, digital twins will be able to gain knowledge from the past, enhance maintenance plans, and enhance decision-making.

By delivering immersive and engaging experiences, augmented reality (AR) and virtual reality (VR) technologies have the potential to improve the maintenance process. Through AR or VR interfaces, maintenance personnel can see digital twins and realistically examine and analyze the various parts and systems of an aircraft. These technologies can facilitate remote collaboration, overlay maintenance instructions, and provide real-time coaching, making maintenance tasks more accurate and efficient.

The seamless exchange of data throughout an aircraft's life cycle, from design through maintenance and beyond, is referred to as the "digital thread." In order to provide real-time feedback and insights on the health and performance of aircraft systems, digital twins can play a key role in the digital thread. Data-driven decisions and advancements are made possible by this integration, which provides a continuous feedback loop between design, manufacturing, operations, and maintenance.

The use of digital twin technology can be expanded to improve maintenance procedures for entire aircraft fleets. Digital twins can uncover common maintenance problems, spot patterns, and offer insights for fleet-wide maintenance programs by evaluating data from many aircrafts. This all-encompassing strategy can result in better resource allocation, cost optimization, and fleet-wide maintenance planning.

The benefit of iterative development and ongoing improvement is provided by digital twins. Digital twins can be improved and updated to increase their accuracy and prediction power as additional data is gathered and examined. This iterative technique enables ongoing learning and modification, resulting in digital twin models for aviation maintenance that are more trustworthy and efficient.

Their powers will be further improved by combining digital twins with IoT devices and big data analytics platforms. While big data analytics can manage massive volumes of data for more in-depth insights and trend analysis, IoT devices can deliver real-time data from multiple aircraft systems and components. Real-time monitoring, anomaly detection, and data-driven decision-making are made possible by this connection for effective and pro-active maintenance.

Aircraft systems are made up of many intricately interrelated parts and are quite complicated. There are many difficulties in creating a complete digital twin that includes all pertinent systems and their interconnections. Three crucial issues that must be addressed are the synchronization of real-time data, the integration of data from numerous sources, and system compatibility.

References

1. Errandonea, I., Beltrán, S., Arrizabalaga, S., Digital Twin for maintenance: A literature review. *Comput. Ind.*, 12, 3, 2020.
2. Wang, T. and Liu, Z., Digital Twin and Its Application for the Maintenance of Aircraft, in: *Handbook of Nondestructive Evaluation 4.0*, pp. 1–19, Springer, New York City, 2021.
3. Lughofer, E. and Sayed-Mouchaweh, M., Prologue: Predictive maintenance in dynamic systems, in: *Predictive Maintenance in Dynamic Systems: Advanced Methods, Decision Support Tools and Real-World Applications*, pp. 1–23, 2019.
4. Al-Ali, A.-R. *et al.*, Digital twin conceptual model within the context of internet of things. *Future Internet*, 12, 10, 163, 2020.
5. Dangut, M.D. *et al.*, Application of deep reinforcement learning for extremely rare failure prediction in aircraft maintenance. *Mech. Syst. Signal Process.*, 171, 2022. https://www.sciencedirect.com/science/article/abs/pii/S0888327022000693#preview-section-cited-by,
6. Berghout, T. and Benbouzid, M., A systematic guide for predicting remaining useful life with machine learning. *Electronics*, 11, 7, 1–31, 2022.
7. Xiong, M. and Wang, H., Digital twin applications in aviation industry: A review. *Int. J. Adv. Manuf. Technol.*, 121, 9-10, 5677–5692, 2022.
8. Zhong, D. *et al.*, Overview of predictive maintenance based on digital twin technology. *Heliyon*, 2023.

9. Rozhok, A.P. *et al.*, The use of digital twin in the industrial sector. *IOP Conference Series: Earth and Environmental Science*, vol. 815, IOP Publishing, 2021.

10. Leng, J. *et al.*, Digital twins-based smart manufacturing system design in Industry 4.0: A review. *J. Manuf. Syst.*, 60, 119–137, 2021.

11. Ren, Z., Wan, J., Deng, P., Machine-Learning-Driven Digital Twin for Lifecycle Management of Complex Equipment. *IEEE Trans. Emerging Top. Comput.*, 10, 1, 9–22, 1 Jan.-March 2022.

12. Srivastav, A.L., Markandeya, Patel, N. *et al.*, Concepts of circular economy for sustainable management of electronic wastes: challenges and management options. *Environ. Sci. Pollut. Res.*, 30, 48654–48675, 2023, https://doi.org/10.1007/s11356-023-26052-y.

13. Tao, F. *et al.*, Digital twin in industry: State-of-the-art. *IEEE Trans. Ind. Inf.*, 15, 4, 2405–2415, 2019.

14. Mendi, A.F., Erol, T., Doğan, D., Digital twin in the military field. *IEEE Internet Comput.*, 26, 5, 33–40, 2021.

15. Mubarak, A., Asmelash, M., Azhari, A., Alemu, T., Mulubrhan, F., Saptaji, K., Digital Twin Enabled Industry 4.0 Predictive Maintenance Under Reliability-Centred Strategy. *First International Conference on Electrical, Electronics, Information and Communication Technologies (ICEEICT)*, Trichy, India, pp. 01–06, 2022.

16. Ma, Z. *et al.*, Data-driven decision-making for equipment maintenance. *Autom. Constr.*, 112, 2020. https://www.sciencedirect.com/science/article/abs/pii/S0926580519308453

17. Xiong, M., Wang, H., Fu, Q., Xu, Y., Digital twin–driven aero-engine intelligent predictive maintenance. *Int. J. Adv. Manuf. Technol.*, 114, 11, 3751–3761, 2021.

18. Motamedi, A., Hammad, A. and Asen, Y., Knowledge-assisted BIM-based visual analytics for failure root cause detection in facilities management. *Autom. Constr.*, 43, 73–83, 2014.

19. Aydemir, H., Zengin, U., Durak, U., The digital twin paradigm for aircraft review and outlook. *AIAA Scitech 2020 Forum*, 2020.

20. Li, L., Aslam, S., Wileman, A. and Perinpanayagam, S., Digital twin in aerospace industry: A gentle introduction. *IEEE Access*, 10, 9543–9562, 2021.

21. Tauqir, A. *et al.*, Causes of fatigue failure in the main bearing of an aero-engine. *Eng. Fail. Anal.*, 7, 2, 127–144, 2000.

22. Roy, M., Failure analysis of bearings of aero-engine. *JFAP*, 19, 6, 1615–1629, 2019.

23. Qin, Y., Wu, X., Luo, J., Data-model combined driven digital twin of life-cycle rolling bearing. *IEEE Trans. Ind. Inf.*, 18, 3, 1530–1540, 2021.

24. Mathew, V., Toby, T., Singh, V., Rao, B.M., Kumar, M.G., Prediction of Remaining Useful Lifetime (RUL) of turbofan engine using machine learning, in: *2017 IEEE International Conference on Circuits and Systems (ICCS)*, pp. 306–311, IEEE, 2017 December.

25. Ahmad, W.M.T.W., Ghani, N.L.A., Drus, S.M., Data mining techniques for disease risk prediction model: A systematic literature review. *Adv. Intell. Syst. Comput.*, 843, 40–46, 2018.

26. Akamine, M. and Ajmera, J., Decision tree-based acoustic models for speech recognition. *EURASIP J. Audio Speech Music Process.*, 2012, 1–8, 2012.

27. Grafmüller, M., Beyerer, J., Kroschel, K., Decision tree classifier for character recognition combining support vector machines and artificial neural networks, in: *Mathematics of Data/Image Coding, Compression, and Encryption with Applications XII*, vol. 7799, pp. 99–106, United States, SPIE, September 7, 2010, 2010.

28. Breiman, L., Random forests. *Machine Learning*, 45, 5–32, 2001.

29. Jalawkhan, M.S. and Mustafa, T.K., Anomaly detection in flight data using the Naïve Bayes classifier, in: *2021 7th International Conference on Contemporary Information Technology and Mathematics (ICCITM)*, pp. 26–30, IEEE, 2021 August.

30. Murty, M.N. and Devi, V.S., Pattern recognition: An algorithmic approach. Springer Science & Business Media, 2011.

31. Tao, F., Zhang, H., Qi, Q.L., Zhang, M., Liu, W.R., Cheng, J.F., Ten questions towards digital twin: analysis and thinking. *Comput. Integr. Manuf. Syst.*, 26, 1, 1–17, 2020.

32. Storhaug, G., Digital-twins-and-sensor-monitoring, 2019. [Online] Available at: https://www.dnv.com/expert-story/maritime-impact/Digital-twins-and-sensor-monitoring/

33. Ibrion, M., Paltrinieri, N., Nejad, A.R., On risk of digital twin implementation in marine industry: Learning from aviation industry, in: *Journal of Physics: Conference Series*, vol. 1357, no. 1, p. 012009, IOP Publishing, 2019 October.

13

Power Energy System Consumption Analysis in Urban Railway by Digital Twin Method

K. Sreenivas Rao[1], P. Harini[2], Srikanta Kumar Mohapatra[3]*
and Jayashree Mohanty[4]

[1]*Department of CSE, Chaitanya Bharathi Institute of Technology, Hyderabad, India*
[2]*Department of Computer Science and Engineering, St Ann's College of Engineering*
and Technology, Chirala, Andhra Pradesh, India
[3]*Chitkara University Institute of Engineering and Technology, Chitkara University,*
Punjab, India
[4]*Department of AIT-CSE, Chandigarh University, Chandigarh, Punjab, India*

Abstract

The railway transport system is the main transport system in the world. The urban railway system is one of the important parts of the railway system, but it goes through a number of challenges to operate smoothly. The main challenges that it faces are the growing population and the developing standard of urbanization. The objective to fulfill the response is to provide a comfort zone which depends on public transportation. The demand is to provide an environment of transport which handles all the sustainable transport modes. The objective fulfillment implies to a secure and safe investment strategy to improve the transport label infrastructure which aims to meet the need of the future generation. This can be achieved by an improved solicit algorithm. Here digital win technology method is used to calculate the energy efficiency along with accuracy estimation. In a nation, the main transport system is bus on roads and railways on tracks. Thus, the main focus is to balance the investment lineup to increase the efficiency of public transportation. The challenges which come are the consumption of energy and handling the capacity in one go. The digital twin technology may solve the issue by considering the energy consumption to energy management issues.

*Corresponding author: srikanta.2k7@gmail.com

Abhineet Anand, Anita Sardana, Abhishek Kumar, Srikanta Kumar Mohapatra and Shikha Gupta (eds.) Simulation Techniques of Digital Twin in Real-Time Applications: Design Modeling and Implementation, (289–300) © 2024 Scrivener Publishing LLC

Keywords: Urban railway, digital twin, TEP, energy traction, energy breaking, driver analysis system, TEM, register breaking energy

13.1   Introduction

The energy demand increases as the population grows, which is directly proportional to the increase in the number of passengers. In the future, it may be required that trains run on electricity only, but the problem is the amount of energy consumption in running the train. Therefore, the goal is to reduce the energy consumption. This may lead to different factors like how the braking system can be optimized, monitoring and making strategies to enhance the energy management, going through the updated train schedule and operational management, and most importantly is to use a renewable energy source. If the goal is achieved, then urban railway may lead to a safe and reliable transport system. This will not only solve the issue related to the transportation system due to the increase in population but will also create a user-friendly and healthy environment.

Electric trains typically derive power from overhead contact lines. These lines can either supply power to the trains or allow the trains to feed energy back into the system through regenerative braking systems. Regenerative braking refers to the process of converting the braking energy of trains during deceleration into electrical energy by utilizing the electric motors as generators. Another option for powering trains is the use of onboard energy storage systems. These systems can operate independently or in conjunction with overhead power lines. They are particularly useful in replacing diesel-powered trains on non-electrified lines.

13.2   Literature Review

The energy flow of the study is analyzed by using the different aspects, i.e., data collected from various sources to relevant research work that searches from the different databases including Google scholar. The relevant keywords which are used for the research-relevant search are 5G, big data, energy efficiency, urban railway, predictive analysis, predictive maintenance, etc. The main objective is to understand the energy consumption in the urban railway and to identify the challenges associated with it to solve the issues. A proper implementation strategy is also important to manage the energy flow within the system. The study enhances with most relevant newer sources with older sources. The goal is to achieve the sensor data to enhance the aspects of utilization of energy in the system. The system emphasizes on how the railway system optimizes its energy system. These depend upon the air conditioning operation, total lighting system in the whole scenario, the elevators, and traction. It is found that the total power system in the train uses 40–60% of whole energy [1, 2]. Thus, powering a train uses the most significant percentage as compared to other forms of energy uses. The aim to work on traction energy consumption in an urban railway system is crucial. It depends on the temperature for regulation, voltage to measurement, and flow of current. These data are considered as true operation data. These data work on the volume of data that is used, velocity and variety of data exercised, and the veracity. The volume of the data is generally considered as the magnitude of data, which increases continuously due to a large number of sensors and data.

Digital twin technology is based upon the velocity dimension which deals with how to handle the high-speed generation and processing of data in real time. This technology diversifies the custom inputs to the desired outputs. The data may be structured or unstructured. The value of the data is derived from the insights and useful information that can be extracted from it [3, 4]. Finally, data segregation to data fulfillment—all of the processes—can be handled by the versatile application of digital twin technology. These veracity aspects relate to biases, noise, and abnormalities in the data, which can introduce inaccuracies and affect its reliability. The combination of these factors often leads to the generation of massive data sets, commonly known as "big data", that surpass the processing capabilities of conventional software tools within a reasonable timeframe [5]. To effectively handle and utilize this wealth of data, advanced data management and analysis techniques are required. This includes employing big data analytics tools and algorithms to process and extract valuable insights from the data. Additionally, data quality assurance measures, such as data cleaning and anomaly detection, are necessary to ensure the accuracy and reliability of the information derived from the data. By effectively managing and analyzing the sensor data generated by urban rail systems, operators can gain valuable insights into the system's performance, identify areas for energy optimization, and make informed decisions to improve energy efficiency and overall operations.

The three main types of traction used in railways throughout history are as follows: steam-powered, diesel-powered, and electrically powered trains. In the mid-1940s, diesel-powered trains became dominant due to factors such as low oil prices and faster refueling times compared to steam-powered trains [6]. However, electrically powered trains have developed over the years and exhibit a significantly higher efficiency, ranging from 65% to 80% compared to 20% to 25% for diesel-powered trains [7]. Despite their higher efficiency and lower greenhouse gas emissions (assuming renewable electricity sources), electric trains only make up 30% of the global rail fleet [8]. However, electric trains have several advantages, especially in urban areas. They produce no exhaust gases and operate silently, making them preferable in cities. Additionally, electric trains have a lower environmental impact compared to other modes of transportation, although there is still room for improvement [9]. In urban rail systems, various types of railway systems are employed, including tramways, light rail systems, metros, and commuter railways. The energy consumption in railways can be divided into two categories: traction and non-traction consumption. Traction energy refers to the energy used to propel the train forward and power the onboard auxiliary systems, such as climate control. Non-traction energy consumption includes the energy used at stations and other subsystems, encompassing signaling, lighting, ventilation, and the operation of groundwater pumps necessary for the functioning of the railway system [10]. Understanding and managing both traction and non-traction energy consumption are essential for optimizing energy efficiency in urban rail systems. By focusing on reducing energy consumption in both categories and exploring renewable energy sources, the sustainability and environmental performance of urban rail systems can be enhanced.

The statement correctly notes that electrically powered trains are more prevalent in Europe and Japan compared to other regions—for example, in Sweden, 95% of trains are electrically powered, and they consume about 2% of the country's total annual electrical energy production [11]. Electric trains offer advantages over diesel-powered trains, particularly in areas with high traffic density and where high power output is preferred, making them well suited for urban use. However, there are several reasons why electric trains are not more widely established globally. One significant factor is the high financial cost of implementing an electric railway infrastructure. The installation of electrified railways can be expensive, with an estimated cost of around one million Euros per kilometer, not including ongoing maintenance expenses. Additionally, each country has its own signaling system standards as well as specific physical and legal requirements for trains. This leads to variations in railway systems, which makes it challenging to establish a global standard. Historical circumstances and differing infrastructure development paths have resulted in various voltage standards in different countries. Replacing existing systems with a standardized one would incur substantial costs, and the potential benefits of one system over another have not been extensively researched. In Europe alone, there are five different power supply systems in use. These complexities and costs associated with infrastructure and standardization pose significant challenges for the widespread adoption of electric trains on a global scale. However, there is ongoing research and efforts to promote interoperability and harmonization of railway systems to facilitate international rail travel and improve energy efficiency [12].

The common types of energy storage systems used onboard trains include supercapacitors, batteries, and fuel cells. There are several benefits associated with using energy storage systems directly on trains. They can extend the range of trains to areas where overhead power lines are not available, such as remote regions or city centers where power lines may be prohibited. Additionally, implementing onboard energy storage systems is often more cost-effective than constructing new infrastructure for power lines. Modern-day digital twin technology is creating a useful environment for the tracking and updating of railway systems [13]. However, there are drawbacks to consider, such as the physical space occupied by the energy storage systems and the added weight, which can potentially limit the benefits of regenerative braking power utilization. Implementing onboard energy storage systems can be challenging due to the constraints of existing train designs [14]. As a result, an alternative approach is to deploy energy storage systems along the tracks. However, this method introduces additional line losses, reducing the overall efficiency of energy transfer. Choosing the most suitable power supply method, whether through overhead contact lines or onboard energy storage systems, depends on various factors such as infrastructure availability, operational requirements, and cost considerations. Balancing these factors is crucial to optimize the energy efficiency and sustainability of electric train systems. Virtual reality can be a part of the digital twin technique to handle such type of queries [15, 16].

13.3   Method

If true operation data were more accessible, it would enable the implementation of several energy-saving measures in the context of train systems. Access to detailed propulsion data would allow for more accurate Train Energy and Performance (TEP) simulations, which can play a crucial role in optimizing energy consumption. Train performance optimization can be analyzed by taking the propulsion data. This leads to tracking the performance of trains in the different conditions upon which they operate. The optimization includes acceleration or deceleration control, thus optimizing the overall speed profile and managing the energy loss.

The energy which is lost can be managed effectively by refining the population data and refining the various energy sources. It can only be possible by tracking and managing the real-time data under the circumstances of energy generation to control the amount of power required or the amount of energy which is stored. It also signifies regenerating the braking energy.

The system design is also an important part of the twining implementation strategy. It can be upgraded as required. It can be achieved by the propulsion data to upgrade the whole train system. In this, engineers can identify the certain components to upgrade in the train system, like traction motor, power electronics, or auxiliary system.

The train system can be emphasized on predictive maintenance. It also depends upon the propulsion data associated with the train system. The operator has to identify the maintenance of the train such that the system can maintained timely.

TEP digital twin simulation also takes a vital part to upgrade or control the energy consumption. TEP collects dynamic data like population, braking energy, and storage system. Then these data are subjected to a preprocess. Overall, simulation strategy is accomplished to predict the correct output. That concludes with a better accuracy.

13.4   Implementation

The data set is implemented on the following criteria. The factors are mentioned in Table 13.1. We have taken two cases to study the performance of the energy system. The general data which were taken are travel time, energy traction, energy breaking, travel distance, etc. TT refers to travel time.

$$\text{NE (net energy)} = \text{ET (energy traction)} - [\text{EB (energy breaking)} + \text{REB (register breaking energy)}] \quad (13.1)$$

$$\text{ACC (accuracy)} = 1 - [\text{TEM (total energy measurement)} / \{(\text{ET (energy traction)} - \text{EB (energy breaking)}\}] \quad (13.2)$$

Use Case
The use case is taken in two rows, R1 and R2, as per the two routes taken for the traveling of the urban railways with a specific time period to calculate the energy sources.

Case 1
This is the system-embedded fastest way of traveling with all the details. All the parameters are simulated. R1 and R2 are two roots are taken for the verify the result set. Table 13.1 is the number of likely methods to be

Table 13.1 Factors associated with the system.

Characteristics	Description
ET	Energy traction
EB	Energy breaking
REB	Register breaking energy
NE	Net energy
TD	Travel distance
TEM	Total energy measurement
ACC	Accuracy
TRD	Total running distance
JT	Journey time
ST	Stop time
EU	Energy usage
RE	Regenerated energy
NE	Net energy

Table 13.2 R1 and R2 with all the parameters.

Route	TT (h:min:s)	ET (kWh)	EB (kWh)	REB (kWh)	NE (kWh)	TD (km)	TEM (kWh)	ACC (%)
R1	00:15:22	7,213	310	3,143	3,760	1,003	7,235	-0.48
R2	00:15:26	7,156	321	3,234	3,601	1,018	6,103	0.11
RT	00:30:48	14,369	631	6,377	7,361	2,021	13,338	0.03

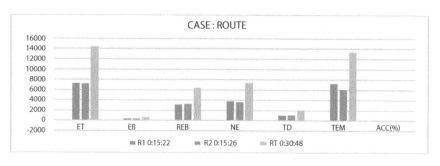

Figure 13.1 Parameter display performances with given time travels.

Table 13.3 Fastest route simulation R1 energy results.

TRD (km)	JT (h:min:s)	ST (h:min:s)	EU (kWh)	RE (kWh)	NE (kWh)
1,023	00:13:20	00:03:10	8,976	6,154	2,822

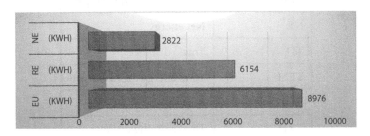

Figure 13.2 Fastest route simulation results R1 with energy results.

Table 13.4 Fastest route simulation R2.

TRD (km)	JT (h:min:s)	ST (h:min:s)	EU (kWh)	RE (kWh)	NE (kWh)
957	00:11:45	00:02:56	9,367	6,246	3,121

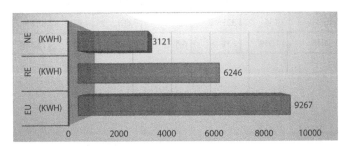

Figure 13.3 Fastest route simulation results R2.

Table 13.5 Driver analysis system R1 energy results.

TRD (km)	JT (h:min:s)	ST (h:min:s)	EU (kWh)	RE (kWh)	NE (kWh)
931	00:14:34	00:03:16	6,826	3,324	3,502

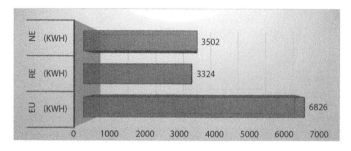

Figure 13.4 Driver analysis system R1 analysis with energy results.

Table 13.6 Driver analysis system R2 energy results.

TRD (km)	JT (h:min:s)	T (h:min:s)	EU (kWh)	RE (kWh)	NE (kWh)
887	00:13:03	00:03:54	5,235	3,024	2,211

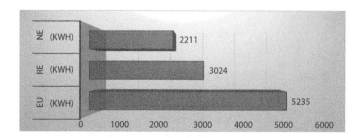

Figure 13.5 Driver analysis system R2 with energy results.

Table 13.7 Real-time operation of trains in railway tracks in R1 with energy results.

TRD (km)	TT (h:min:s)	TST (h:min:s)	EU (kWh)	RE (kWh)	NE (kWh)
943	00:13:02	00:03:23	6,378	3,821	2,557

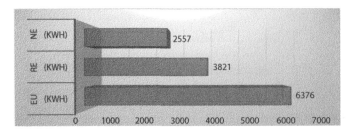

Figure 13.6 Real-time operation of trains in railway tracks in R1 with energy results.

Table 13.8 Real-time operation of trains in railway tracks in R2 with energy results.

TRD (km)	JT (h:min:s)	JT (h:min:s)	TEL (kWh)	RE (kWh)	NE (kWh)
902	00:12:32	00:02:42	6,797	3,443	3,354

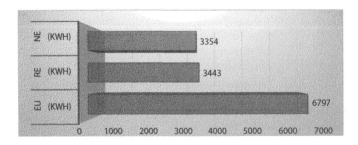

Figure 13.7 Real-time operation of trains in railway tracks in R2 with energy results.

used and Table 13.2 shows the parameters which are used in the R1 and R2. Tables 13.3 and 13.4 shows the fastest root energy consumption. Tables 13.5 and 13.6 refers to driver analysis report. The Tables 13.7 and 13.8 implies the real-time root analysis of R1 and R2.

The Figures 13.1–13.7 are the real time analysis of corresponding Tables 13.2 to 13.8.

Case 2: Driver Analysis System
This case is based upon the driver analysis system which analyzes both the journey time and the net energy which is required.

Case 3: Real-Time Operation of Trains in Railway Tracks

13.5 Conclusion

The energy consumption which is directly related to the power consumption in urban railway depends upon the population growth. The energy performance in the system shows that the energy is gradually increasing in both reference cases. Accuracy is also shown, with an error result of less than 1%. Thus, the power consumption or energy utilization is a concerning factor. These results can be useful for the concerned authorities of railways to depict the user label experience. These data also show that some preventive methods can be implemented for the simulation. The effective way of operations may result in increased and adequate performance. The digital twin technology used to calculate the value in energy efficiency can be improved with other embedded technology.

References

1. Su, S., Tang, T., Wang, Y., Evaluation of strategies to reducing traction energy consumption of metro systems using an optimal train control simulation model. *Energies*, 9, 2, 105, 2016.
2. González-Gil, A., Palacin, R., Batty, P., Powell, J.P., A systems approach to reduce urban rail energy consumption. *Energy Convers. Manag.*, 80, 509–524, 2014.
3. Kumar, A., Kumar, S.A., Dutt, V., Shitharth, S., Tripathi, E., IoT based arrhythmia classification using the enhanced hunt optimization-based deep learning. *Expert Syst.*, 40, 7, e13298, 2023, https://doi.org/10.1111/exsy.13298.
4. Zhou, H., Yan, Z., Jing, X., Chen, Y., Liu, J., Zou, X., Kang, C., Li, B., Xie, Y., Yan, D., Research on the three-dimensional visual management and control

for marine intelligent mould bed based on digital twin. *Ships Offshore Struct.*, 18, 1–13, 2023.

5. Grover, V., Chiang, R.H., Liang, T.P., Zhang, D., Creating strategic business value from big data analytics: A research framework. *J. Manage. Inf. Syst.*, 35, 2, 388–423, 2018.

6. Allen, J.G. and Newmark, G.L., Commuter Rail Electrifications That Never Were and What They Teach Us. *Transp. Res. Rec.*, *2677*, 1, 639–652, 2023.

7. Yang, N., Wang, L., Geraci, G., Elkashlan, M., Yuan, J., Di Renzo, M., Safeguarding 5G wireless communication networks using physical layer security. *IEEE Commun. Mag.*, *53*, 4, 20–27, 2015.

8. Kumar, A., Rathore, P.S., Dubey, A.K. *et al.*, LTE-NBP with holistic UWB-WBAN approach for the energy efficient biomedical application. *Multimed. Tools Appl.*, 82, 39797–39811, 2023, https://doi.org/10.1007/s11042-023-15604-6.

9. Kumlin, J., True operation simulation for urban rail: Energy efficiency from access to Big data, Thesis, Master of Science program in Industrial Engineering of Malardalen University Sweden, 2019.

10. Chandrasekaran, S., Dutt, V., Vyas, N., Kumar, R., Student Sentiment Analysis Using Various Machine Learning Techniques. *2023 International Conference on Artificial Intelligence and Smart Communication (AISC)*, pp. 104–107, Greater Noida, India, 2023, doi: 10.1109/AISC56616.2023.10085018.

11. Tu, M. and Olofsson, U., PM10 in underground stations from different types of trains. *Transp. Res. Part D Transp. Environ.*, 95, 102867, 2021.

12. Ilyas, B., Kumar, A., Setitra, M.A., Bensalem, Z.E.A., Lei, H., Prevention of DDoS attacks using an optimized deep learning approach in blockchain technology. *Trans. Emerging Telecommun. Technol.*, 34, 4, e4729, 2023.

13. Ahmadi, M., Kaleybar, H.J., Brenna, M., Castelli-Dezza, F., Carmeli, M.S., Adapting digital twin technology in electric railway power systems, in: *2021 12th Power Electronics, Drive Systems, and Technologies Conference (PEDSTC)*, IEEE, pp. 1–6, 2021, February.

14. Srivastav, A.L., Markandeya, Patel, N. *et al.*, Concepts of circular economy for sustainable management of electronic wastes: challenges and management options. *Environ. Sci. Pollut. Res.*, 30, 48654–48675, 2023, https://doi.org/10.1007/s11356-023-26052-y.

15. Kumar, A., Kumar, S.A., Dutt, V., Dubey, A.K., Narang, S., A Hybrid Secure Cloud Platform Maintenance Based on Improved Attribute-Based Encryption Strategies. *Int. J. Interact. Multimed. Artif. Intell.*, 8, 2, 150–157, 2023, http://dx.doi.org/10.9781/ijimai.2021.11.004.

16. Benkhaddra, I., Kumar, A., Setitra, M.A. *et al.*, Design and Development of Consensus Activation Function Enabled Neural Network-Based Smart Healthcare Using BIoT. *Wirel. Pers. Commun.*, 130, 1549–1574, 2023, https://doi.org/10.1007/s11277-023-10344-0.

14

Based on Digital Twin Technology, an Early Warning System and Strategy for Predicting Urban Waterlogging

Shweta Thakur

Chandigarh University, Mohali, Punjab, India

Abstract

By gathering data from the actual environment and simulating it, digital twin (DT) technology portrays the twinning behavior of a tangible thing or process, i.e., the current and future behavior. In a variety of fields and industries, including industrial, automotive, medical, smart cities, etc., it is utilized for predictive analysis. In the age of a growing urban population, it is a challenge not only to maintain water quality but also to develop a system that manages water logging-related problems like sewage overflows and flash floods. Numerous initiatives have failed to meet the needed performance standards because there is insufficient ongoing monitoring of data in real time and a poor knowledge of self-propelled systems. To address these issues, engineers are seeking to build a network embedded with data sensors and online models using digital twin technology for real-time monitoring of system dynamics. Operators can use this technology to spot odd sewer network conditions and then dispatch a maintenance crew to conduct repairs before damage is done. It results in reducing the operational cost of the system and preventing sewer overflows and waterlogging to a large extent. The main challenge of DT technology in social adoption is the lack of standardization of definitions and characteristics. Performance digital twin (PDT) methodology can be utilized to monitor the information from physical counterparts and produce actionable data for optimizing product design, generating strategy, and drawing conclusions. Instead of achieving economic efficiency, the methodology has provided quality of life and services to the citizens. The DT's infrastructure includes various data

Email: shweta.e12791@cumail.in

Abhineet Anand, Anita Sardana, Abhishek Kumar, Srikanta Kumar Mohapatra and Shikha Gupta (eds.) Simulation Techniques of Digital Twin in Real-Time Applications: Design Modeling and Implementation, (301–318) © 2024 Scrivener Publishing LLC

mining and modeling techniques for prediction and optimization, and sensors, actuators, and IoT can be used for data acquisition methods.

Keywords: Digital twin, prediction, warning system, water logging, urban area

14.1 Introduction

Digital twin technology focuses on the predictive analysis and fault tolerance of various systems in the industrial domain due to IOT-rich environments and advanced data analytics.

14.1.1 Definition

According to the author in [1], the digital twin is essentially a living simulation of a tangible asset or system that can predict the future of its physical counterpart and continuously adjusts to accommodate changes based on data and information gathered online. The author in [2] describes it as follows: "A digital twin is a model of a physical component or assembly created digitally utilizing service information and integrated simulations. The digital representation contains data that is gathered from various sources during the course of a product's life cycle. In order to improve decision-making, this data is constantly revised and presented in a number of ways to forecast current and future situations in both the architectural and operating environments."

14.1.2 Application Areas of Digital Twin Technology

The primary area of applications includes smart cities and industrial manufacturing with some healthcare-related applications:

1. Smart cities: The application of digital twin technology is growing along with the emergence of smart cities. The development of sophisticated AI algorithms is aided by the data collected from IoT devices. Smart city planning and development are aided by a surveillance system of IoT sensors. It provides a living testbed inside a simulated twin that may be used to test situations and, secondly, to enable digital twins to acquire knowledge from their surroundings by examining alterations to the data gathered [3]. Digital twins of cities help in urban planning, infrastructure management, and optimizing resource allocation. They enable simulations,

monitoring of energy usage, traffic management, and prediction of environmental conditions [4].

2. Manufacturing: Digital twin technology has significant applications in the manufacturing industry, offering numerous benefits in optimizing processes, improving efficiency, and enhancing overall performance. Digital twins enable manufacturers to create virtual replicas of their products, allowing for detailed design analysis, simulation, and testing before physical production begins. This helps identify design flaws, optimize performance, reduce time to market, and minimize costs associated with physical prototyping [5]. Manufacturers can track and analyze production performance, spot bottlenecks, anticipate maintenance requirements, optimize scheduling, and streamline processes by integrating real-time information from sensors and manufacturing equipment. This results in more production, less downtime, and better resource use [6]. Through real-time equipment and machinery monitoring, digital twins enable predictive maintenance. Manufacturers can predict impending failures or maintenance requirements by analyzing sensor information and performance indicators. In addition to minimizing unplanned downtime, cutting repair costs, and maximizing equipment longevity, this enables proactive maintenance scheduling [7]. Digital twins can provide visibility and optimization capabilities across the supply chain. By creating a virtual representation of the supply chain, manufacturers can track inventory levels, analyze demand patterns, optimize logistics, and simulate different scenarios to improve overall supply chain efficiency, minimize inventory holding costs, and enhance customer satisfaction [8]. Digital twins enable manufacturers to keep track of and analyze production processes in real time to discover anomalies, defects, or quality issues. By integrating data from sensors, cameras, and other sources, manufacturers can implement automated quality control measures, perform root cause analysis, and optimize production parameters to improve product quality and reduce waste. Digital twins facilitate continuous improvement efforts by providing a platform for experimentation and simulation. Manufacturers can test different process modifications, evaluate the impact of changes, and simulate scenarios to optimize performance, energy

consumption, or resource allocation without disrupting actual production [9].

3. Healthcare: Digital twins of human organs or body systems are utilized for personalized medicine, treatment planning, and simulation of surgical procedures. They can aid in diagnosis, monitoring, and optimization of patient care [10]. By integrating real-time data from wearables, sensors, and medical records, healthcare providers can track patient conditions, detect early warning signs, and intervene proactively, leading to improved disease management and personalized interventions [11]. Digital twins of virtual patients and organ models are utilized in drug discovery and clinical trials. They aid in the prediction of drug efficacy, optimization of dosage, and identification of potential adverse reactions, thereby accelerating the drug development process and reducing costs [12]. Digital twins can be employed to model and optimize healthcare systems, including hospitals, clinics, and emergency response systems. They facilitate resource planning, patient flow management, and capacity optimization, leading to more efficient healthcare delivery and improved patient outcomes [13].

4. Energy systems: Digital twins are used to model and optimize energy generation, distribution, and consumption. They aid in demand forecasting, energy grid management, and integration of renewable energy sources [14]. Digital twins of energy grids enable real-time monitoring, control, and optimization of grid operations. They facilitate load balancing, fault detection, and predictive maintenance, leading to improved grid reliability, efficiency, and resilience [15]. Digital twins facilitate the grid's incorporation of renewable energy resources like solar and wind. They manage intermittency, support decision-making for energy storage systems, and demand response programs [16]. Immediate tracking and administration of the consumption of energy are possible, thanks to digital twins. They enable energy-efficient building management, optimize HVAC systems, and provide insights for occupant behavior analysis and energy-saving strategies [17]. Digital twins support the modeling and simulation of virtual power plants (VPPs), which aggregate and coordinate distributed energy resources. They optimize energy dispatch, predict energy generation, and enable

virtual power trading, promoting flexibility and stability in the energy system [18]. Digital twins provide a virtual environment for energy market analysis and planning. They facilitate scenario analysis, policy evaluation, and investment decision-making, enabling stakeholders to assess the impact of different energy policies and market dynamics [19].

5. Transportation and logistics: Digital twins of vehicles, transportation networks, and supply chains help in optimizing routes, improving logistics efficiency, and enhancing fleet management. They enable the real-time monitoring and predictive maintenance of vehicles [20]. Through the integration of data from numerous sources, including suppliers, storage facilities, and transportation systems, digital twins provide a comprehensive perspective of the supply chain. They enhance demand forecasting, regulate inventory levels, and provide real-time tracking of commodities. Digital twins also support scenario modeling and simulation to identify bottlenecks and optimize logistics processes [21]. Digital twins help optimize port and terminal operations by simulating and monitoring activities such as container handling, berth scheduling, and cargo flow. By analyzing real-time data from sensors, digital twins can improve resource allocation, reduce congestion, and enhance safety and security. They enable better coordination among various stakeholders within the port ecosystem [22]. Digital twins enable the proactive maintenance of transportation assets, such as engines, railway tracks, and airport infrastructure. Digital twins can anticipate equipment problems, optimize maintenance schedules, and reduce downtime by constantly recording sensor data and examining performance patterns. This results in cost savings, improved safety, and increased asset lifespan [23]. In order to improve traffic flow, lessen congestion, and increase the effectiveness of transportation, digital twins are used in traffic management systems. Digital twins allow for real-time traffic monitoring by fusing data from numerous sources, such as sensors, camera footage, and GPS units. They support predictive modeling and simulation to optimize traffic signal timings, manage road networks, and provide dynamic routing recommendations [24].

14.2 Literature Review

In the context of urban waterlogging, researchers have explored the utilization of digital twin technology to develop early warning mechanisms and strategies. These systems aim to predict and mitigate the risks associated with water logging in urban areas, helping authorities and stakeholders to take preventive measures. The research in this area typically involves integrating various data sources, such as weather data, hydrological information, topographic data, and infrastructure data, into the digital twin model. By analyzing and simulating these data, researchers can identify potential water logging hotspots, assess the vulnerability of different areas, and develop strategies for effective water management.

A quick, reservoir-based surrogate forecast model was created in 2019 by researchers Lund *et al.* from a 1D hydrodynamic metropolitan drainage model. Each forecast is preceded by an update to the surrogate model using the Ensemble Kalman filter. Using rating curves, water level observations were incorporated, and the model was validated. The findings demonstrate that more recent water level data aided in improving flow forecasts [25]. A digital twin model was presented by Bartos *et al.* in 2021 for stormwater systems. In this, the data assimilation process was combined with a new hydraulic solver to complete the model. Additionally, they made use of the Kalman filtering technique, which effectively updates hydraulic states in response to observed data. Their software allowed for quick flood warnings and enhanced characterization of maintenance and remediation requirements. Additionally, it offered dependable real-time management for both small and big networks, such as rivers and reservoirs, as well as stormwater systems [26]. A similar type of study is concluded by incorporating water level readings into a collection of hydrodynamic models by the scientists Palmitessa *et al.* that made them possible to do soft sensing of urban drainage tunnels. It offers practical uncertainty estimates and is most appropriate for non-linear models. Two sensors were placed 3.4 km apart in a combined sewer overflow tunnel in Copenhagen, Denmark, where the plan was tested. While the upstream observations were used for validation, the downstream observations were taken into account. Their method successfully identified flaws in the upstream sensor and could give soft sensing [27].

In the year 2022, the vast amount of data produced by the Internet of things (IoT) in smart cities was subjected to a big data analysis by Xiaoming Li *et al.* They introduced the convolutional neural network's (CNN) distributed parallelism method and the deep learning algorithm. To build the smart city digital twins multi-hop transmission IoT-BDA system based on Deep Learning, digital twins (DTs) and multi-hop transmission technology is introduced. The findings show that, as the minimum energy collected increases, the model's energy efficiency first rises and subsequently falls. The model's prediction accuracy was 97.80%, and the data transfer performance was the most accurate [28]. In another work, a thorough analysis of 3D city modeling, developing early warning systems, digital replicas, and climate resilience technology was provided by Riaz K. *et al.* in which 37 case reports were selected among the 68 papers that were found using the PRISMA method. The analysis discovered a new concept for enhancing climate resilience: a bidirectional flow of information between the computerized model and the actual physical environment; however, there are still research gaps about how to implement and use a true digital twin with a bidirectional data flow [29].

14.3   Methodology

Digital twin technology can be a valuable tool for developing an early warning system and strategy for predicting urban waterlogging. A step-by-step approach to implementing such a system includes the following:

1. Data collection: Gather relevant data about the urban area prone to water logging. This includes information on topography, drainage systems, rainfall patterns, land use, and infrastructure. Remote sensing techniques, IoT sensors, weather stations, and historical data can be used for data collection [30].

2. Digital twin creation: Develop a digital twin of the urban area, which is a virtual replica that mirrors the physical environment. The digital twin should incorporate the collected data and accurately represent the urban infrastructure, such as buildings, roads, drainage networks, and water bodies [31].

3. Model development: Create a hydrological model that simulates the flow of water in the digital twin. This model should take into account rainfall data, land characteristics, drainage network capacity, and other relevant factors. Various modeling techniques, such as hydraulic models or hydrodynamic simulations, can be employed to predict water logging scenarios [32].

4. Data integration and analytics: The digital twin incorporates real-time data from numerous sources, including precipitation sensors, riverbed levels, and drainage networks. The data is analyzed to find prospective scenarios using sophisticated data analytics techniques like artificial intelligence or machine learning and hydrological models. These models can take into account factors like rainfall intensity, soil permeability, and the capacity of drainage systems [33].

5. Calibration and validation: Calibrate the model using historical data and validate it against observed water logging events in the past. This step ensures that the model accurately represents real-world conditions and improves the reliability of predictions [34].

6. Early warning system: Implement an early warning system based on the digital twin and the calibrated model. The system should monitor real-time data from sensors, weather forecasts, and other relevant sources. When specific thresholds are exceeded (e.g., rainfall intensity, the water level in drainage channels), the system should generate alerts or notifications to relevant stakeholders, such as city authorities, emergency services, or residents [35].

7. Decision support: Integrate the digital twin and the early warning system into a decision support platform. This platform should provide stakeholders with visualizations, real-time data, and actionable insights to facilitate decision-making—for example, it can suggest optimal evacuation routes, identify areas prone to water logging, or recommend infrastructure improvements.

8. Continuous monitoring and improvement: Regularly update and improve the digital twin and the predictive model based on new data, feedback, and lessons learned from previous water logging events. This iterative process helps refine the accuracy of predictions and enhances the effectiveness of the early warning system.

9. Stakeholder engagement and education: Educate and involve the community, city officials, and other relevant stakeholders in the early warning system. Raise awareness about water logging risks, provide guidance on response actions, and encourage proactive measures, such as proper waste management, maintenance of drainage infrastructure, and urban planning considerations.

By leveraging digital twin technology, a comprehensive early warning system and strategy for predicting urban waterlogging can be developed. This approach enables proactive planning, risk mitigation, and timely response to protect urban areas from the damaging effects of water logging.

There are various methods to build a digital model that collects the data in real time through sensors and intimate the levels of water logging to the stakeholders so that necessary action can be taken to avoid the consequences, namely:

1. Surrogate models: Using an abstract piecewise-linear storage tank system that is geographically distributed as a substitute for a high-fidelity methodology, this study provides a method to estimate the two types of flows and overflows without relying on lengthy time series of history for the model's development or calibration. The surrogate model uses tabulated storage–discharge relationships to calculate outflows from compartments, extracting them from the HiFi model. Interpolating between the closest numbers yields the flow rate. The characteristics of the HiFi surface model are used to calculate the surface runoff compartments, which are subsequently transmitted to the mesh model applying a temporal area model as well as a single linear reservoir having a 0.5Tc time constant. The states of the surrogate model are updated utilizing the EnKF as a data aggregation approach each time a freshwater level or flow record is available, even though the surrogate system is created solely from the set of variables and outcomes from the HiFi representation. The revised states serve as the starting point for the surrogate model's prediction. In order to predict flows and spillage in densely populated sewer systems, this work built a quick, reservoir-based substitute prognosticate model based on a 1D hydrodynamic metropolitan drainage model. The findings demonstrated that paradigm upgrading enhanced the prediction by up to 2 h in advance, but they also demonstrated that updating based on water level examination produced higher-quality flow estimates than integration built on flow data. This approach is appropriate for operational situations where there is frequently insufficient time and information for finetuning [25].

2. Hydraulic models: Firstly, a reliable hydraulic solver is put into place to provide an accurate state-space model

of the drainage system, which makes it easier to assimi-
late data. The hydraulic solver is then paired with an intuitive Kalman filter to make it easier to incorporate sensor
data in real time within the dynamical model. Finally, the
data assimilation approach is assessed based on how well
it interpolates and forecasts system states using data from
sensors from an actual-world stormwater network. The
hydrodynamic solver developed in this paper is based on
an implicitly staggered-grid method and is used to solve
the single-dimensional Saint-Venant parameters in sewer/
channel networks. It is a limited difference model with
links, intersections, super links, and hyper-junctions as its
four different computational element types [26]. In order to
simplify the computation of pressured flow, each link incorporates a Priessman slot. An example network from [36] is
depicted in Figure 14.1.

The Saint-Venant equations in one dimension are used in this model. It
is split into two sections: the equation of continuity (14.1), which depicts
the mass equilibrium for a limited volume, and the equation for momentum (14.2), which describes the force balance:

$$\frac{\partial A}{\partial t} + \frac{\partial Q}{\partial x} = qin \tag{14.1}$$

$$\frac{\partial Q}{\partial t} + \frac{\partial}{\partial x}(Qu) + g(A)\left(\frac{\partial h}{\partial x} - S0 + Sf + Sl\right) = 0 \tag{14.2}$$

where Q is the discharge process, A is the cross-sectional
area of the flow, u is the mean velocity, h is the measurement

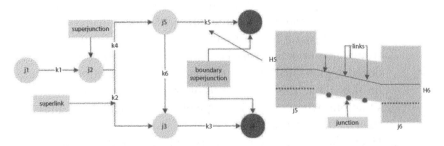

Figure 14.1 Basic computational elements of a model [36].

of the depth, x is the length of the stream, t is the length of time, and qin is the lateral inflow per unit width; Sf and SL represent the dimension of the channel bottom slope, frictional slope, and local loss of head slope, respectively [26].

3. Kalman filter: Quick assimilation of data from sensors is made possible by this methodology while still respecting the physical system's dynamics. A Bayesian estimation process called Kalman filtering creates a posterior estimate of the system states by updating the prior estimate with observed data. It accomplishes this by creating an earlier prediction of the system behaviors within a dynamical system paradigm. This is the best linear estimator for the system's state if the dynamical system organization is highly accurate and the variability is white and uniform with a specified covariance [26]. The implicit status equation can be stated as follows to get started:

$$X_{t+\Delta t} = A_t X_t + B_t U_{t+\Delta t} + Y_t$$

where $A_t = Z_t^{-1} Y_t, B_t = Z_t^{-1}$, and $Y_t = Z_t^{-1} S_t$. Thus, using an equation for the observed output and an equation for the "hidden" state of the system, we can describe the inner workings and observable outputs of the system. Assuming that some unpredictable disturbance W_t corrupts the state equation while noise from measurement V_t corrupts the output equation.

$$X_{t+\Delta t} = A_t X_t + B_t U_{t+\Delta t} + Y_t + W_t$$
$$Z_t = H_t X_t + V_t$$

Here X_t is the current time step's n-dimensional state vector, U_t is the input vector's ℓ dimensions, W_t is the stochastic disturbance's p dimensions, Z_t is the current time step's m-dimensional recognized state, and V_t is the measurement noise vector's m dimensions. The $(n \times n)$ matrix of state transitions A_t, the $(n \times \ell)$ input transition matrix B_t, the $(n \times 1)$ constants vector Y_t, and the $(m \times n)$ measurement transitional matrix H_t are all represented by matrices. The measurement noise V_t and stochastic disturbance W_t are thought to be arbitrary vectors of known-covariance zero-mean stochastic white noise [26].

The Kalman filter integrates these readings into the hydraulic solution by capturing inputs in the configuration of depth or oppression data collected by sensors at super junctions. Interpolated and projected system states are more accurate, thanks to the Kalman filter, which also lowers the mean absolute error brought on by unsure dynamic inputs. It improves system behavior prediction by real-time correcting system states by integrating and subtracting lumps from the complete system to correlate with field investigation data.

4. Early warning systems: Low-lying locations are more susceptible to environmental risks such as storm surges, coastal floods, and erosion as a result of climate change [4]. Globally, 40% of the population live within 100 km of a shore. These populated regions with low elevations need dependable early-alert mechanisms that appropriately consider the region's compounded processes to avert the deprivation of lives and assets as a consequence of devastating climatic occurrences in waterfront zones. In earlier times, models were utilized to predict environmental disasters, but their accuracy was constrained by the scarcity of data at regional sizes. Both the immediate and future disaster predictions made by these models are erroneous because of how cities' parameters are constantly changing. Early warning system real-time data is thought to be extremely dependable. The difficulties of analyzing such data and figuring out how to use it to provide accurate early warnings, however, is a bigger issue. Technology improvements have led to the creation of "digital twins" or virtual city models that incorporate real-time sensor data in many cities [37]. Sensors can measure the infrastructure's real-time resilience, enabling specialists to analyze how well it performs in the face of catastrophic occurrences like climate change. It is simpler to keep track of performance and find defects when all components of a city are connected to a cloud-based digital twin [38]. Cities can use sensors and cameras scattered throughout the city to collect actual-time geographic information that is up to date, thanks to wireless, IoT, and 5G technology for sensors. This makes it easier for stakeholders and urban designers to collaborate on approaches to managing cities.

A representation of the same can be shown in Figure 14.2. Sensors can collect data about coastal threats, which can be

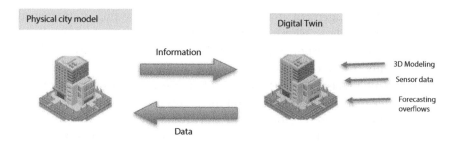

Figure 14.2 Using sensor data to transfer a physical municipal infrastructure to a digital replica model [4].

utilized to inform stakeholders and decision-makers about how to put mitigating measures into place. Virtual and physical twins can teach smart cities how to better prepare for and respond to calamities. The top three adopters, with $73 million spent in the Virtual Singapore initiative, are Singapore, Zurich, and Oslo [39]. End-to-end early-warning notifications for hazard prediction, consisting of an on-site unit and a web-based interface, require the collection of data in real time. Sensors are used to measure things like water level, tides, rainfall, temperature, and humidity [40]. Due to their low price and small size, micro-electro-mechanical system (MEMS) sensors are becoming more and more attractive for early detection methods for earthquake and flooding incidents. A system for early warning has been developed through research in the Indian Himalayan region [41]. Through the use of a micro-SD card along with GSM, sensor data can be locally recorded and sent to a distant server by being preserved in a local or Internet-based data logger. To establish an acceptable level for hazard warnings, this is done. The threshold limit for a particular location or city is compared to the benchmark limit in the last phase, which also uses predictive modeling and statistical analysis to establish limits of threshold for natural disasters. Early warning systems are being investigated with digital twin technology [42].

14.4   Discussion and Conclusion

Pipedream is a novel technology that allows for the forecasting and interpolation of hydraulic states in real time for urban rapid flood nowcasting.

Emergency management may estimate localized flooding at ungauged places using the data assimilation process in the pipedream toolset, allowing for quick flood response and focused emergency service dispatch [43]. Additionally, the toolkit aids in spotting maintenance crises, enabling prompt and precise diagnosis of maintenance problems for successful stormwater management. Pipedream integrates information from sensors with a dynamic representation of the stormwater system in order to provide two separate estimates of the state of the system, making it simpler to track irregularities and distinguish between real emergencies and false positives. The basis for real-time management of urban drainage systems is also provided by the pipedream toolbox, which has been shown to reduce overflows of combined sewers and enhance urban water quality [44]. This study compares pipedream to SWMM and pySWMM to assess pipedream's functionality for networks with up to 210 super junctions. Larger networks, however, might necessitate specialized techniques for sparse matrix equations. Improvements to the standard Kalman filter may be required for huge systems, such as those with many states and negligible process noise covariance. Future research ought to look into these additions and include them in current modeling frameworks. Future studies should investigate different numerical techniques for Saint-Venant computations in real-time data integration. An upwind formulation of a first-order implicit system remains constant, but higher-order systems may be more accurate and have less mass balance error. Future research should also look at the boundary constraints for the hydraulic solution while taking into account the inertial element of the motion balance at the point of contact across superlinks and superjunctions. HiFi models cannot be used for predictive purposes in urban drainage systems due to their slow computational performance. Surrogate models can be utilized for streamlined systems though. Without using historical data, a study coupled a surrogate model and the Ensemble Kalman filter. The method was evaluated on a watershed near Copenhagen by comparing actual flow and level data to anticipated flows and overflows. The study suggests that calibrating the HiFi model to actual observations would be advantageous. Enhancing the surrogate model outperformed both the ordinary and HiFi models with projections accurate to 2 h in advance. Because level sensors are more affordable and dependable, water level measurements have enhanced forecasts in addition to flow data. This robust setup requires less tuning, making it valuable for operational implementations with limited time and data. Updating surrogate models can create robust and efficient flow and overflow forecasts.

This systematic investigation looks at the possibilities of computational twin technologies, 3D urban simulation, and early alerting technologies in climate-resilient metropolitan settings. It focuses on severe climate issues such as sea level rise, coastal erosion, flooding, and storm surges. The analysis emphasizes how early warning systems, digital twins, and 3D city models may improve climate adaptability in smart cities. The advantages of the use of digital twins must, however, be fully realized until data handling and oversight challenges can be resolved. The outcomes could be used as a road map for developing and implementing a climate-resilient digital twin mechanism in modern cities. Case studies, social and economic ramifications, and in-depth analysis of data management and oversight challenges should all be part of future research.

References

1. Liu, Z., Meyendorf, N., Mrad, N., The role of data fusion in predictive maintenance using digital twin. *Proc. Annu. Rev. Prog. Quant. Nondestruct. Eval.*, 1949, 1, 2018.

2. Vrabič, R., Erkoyuncu, J.A., Butala, P., Roy, R., Digital twins: Understanding the added value of integrated models for through-life engineering services. *Proc. Manuf.*, 16, 139–146, Jan. 2018.

3. Fuller, A., Fan, Z., Day, C., Barlow, C., Digital Twin: Enabling Technologies, Challenges and Open Research. *IEEE Access*, 8, 108952–108971, 2020, doi: 10.1109/ACCESS.2020.2998358.

4. Riaz, K., McAfee, M., Gharbia, S.S., Management of Climate Resilience: Exploring the Potential of Digital Twin Technology, 3D City Modelling, and Early Warning Systems. *Sensors 2023, 23*, 2659, https://doi.org/10.3390/s23052659, 2023.

5. Tao, F., Cheng, J., Qi, Q., Zhang, M., Zhang, H., Sui, F., Digital twin-driven product design, manufacturing and service with big data. *Int. J. Adv. Manuf. Technol.*, 94, 9-12, 3563–3576, 2018.

6. Sallez, Y., Tamayo-Giraldo, S., Bernard, A., Digital Twin for Smart Manufacturing: A Literature Review. *IEEE Trans. Ind. Inf.*, 15, 6, 3701–3717, 2018.

7. Wang, J., Chen, S., Wan, J., Digital Twin-Driven Production Process Optimization in Smart Manufacturing. *IEEE Trans. Ind. Inf.*, 16, 10, 6471–6483, 2020.

8. Jia, Y., Wang, Z., Xu, X., Li, H., Xu, X., Sun, Y., A review of digital twin framework for quality control in smart manufacturing. *Int. J. Adv. Manuf. Technol.*, 97, 1-4, 139–153, 2018.

9. Xu, X., Jia, Y., Xu, X., Wang, Z., Smart manufacturing and digital twin: A review. *J. Intell. Manuf.*, 29, 3, 501–514, 2018.

10. Benkhaddra, I., Kumar, A., Setitra, M.A. *et al.*, Design and Development of Consensus Activation Function Enabled Neural Network-Based Smart

Healthcare Using BIoT. *Wirel. Pers. Commun.*, 130, 1549–1574, 2023. https://doi.org/10.1007/s11277-023-10344-0.

11. Hoang, N.D., Sato, H., Barolli, L., Pham, T.D., Digital Twin and Artificial Intelligence for Healthcare Internet of Things: A Survey. *IEEE Internet Things J.*, 8, 6, 4753–4766, 2020.

12. Bala, S., Spilker, M.E., Goonewardene, S.S., Franke, J., Digital twin and personalized clinical trials in drug development. *Clin. Trans. Sci.*, 13, 5, 867–874, 2020.

13. Alharbi, A., Alharbi, M., Alharbi, K., Cruzes, D.S., Leveraging digital twin technology to improve healthcare system responsiveness during pandemics. *IEEE Access*, 8, 192407–192414, 2020.

14. Chen, S., Xu, Y., Ma, C., Chen, N., Wang, J., Digital Twin and its Application in Energy Internet: A Comprehensive Survey. *IEEE Access*, 8, 65429–65441, 2020.

15. Huang, Y. and Zhang, Y., Digital twin for smart grid operation and control in the internet of energy. *IEEE Trans. Ind. Inf.*, 15, 6, 3634–3643, 2020.

16. Zhang, W., Li, W., Zhuang, J., Hu, Y., Ma, F., Digital twin for renewable energy systems: A review. *Appl. Energy*, 275, 115342, 2020.

17. Ahamed, S.A., Sreeram, V., Manic, M., Digital Twin-Based Building Energy Management System: A Comprehensive Survey. *IEEE Access*, 9, 30000–30013, 2021.

18. Zhou, K., Zeng, J., Gao, X., Liu, H., Hu, Z., Digital twin and distributed artificial intelligence for virtual power plants: Opportunities, challenges, and enabling technologies. *Appl. Energy*, 265, 114814, 2020.

19. Srivastav, A.L., Markandeya, Patel, N. *et al.*, Concepts of circular economy for sustainable management of electronic wastes: challenges and management options. *Environ. Sci. Pollut. Res.*, 30, 48654–48675, 2023. https://doi.org/10.1007/s11356-023-26052-y.

20. Leng, Y., Gu, Y., Li, Y., Digital Twin: A Comprehensive Survey from Logistics Perspective. *IEEE Access*, 8, 133141–133157, 2020.

21. Lu, Y. *et al.*, Digital Twin-Enabled Smart Supply Chain: A Comprehensive Review and Future Research Directions. *IEEE Trans. Ind. Inf.*, 37, 690–708, 2021, doi: 10.1109/TII.2021.3055369, 2021.

22. Russo, G. *et al.*, Digital Twins for Smart Ports: A Review. *IEEE Access*, 22, 3216, 2020, doi: 10.1109/ACCESS.2020.2990766.

23. Ilyas, B., Kumar, A., Setitra, M.A., Bensalem, Z.E.A., Lei, H., Prevention of DDoS attacks using an optimized deep learning approach in blockchain technology. *Trans. Emerging. Telecommun. Technol.*, 34, 4, e4729, 2023.

24. Islam, M.M. *et al.*, Digital Twin-Based Urban Traffic Control: A Comprehensive Review. *IEEE Access*, 9, 143580–143591, doi: 10.1109/ACCESS.2021.3080357, 2021.

25. N.S.V., Lund, Madsen, H., Mazzoleni, M., Solomatine, D., Borup, M., Assimilating flow and level data into an urban drainage surrogate model

for forecasting flows and overflows. *J. Environ. Manage.*, 248, 109052, 2019. ISSN 0301-4797.

26. Bartos, M. and Kerkez, B., Pipedream: An interactive digital twin model for natural and urban drainage systems. *Environ. Model. Softw.*, 144, 105120, 2021. ISSN 1364-8152.

27. Kumar, A., Rathore, P.S., Dubey, A.K. *et al.*, LTE-NBP with holistic UWB-WBAN approach for the energy efficient biomedical application. *Multimed Tools Appl.*, 82, 39813, 2023. https://doi.org/10.1007/s11042-023-15604-6.

28. Li, X., Liu, H., Wang, W., Zheng, Y., Lv, H., Lv, Z., Big data analysis of the Internet of Things in the digital twins of smart city based on deep learning. *Future Gener. Comput. Syst.*, 128, 167–177, 2022. ISSN 0167-739X.

29. Li, L., Zhang, H., Wang, X., Zhang, J., Shen, W., Digital twin-driven smart city framework: a case study of Yanbu, Saudi Arabia. *IEEE Access*, 7, 12221–12233, 2019.

30. Kumar, A., Kumar, S.A., Dutt, V., Shitharth, S., Tripathi, E., IoT based arrhythmia classification using the enhanced hunt optimization-based deep learning. *Expert Syst.*, 40, 7, e13298, 2023. https://doi.org/10.1111/ exsy.13298.

31. Li, Z. *et al.*, Digital Twin-Enabled Early Warning System for Urban Waterlogging in China. *IEEE Access*, 13, 1432–1447, 2020, doi: 10.1109/ ACCESS.2020.3036850.

32. Mao, S. *et al.*, Digital Twin-Enabled Early Warning System for Urban Rainfall- Induced Waterlogging. *IEEE Trans. Ind. Inf.*, 5, 10, 822–829 2020, doi: 10.1109/TII.2019.2945998.

33. Kumar, A., Swarn., A., Dutt., V., Sitharth., S., Triapthi., E., IoT based Arrhythmia Classification Using the Enhanced Hunt Optimization based Deep Learning, Expert Systems. *J. Knowl. Eng.*, 40, 7, e13298, 2023, ISSN:1468-0394.

34. Zhu, J. *et al.*, Development and Application of a Digital Twin-Based Flood Early Warning System. *J. Hydrol.*, 12460, 1091–1096, 2021, doi: 10.1016/j. jhydrol. 2021.126206.

35. Zhou, P. *et al.*, A Digital Twin-Enabled Early Warning System for Urban Flooding. *J. Hydrol.*, 609, 127834, 2020, doi: 10.1016/j.jhydrol.2020.125306.

36. Dutt, V. and Sharma, S., 9 - Artificial intelligence and technology in weather forecasting and renewable energy systems: emerging techniques and worldwide studies, in: *Woodhead Publishing Series in Energy, Artificial Intelligence for Renewable Energy Systems*, pp. 189–207, Woodhead Publishing, New Delhi, 2022, ISBN 9780323903967, https://doi.org/10.1016/ B978-0-323-90396-7.00009-2.

37. Mashaly, M., Connecting the Twins: A Review on Digital Twin Technology & Its Networking Requirements. *Proc. Comput. Sci.*, 184, 299–305, 2021.

38. Gowran, L.M., EU to Develop a Digital Twin of Earth to Better Predict Climate Impact, Darren Mc Auliffe, Ireland, 2022. 2022, https://www.siliconrepublic. com/innovation/eu-commission-digital-replica-earth-climate.

39. Deng, T., Zhang, K., Shen, Z.-J., A Systematic Review of a Digital Twin City: A New Pattern of Urban Governance toward Smart Cities. *J. Manage. Sci. Eng.*, 6, 125–134, 2021.

40. Kumar, A., Kumar, S.A., Dutt, V., Dubey, A.K., Narang, S., A Hybrid Secure Cloud Platform Maintenance Based on Improved Attribute-Based Encryption Strategies. *Int. J. Interact. Multimed. Artif. Intell.*, 8, 2, 150–157, 2021, http://dx.doi.org/10.9781/ijimai.2021.11.004.

41. Dikshit, A., Satyam, D.N., Towhata, I., Early Warning System Using Tilt Sensors in Chibo, Kalimpong, Darjeeling Himalayas, India. *Nat. Hazards*, 94, 727–741, 2018.

42. Chandrasekaran, S., Dutt, V., Vyas, N., Kumar, R., Student Sentiment Analysis Using Various Machine Learning Techniques. *2023 International Conference on Artificial Intelligence and Smart Communication (AISC)*, Greater Noida, India, pp. 104–107, 2023, doi: 10.1109/AISC56616.2023.10085018.

43. Hapuarachchi, H.A.P., Wang, Q.J., Pagano, T.C., A review of advances in flash flood forecasting. *Hydrol. Process.*, 25, 18, 2771–2784, 2011.

44. Montestruque, L. and Lemmon, M.D., Globally coordinated distributed storm water management system. *Proceedings of the 1st ACM International Workshop on Cyber-Physical Systems for Smart Water Networks*, ACM Press, 2015.

15

Advanced Real-Time Simulation Framework for the Physical Interaction Dynamics of Production Lines Leveraging Digital Twin Paradigms

Neha Bhati[1], Narayan Vyas[2*], Vishal Dutt[2], Ronak Duggar[1] and Aradhya Pokhriyal[1]

[1]Department of Research and Development, AVN Innovations, Ajmer, Rajasthan, India
[2]Department of CSE, Chandigarh University, Mohali, Punjab, India

Abstract

This chapter delves into the cutting-edge world of advanced real-time simulation frameworks, focusing on how they can revolutionize the dynamics of production lines through the adoption of digital twin paradigms. This chapter provides an in-depth look at the ideas behind digital twins, how they are built, and why they are so crucial to the manufacturing process. It sheds more information on the complexities of physical interaction dynamics while stressing the difficulties of more conventional approaches. The advanced framework's design, principles, and practical implementation are the focus of this chapter, which is bolstered by examples drawn from actual applications. Finally, a future in which cutting-edge simulations power revolutionary production lines is envisioned, complete with its associated obstacles, future opportunities, and ethical considerations.

Keywords: Advanced real-time simulation framework, digital twin paradigms, production line dynamics, physical interaction dynamics, real-time feedback mechanisms, production simulations sustainability

*Corresponding author: narayanvyas87@gmail.com

Abhineet Anand, Anita Sardana, Abhishek Kumar, Srikanta Kumar Mohapatra and Shikha Gupta (eds.) Simulation Techniques of Digital Twin in Real-Time Applications: Design Modeling and Implementation, (319–344) © 2024 Scrivener Publishing LLC

15.1 Introduction

Innovative technologies and practices have emerged as the industrial production landscape has shifted in search of more efficiency, accuracy, and flexibility. Among these, the advanced real-time simulation framework stands out as a model of innovation due to the unique perspective that it provides into the inner workings of manufacturing facilities. In this section, the layers of this framework are discussed, focusing on how it interacts with the digital twin paradigms. The setting is set for a deep dive into the world of digital twins to understand their distinguishing characteristics, architectural intricacies, and revolutionary impact on manufacturing, from the historical history of production line simulations to the transformative potential of real-time analysis [1]. As the story progresses, readers learn about the complexities of traditional simulation approaches, the revolutionary potential of the advanced framework, and the nature of physical interactions in manufacturing lines. The approach's tangible benefits are

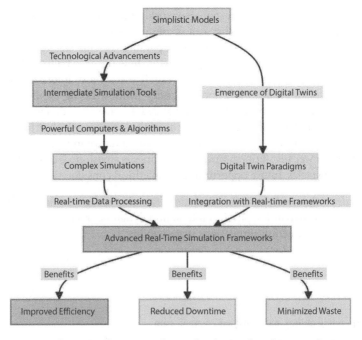

Figure 15.1 From basic simulations to advanced real-time digital twin evolution.

made clear through examples of their use in the actual world. Like any new idea, it has its drawbacks, but these are discussed openly, along with potential remedies and workarounds. It also considers production simulations' ethical implications and sustainable future [2].

Figure 15.1 traces the transformative progression of production simulations, high-lighting technological leaps and the integration of real-time analysis with digital twin paradigms.

15.2 Introduction to Advanced Simulation Frameworks

The convergence of technology and production processes has ushered in a new era of efficiency and precision in the manufacturing sector. In this revolutionary process, advanced simulation frameworks have come to play a crucial role by providing access to information and options that were previously out of reach [3].

15.2.1 The Evolution of Production Line Simulations

Production line simulations were traditionally simplistic models used solely for output prediction and bottleneck identification. The need for increasingly complicated simulation tools increased as technology advanced and the manufacturing line complexity increased. The development of powerful computers and sophisticated algorithms allowed for the creation of simulations that simulate complex processes, consider a wide variety of variables, and yield valuable insights. The advancements that led to today's advanced simulation frameworks were not simple steps in a predetermined direction but rather a sequence of revolutionary advances built upon one another [4].

15.2.2 The Promise of Real-Time Analysis

The capacity to perform studies in real time has been a game-changer for production simulations. Unlike conventional models, which rely on past data and hindsight, real-time analysis processes data as it is being collected. It allows factories to monitor production lines in real time, make adjustments on the fly, and fine-tune their processes as they go.

Table 15.1 summarizes the development of simulation frameworks, drawing attention to the significant step forward represented by the shift from static models to those that incorporate real-time analysis.

There will be far-reaching effects, such as increased productivity and output and decreased downtime and waste. As more and more industries move into the digital era, real-time analysis in state-of-the-art simulation frameworks will play a crucial part in deciding the direction of future production [5].

Figure 15.2 compares and contrasts two common approaches to manufacturing simulation, highlighting the advantages and disadvantages of each with regard to data processing, efficiency, and the ability to conduct analyses in real time.

Table 15.1 Evolution of simulation framework advancements.

Advancement in simulation frameworks	Description
Traditional simulation models	Simplistic models for output prediction and bottleneck identification
Early computational advances	Use of high-powered computers and standard algorithmic approaches for conducting in-depth simulations.
Integration of sophisticated algorithms	Implementation of state-of-the-art algorithms for modeling interdependent processes and parameters.
Real-time analysis implementation	The implementation of real-time analysis has opened the door to near-instantaneous data processing and improvisation.

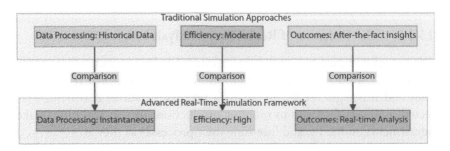

Figure 15.2 Analyzing the differences between classical models and state-of-the-art real-time digital frameworks.

15.3   Digital Twins: A Comprehensive Analysis

Digital Twins has evolved as a revolutionary paradigm in the modern industrial landscape, changing how industries view and engage with their production processes. This chapter digs into the nitty-gritty details of digital twin paradigms, explaining what they are, how they work architecturally, and the many benefits they provide to the industrial industry [6].

15.3.1   What Defines a Digital Twin?

A digital replica of a physical thing or system is called a "digital twin." It replicates the real thing digitally, right down to its current condition, ambient conditions, and performance metrics. Digital twins enable predictive analysis, performance monitoring, and proactive interventions by visualizing an item in real time using data collected from sensors and other sources. It provides a more comprehensive picture than conventional monitoring systems by including the entity's activity, relationships, and life cycle activities in addition to its representation [7].

Figure 15.3 depicts the digital twin process, showcasing data collection, real-time representation, and the power of predictive analysis in modern industrial applications.

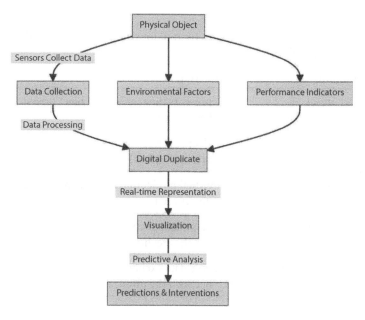

Figure 15.3 Digital twin: from physical object to predictive analysis visualization.

15.3.2 The Architecture and Components of Digital Twins

Digital twin's foundational architecture comprises physical objects, data, and digital duplicates. Sensors are built into the machine, system, or process and collect real-time data.

Table 15.2 elucidates the core components essential to the functioning of digital twins, bridging reality and virtuality in industrial contexts.

Parameters such as temperature, pressure, speed, and efficiency are measured and communicated to the digital duplicate. Sophisticated algorithms and computational models then process this information to ensure that the virtual model closely resembles the physical thing in real time. Strong communication networks allow for smooth information exchange and synchronization between the actual and digital worlds [8].

Figure 15.4 showcases the intricate interplay between physical entities and their digital counterparts, emphasizing real-time data collection, processing, and representation in the digital twin system.

15.3.3 Advantages of Integrating Digital Twins in Manufacturing

There will be several benefits to using digital twins in production. For starters, they facilitate predictive maintenance, which aids businesses in

Table 15.2 Digital twin components for building the bridge between the physical and virtual world.

Component	Function
Physical object	Represents the real-world object or system being duplicated
Data sensors	Collect real-time data (e.g., temperature, pressure, speed)
Digital duplicate	A virtual model that mirrors the physical object's state
Computational models	Process data to ensure that the virtual model matches reality
Communication networks	Enable data exchange and synchronization between the physical and digital worlds

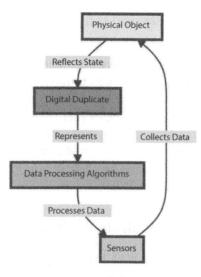

Figure 15.4 Digital twin system: components linking physical objects to their virtual representation.

anticipating and resolving problems before they even occur. The second benefit is that they allow for data-driven decisions, improving real-time resource management and process optimization [9]. In addition, digital twins encourage creativity by serving as a virtual test bed for new ideas, procedures, and tactics before they are put into action. Finally, they make the production process more agile, allowing businesses to respond quickly to shifting consumer preferences and technology developments [10].

15.4 Physical Interaction Dynamics in Production Lines

Complex physical interactions regulate the delicate choreography of machines, parts, and human workers throughout a manufacturing line. To maximize effectiveness, guarantee security, and boost the manufacturing output, it is critical to comprehend these interrelationships. This chapter delves into the specifics of these physical interaction dynamics to learn more about their nature, how they affect production efficiency, and the difficulties inherent in using conventional simulation techniques to study them [11].

15.4.1 The Nature of Physical Interactions

Forces, motions, and reactions cover a wide range of physical interactions on a production line. Assembly line interactions range from simple mechanical motion on a conveyor belt to intricate coordination between robotic arms. Object and machine behavior is greatly influenced by friction, gravity, and electromagnetic fields [12].

Human interaction with machines, tools, and components, each with its dynamics, also generates uncertainty. Predicting system behavior, maintaining consistent operations, and avoiding disruptions necessitate awareness of these interrelationships [10].

15.4.2 The Role of Dynamics in Production Efficiency

The effectiveness of assembly lines heavily depends on dynamics or the study of forces and their effects on motion. Machinery with well-tuned dynamics runs more efficiently, uses less energy, and has less wear and tear. Better layout designs, quicker workflows, and improved synchronization between various production line components are all possible when one has a firm grasp of the dynamics of physical interactions. By fine-tuning these dynamics, manufacturing facilities can shorten their production cycles, reduce waste, and improve the quality of their final goods [13].

Figure 15.5 visualizes the steps to understand and enhance physical interactions, emphasizing dynamics and optimization in production processes.

15.4.3 Challenges in Traditional Simulation Methods

While helpful, traditional simulation approaches sometimes need to model the complex physical interactions in production lines adequately. Many of these approaches are based on static models that do not consider the inherent uncertainty in some interactions or that they can change at any moment. Furthermore, they may simplify complex circumstances in ways that lead to discrepancies between what the simulation predicts and what really occurs. Complex dynamics were difficult to represent because of the limited computer power and lack of advanced algorithms in early simulation systems. In order to fill these gaps and provide a more precise representation of physical interaction dynamics in manufacturing settings, more sophisticated, real-time simulation frameworks were urgently required [14].

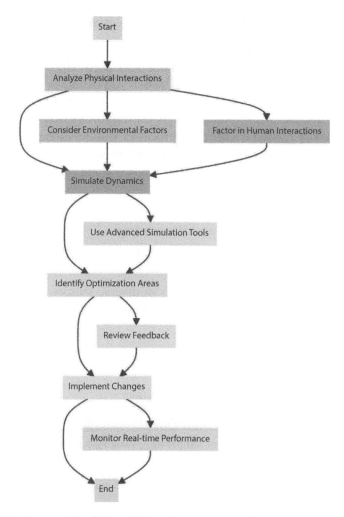

Figure 15.5 Optimized workflow of physical interactions in the production line.

15.5 Building the Advanced Real-Time Simulation Framework

The advanced real-time simulation framework is a cutting-edge tool in industrial production, created with painstaking care to record, examine, and enhance the myriad dynamics of assembly lines. This chapter provides an in-depth look at the design and workings of this groundbreaking framework, explaining its key ideas, data processing processes, and high-level real-time feedback mechanisms [15].

15.5.1 Core Principles and Design Objectives

The advanced real-time simulation framework's guiding principles and design goals are at the heart of the framework itself. The ultimate goal is to model manufacturing dynamics as closely as possible in a digital environment. It calls for a dedication to perfection in precision, scalability, and flexibility. Because of its modular design, the framework may easily accommodate new or revised features and processes without disrupting existing ones. A constant focus on real-time responsiveness ensures that simulations remain flexible, adjusting on the fly to any changes in the production environment [16].

15.5.2 Data Integration and Processing

The system relies on data, both in its breadth and depth, to drive simulations and provide crucial insights.

Table 15.3 outlines the pivotal roles of diverse sensors and IoT infrastructure in seamlessly integrating real-time data within the advanced real-time simulation framework.

Table 15.3 Sensors and IoT in data integration.

Sensor type	Role in data integration and processing
Temperature	Monitor temperature variations in machinery and manufacturing processes
Pressure	Measure pressure levels to ensure safe and efficient operations
Speed	Monitor machine speed and performance for real-time adjustments
Efficiency	Gather data on equipment efficiency to optimize production
IoT infrastructure	Facilitate reliable and real-time data transmission to the framework

15.5.2.1   Role of Sensors and IoT

Sensors and Internet of Things (IoT) devices are vital tools for data collection. These sensors are always at work, strategically placed throughout machinery and key manufacturing components, and gather various data points. With the help of the IoT infrastructure, this data may be sent to the framework reliably and in real time [17].

Figure 15.6 showcases the simulation framework's data flow and feedback mechanisms.

15.5.2.2   Algorithmic Foundations for Feedback

The computational underpinnings of the feedback mechanism are crucial to its success in a cutting-edge real-time simulation context. These algorithms are dynamic, continually learning and improving their ability to predict future outcomes in response to new information [18].

Nature of algorithms: Adaptability is a critical factor in selecting these algorithms, which analyze past events and current conditions to foresee potential problems and offer solutions.

Integration with other systems: To react in real time to any changes in the data, feedback algorithms are connected with sensors, IoT devices, and data processing units.

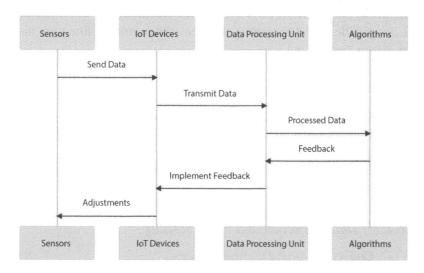

Figure 15.6 Framework component interactions over time.

15.6 Types of Algorithms

- Predictive algorithms: Forecasting algorithms analyze the present and past to foretell the future.
- Reinforcement learning: In reinforcement learning, algorithms learn from their mistakes and improve their methods accordingly.
- Neural networks: Neural networks are advanced algorithms for identifying patterns in large datasets.
- Decision trees: Decision trees can better analyze the causes of problems.
- Continuous refinement: Algorithms are continually updated to improve accuracy as the production environment and data change.

In essence, these algorithmic underpinnings guarantee a quick and effective response from the framework, maximizing the assembly line's efficiency [19].

15.6.1 Pseudocode for Real-Time Adjustments

Immediate and accurate responses to any deviations or changes in the manufacturing line necessitate real-time adjustments in the simulation framework. The pseudocode is a logical representation of the mathematical computations and reasoning that the system uses to fine-tune itself. Here is how it works out.

15.6.1.1 Initialization

- Set a threshold value, typically 0.95, to determine anomalies.
- Define a learning rate, often set at 0.01, which dictates how quickly the system adapts.
- Initialize a weight matrix (W) and a bias vector (b) for data processing.

15.6.1.2 Data Collection and Pre-Processing

- Collect real-time data from sensors.
- Normalize this data using the formula: "normalized _ data _point = (data _point - MEAN(real-time _data)) / STANDARD_DEVIATION (real-time _data)"

15.6.1.3   Analysis Using Bayesian Inference

- Calculate the probability distribution of the normalized data point using Bayesian methods and the weight matrix and bias vector.

15.6.1.4   Anomaly Detection and Root Cause Analysis

- If the maximum value of the probability distribution is less than the threshold, an anomaly is detected.
- The anomaly score is calculated as "anomaly _score = 1 – MAX (probability_distribution)".
- The root cause of the anomaly is then determined using decision trees.

15.6.1.5   Corrective Action Using Gradient Boosting

- The gradient of the root cause is calculated using gradient boosting, factoring in the learning rate.
- The corrective action is then determined as "corrective _ action = - learning _rate* gradient."

15.6.1.6   Update and Implement

- The weight matrix and bias vector are updated using the learning rate and gradient to improve future predictions.
- The determined corrective action is implemented on the production line.

15.6.1.7   Continuous Monitoring

- The updated weight matrix and bias vector continuously monitor the production line for further anomalies.
- With its mathematical formulas, this pseudocode offers a systematic approach to real-time adjustments, ensuring that the production line operates optimally and efficiently.

This state diagram in Figure 15.7 illustrates transitions within the advanced real-time simulation framework, from initialization to monitoring, with a forest-themed palette for clarity [20].

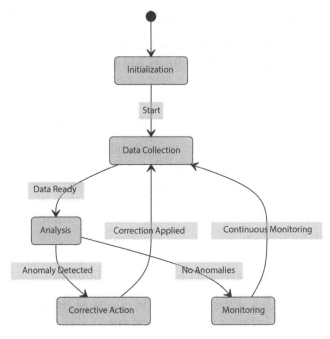

Figure 15.7 State diagram.

15.7   Practical Implementations and Case Studies

While the theory behind the advanced real-time simulation framework is solid, it is in its practical applications where it truly shines. This part digs further into the practical use of the framework, explaining its nuances, providing examples of its deployment in other fields, and emphasizing the real benefits businesses have gained from adopting it [21].

Figure 15.8 shows the framework's implementation steps, industry applications, and the tangible benefits it offers businesses for enhanced productivity.

15.7.1   Implementing the Framework: A Step-by-Step Guide

The advanced real-time simulation framework requires a methodical strategy for deployment to be successful.

- Requirement analysis: Setting measurable goals for adopting the framework includes locating potential bottlenecks, gaining insight into areas that need optimization, and so on.

Figure 15.8 Overview of advanced real-time simulation framework and its impact.

- Infrastructure setup: Putting in sensors, connecting Internet of Things gadgets, and setting up data centers all fall under this category. Ensuring that these parts work in tandem with the current infrastructure is crucial.
- Data collection and normalization: After collection, this information needs to be prepared for analysis by being thoroughly scrubbed, standardized, and arranged.
- Algorithm integration: It is critical to modify these algorithms to address the specific needs of the manufacturing setting.
- Testing and validation: Thorough testing should be performed before a full-scale deployment. Evaluation is essential to determine the framework's success, find places for enhancement, and optimize the system for maximum efficiency [22].
- Deployment and continuous monitoring: Once the framework has been tested and proven to work, it should be rolled out across the whole production line and monitored continuously. After a system has been implemented, it must be monitored in real time to make adjustments as needed [23].

The framework's adaptability is demonstrated by its widespread use in several fields.

- Automotive manufacturing: One of the world's leading automakers used the framework to improve its production line procedures. As a result of this tactical adjustment, manufacturing efficiency increased by an astounding 15%.

- Pharmaceuticals: A major pharmaceutical company adopted the system to streamline drug manufacturing. This resulted in tighter control over its drug formulation procedures, which led to consistent quality and far less waste.
- Electronics production: A significant electronics manufacturer used the framework to modernize its approach to making circuit boards. The result was a noticeable reduction in product faults and a speeding up of production timetables.

15.7.2　Measurable Benefits and Outcomes

The benefits of using the framework are numerous, namely:
- Augmented efficiency: After using the framework, businesses typically see an increase in output efficiency of 10–25% [24].
- Diminished downtime: Real-time alterations mean fewer operational disturbances, leading to less unscheduled downtime.
- Economic advantage: Greater manufacturing efficiency and less wasteful practices result in significant business savings.
- Elevated product quality: The framework's emphasis on constant monitoring and immediate feedback guarantees superior quality products at all times, which is excellent for the reputation of the business and the retention of loyal customers.

To sum up, the advanced real-time simulation framework can revolutionize the production environment, ushering in an era of unprecedented efficiency, cost-effectiveness, and product quality if it is carefully controlled with care [25].

15.8　Overcoming Challenges and Limitations

The advanced real-time simulation framework can significantly improve assembly lines, but putting it to use is not without its difficulties. In this section, researchers explore the obstacles that may develop during the deployment of the framework, provide suggestions for resolving these issues in real time, and stress the significance of maintaining the confidentiality and integrity of the data.

15.8.1 Potential Roadblocks in Framework Implementation

There may be many challenges along the way to complete the framework integration, namely:

- Technological constraints: Because of limitations in available technology, not all production environments can meet the specifications of the framework.
- Resistance to change: Employees and management may hesitate to embrace new technologies for fear of upsetting established procedures.
- Data overload: Mistakes and delays in processing can result from the overload caused by the constant stream of real-time data.
- Integration issues: Compatibility issues with preexisting systems may arise during the integration of the framework, resulting in downtime and inefficiency.

Table 15.4 offers insights into potential implementation hurdles and practical solutions for ensuring the success of the advanced real-time simulation framework.

15.8.2 Solutions and Workarounds for Real-Time Challenges

The framework's success depends on how well it handles the difficulties introduced by instantaneous modifications [26].

Table 15.4 Addressing challenges in framework implementation.

Potential challenges in implementation	Solutions and workarounds
Technological constraints	Invest in scalable technologies to accommodate the framework's requirements
Resistance to change	Provide continuous training to staff for better adoption and understanding
Data overload	Implement hybrid approaches to balance real-time data processing demands
Integration issues	Set up feedback loops for constant adaptation and resolve compatibility issues

- Scalable systems: Scalable technologies should be implemented to ensure that real-time modifications are not slowed down by the need to process enormous amounts of data.
- Continuous training: Offer ongoing training to staff to ensure that they are familiar with the framework's features and making the most of their potential.
- Hybrid approaches: Combining different strategies when making changes in real time could cause too much disruption. Make smart choices based on real-time data, yet roll out new features during off-peak times.
- Feedback loops: Set up feedback loops to ensure that the framework constantly adapts to local conditions and receives input from those closest to the action.

15.8.3   Ensuring Data Security and Integrity

- Given the framework's reliance on information, protecting that information is paramount.
- Encryption: All information should be encrypted with modern cryptographic methods, whether in motion or stored.
- Access control: Ensure that only authorized individuals have access to private information by enforcing tight access control procedures.

15.9   Regular Audits: Schedule Frequent Audits to Help Find Security Flaws Before They Cause Problems

- Data validation: Data should be checked for accuracy and relevance before processing. Inaccurate real-time modifications could halt production if based on inaccurate data.
- Backup and recovery: Having data backed up means that business may continue with minimal interruption in the case of data loss.

While the advanced real-time simulation framework holds great promise for improving the efficiency of production lines, it is essential to be aware of the obstacles that may arise. Companies can realize the full potential of the framework by aggressively tackling these difficulties and establishing strong data security safeguards.

15.10   The Future of Production Simulations With Digital Twins

Thanks to the use of digital twins in production simulations, a new era in manufacturing and production is upon us. The use of digital twins to revolutionize the field of production simulations has excellent promise as technology advances. Insights into recent developments in digital twin technology, the growing capabilities of real-time simulations, and the associated ethical and sustainability concerns are provided in this part.

The Gantt chart in Figure 15.9 provides a projected timeline for developing and implementing various digital twin technologies. It is essential to note that these dates are tentative and may change based on various factors.

15.10.1   Emerging Trends in Digital Twin Technology

Rapid progress is being made in the field of digital twin technology:

- Integration with artificial intelligence (AI): Digital twins of the future are anticipated to feature extensive integration

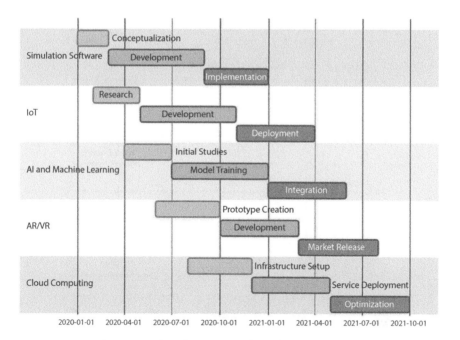

Figure 15.9 Development and implementation of digital twin technologies.

with AI, allowing them to make autonomous decisions based on real-time data.

- Augmented and virtual reality (AR/VR) interfaces: Augmented and virtual reality (AR/VR) interfaces may be the next step in digital twin development, giving users a more lifelike experience while interacting with the digital twin.
- Predictive maintenance: Digital twins can use previous data to foresee when a component is about to break, allowing for preventive maintenance and cutting down on downtime.
- Interconnected digital twins: A networked ecosystem of digital replicas replicating complex real-world systems may form in the future thanks to the interaction of numerous digital twins [27].

The diagram in Figure 15.10 depicts the intricate network of digital twins and their interaction with a central server. Each digital twin sends data to and receives updates from the central server, highlighting the collaborative nature of the ecosystem.

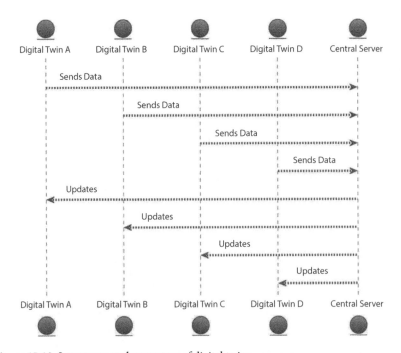

Figure 15.10 Interconnected ecosystem of digital twins.

15.10.2   Expanding the Scope of Real-Time Simulations

Real-time simulations are expected to grow in complexity and application with time.

- Simulating entire supply chains: One potential application of real-time simulations is to cover the entire supply chain, from the procurement of inputs through the shipment of finished goods.
- Integration with smart cities: To further optimize city-wide processes, such as traffic flows, energy consumption, and public services, real-time simulations could be integrated with smart cities.
- Personalized production: Production lines use real-time data to generate items that are unique to each user.

15.10.3   Ethical Considerations and Sustainability

There is a price to pay for having so much influence, namely:

- Data privacy: Since digital twins depend on data, protecting its confidentiality is critical. Organizations must be open and honest about how they use data and comply with international privacy laws.
- Impact on the environment: While digital twins can improve production efficiency, it is crucial to ensure that doing so does not compromise environmental sustainability.
- Workforce implications: The workforce may be affected by digital twins' increased automation and optimization. Workers must receive retraining and skill upgrades to collaborate effectively with their digital counterparts.
- Ethical use of AI: Ensuring that AI is utilized responsibly, without bias, and in a way that benefits all stakeholders is essential as the technology becomes increasingly embedded in digital twins.

Digital twins present an exciting new frontier for production simulation. To ensure that progress is both responsible and inclusive, however, it will be necessary to face the ethical and sustainability concerns of the future with an eye toward the present.

15.11   Conclusion: Revolutionizing Production Lines With Advanced Simulations

All signs point to advanced real-time simulation frameworks taking center stage in the future of today's production lines. These frameworks, founded on the ideas of digital twins, have ushered in a new era in which real-time data synthesis and immediate feedback are not merely helpful but indispensable. Digital twins have improved production simulations' realism, accuracy, and thoroughness. Industries can now anticipate problems, make accurate predictions, and base decisions on real-time data thanks to the widespread adoption of digital twins of traditionally physical systems.

These cutting-edge simulations go far beyond the realm of simple productivity boosts. They can transform supply chains as a whole, fit in easily with the systems of upcoming smart cities, and allow producers to cater to specific customers' preferences.

However, there are obstacles along the way to optimization. Data security, the moral implications of these technologies, and their possible social and economic effects on the labor force all rank high on the list of significant worries. The responsibility for overcoming these obstacles and keeping the development of these simulations in line with ethical and sustainable standards falls on academics, industry leaders, and regulatory agencies.

To sum up, cutting-edge simulation tools are driving a sea change in factories' operations, and this trend is only expected to accelerate. As advancements in technology multiply, they present a picture of a future in which production methods are efficient, self-aware, flexible, and fundamentally committed to making the world a better place for future generations.

References

1. Srivastav, A.L., Markandeya, Patel, N., Pandey, M., Pandey, A.K., Dubey, A.K., Kumar, A., Bhardwaj, A.K., Chaudhary, V.K., Concepts of circular economy for sustainable management of electronic wastes: challenges and management options. *Environ. Sci. Pollut. Res. Int.*, 30, 17, 48 654–48 675, 2023.

2. Punugoti, R., Vyas, N., Siddiqui, A.T., Basit, A., The Convergence of Cutting-Edge Technologies: Leveraging AI and Edge Computing to Transform the Internet of Medical Things (IoMT), in: *2023 4th International Conference on Electronics and Sustainable Communication Systems (ICESC)*, pp. 600–606, 2023, doi: 10.1109/ICESC57686.2023.10193047.

3. Wang, Z., *et al.*, A Digital Twin Paradigm: Vehicle-to-Cloud Based Advanced Driver Assistance Systems, *2020 IEEE 91st Vehicular Technology Conference (VTC2020-Spring)*, pp. 1–6, Antwerp, Belgium, 2020, doi: 10.1109/VTC2020-Spring48590.2020.9128938.

4. Chandrasekaran, S., Dutt, V., Vyas, N., Kumar, R., Student Sentiment Analysis Using Various Machine Learning Techniques. *2023 International Conference on Artificial Intelligence and Smart Communication (AISC)*, pp. 104–107, 2023, doi: 10.1109/AISC56616.2023.10085018.

5. Anumbe, N., Saidy, C., Harik, R., A Primer on the Factories of the Future. *Sensors*, 22, 15, 5834–5834, 2022.

6. Ilyas, B., Kumar, A., Setitra, M.A., Bensalem, Z.A., Lei, H., Prevention of DDoS attacks using an optimized deep learning approach in blockchain technology, *Transactions on Emerging Telecommunications Technologies*, vol. 34, no. 4. Wiley, Jan. 25, 2023. doi: 10.1002/ett.4729.

7. Singh, M., Fuenmayor, E., Hinchy, E.P., Qiao, Y., Murray, N., Devine, D., Digital twin: Origin to future. *Appl. Syst. Innov.*, 4, 2, 36–36, 2021.

8. Raturi, R., Kumar, A., Vyas, N., Dutt, V., A Novel Approach for Anomaly Detection in Time-Series Data using Generative Adversarial Networks, in: *2023 International Conference on Sustainable Computing and Smart Systems (ICSCSS)*, pp. 1352–1357, 2023, doi: 10.1109/ ICSCSS57650.2023.10169365.

9. Boyapati, S., Swarna, S.R., Dutt, V., Vyas, N., Big Data Approach for Medical Data Classification: A Review Study, in: *2020 3rd International Conference on Intelligent Sustainable Systems (ICISS)*, pp. 762–766, 2020, doi: 10.1109/ ICISS49785. 2020.9315870.

10. Bao, J., Guo, D., Li, J., Zhang, J., The modeling and operations for the digital twin in the context of manufacturing. *Enterp Inf. Syst.*, 13, 4, 534–556, 2019.

11. Kumar, A., Rathore, P.S., Dubey, A.K., Agrawal, R., Sharma, K.P., LTE-NBP with holistic UWB-WBAN approach for the energy efficient biomedical application, *Multimedia Tools and Applications*, vol. 82, no. 25. Springer Science and Business Media LLC, pp. 39797–39811, Mar. 29, 2023. doi: 10.1007/s11042-023-15093-7.

12. Burri, S.R., Kumar, A., Baliyan, A., Kumar, T.A., Predictive intelligence for healthcare outcomes: An AI architecture overview, in: *2023 2nd International Conference on Smart Technologies and Systems for Next Generation Computing ({ICSTSN})*, IEEE, 2023.

13. Burugadda, V.R., Jadhav, N., Vyas, N., Duggar, R., Exploring the Potential of Deep Reinforcement Learning for Autonomous Navigation in Complex Environments, *2023 7th International Conference On Computing, Communication, Control And Automation (ICCUBEA)*, Pune, India, 2023, pp. 1–6, doi: 10.1109/ICCUBEA58933.2023.10392109.

14. Burri, S.R., Agarwal, D.K., Vyas, N., Duggar, R., Optimizing Irrigation Efficiency with IoT and Machine Learning: A Transfer Learning Approach for Accurate Soil Moisture Prediction, in: *2023 World Conference on*

Communication & Computing (WCONF), pp. 1–6, 2023, doi: 10.1109/WCONF58270.2023.10235220.

15. Kumar, A., Kumar, S.A., Dutt, V., Shitharth, S., Tripathi, E., IoT based arrhythmia classification using the enhanced hunt optimization-based deep learning. *Expert Syst.*, 40, 7, e13298, 2023, https://doi.org/10.1111/ exsy.13298.

16. Burri, S.R., Kumar, A., Baliyan, A., Kumar, T.A., Transforming payment processes: A discussion of AI-enabled routing optimization, in: *2023 2nd International Conference on Smart Technologies and Systems for Next Generation Computing ({ICSTSN})*, IEEE, 2023.

17. Zhao, Z.., Shen, L., Yang, C., Wu, W., Zhang, M., Huang, G.Q., IoT and digital twin enabled smart tracking for safety management, *Computers & Operations Research*, vol. 128, p. 105183, Elsevier BV, Apr. 2021. doi: 10.1016/j.cor.2020.105183.

18. Kumar, A., Kumar, S.A., Dutt, V., Shitharth, S., Tripathi, E., IoT based arrhythmia classification using the enhanced hunt optimization-based deep learning. *Expert Syst.*, 40, 7, Apr. 16, 2023. doi: 10.1111/exsy.13298.

19. Burri, S.R., Ahuja, S., Kumar, A., Baliyan, A., Exploring the effectiveness of optimized convolutional neural network in transfer learning for image classification: A practical approach, in: *2023 International Conference on Advancement in Computation & Computer Technologies ({InCACCT})*, IEEE, 2023.

20. Benkhaddra, I., Kumar, A., Setitra, M. A., Hang, L., Design and Development of Consensus Activation Function Enabled Neural Network-Based Smart Healthcare Using BIoT, *Wireless Personal Communications*, vol. 130, no. 3, pp. 1549–1574, Springer Science and Business Media LLC, Mar. 20, 2023. doi: 10.1007/s11277-023-10344-0.

21. Dutt, V. and Sharma, S., 9 - Artificial intelligence and technology in weather forecasting and renewable energy systems: emerging techniques and worldwide studies, in: *Woodhead Publishing Series in Energy, Artificial Intelligence for Renewable Energy Systems*, pp. 189–207, Woodhead Publishing, Sawston, Cambridge, 2022, ISBN 9780323903967, https://doi.org/10.1016/B978-0-323-90396-7.00009-2.

22. Chandrasekaran, S., Dutt, V., Vyas, N., Anand, A., Fuzzy KNN Implementation for Early Parkinson's Disease Prediction, in: *2023 7th International Conference on Computing Methodologies and Communication (ICCMC)*, pp. 896–901, 2023.

23. Liu, M., Fang, S., Dong, H., Xu, C., Review of digital twin about concepts, technologies, and industrial applications. *J. Manuf. Syst.*, 58, 346–361, 2021.

24. Kumar, A., Kumar, S. A., Dutt, V., Dubey, A. K., Narang, S., A Hybrid Secure Cloud Platform Maintenance Based on Improved Attribute-Based Encryption Strategies. *International Journal of Interactive Multimedia and Artificial Intelligence (IJIMAI)*, 8, 2, 150, Universidad Internacional de La Rioja, 2023. doi: 10.9781/ijimai.2021.11.004.

25. Leng, J., Zhang, H., Yan, S., Liu, Q., Chen, X., Zhang, D., Digital twin-driven manufacturing cyber-physical system for parallel controlling of smart workshop, *J. Ambient Intell. Humaniz. Comput.*, 10, 3, 1155–1166, Springer Science and Business Media LLC, Jun. 02, 2018. doi: 10.1007/s12652-018-0881-5.

26. Sekhar, U.S., Vyas, N., Dutt, V., Kumar, A., Multimodal Neuroimaging Data in Early Detection of Alzheimer's Disease: Exploring the Role of Ensemble Models and GAN Algorithm, *2023 International Conference on Circuit Power and Computing Technologies (ICCPCT)*, Kollam, India, 2023, pp. 1664–1669, doi: 10.1109/ICCPCT58313.2023.10245177.

27. Fang, X., Wang, H., Liu, G., Tian, X., Ding, G., Zhang, H., Industry application of digital twin: From concept to implementation. *Int. J. Adv. Manuf. Technol.*, 121, 7–8, 4289–4312, 2022.

Index